KINGS SUTTON
CHURCHWARDENS' ACCOUNTS
1636-1700

Appointment of churchwardens and overseers of the highways, 1658. The first entry was written by the vicar. The last entries are the signatures of some of those who attended the parish meeting on 13 April 1658 and chose John Waters to be churchwarden (page 79).

The Banbury Historical Society

General Editor: J.S.W. Gibson

KINGS SUTTON
Northamptonshire

CHURCHWARDENS' ACCOUNTS
1636 - 1700

Transcribed and Edited by Paul Hayter

Volume 27

2001

Published by
The Banbury Historical Society,
c/o Banbury Museum, Spiceball Park Road, Banbury OX16 2PQ

This edition © Banbury Historical Society, 2001

ISBN 0 900129 25 5

Typed to disc by Paul Hayter,
with minor editing by Jeremy Gibson

Printed by
Parchment (Oxford) Limited

Cover illustration:

A full page illustration of Kings Sutton church from the west end ('drawn and engraved by W.S. Wilkinson from a sketch by A.E.B.') in George Baker's *The History and Antiquities of the County of Northampton*, vol. 1, London, 1823-1830, facing page 692.

This is no longer a familiar aspect of the church, since the view is obscured by trees around the churchyard. Nevertheless the sketch by 'A.E.B.', *c.*1820, was nearer in time to the churchwardens who kept these accounts than we are today. This view of the church would have been familiar to them.

Acknowledgments:

This edited transcript from the first volume of Kings Sutton churchwardens' accounts is published by kind permission of the Vicar and Churchwardens of Kings Sutton.

CONTENTS

(*Note.* The Introduction has been paginated in **bold** figures, and references to it are shown as such in the indexes.)

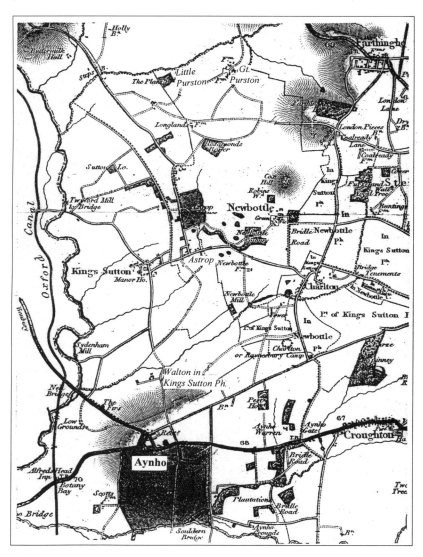

Kings Sutton parish after the enclosures, based on Bryant's map of 1827, but with clarified legends. In the seventeenth century, the common fields of Astrop and Charlton were split between Kings Sutton and Newbottle, as were tithes of Purston. This intermingling of the parishes is reflected in the post-enclosure awards. The boundaries of Kings Sutton parish stretched from the River Cherwell in the west to the east of Charlton, and from the stream by Little Purston in the north to the edge of Aynho in the south.

Bryant's map is reproduced by kind permission of Northamptonshire Record Office.

Kings Sutton Churchwardens' Accounts

Among the archives of the parish church of St Peter and St Paul, Kings Sutton, in Northamptonshire, are a series of account books used by the churchwardens to record the receipts and expenditure of the church. The first volume covers the period from 1636 to 1713; then there is a gap from 1713 to 1759; after that three volumes cover the years from 1759 to 1927.

The first volume is a leather bound book, measuring 37.5 cm by 15 cm, bought by the churchwardens in 1636 for 3s 6d (see p. 5). The opening few pages are in very poor condition, but generally it is well preserved and its entries are meticulously kept until shortly after 1700 when they become more hit and miss. The exceptions to this are the years from 1642 to 1648, evidently because of the Civil War, and 1688 to 1690 when most of the accounts are missing. Because one loose page also survives from 1629, in a format similar to the volume transcribed here, there was probably an earlier volume now lost. The volume from 1713 to 1759 has also disappeared.

The book records the appointment of the churchwardens and other parish officials each year at the parish meeting in the week after Easter. To this extent it acted as a parish record book. The appointment of the Overseers of the Poor, for instance, was recorded here, even though they kept their accounts separately, some of which are in the Northamptonshire Record Office. The book, which was transferred from one pair of churchwardens to the next, acted as a badge of office, and it is evident (e.g. p. 97) that any spare cash held by them went with the book. This is in contrast to practice at the nearby parish of South Newington in Oxfordshire, for example, where the cash was kept in a church box until at least the late seventeenth century.[1] The book was also used as a receipt book for church levies (see below).

The parish of Kings Sutton covered both the village of Kings Sutton, which then had a population of about 500-600,[2] and also the hamlets of Astrop and Walton and parts of Purston and Charlton. Other parts of Purston and Charlton were in the parish of Newbottle.

---

[1] E R C Brinkworth (ed.), *South Newington Churchwardens' Accounts 1553 – 1684*, Banbury Historical Society vol 6 (1964), pp. 2-10 and 62

[2] This estimate is based on the hearth tax returns for 1662 [PRO E179/254/11], which recorded 133 households in Kings Sutton, paying or exempt from the tax

Role of the Churchwardens

The two churchwardens had a threefold role. First and foremost they were the lay leaders of the congregation, with responsibility for the church's property and the fabric of the church except the chancel; the latter was the responsibility of the rector. Secondly, as a result of this, they became the agents of the ecclesiastical courts which imposed on them duties such as enforcing uniformity and good behaviour. Thirdly they became the agents of the secular authorities from the sixteenth century on, when there was no secular parish council and the state was beginning to need local administrative machinery to implement the poor laws, restrict vagrancy or control vermin.

The churchwardens had a pivotal role from the early days of the Elizabethan Reformation settlement. The Act of Uniformity of 1559 provided that "every person [absent from divine service] shall forfeit for every such offence twelve pence, to be levied by the churchwardens of the parish where such offence shall be done, to the use of the poor of the same parish, of the goods, lands and tenements of such offender by way of distress."[3]

The influence of the church courts was particularly strong in the life of a churchwarden, when civil law and ecclesiastical law operated side by side. The newly appointed churchwardens had to take an oath of office in court at the time of their election; they had to enforce the orders of the archdeacon's and the bishop's courts; and in response to the archdeacon's questions at Visitations they were expected to make presentments twice yearly about the state of the church's fabric and services and the parish's morality. Among the Canons of the Church of England of 1603 were orders that the churchwardens "shall not suffer any idle persons to abide either in the churchyard or church porch during the time of divine service, or preaching, but shall cause them to either to come in, or to depart" (19); they had to present those who "offend their brethren, either by adultery, whoredom, incest or drunkenness, or by swearing, ribaldry, usury and any other uncleanness, and wickedness of life" (109) or "behave themselves rudely and disorderly in the church" (111); they would be excommunicated if "having taken their oaths to present to their ordinaries[4] [at least twice a year] all such public offences as they are particularly charged to inquire of in their several parishes, [they] shall (notwithstanding their said oaths, and that their faithful discharging of them is the chief means whereby public sins and offences may be reformed and punished) wittingly and willingly, desperately and irreligiously, incur the horrible crime of perjury [by] refusing to present such enormities and public

---

[3] 1 Eliz cap 2, s. 3
[4] i.e. their bishops

offences" (26); and they had to "take care and provide that the churches be well and sufficiently repaired, and so from time to time kept and maintained that the windows be well glazed, and that the floors be kept paved, plain, and even, and all things there in such an orderly and decent sort, without dust, or anything that may be either noisome or unseemly, as best becometh the House of God" and keep the churchyards "well and sufficiently repaired, fenced and maintained with walls, rails or pales" (85).

It was both a troublesome and expensive business complying with all these regulations. The accounts are full of payments to the "parritor" or apparitor, who acted as the messenger of the court, giving notice of its meeting, instructing the clergy, churchwardens and others to appear, and conveying the Visitation Articles to which the churchwardens had to respond. For most of the century there were payments when the churchwardens took their oaths, and heavy charges at visitations, and since the visitations often took place in distant parts of the Archdeaconry of Buckingham, such as Aylesbury and Stony Stratford, there were travel costs as well. (Kings Sutton church was annexed with Buckingham to endow a prebend of Lincoln Cathedral in the twelfth century and thereafter the Archdeacon of Buckingham was usually also the Rector of Kings Sutton.) The exception was between 1641 and 1661 when visitations ceased; Parliament ended episcopal disciplinary authority and made it illegal for church courts to "minister unto any churchwarden ..... any corporal oath" to make presentments. The accounts reflect this. Until 1641 and after 1661 they record visitations at Banbury and numerous towns in Buckinghamshire. From 1642 to 1650 there is none, and from 1651 to 1660 there are "sittings", all closer to home in Northamptonshire, at Culworth, Moreton Pinkney, Daventry, Brackley and Northampton. At the same period and probably in connection with those sittings, the accounts had to be approved. The signatures of Jo. Cartwright and Hen. Barkelry, for instance, in 1656 (p. 73) are the same signatures as those approving the Culworth churchwardens' accounts that year.[5] They were presumably justices of the peace, who at this period were required to certify the accounts of the overseers of the poor.

The quality of the presentments by churchwardens was variable, which is hardly surprising, given that they were being asked to tell tales on their neighbours. Officiously discharging this duty was a sure route to unpopularity. So the Bishop of Peterborough wrote to the Archbishop of Canterbury in 1680 that "defects can never be known by the presentments of the churchwardens [who] will forswear themselves over and over

---

[5] Northamptonshire Record Office 94P/22

rather than bring expense on themselves or their neighbours".[6] Corroboration of this can be found in the presentments which the churchwardens of Kings Sutton made to the Peculiar Court of Banbury. (When the diocese of Oxford was created out of the diocese of Lincoln in 1542, Banbury retained its status as a peculiar or exempt jurisdiction within the diocese of Lincoln, a jurisdiction which extended to Kings Sutton and also to Horley, Hornton and Cropredy and their related hamlets.) Henry Johnson in 1611 presented various parishioners for Sunday dancing, keeping "ill rule in his howse in time of divine prayer", for fornication, for being a common scold and for not paying their levies and he presented his fellow churchwarden George Jennings for "seinge John Pillie & others & will not present them ..... George Jennings is a good fellowe & will not willingly present any thinge".[7] The outcome of a few of the presentments can be found in the Act Book of the Peculiar Court of Banbury 1625 – 1638;[8] R.K. Gilkes in his Introduction gives a very full explanation of the workings of the Court, which therefore does not need to be repeated here.

As mentioned above, the churchwardens were elected each year at a parish meeting in Easter week. There were two of them and generally they served for one year only. Occasionally they might be re-elected but that was the exception, reflecting the fact that the post was no sinecure and, if the churchwardens were unlucky enough to hold office in a year of high expenditure, they could find themselves acting as moneylenders to the parish until reimbursed by their successors in office. The only churchwardens to remain in office for several years were Richard Taylor and Thomas Rawlins, who were elected in April 1641 and were still in office in 1648 as a result of the disruption caused by the Civil War; and their successors John Phipps and John Haynes, who were not replaced for three years.

Canon 89 of the Church of England provided for the churchwardens to be chosen by the minister and parishioners jointly each year "but if they cannot agree upon such a choice, then the minister shall choose one, and the parishioners another". In Kings Sutton there may not have been disagreement but, during the incumbency of Rev. Robert Mansell from

---

[6] Quoted in Eric Carlson: 'The origins, function and status of the office of churchwarden with particular reference to the diocese of Ely', in M Spufford *The World of Rural Dissenters, 1520 – 1725* (Cambridge 1995), p. 177

[7] S A Peyton (ed.), *The Churchwardens' Presentments in the Oxfordshire Peculiars*, Oxfordshire Record Society vol 10 (1928) pp. 288-9

[8] R K Gilkes (ed.), *The "Bawdy Court" of Banbury: The Act Book of the Peculiar Court of Banbury 1625 – 1638*, Banbury Historical Society vol 26 (1997)

*c.*1657 to *c.*1662, the vicar often recorded that he had chosen one of the churchwardens "according to the custom used in Kings-Sutton" (p. 87).

Canon 89 further decreed that "all churchwardens at the end of their year, or within a month at the most, shall before the minister and the parishioners give up a just account of such money as they have received, and also what particularly they have bestowed in reparations and otherwise, for the use of the church" and hand over any money or other church possessions to the next churchwardens. Occasionally the accounts show that they were audited at this stage (pp. 73, 81); and on a single occasion in 1641 the accounts record that some expenditure incurred by the churchwardens was disallowed (p. 45).

From the handwriting of the accounts, one can see that in many years they were copied out fair at the end of the year but in others the churchwardens or their amanuenses wrote in entries as they went along. In 1692 no fewer than six different hands can be identified in the expenditure accounts. One of these belonged to John Whitaker, the glazier, whose handwriting appears in several years and who was paid 3s in 1692 for "Righting our leveys & setting down our layings out" (p.182). Another belonged to George Maule, the innkeeper, who was evidently asked to write down the fact that he had just been paid 1s 6d "for a hondred of colls for the plomers yuse" (p. 181). The vicar, William Bradley, wrote the expenditure accounts for 1694, 1695 and part of 1696. Mr Bradley also wrote out the levy of 25 November 1697, but that was unusual; the levies were generally written by someone with professional skills in writing. The vicar (except John Creeke) wrote most of the entries about the appointment of churchwardens, and the lists of names which followed were normally the signatures of those concerned (or their marks). The majority of churchwardens were literate, though not necessarily to the extent of writing out the accounts, and one (probably Edward Toms) who wrote most of the accounts for 1636-48 had an exquisite hand. He was followed in 1651-52 by another, John Quatermaine, whose handwriting and spelling were definitely not so good.

What kind of people were the churchwardens? This has been a subject of some debate, effectively summarised by J S Craig in 'Co-operation and initiatives: Elizabethan churchwardens and the parish accounts of Mildenhall',[9] who says that "By the late sixteenth century, it is clear the office of churchwarden was commonly staffed by the middling sort of people, although this is to use a term that was not yet in common currency." This is borne out by the experience of Kings Sutton, where almost every churchwarden was a landowner in a small way or at least a

---

[9] *Social History* vol 18 No 3 (1993). The quotation comes from p. 363.

householder but was never from the family of the lord of the manor and seldom from the biggest houses. It is possible to tell this from the 22 single or multiple levies which are recorded. Only three churchwardens (Richard Taylor 1641, Christopher North 1658 and John Meacocke 1699) appear not to have been liable for the levy, and the other 76 were the owners on average of one or two yardlands. Every year at least one of those elected lived in Kings Sutton, but the other frequently came from Astrop or less often Charlton or Purston. Walton, which was depopulated and owned by an absentee landlord, was never represented.

Since the parish officials who had to be appointed each year included not only the churchwardens but also sidesmen, overseers of the poor, surveyors of the highways and a constable, and most were annual appointments, they must have taken up most of the able-bodied men available. (They were always men.) Of the appointments, the churchwardens were probably the most senior but there is no discernible progression of individuals from one appointment to another.

As J S Craig has said, "holding the office of churchwarden was a mark of status and honour within local communities that was rarely spurned".[10] Although fines could be imposed in some parishes on those who refused to serve (which in itself is an indication that those chosen had to be men of some substance) there is some evidence of men going out of their way to get elected. Two examples from the 1630s may be quoted: a resident of March in Cambridgeshire was presented for alleging that one of the churchwardens had bribed the curate in order to obtain his office;[11] and William Parker of Myddle in Shropshire was alleged to have given the rector's brother a side of bacon "to the end hee would persuade his brother the Rector to choose him Churchwarden, and afterwards hee made that yeare the epoch of his computation of all accidents, and would usually say such a thing was done soe many yeares beefore or after the yeare that I was Churchwarden".[12]

RECEIPTS

Among the receipts which the churchwardens accounted for, the most important were the church levies. Apart from the Civil War period, one or more were levied in most years "by the minister and major part of the parish present for necessary uses and repairs of our parish church of King Sutton". Church rates originated in the common law duty of parishioners to repair the nave of the church, where they sat. John of Athon, writing about 1340, said "Every parishioner is bound to repair the church

---

[10]   *Social History*, as fn. 9, p. 364
[11]   Eric Carlson (fn. 6): p. 182
[12]   Richard Gough: *The History of Myddle (1701)*, ed. David Hey (1981), p. 239

according to the portion of land he possesses ...... and the number of animals he keeps and feeds there". In 1342 John Stratford, Archbishop of Canterbury, gave a ruling that all having any property in a parish except the glebe, whether resident or not, must pay towards the repair of the church according to their possessions and revenues.[13] Before 1600 a major source of revenue came from church ales, when the village gathered for communal celebrations and clubbed together to produce, sell and drink ale and to sell any malt left over; but as church ales went out of fashion levies took over as the main source of revenue. In South Newington the process can be seen taking place in the churchwardens accounts, with the last recorded sale of malt in 1606,[14] and the same may have occurred in Kings Sutton. In any event the practice of church levies was well established by 1636.

The levy was payable by all the owners of yardlands in the common fields according to their holdings, by the holders of certain enclosed land (presumably on account of the fact that it was once part of the common fields), and by the occupiers of numerous houses belonging to one or other of the two manors in Kings Sutton. Throughout the seventeenth century those liable were listed in the accounts and so it is possible to trace the passing of property ownership from one hand to another. With the property went the liability to pay. The lists were used by the churchwardens to record payments as they came in. Against each entry an 'X' was marked on payment, or in the case of those with bigger liabilities two Xs, suggesting that they paid in instalments. Defaulters, of whom there were a few each year, could be identified by the absence of the X. An indication of the amount of effort that was involved in collecting the levies can be got from the list in April 1639 (pp. 25-7) of those who had still not paid the levy imposed in October 1638; and from the defaulters in 1692 (pp. 187-8).

The amount of the levy was determined by custom at so much a holding, and then the parish would decide whether to call for a single, double or greater levy. The normal payment was a double levy, when those in Kings Sutton paid at a rate of 2s a yardland, Astrop at 1s a yardland, and Charlton at 6d a yardland. The explanation for the differences is unknown, though it might be partly related to the distance of the settlements from the church; moreover the yardlands in Kings Sutton were almost certainly larger than in Astrop and Charlton.[15] The

---

[13]   W E Tate *The Parish Chest* (Cambridge Univ. Press 1969 (1st ed 1946)) p. 93

[14]   *South Newington Churchwardens' Accounts* (as fn. 1), pp. 3-44

[15]   Yardlands were units of landholding whose size varied from place to place. Kings Sutton was unusual in having large areas of meadow and pasture, alongside the river Cherwell, compared with Astrop and Charlton, and in having far fewer yardlands, that is arable land in the common fields. At enclosure at the end of the

Lord of the Manor (Richard Kenwrick and his descendants) paid 9s for his land. The single occupier of Walton paid a hefty £2 13s 4d for his old enclosures and the occupiers of Purston shared a payment of £1 6s 8d for theirs. The exact number of yardlands in each person's ownership can be traced from the levy of August 1675 (pp. 124-6) which specifies them; it also highlights the fragmentation of holdings, as in the case of one of the Thomas Toms in Kings Sutton who owned half a yardland, one cottage and "sume od land", or Widow Pargiter who had "3 qurt & a halfe", i.e. seven eighths of a yardland.

Then there were cottagers in Kings Sutton, who paid at the rate of 6d a cottage if it belonged to the Lord's manor, or 4d if it belonged to the Parsonage manor. But some of these payments were also broken down into fractions, with people paying 3d or 2d, presumably because cottages were shared. In a last category which was liable to levy were the two mills, Twyford mill, with its meadow and the unidentified "Garrett's acres", and the little mill, which must have been in the dip of Mill Lane on the way to Walton.

The total amount which could be raised by a double levy was £11 4s 8d, no small amount when one remembers that the church rate was not the only levy to which the villagers were subject. The poor rate was levied on many of the same people, and for example the poor rate levy of March 1652 raised £7 0s 10d,[16] and after 1654 highway rates were introduced so that the Surveyors of the Highways, who were responsible for the village roads, were no longer dependent on voluntary labour. The parish was also liable to rates each year for the county ḡaol and for the relief of "maimed soldiers" and mariners, which the churchwardens were required to collect (see below).

The other sources of revenue which Kings Sutton church enjoyed on a regular basis were the proceeds from letting the church barn at £1 a year; selling the grass in meadows belonging to the church – Lady Mead, the Nothings in Lake Mead, Wet Ham and a ley on Rye Hill; and the rent of 4s for two lands (or strips) in the common fields of Kings Sutton. The most lucrative of these was the church grass which was let to one or two different parishioners each year and brought in between £3 17s and £7 6s 8d, depending on the size of the crop. Baker's *History and Antiquities of the County of Northampton* (1822-30)[17] described an Inquisition at Northampton in 1630, before commissioners appointed by the court of

---

eighteenth century, Kings Sutton, Astrop and Charlton had 1,185, 1,565 and about 1,000 acres respectively of land enclosed, which incorporated 17, 77 and 59 yardlands. This suggests that Kings Sutton's yardlands could have been about twice the size of the others.

[16]   Northamptonshire Record Office 188P/11
[17]   Baker, vol 1, p.702

Chancery, which found that the churchwardens of Kings Sutton had from time immemorial received rents from various properties in the village until these were misappropriated by a churchwarden called Richard Chambers in 1564, and the court ordered their reinstatement. The properties were an ancient messuage called the Great Church House, with doles of meadow called the Nothings in Lake Mead and Wethames; the Little Church House with further doles of meadow in the same places; the Church Barn; the Church kitchen; and the Church Chamber and Church Shop. They belonged to the church and the parishioners in trust for the repair of the church, its bells and its clock. Baker went on to say that the houses were no longer standing but "there are five cottages, probably on their site, adjoining the churchyard, and 3 acres 3 roods of land in the meadow near Twyford, vested in the churchwardens for the above purposes".

Some at least of these properties were standing throughout the time of the accounts in this volume. Occasional receipts came from rent from church houses, and from sales of old thatch off the houses (p. 179) and the church barn (p. 217). There are references to four or five houses (or dwellings) belonging to the church (see pp. 60, 69-70) but the records of rent paid are very few. It may be significant that in 1687 payments were received from the overseers of the poor for two of the houses; perhaps the houses were usually occupied rent free. Other receipts came from burials in the church where the standard cost of opening up a grave was 6s 8d; sales of wood growing on church property; and the sale of two pewter bottles (p. 74) and an old bible (p. 219).

The last source of revenue was the Easter collection when each communicant was expected to contribute a halfpenny. For most years between 1636 and 1648 a receipt of 10s is noted, with in addition in 1649-51 the information that "there are three yeares halfpence for the easter communion in Mr Creekes hand" (p. 61). Since it is unlikely that there were exactly 240 communicants each year, this may have been a conventional way of recording the collection which was then passed to the vicar, though in 1639 the recorded collection was 10s 6d. From 1652 on no mention of the Easter collection is made. This does not necessarily indicate that the practice ceased, or that it was not resumed at the Restoration. But there does seem to have been one or more periods in the 1650s when the parish was without a vicar. Although John Creeke's death appears in the Kings Sutton burial register in 1655, his wife's appears there in 1652 when she was described as wife of the "late vicar of Kings Sutton". No name of a successor is found in the accounts until Robert Mansell in 1657 (p. 77). The churchwardens were chosen by the minister and major part of the parish in 1652 and 1656, but in between the minister is missing. (Further interregnums may have occurred during the periods from 1663-68, and from 1669-74.)

EXPENDITURE

1 Fabric

Apart from complying with the requirements of the church courts, the churchwardens' main expenditure was on the fabric of the church. This they undertook both as a matter of necessity and of pride in their church and also because the archdeacon's Visitations obliged them to do so.

In most years there was work to be done on the roof and on the windows. The churchyard wall and the church gate needed repair every two or three years, except in the period between the Civil War and the Restoration when they were largely neglected. Exceptionally paving stones had to be brought in to stop up the path "when the gate was burnt by the souldiers" (p. 53) in 1643; and the gate was replaced in 1648 (p. 61). Inside, there were replastering and whitewashing to be done in 1638/9, 1648, 1660, 1686 and 1699. And in many years there was "work done about the church" by a variety of masons, carpenters and labourers.

Major structural work occurred towards the end of the century. The spire and the steeple were repaired in 1687; the nave was partly reroofed in 1692; and further reroofing and structural work were done in 1697. In this last year expenditure on the church fabric was over £80, compared with more normal expenditure of perhaps £3-£4. It was no doubt with feeling that on 17 June 1698 John Haynes and Charles Wheeler, the churchwardens for that year, made a presentment to the Peculiar Court of Banbury of "Mr Thomas Margetts Tent to the Impropriator [of the Rectory of Kings Sutton] for not repaireing of the Roofe of the Chancell being so much out of repaire that it raines in, & for not mending of the windows. Wee present Edward Wyatt for not paying of 9 Taxes [i.e. levies] made towards the repaire of the Church each Tax amounting to 10d in the whole 7s 6d".[18] The parish had clearly made a superhuman effort to raise money for making the nave watertight and Thomas Margetts, who was responsible for the chancel, had not done his bit. Indeed in 1699 the churchwardens were presenting Thomas Margetts for not paying his "tenn Rattes or taxes made for the reparacons of the church being 1s 8d". And the work did not end there, because in 1704 two exceptional entries noted £56 19s 10d "paid to Mr Watts for ye ploming work done at ye Church", and £7 3s 0d "paid to Mr Watts for 13 hundered futt of ocken bords at eleven shillings a hundered".

Most of the work was done by men from the parish. Only the plumber whose job it was to lay and repair lead on the roof regularly came from outside. The painter employed in 1686, John Jameson, may also have been an outsider. The Kings Sutton glaziers were members of the Whitaker family, John, Michael and then John again; and the demand for

---

[18]   *Churchwardens' Presentments* (fn. 12), p. 303

their services was so great that until the Civil War John Whitaker was paid an annual wage. Thereafter the glaziers were paid piece work, beginning with the replacement of all the windows in 1648, no doubt to put right Civil War damage. The blacksmiths were mostly members of the Upstone family, and there appear to have been two smithies in Kings Sutton. In the earlier years of the accounts the blacksmiths were Edward Upstone and Michael Upstone; and in the later years Ladowick Upstone and William Upstone. A third blacksmith, Robert Lucas, came from Charlton.

Among at least nine carpenters the most important were William Dolton, Thomas Williams and Thomas Ward. Masons included Thomas Allibone, Daniel Smith, John Stratford and John and George Fathers. The chief supplier of oil and nails was latterly Robert Jennings but before him it was, unusually, a widow, Margaret Pillie. Another female supplier was Gooddie Gervise who provided "youllming", i.e. thatching material, for the church barn in 1658. Leather was supplied by a variety of people in Kings Sutton – Austin Smallbone, Thomas Clements, Edward Watson and Robert Kerby. Beer was provided by three innkeepers, George Clarke, and John and George Maule, all of whom were active in the church.

The accounts can give an idea of wage rates, which varied according to skills. A labourer's wage might be 6d-10d a day (1692); a mason 1s 4d (1653, 1694); a carpenter 1s 4d-1s 6d (1655, 1673); a slatter 1s 2d-1s 6d (1662, 1692); and, most expensive, the plumber 2s (1656). But these compare unfavourably with the sum of 8s paid to "Mr Yomanes for preching one time" in 1679 (p. 138).

2 Bells

Another major item of expense in the church was the bells, which reflected what an important place they occupied in the life of the parish, summoning the faithful to church, marking the most sacred part of the communion service, or helping the village to celebrate special occasions.

The most consistent outgoings paid for bellropes. Until 1657 about three ropes were replaced every year at a cost of 2s 6d-3s 0d per rope (or 1s 6d for second hand ropes in 1643 and 1648). Then the pattern changed and replacements took place on average every three years, and usually a whole set of six was bought, at a price which settled down at 22s 6d for a set.

This change of practice may have been the result of good housekeeping, but it may also have been influenced by the rehanging of the bells in 1653, when the accounts contain no fewer than 23 entries, the building or rebuilding of a new ringing floor in 1654, and the mending of two bell wheels and adjustments to the bell hangings in 1655.

These major works were not unique. Something was done virtually every year, apart from the purchase of grease for the bells. (Greasing the bells, and oiling the church clock, were duties of the clerk.) On four occasions leather was bought for the baldricks, which were inserted into the joint between the bell and its clapper to reduce friction and provide insulation, and in three other years money was paid for linings, which may have been the same; and on ten occasions work was done on the clappers themselves. In 1657 leather was bought "for ye bathering of ye bells" – a process which is not identifiable now. In eleven years, work on the bell wheels was specifically mentioned.

In the bell tower one of the major events of the period of these accounts was the "casting of the gt bell & for mettell as was put in" in 1666 at a cost of £1 3s 10d and 2s 2d for "bringing it home" (p. 103). It seems that this was probably a recasting of the present No 8 bell, made in 1602 by Bartholomew Atton of Buckingham, and it had to be sent away to be done. In the same year Ladowick Upstone, the Kings Sutton blacksmith, charged 14s 6d for the great bell clapper and other ironwork.

The peal of eight bells in Kings Sutton tower now includes four seventeenth century bells and the venerable No 7 made by J Rufford of London in about 1350. Two (Nos 4 and 5) were made by James Keene of Woodstock in 1626; and No 3 was cast by an itinerant bell founder Michael Darbie in 1655. That there was a Sanctus or "Saints" bell in the seventeenth century is confirmed by entries in the accounts for 1655 and 1684, but this was replaced in 1738. The Darbie bell creates something of a mystery since there is no reference to it in the accounts, apart from the blacksmith making wedges for it; maybe it was paid for privately.

Another year of extensive work on the bells was 1675. Robert Lucas, the blacksmith, mended most or all the bell clappers, while Thomas Williams the carpenter mended the bells (on three separate occasions), the treble gudgeons,[19] the bell frames and garters[20] and the ringing floor.

3   Clock

The church clock also required regular maintenance, both by oiling or the replacement of wires. In four years – 1640, 1648, 1665 and 1693 – the dial needed attention, and in 1680 the clock was in such a bad state that it had to be taken away for mending. Then in 1696 it was replaced altogether. The entries begin with a deal being made with the clockmaker in Banbury, Mr Parish, at a cost of 6s 2d; then a down payment of £1, to confirm that the churchwardens were in earnest; followed by payment of

---

[19]   Gudgeons are part of the bearings on which the bell swings on the headstock

[20]   The garter hole is where the rope joins the bell wheel. The wheel is invariably made of wood

the outstanding balance of £9; and lastly 4s spent in the inn when Mr Parish was paid. Mr Parish kept the old clock in part exchange (p. 198).

4   Furniture and furnishings

In 1640 the outgoing churchwardens, George Toms and Thomas Tayler, recorded (p. 40) that "we have delivered to the new Churchwardens Richard Haynes and Robert Toms all the Church goods that is to say the Church Bookes a surplis a table Cloath a Carpet the pulpit Cloath and the Cushion wth other necessaries belonging to the Church". This list is valuable, first for showing that custody of these items was the churchwardens' responsibility, and secondly because it is so short. It may of course be incomplete: there is no mention of any cross, chalice or candlesticks, for example, and it does not explain what was included in the church's "necessaries". But the church must have been sparsely furnished.

The surplice and the table cloth appear regularly in the accounts. Someone in the parish was paid for washing them several times a year, and the surplice was often in need of mending as well. Indeed the surplice, which was supplied by the church for the priest to wear, was evidently an important part of the ritual of the church. In 1642 it was taken away as part of the Puritan purge, though prudently the churchwardens paid Bess Harris to wash and mend it first in case it should be needed again (p. 53); and after the Restoration a new one which was ordered from Oxford cost the massive sum of £3 10s (p. 96). At that price, equivalent to several hundred pounds in modern terms, the surplice must have been heavily decorated with lace. Another replacement was bought in 1694 for £2 9s 6d and a special box was bought to keep it in (p. 195).

A new table cloth for the Communion table (i.e. an altar cloth, but it was considered too "Papist" to call it that) was bought in 1639 for 5s 7d (p. 29). At the same time a prayer book for the commemoration of the gunpowder plot on 5th November and a new parchment register for christenings, marriages and burials were bought and four shillings was "given to the bookbinder in change betweene the old Common prayer booke and a booke for the Clarke to answer in" (p. 29). This followed the purchase in 1638 of a great bible and a Book of Common Prayer for £3 7s (p. 17). Some of these books may have been discarded during the Civil War; in 1662 there is a record of the purchase for 10s of the newly appointed Book of Common Prayer, a book of Canons and a table of marriages (presumably the list of those degrees of kindred and affinity within which marriage was or was not allowed) (p. 96). Another Book of Common Prayer was bought in 1682 (p. 152) and another in 1693; and in 1693 a bible as well, and a chained book in the church was bound and a new chain was bought (pp.188-9). The only purchase of a book recorded during the Interregnum was one "which was anact for ye sabbath" in 1657 (p. 78); this was a requirement of an Act of the Protectorate (1657 c.XV) for the better observation of the Lord's Day – the churchwardens were supposed to enforce the Act, and to cause it to be read in church annually. In 1678 a register was bought for recording that burials had taken place in woollen shrouds, as required by an Act of that year (p. 135). Then in 1694 the churchwardens had to buy a "paper of alterations" following the death of Queen Mary, presumably to change the prayers for the Royal Family (p. 195).

The biggest expense which recurred regularly was for bread and wine for the communion. Annual expenditure on this before the Civil War was between £3 10s and £4 10s, apart from an astonishing £10 2s at Easter 1638 (p. 14). By the end of the century the amount spent had fallen to about £1 a year. There must have been a number of factors contributing to this reduction. One was a fall in the number of Communion services (see below), and another might have been a decline in the number of communicants; but these cannot be the only explanation. One cause might have been a reduction in the cost of wine: either the cost fell nationally, or the parish took to buying cheaper wine. However, the latter seems unlikely since the cost of wine in Kings Sutton in the 1680s and 1690s was about the same as in South Newington and Culworth[21] at 1s a pint or 2s a bottle. Perhaps the communicants simply started to drink less. (Consumption at the communion service then must have been nearer a glassful of wine than the modern day sip. In Culworth in 1662 two gallons of wine were bought for Christmas, and at Easter "four gallons and one pint".) At Easter 1686 seven bottles were consumed in Kings Sutton; this expenditure of 14s compares with £2 5s, that is more than three times as much, at Easter in the 1630s. Easter expenditure fell slightly in the later 1650s and 1660s to around £1 19s, and then suddenly halved after 1670, seldom exceeding £1. Suppliers of wine included in particular Thomas Norris of Aynho (mentioned in 1642, 1648, 1662-6 and 1676),[22] and also suppliers in Banbury (pp. 29, 53, 164) and Charlton (p. 195). Bread was baked in Kings Sutton, for instance by Edward Williams the village baker (pp. 96, 105, 112) and his son John (p. 196).

Miscellaneous items which appear in the accounts include the church ladder (p. 71), another ladder belonging to Mr Kenwrick, the lord of the manor, which the church had to repair (p. 71), and "a tree to make a

---

[21] Wine in South Newington cost 1s a pint in 1664 (*op. cit.* (fn. 1) no. 70); in Culworth it cost 1s a pint in 1662 and 2s a bottle in 1676 (Northamptonshire Record Office 94P/22)

[22] Thomas Norris was landlord of the Red Lion at Aynho, and churchwarden in 1684 (N. Cooper, *Aynho*, Banbury Historical Society vol. 20 (1984), pp. 112-3, 171)

ladder" (p. 104); the church leather buckets (p. 69); and the coals which had to be bought from time to time to provide heat for workmen, and especially the plumber who needed fire to solder the lead of the roof (pp. 142, 181).

The quality of accounting was generally good, but after what was evidently a rocky patch the churchwardens in 1655 recorded a payment of 2d to the carpenter for "I know not what" (p. 71); and in the same year declared that "there is behinde for the Church barne we know not what, and there wilbe a true Accompt made of all particulers wee know not when" (p. 68).

5 Secular property

Expenditure on property outside the church and churchyard took two forms. First the church meadows had to be maintained and this involved scouring the drainage ditches in Lady Mead every few years, or in 1656 "scowering of the river" (p. 74). Secondly the church barn and the church houses needed repair. The barn was reroofed in 1636 (p. 5) and rethatched in 1658 (p. 80), and in 1664 modest repairs were funded by coming to an arrangement with Mr Kenwrick, who was given the use of the barn at a reduced rent for a number of years (p. 101), provided he kept it in repair. Very little was spent by the churchwardens on the church houses until 1699-1700 when they were reroofed (pp. 221-3).

6 Beer

The importance of beer as a village lubricant is apparent from the frequency with which it was bought by the churchwardens to reward workmen, to seal a deal or just to mark a special occasion. Thus in the 1690s "gave the carpntors in beere" 6d (p. 188); 3s "pd for Ale given to ye workemen when they ware at worke at ye church" (p. 207); or simply 6d "spent on beere" (p. 189). George Maule was the innkeeper at whose inn 1s was "spent att Geo: Maules making the Levey" (p. 195); 5s 4d "paid at George Mauls at severall times with the plomer and other worckmen & bargning" (p. 198); and 4s "paid at George Maules what was spent when we paid mr paris for the neu clock" (p. 198). It seems likely that beer was again the explanation for the entry that 5s 6d was "spent upon the Neighbrs about disposing Mr Heynes money"[23] (p. 194) and when 10s was "spent when the towensmen dide mett abut the Repares of the Church" (p. 180). And every year from 1675 to 1700 a sum, initially of 2s 6d rising in 1682 to 6s, was paid for ale to reward the

---

[23]   This refers to the setting up of the Haynes charity in Kings Sutton. John Haynes in 1688 left £100, which funded payments of 10s each to ten of the oldest and most deserving inhabitants of the parish on Easter day.

ringers for a peal to commemorate the Gunpowder Plot on 5 November (p. 127).

7 Secular duties

Several secular duties were imposed on the churchwardens which became more visible in the accounts as the century wore on. First of these was the statutory duty to make payments, usually of 6d or so, to travellers who had a pass. These would usually be people returning to, or being returned to, their home parish under the terms of the poor laws......
Other travellers were men such as six soldiers returning from hospital in Ostend (p. 195), or a woman who stayed overnight with three children (p. 179). No explanation is given why one payment of 6d to some travellers was disallowed (p. 45). The frequency with which payments were made in Kings Sutton, for instance to 44 passengers in 1691-2, compared with the small numbers recorded by other local churchwardens[24] may reflect the size of Kings Sutton and its geographical position, though it is also probable that payments were sometimes recorded separately from the main church accounts.

A second duty was the collection and distribution of money to letters of request or briefs. These were officially authorised or private collections for charitable purposes, and the accounts show what a large-scale network of collections existed, especially for disaster relief. Many of the Kings Sutton entries are anonymous – simply "paid to a letter of request" – but the records of the neighbouring parish of Newbottle[25] for the years 1660-76 show that, out of 125 collections there, 56 were for fire damage (including the Great Fire of London in 1666), 15 for rebuilding or repairing churches, 3 for foreign hostages and 4 for those sick of the plague in London in 1665. The Kings Sutton collections will probably have included many of the same items, as well as one for a shipwreck (p. 190), two for breaches of sea defences in Lincolnshire (p. 182) and the Fens (p. 189), another for the release of merchants held hostage in Turkey (pp. 162, 164) and again "for sume that were taken by the turk" (p. 180). These were not the only international requests. Collections were made for Poland and Bohemia in 1658 (p. 81), French protestants in 1688 after the revocation by the French king of the Edict of Nantes (p. 162), and a request from Flanders (p. 195). In England requests came from nearly every county, not just locally. Moreover the numbers mounted fast towards the end of the century, with a peak in the years 1693-6: in 1696 81 payments are recorded, amounting in all to £7 10s 5¼d.

---

[24]   For example Culworth and Eydon; see Northamptonshire Record Office 94P/22 and 120P/46

[25]   Northamptonshire Record Office 219P/2

Another duty which became prominent after 1674 was payment for vermin. To modern eyes, hedgehogs and sparrows are surprising targets for official disapproval, and so are the numbers taken. The churchwardens paid 4d a piece for 68 hedgehogs in 1696, and 2d a dozen for 1,368 sparrows in 1699-1700. The practice of paying a bounty on vermin originated in an Act of Parliament of 1532 (24 HVIII c. 10) which obliged each parish, township or hamlet to provide itself with a net to destroy rooks, crows and choughs, in order to protect the seed corn. Twopence a bird was payable by the lord of the manor. In 1566 another Act (14 Eliz c.11) renewed the earlier Act and transferred the duty of payment to churchwardens, who had to set up a fund for the purpose, assessed on all holders of land or tithes; magpies and owls were added to the list. By the eighteenth century, vermin with a price on their head included sparrows, foxes, hedgehogs, woodpeckers and jays. Why the payments in Kings Sutton for hedgehogs and sparrows did not occur before 1674 and then grew so strongly − apart from the fact that they offered the boys of the village a good source of money − is unclear, especially since in Eydon nearby a payment for three hedgehogs was made in 1666 and for sparrows in 1667,[26] and in Culworth a payment for sparrows was made in 1654.[27]

A fourth duty, which was regular at first and then disappeared after 1663, was the annual payment for the "gaol and maimed soldiers". This was actually two separate payments which became lumped together and cost the parish an average of 4s 4d a year in normal times, and more in the 1650s, peaking at 12s in 1657. The gaol payment was started under an Act of 1531-2 (23 HVIII c. 2) which ordered county gaols to be built, funded by taxes on the inhabitants of the county at a level set by the justices of the peace. An Act of 1601 "for the necessary relief of soldiers and mariners" (43 Eliz c. 3) decreed that parishes should be charged between 2d and 10d a week towards "the relief of sick, hurt and maimed soldiers and mariners", the money to be assessed by agreement of the parishioners and to be collected by the churchwardens and petty constable of each parish. Since the obligation to pay for gaols and maimed soldiers did not end in 1663, it must be assumed that Kings Sutton accounted differently for the payment after that date. As the money was paid to the constable (see for example p. 61), it probably appeared in the constable's accounts.

The last secular items of expenditure to note are those concerned with royal celebrations. The annual celebration on 5 November has already been mentioned. In 1687 a peal of thanksgiving was rung for "ye queene

---

[26]   Northamptonshire Record Office 120P/46

[27]   Northamptonshire Record Office 94P/22

being with child" (p. 164); on 10 June 1688 a male heir was born to James II and Mary of Modena. This was James Stuart, who as the Old Pretender led the 1715 Jacobite rebellion. In 1692 two shillings was "given to the Ringers for the victory against the French" (p. 182); this marked the naval victory against Louis XIV at the battle of La Hogue in the English Channel. In 1693 there was a celebration of a different kind when the ringers got three shillings on "the thanks giving day for king Wiliams safe return" (p. 189) after William III had been defeated by the Marshal de Luxembourg at the battle of Neeuwinden.

OTHER TRANSACTIONS

Whenever expenditure was high, the churchwardens imposed levies to cover the cost. Only in the 1650s did they experience the opposite, an excess of income over expenditure. So for a short period they took to lending out their spare cash at interest. It appears that between 1659 and 1662 £10 was lent out on bond, first to Christopher North (who had been churchwarden in 1658) and then to the vicar, Mr Mansell, and the parish received 12s per annum interest (pp. 82-3, 85, 90-1). Memoranda in the account book recorded the loans and each was crossed out when the money was repaid.

ARMINIANISM, PURITANISM AND THE CIVIL WAR

The contents of the Kings Sutton churchwardens' accounts differ little in broad outline from those of other parishes which have survived. However they are distinctive because of their detail and completeness, and they also cover the period of the Civil War, Interregnum and Restoration. This makes it possible to get some insight into the impact of the ecclesiastical upheavals of the time and how they affected Kings Sutton.

First it is no surprise to find evidence of the changes associated with Arminianism and imposed by Archbishop Laud on the Church of England in the decade before the Civil War. Arminianism was a reaction against the stark Calvinist doctrine of the Anglican church at the end of the sixteenth century and its emphasis on predestination. The Arminians discouraged the individualism which went with preaching and bible readings, and in their place laid more emphasis on ritual, the sacraments and the ceremonial of the liturgy. Especially after Laud became Archbishop of Canterbury in 1633 and Neile became Archbishop of York in 1632, non-conformity was expected to give way to conformity, and severity to the "beauty of holiness".

As a result, during the 1630s the interiors of many English parish churches were transformed. The main change involved the conversion of communion tables into altars, their removal from the middle of the chancel to the east end, and their enclosure with rails. The Bishop of Bath and Wells was one of the first to draw up a schedule of "reasons why the communion table in every church should be sett close under the east-window or wall with the ends north and south, and railed in" to underline its sanctity. One reason given was that "Daughters should be like their mother, the parochial churches should be like the cathedral churches, that soe there may be an uniformity in this respect in any church".[28] In the diocese of Peterborough, the bishop Francis Dee undertook a major drive in August 1637 to require the removal of communion tables to the east end – where they had been before the Reformation.[29] This led to a repeated tug-of-war between the diocese and the churchwardens of All Saints Northampton, where the communion table was moved back and forth.

In Kings Sutton a new communion table was bought from Bicester in 1636 and installed within a rail (p. 5). Since this was before Bishop Dee's campaign of 1637, it implies that Kings Sutton was quick to adopt the new Arminian practices without outside pressure. New books were bought in 1638-9 and a new table cloth for the communion table in 1639 (see above).

But this change was short-lived. The Laudian reforms were closely identified with the personal rule of Charles I and hostility to one soon became associated with hostility to the other. Parliamentary resistance to the king and Puritan resistance to the bishops united. In Kings Sutton the rails went in 1641, following a Parliamentary decision: "a Proclamation and confirmation concerning the takeing away the Rayles in the Chancell commanded to be read in the Church" (p. 46). In 1643 a Parliamentary Ordinance declared that "all monuments of idolatry and superstition should be removed and abolished", including all fixed altars, rails, chancel steps and "all crucifixes, crosses, and all images and pictures of any one or more persons of the Trinity, or of the Virgin Mary and all other images and pictures of Saints". The task of removal was laid on the churchwardens, who could levy a parish rate to cover the cost.[30] The expenditure on lime and plastering in 1648 (p. 60) may have reflected the painting out or removal of images. Certainly the item in 1650 "Ite to Robert Bricknell for washing out ye Kings armes" (p. 61) refers to whitewashing over the Royal Coat of Arms on the wall of the church after the king's execution and the abolition of the monarchy in 1649. Robert Bricknell was the constable.

---

[28] N Tyacke: *Anti-Calvinists. The Rise of English Arminianism c.1590-1640*, p. 203 (Oxford 1987)

[29] *ibid* p. 205

[30] *Public Duty and Private Conscience in Seventeenth Century England*, ed. Morrill, Slack and Woolf (1993) pp. 188-9

Other signs of the disruption caused by the Civil War appear from time to time. In 1642, a levy was written into the accounts but a note was added at the bottom of the list: "Memorandum this levie was written and made in the time of Warre and never gathered" (p. 53). As mentioned above, the surplice used in church services was taken away in 1643 and the church gate was burnt by soldiers in the same year.

What about the pattern of church services? The Parliamentarian leaders sought to suppress the Book of Common Prayer in favour of their Directory of Public Worship, to discontinue old Christian festivals such as Christmas, Easter and Rogationtide and to make admission to Holy Communion dependent on approved behaviour instead of being open to all (apart from the excommunicated). Except locally they were not very successful; and the speed of the Anglican restoration in 1660 confirmed that change had not gone deep. The bishops' diocesan institutions collapsed in 1642-3 and the bishops themselves were abolished in 1646. But the clergy mostly stayed in place. It has been calculated by John Morrill that less than 20 percent of clergy were dispossessed and that, assuming the normal death rate of ministers, 60-66 percent of all parishes had the same minister in 1649 as in 1642.[31]

Certainly Kings Sutton kept the same vicar, Mr Creeke, until at least 1651 (p. 62). But, as mentioned above, there may have been an interregnum before his successor was appointed and it could be significant of Puritan leanings that in 1654 an entry records a schoolmaster being fetched "to officiate here one sabbath" (p. 69).

John Morrill also deduces from wine and bread purchases that in 85 percent of parishes the pattern of communion services remained unchanged till 1646 and that when the nadir of services was reached in 1650 Easter was recorded in 43 percent of parishes. The Easter communion was certainly the great festival in Kings Sutton throughout the century and was not interrupted. But whereas until 1642 celebrations of Communion took place at four festivals – Easter, Midsummer (Whitsun), Michaelmas and Christmas – from 1644 onwards only an Easter Communion was recorded, until 1682 when the purchase of bread and wine for Christmas reappears.

The quantities of wine bought for Easter did not change during the Civil War or the Interregnum, which implies that the number of communicants was fairly constant. The only marked difference was the emergence of "other needful communions to poore people diseased" in 1645 (p. 54), "twelve private Communions to diseased people" in 1648

---

[31] 'The Church in England 1642-49', by John Morrill, in *Reactions to the English Civil War 1642-9*, ed. Morrill (1982)

(p. 59) and "many private communions" in 1649 (p. 60). If such sick communions took place before or after, they were not noted down.

Following the Restoration the old patterns were quickly reestablished, except in respect of the number of communions. Visitations restarted in 1661 (p. 91), and in 1662 a new surplice was bought along with the new Book of Common Prayer (p. 96).

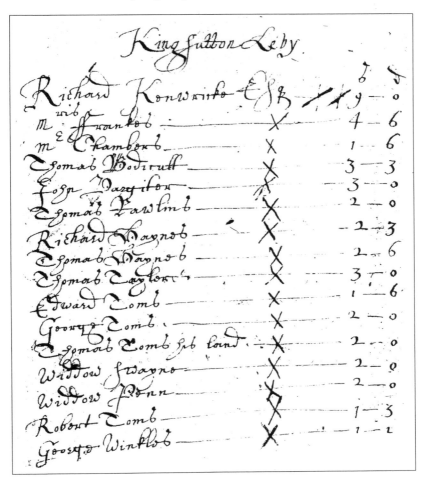

Extract from the levy of March 1639/40, showing contributors from Kings Sutton and the amount they had to pay. Each cross is the churchwardens' record that they had received the money. Richard Kenwricke paid in two instalments (pages 31-32).

The text of the accounts has been transcribed, so far as possible, exactly as written, even when the text was clearly not exactly what the author intended. Since some pages were written in several different hands, it is not uncommon to have the same word spelt in more than one way in close proximity. In the index however spellings have been harmonised around the most common form, or its modern equivalent, to make it easier to trace names and to avoid artificial differences arising from odd spellings. Three examples may be given to indicate why this is desirable. The surname of Thomas Allibone, the stonemason, is spelt nine different ways in the accounts, although phonetically they all produce the same result. The ground called Garretts Acres is referred to in 22 entries and is spelt in 14 different ways. Generally, as in these cases, the phonetic result is the same. But the blacksmith, Ladowick Upstone, has a Christian name which appears in 13 forms, including Laddicke, Ladvike, Ladwecke, Lodowick, Lodwick and Ludawick. It is hard to see a common pronunciation. Since the abbreviation Lad also appears, the version with an "a" has been preferred in the index.

Most of the accounts are in good condition. When the text is damaged so that words are missing, this is marked with an *. Where the text is not decipherable or is uncertain, the apparent spelling is given in square brackets, thus [Thealos] and [sallow]. Editorial comment or explanation is given in square brackets and italics, thus [*Page torn and missing*] and [*Harrogate*].

Money values are in £ s d (with 12d, that is pence, in the shilling and 20s in the pound). In the first years of the accounts most numbers were written in small Roman numerals, "xvjs iijd" for example. Very soon a mixture of Roman and Arabic numbers was introduced and after 1640 only solitary Roman numerals survived. After a few years in which the format fluctuated and pounds were usually not recorded – thus 25s 4d for example – a regular format was adopted with figures recorded in three columns, which might or might not be headed £ s d.

The sequence of items in the book is not always straightforward. Items of revenue and expenditure are mixed with items about the appointment of churchwardens and others. The transcription follows the sequence of the book, even though this occasionally results in entries appearing out of their natural order, because churchwardens have sometimes begun entries on a right-hand page before returning to the previous left-hand page. Only where a levy spreads over three right-hand pages, for example, interspersed with expenditure records on the left-hand pages, has the sequence of the book been broken, so that the text of the levy is kept continuous.

Kings Sutton
Churchwardens' Accounts
1636-1700

Kingsutton
October the 23rd Anno Dm 1636
A levie made by the maior part present for necessary uses and repaires of
our parish Church of Kingsutton aforsaid By us whose names are
subscribed   vzt

Kingsutton at two shillings ye yardland
Astrup at twelvepence the yardland
Charlton at six pence the yardland
Cottages of the Lords hold vjd a peece
Cottage of the Parsonage hold iiijd a peece
Walton levie   53s 4d
Purston levie   26s 8d
      Richard Kenwricke
      John Creeke minister

      Churchwardens   John [Pargiter]}

             *** ***}

[*Page torn and missing*]

    ***   ***

Edward Toms
George Toms
John Carpenter
Charles Butcher
Robert Toms
Thomas Haines
William Wyat
John Warner

[Page torn and missing]

[King Sutton levie]	
*** ***	*
Charles Butcher	*
Edward Williams	xd
francis Davis	xd
Richard Rawlins	vjd
Widdo: Colgrove	vjd
John Jenings	vjd
William Bricknell	vjd
John Upston	vjd
Willi: Peedle	vjd
John Sworder	vjd
John Clemens	vjd
Johon Rawlins	vjd
frances Whitby	iijd
William ***	iijd
*** ***	**

[This may be part of the same levy as above]

*** ***	**
William Pecover	vjd
Richard Arlatch	vjd
Henry Heritage	vjd
Robert Castell	vjd
Thomas field	vjd
Robert Bricknell	iiijd
Roger Jarvis	iiijd

Michaell Upston	iiijd
William Owers	iiijd
George Maule	iiijd
Thomas Wyatt	iiijd
Widdo: Price	iiijd
William Bett	iiijd
John Whitaker	iiijd
Thomas Harrise	iiijd
Widdo: longe	iiijd
John Kirby	ixd
Mr Creeke	iijd
Henry Bigge	iijd
George Andros	iijd
Thomas Darby	iijd
William fathers	ijd
William Cooper	ijd
Richard Yeats	ijd
[John Clemens]	ijd
Widdo: Stacie	ijd
William Peedle for Bishop house	ijd
William Peedle	ijd
[Richard] Nevells house	ijd
Allexander Smith	ijd
Henry Paynter	ijd
* Williams	ijd
Symon Wheler	ijd
William Hawese	ijd
William Pillie	ijd

[This may be part of the same levy as above]

Astropp levie

Mr Steward's land	xviijs
Mr Cartwright's land	ixs
Mr Hygherns	vs
Edmund Carpenter	iiijs
John Carpenter	iiijs vjd
John Wyatt	iiijs
Mr Chambers	iijs
Thomas Taylor	iijs iiijd
Mr Crew	ijs

William Newman	ijs
George Toms	ijs
William Wyatt	js
Mr Piggot	js
Edward Toms	js
John and Thomas Wyatt	vjd
Thomas Durman	vjd
Thomas Wyatt	vjd
*** ***	**
[Charlton levie]	
*** ***	**
Thomas Hobcroft	jd
John Garner	jd
William Flecknoll	jd
Robert Glase	jd

£11 3s 11d ob

Item received of Thomas Bodicott for the churche barne

                                                 xvis

Item received of the old churchwardens   vs ixd

Item received of widdo: Lucas for her husband's grave

           in the church   vjs viijd

Item for Mr Pargiters grave   vjs viijd

Item received of a former levy due [in the old]

           churchwardens tyme   xvs

Item received of the communicants at Ester   xs

                                         £3 0s 1d

The layinges forth of us John Pargiter and Edmund Carpenter for this our
yeare 1636

Inprimis to the bookbinder for this booke	iijs vjd
for bread and wine at Midsomer Communion	viijs xjd
Item for nayles to mend the bell whell	ijd
to Edward Upston for loocking to the clocke	js
Item bread and wine at Michaellmas	xs xd
Item at Michaellmas visitation for our dinners	viijs vjd
Item to the Register for our oathes	ijs
to the parrytor for warning the Court	viijd
Item William Dolton for worke about the Church and the Church barne	ixs
Item for Rafters for the Church barne	xjs *d
Item for lathes for the barne	vjs xd
Item for lath nayles	iijs
to Richard Andros wife for her worke about the barne	iijs
Item William Hogges and his wife for theire worke about the barne	vs vjd
Item the carryage of the Rafters from Brackly and other caryag	xs
Item to George Toms for butts of hall[me]	*
Item to John Warner for on load [of] hallme for the Church barne	*
Item to Edmund Carpenter for [caryage] of that load of hallme	*
Item to William Wyatt for on land of * * *	*
Item to Edmund Carpenter for on [land] *	*
Item to John Carpenter for on [land *	*
Item to John Pargiter for [caryage]	*
Item to Edward Stone for mending the Church wall	*
Item John Upston for nayles	*
Item to a poore man haveing a p* to shew of his very greate lose *	*
Item to the plumer for soder and his worke about the church	*
Item Michaell Upston for two yron hookes	*
Item to John * * * Bister for the New Communion Table and the Raill	*
Item spent at Bister when we went for it	*
Item for the carrage of it home	*
Item to the * * * soldiers	iiijs *
Item Edward Stone for worke about the Raile and other worke	ijs vjd

Item spent in bread and beare when John George came to take the worke	ijs
and when he came to set it up after it came home	js
Item to Thomas Darby for worke	ijs vjd
To Edward Rowsam for ridinge the Chancell and other worke	ijs
Item to Edward Upston for plates for the bellwheell	iijs
Item Thomas Durman for his worke about the Church barne	vjs vjd
Item for fower loads of stones for the Church wall	js
Item for caringe of the stones	iijs iiijd
Item to Edward Ston for on days worke about the Church wall	js
Item for bread and wine for Chrismas Communion	xiijs vd
Item to Joale and lame soldiers	iiijs iiijd
Item to Edward Upston for nailes and hinges for the Raile	ijs
Item paide for the washing of * * * clothes six tymes	ijs
* * pounds of grease * * bells	js
* * Clarke for his wages	iijs iiijd
* * William Dolton for his * * of the seats	viijs
* * Edmund Carpenter for * * the Church seats	ixs xd
* * Whitakers his yeares wages	viijs
* * John Upston for nailes	vijd
* * * two poore men	viijd
paid John Watters for the [mats] about the Raill	iiijs xd
for bread and wine on palme Sunday and on Ester day	xlvijs vjd
for nailes	ijd
to widdo: pillie for oyle	ijd
Item payd for the carriing of the [register]	iijs
*** for the wrighting of the Registers	*

King Sutton levie   1636

Mr Richard Kenwricke esq	ixs
Mrs ffrankes	iiijs vjd
Mr Mychaell Chambers	is vjd
Thomas Bodicott	ijs
Mr Pargiter	ijs
John Pargiter	iijs
Richard Haynes	ijs iiijd
ffoulke Meacoke	iijs
Thomas Haynes	ijs vid
Edward Toms	ijs
George Toms	ijs
Thomas Toms	ijs
Widdo: Swaine	ijs
Thomas Penn	ijs
Robert Toms	js vjd
George Winckles	js
Widdo: Price	vid
Thomas Haynes for little mill	*
Richard Hanly	*
Charles Butcher	*
Edward Williams	*
Jeromie Parishe	*
ffrances Davis	*
Richard Rawlins	*
Widdo: Colgrove	*
John Jenings	*
William Bricknell	*
John Upston	*
William Peedle	*
John Sworder	*
John Clemense	*
John Rawlins	*
ffrances Whitby	*
William Parish	*
Katherine Jenings	*
Symon Watts	*
Elizabeth Darby	*
Widdo: Bett	*
Edward Upston	*
John Warner	*
[William] Whitwell	*
William Pecover	vjd

Richard Arlatch	vjd
Henry Herytage	vjd
Robert Castill	vjd
Thomas field	vjd
Robert Bricknell	iiijd
Roger Jarvis	iiijd
Michaell Upston	iiijd
William Owers	iiijd
George Maule	iiijd
Thomas Wyatt	iiijd
Widdo: Price	iiijd
William Bett	iiijd
John Whitakers	iiijd
Thomas Harris	iiijd
Widdo: Longe	iiijd
John Kirby	ixd
Widdo: Bigge	iijd
Mr Creeke	iijd
George Andros	iijd
Thomas Darby	iijd
William fathers	ijd
William Cooper	ijd
Richard Yeates	ijd
John Clements	ijd
Widdo: Statie	ijd
Willi: Peedle for Bish**	*
Richard [Nevell]	*
*** ***	*
[Astrop levy] * * * *	
John Wyatt	iiijs
Mr Chambers	iijs
Thomas Taylor	ijs iiijd
Mr Crew	ijs
William Newman	ijs
George Toms	ijs
William Wyatt	ijs
Mr Pigott	js
Edward Toms	js
John Wyatt & Thomas Wyatt	vjd
Thomas Durman	vjd
Thomas Wyatt	vjd
Thomas Penn	vjd
William Smith	ijd

Walton levie

[Sir] Thomas Pope	liijs iiijd

Purston

Mr Blincow	xs
Mr [Blincow]	xiijs iiijd
Mr Craswell	iijs iiijd

Charleton

Mr Craswelles land	iijs iiijd
* Haddon	iijs ijd ob
*	ijs iiijd ob

Undecimo die Aprilis 1637

Churchwardens chosen by the minister and maior part of the parish
the day and yeare aforsaid

Churchward: { John Pargiter
{ Edmund Carpenter

Sidsmen { Edward Toms
{ Richard Haines

Overseeres for the
poor { Edward Williams
{ Richard Taylor

Overseeres for
the highways { George Jenings
{ Robert Bricknell

John Creeke vicar

Richard Kenwricke
John Carpenter
Thomas Rawlines
Thomas Haynes
John Warner

Decimo octavo ffebruarii 1637
A levie made by the minister & maior part of the parish present for
necessary uses and repaires of our parish Church of Kingsutton
that is to say

KingSutton levied at ijs the yardland
Astrup at twelvepence the yardland
Charlton at six pence the yardland
Cottages of the Lords hold vjd a peece
Cottages of the Parsonage manus 4d a peece
Walton levie   53s 4d
Purston levie   26s 8d
            By us
            John Creeke vicar

            John Pargiter   }
            Edmund Carpenter} Churchwardens
            Richard Haines   }
            Edmund Toms   } Sidsmen
            George Toms
            Charles Butcher
            Robert Toms
            John Carpenter

King Sutton levy   1637

Mr Richard Kenwricke esq	ixs
Mrs ffrankes	iiijs vjd
Mr Chambers	js vjd
Thomas Bodicott	ijs ixd
Tho: Bodicott	vjd
John Pargiter	iijs
Thomas Rawlins	ijs
Richard Haynes	ijs iijd
ffoulke Meacoke	iijs
Thomas Haynes	ijs vid
Edward Toms	js vid
George Toms	ijs
Thomas Toms his land	ijs
Widdo: Swayne	ijs
Thomas Penne	ijs
Robert Toms	js iijd

George Winkles	js jd
Widdo: Price	vid
Thomas Haynes for little mill	iiijd
Richard Hanly	js
Charles Bucher	js
Edward Williams	xd
frances Davis	xd
Richard Rawlins	vjd
Widdo: Colgrove	vjd
John Jenings	vjd
William Bricknell	vjd
John Upston	vjd
William Peedle	vjd
John Sworder	vjd
John Clemens	vjd
John Rawlins	vjd
frances Whitbye	iijd
William Parrish	iijd
Katherine Jenings	vjd
Symon Watts	vjd
Elizabeth Darby	vjd
Widdo: Bett	vjd
John Warner	[vjd]
[William] Whitwell	[vjd]
William Pecover	vjd
Richard Arlatch	vjd
Henry Herytage	vjd
Widdo: Castill	vjd
George Jenings	vjd
Robert Bricknell	iiijd
Roger Jarvis	iiijd
Michaell Upston	iiijd
William Owers	iiijd
George Maule	iiijd
Thomas Wyatt	iiijd
Widdo: Price	iiijd
William Bett	iiijd
John Whitakers	iiijd
Thomas Harris	iiijd
Widdo: Longe	iiijd
frances Bigg	iijd
Edward Upston	iijd
George Andros	iijd

Thomas Darby	iijd
William fathers	ijd
William Cooper	ijd
Richard Yeates	ijd
John Clements	ijd
Widdo: Statie	ijd
William Peedle for Bishops house	ijd
Richard Nevell	ijd
Alexander Smith	ijd
Henry Paynter	ijd
John Williams	ijd
Symon Wheelor	ijd
William Hawese	ijd
William Pillie	ijd
William Peedle	ijd
Astroppe	Received
Mr Stewards land	xviijs
Mr Cartwrights land	ixs
Mr Higherns	vs
Edmund Carpenter	iiijs
John Carpenter	iiijs vjd
John Wyatt	iiijs
Mr Chambers	iiijs
Thomas Taylor	ijs iiijd
Mr Crew	ijs
John Newman	ijs
George Toms	ijs
William Wyatt	ijs
Mr Piggott	js
Edward Toms	is
John Wyatt & Thomas Wyatt	vjd
Thomas Durman	vjd
Thomas Wyatt	vjd
Thomas Penn	vjd
William Smith	ijd
Walton levy	
Sir Thomas Poope	liijs iiijd
Purston levy	
Mr Craswell	iijs iiijd
Mr Blincow	xs
Mr Blincow	xiijs iiijd

Charleton

Mr Craswells land	iijs iiijd
William Haddon	iijs vijd ob
George flowers	ijs iiijd ob
Mathew Haddon	ijs iiijd *
John Phipps	ijs
Robert lucas	js
Dennice Emberly	js
Mr Marshall	xd ob
Al[ce] Yeomans	iiijd
Thomas Hobcroft	jd
John Garner	jd
William flecknole	jd
Robert Glase	jd

Item received of the Communicants at Easter   xs

The layings out of John Pargiter
and Edmund Carpenter for this
our yeare 1637

Inprimis payd at the Court for our oathes and other charges	xiiijs vjd
Item payd for breade and wine at Midsomer Comunion	ixs xd
Item John Upston for nayles	vjd
Item for oyle for the clocke	ijd
Item for three bellroopes	ixs
Item to Edward Stone for worke about the church	vjd
Item to William Dolton for worke about the bells	iijs
Item to the Jayle and lam souldiers	iiijs iiijd
Item for bread and wine Mychaellmas Comunion	xijs vd
Item for washing the church clothes three tymes	js vjd
Item payd to Edward Upston for mendinge the church grate	iijs
Item payd for oyle for the clocke	ijd
Item payd for oyle for the bells	vjd
Item to William Dolton for mendinge the bell wheeles	iijs
Item to Edward Upston for a worke about the church	js vjd
Item for bread and wine at Christmas Comunion	14s 7d
Item for nayles for the church	vjd
Item to Edward Upston for worke about the bells	ijs
Item at the Court for our dinners and other charges	xiijs iiijd
Item to the Register and aparrytor for fees	iijs viijd

Item for wrighting our presentments	vjd
Item to Thomas Allibone for one dayes work	js
Item to widdo: pillie for oyle	ijd
Item to John Upston for nayles	iiijd
Item to Tymothy Chester for mending a bell wheel	js vjd
Item for washing the church clothes	js
Item for wrighting of the Regester	iiijs
Item for sending in the regester	iijs
Item at the bishops vissitation for our oathes the aparitors fees and other charges goeing and coming: is in all	£iij iiijs viijd and ijs
Item for bread and wynne on palme sundaye and upon Ester daye	£x ijs
Item the Clarkes wages	iijs iiijd
Item to John Whitakers his wagges	viijs
Item to Edmund Upston for looking to the Clocke	js
Item to widdo: Pilly for oyle	ijd
Item to the Joyle and lam soldiers	iiijs iiijd
Item Edward Upston for mending the Church gate	js

£11 17s 0d

The accompte of John Pargiter and Edmund Carpenter for this two yeares past 1636 and 1637: given to the parish the two and twenty day of April 1638

All our receits are	£32 7s 0d
and our layings out are	£31 12s 1d
for that there remaynes to be delivered to the next Churchwardens the sum of	14s 11d
which we now have delivered	
Item the old Churchwardens have received of the last levie the sum:	£6 12s 1d
and there is left unpaid of the said levy to be gathered up by the new Churchwardens	£4 14s 4d ob
and of one old levie	1s

Vicesimo septimo die Martii
Anno dni 1638

Churchwardens chosen by the minister
and maior part of the parish present
the day and yeare aforsaid vzt

Churchwardens { Edward Toms
               { Mathew Neale

Sidsmen   { George Toms
            { John Jenings

Overseeres for the { William Wyatt
poore   { Alexander Smith

Overseeres for   { William Bett
the highway   {John Walters

John Pargiter
Edmund Carpenter
John Jeninges
Richard Taylor   John Carpenter
Richard Bricknell
William Whitwell   Thomas Rawlins
Charles Butcher
ffrances Davies
Edward Williams

The laying forth of Matthew Neale and Edward Toms
churchwardens of the parish of King Sutton for the yeare
1638

Imps ffor half a quarter of lime	3s
ffor dressing of the Church	5s xd
ffor bread and wine	xd
ffor gryas for the clocke	xd

ffor 4 Iron Houckes	5d
ffor nailes for the Church Dores	3s 4d
ffor bread and wine at Micallmas	1s 4d
ffor Bords for the Church dore bought off William Haffe	13s
Charges att Aylsbury conserning the visitation of the Court and ourselves	33s xd
our charges and Bambery Court	xs 7d
ffor Grease for the Bells	4d
It paid to William Dolton for making the Church dores, a bell wheele and other worke about the churche	32s 3d
It ffor tow strike of lime and carriage	1s 6d
It paid to Thomas Alibon for worke about the Church dore	8s 4d
It paid to Richard Taylor for 6 pounds of lead for the dores	xs
It laid forth for bread and wine at Crismas Comunion	xiiijs iiijd
It paid to Bowers for worke and for a eleven pound *****	xiiijs
It paid to Upston for his years keeping of the Clocke	1s
It paid to Upston for iron worke for the porch dores	39s 6d
It paid to Evans for 2 bellropes	5s
It paid to Thomas Tomes for worke	xjs 2d
It for oyle for the clocke	2d
It ffor charges about the Court at Laytonn [*Leighton Buzzard?*]	30s
ffor wine att Easter Communion	40s 10d
ffor bread att the same time	1s 8d
Item payd Rousam his wayges	3s 4d
It payd for half a days worke of the plummer	4d
To Thomas Alibonn for paving of the Church	1s
Payd to the House of Correctio	4s 4d
To Edw: Upston for a barr for the Church window	4d
To Elsabeth Harris for mending of the surplis	2d
ffor washing of the surplis twise	1s
It to John Witaker His whole yeares wages	8s
to Robert Bricnell for pavments for the Church	9d
tem paid to Thomas Rawlins for bordes	25s 4d
Item paid to John Whittaker	1s 2d
Item payd to William haryes for halfe a hundred and 4 foutt of Bordes	7s 4d
Item for mendinge ye Xchyard wall	3d
Item for writinge the Registers	4s
for expenses at the last court *** to the Regesters	3s 4d
for the old Churchwardens oatthes	1s 4d
for the new Churchwardens oathes	1s 4d
for the Booke	1s

for our Dinners	18s 4d
for the apparitors fees	2s
for oyle for the clocke	ijd
to Willia Pilly for 2 Cotters	4d
to Ned Upston for mending the Church dore lock	2d
ffor midsomer Comunio	12s 2d
for a greate bible and a comon prayer book	£3 7s
for the bringing home of the same	1s
Item for washinge the surplice four tims	ijs
Item to the clockmaker	vijd
Item to George Toms for two [Thealos]	iijs
Item to Thomas Bodicott for [sallow] Pole	vjd

Vicesimo die Octobris anno 1638

A levie made by the minister and maior part of the parish present for necessary uses and repayres of our parish Church of Kingsutton vzt

Kingsutton levied at ijs the yeardland
Astrup at xijd the yardland
Charlton at vjd the yardland
Cottages of the Lords hold vjd a peece
Cottages of ye Parsonage hold iiijd a peece
        Walton levie   53s 4d
        Purston levie   26s 8d
        By us
             John Creeke vicar
             Edward Toms }
             Mathew Neale } Churchwardens
             Gorg Toms
             John Genenes
             Thomas Bodicott

King Sutton levy

Mr Richard Kenwricke	ixs
Mrs ffrankes	iiijs vjd
Mr Chambers	js vjd
Thomas Bodicott	iijs iiijd
John Pargiter	iijs
Thomas Rawlinges	ijs
Richard Heines	ijs iijd
ffoulke Meacoke	iijs
Thomas Heines	ijs vid
Edward Tomes	js vid
Georg Tomes	ijs
Thomas Tomes his land	ijs
Widdow Swaine	ijs
Thomas Penne	ijs
Robert Tomes	js iijd
Georg Winckles	js jd
Widdow Price	vid
Thomas Heines for little mill	iiijd
Richard Hanly	js
Charles Butcher	js
Edward Williams	xd
ffrancis Davis	xd
Richard Raulinges	vjd
Widdow Colegrave	vjd
John Jenninges	vjd
Willia Bricknell	vjd
John Upstonn	vjd
William Peedle	vjd
John Sworder	vjd
John Clemans	vjd
John Raulinges	vjd
fransis Whittbee	iijd
William Parrish	iijd
Katherinn Jenninges	vjd
Simon Wattes	vjd
Elsabeth Darby	vjd
Widdow Brett	vjd
John Warner	vjd
William Whitwell	vjd
William Pecover	vjd
Richard Arlatch	vjd
Henry Herytage	vjd

Widdow Castill	vjd
George Jenninges	vjd
Robert Bricknell	iiijd
Roger Jerviss	iiijd
Micaell Upstonn	4d
William Owers	4d
Georg Maule	4d
Widdow Price	4d
William Brett	4d
John Whitakers	4d
Thomas Harris	4d
Widdow Long	4d
ffransis Bigg	3d
Edward Upstonn	3d
Georg Andrewes	3d
Thomas Darby	3d
William ffathers	2d
William Cooper	2d
Richard Yeattes	2d
John Clemans	2d
Widdow Stasye	2d
William Peedle for Bisshops House	2d
Richard Nevill	2d
Allexander Smith	2d
Henry Painter	2d
John Williams	2d
Simon Wheeler	2d
William Hause	2d
William Pilly	2d
William Peedle	2d

Astrop Levy

Mr Steward land John Quatermaine	12s
Mr Cartwrights land	9s
Mr Hygherns land	5s
Edmund Carpenter	4s
John Carpenter	4s 6d
John Wyatt senior	4s
Mr Chambers	3s
Mr Crew land	2s
Thomas Taylor	2s 4d
John Newman	2s

Georg Tomes	2s
Edward Tomes	1s
Mr Piggott	1s
John Wyatt & Thoma Wyatt	6d
Thomas Wyatt	6d
Thomas Durman	6d
Thomas Penn	6d
John Kyrby	6s
William Wyatt	2s
William Smith	2d

Waltonn levy

Sir Thomas Poope	liijs 4d

Purston levy

Mr John Cresswell	3s 4d
Mr John Blinco	13s 4d
Mr Wauker	xs

Charletonn

Mr Cresswell land	3s 3d	
William Haddo land	3s 7d	ob
Georg fflowers	2s 4d	ob
Mathew Haddon	2s 4d	ob
John Phippes	2s 3d	
Widdow Lucas	1s	
Dennise Emerly	1s	
Mr Marshall	xd	ob
Alce Yeomans	3d	
Thomas Hopcroft	1d	
John Garner	1d	
Willia fflecnole	1d	
Robertt Glase	jd	

Received of the Communicants   xs

Decimo quinto die
Aprilis 1639

A levie made by the minister and maior part of the parish present for
necessarie uses and repaires of our parish Church of Kingsutton, that is to
say

Kingsutton levied at ijs the yard land
Astrup at xijd the yard land
Charlton at vjd the yard land
Cottages of the Lords hold vjd a peece
Cottages of the Parsonage hold iiijd
Walton   53s 4d
Purston levie   26s 8d

       Jo: Creeke vic
       Edward Toms }
       Mathew Neale } Churchwardens

       Thomas Heaines
       Richard Harris
       George Toms
       Robert Toms his marke
       John Pargiter

King Sutton levy

Richard Kenwricke Esq	ixs
Mrs ffrankes	4s 6d
Mr Chambers	1s 6d
Thomas Bodicott	3s 3d
John Pargiter	3s
Thomas Rawlins	2s
Richard Haines	2s 3d
ffulk Macoke	3s
Thomas Haines	2s 6d
Edward Toms	1s 6d
George Toms	2s
Thomas Toms his land	2s
Widdow Swayne	2s
Thomas Pen	2s
Robert Toms	1s 3d
George Winckles	1s 1d
Widdow Price	6d

Thomas Haines for little mill	4d
Richard Hanley	1s
Charles Butcher	1s
Edward Williams	10d
ffrancis Davies	7d
Richard Rawlins	9d
Widdow Colgrave	6d
John Jeninges	6d
William Bricknell	6d
John Upston	6d
William Peedle	6d
John Sworder	6d
John Clemens	6d
John Rawlins	6d
Francis Whittby	3d
William Parrish	3d
Katherinn Jeninges	6d
Simon Watts	6d
Elsabeth Darby	6d
Widdow Bett	6d
John Warner	6d
William Whittwell	6d
William Peckover	6d
Richard Arlatch	6d
Henry Heritage	6d
Widdow Castile	6d
George Jeninges	6d
Robert Bricknell	4d
Roger Jarvis	4d
Michaell Upston	4d
William Oares	4d
George Maule	4d
Widdow Price	4d
William Bet	4d
John Whitaker	4d
Thomas Harris	4d
Widdow Longue	4d
ffrancis Bigg	3d
Edward Upston	3d
George Andrewes	3d
Thomas Darby	3d
William ffathers	2d
William Cooper	2d

Richard Yates	2d
John Clemens	2d
Mathew Stacie	2d
Simon Dumbleton	2d
Richard Nevill	2d
Alexander Smith	2d
Henry Painter	2d
John Williams	2d
Simon Wheeler	2d
William Hawes	2d
William Pillie	2d
William Peedle	2d

Astrop Levy

Mr Steward's land John Quatermaine	12s
Mr Cartwright his land	9s
Roger Jarvis behinde	js
Thomas Warner	5s
Edmund Carpenter	4s
John Carpenter	4s 6d
John Wyatt	2s
Thomas Bodicott	2s
Mr Chambers	3s
Mr Crew his land	2s
Thomas Taylor	2s 4d
John Newman	2s
George Toms	2s
Edward Toms	1s
Mr Piggott	1s
John Wyat et Tho: Wyat	6d
Thomas Wyat	6d
Thomas Durman	6d
Thomas Pen	6d
John Kirby	6s
William Wyatt	2s
William Smith	2d

Walton Levie

Sir Thomas Pope	liijs 4d

Purston Levie

Mr Crasswell	3s 4d
Mr John Blincoe	13s 4d
Mr Walker	10s

Charlton Levie

Mr Crasswells land	3s 3d
William Haddons land	3s 7d ob
George fflowers	2s 4d ob
Mathew Haddon	2s 4d ob
John Phipps	2s 3d
Widdow Lucas	1s
Dennise Emberly	1s
Mr Marshall	10d ob
Alce Yeomans	3d
Thomas Hopcraft	1d
John Garner	1d
Willia fflecnole	1d
Robert Glaze	1d

George Toms & Thomas Tayler have reteined of this levy wch was left ungathered by Mathew Neale & Edward Toms the sume of £4 4s 4d and there is yet left ungathered of the said levy 2s 1d

The accoumpts of Mathew Neale and Edward Toms Church Wardens for the parish of King Sutton for the yeare 1638 given the two and twentieth day of September 1639

All our receipts are	£23 9s 1d
All our layings out are	£23 10s 11d
Soe there is due to be paide backe to the old Churchwardens by the new	1s 10d
wch is payd as appears in the layings out of us George Toms & Thomas Tayler	
And their remains due to the Church from Edmund Carpenter and John Pargiter of their accoumpts	8s 4d
wch is now payde to George Toms and Thomas Taylor	
The old Church Wardens have received of this last levy	£6 18s 9d
And theire is left of the saide levy unpaid to be gather up of the new	£4 5s 5d

Soe that this whole levy comes to   £11 4s 2d

That is to say Sutton at	£3 4s 10d
Astrup at	£3 2s
Walton at	£2 13s 4d
Purston at	£1 6s 8d
Charlton at	£0 17s 4d

The names of those wch are behinde & unpayde of the last levy
made in Mathew Neale and Edw Toms ther time
Aprill the 15th 1639

Thomas Rawlins	ijs
Richard Haynes	ijs iijd
Thomas Taylor	iijs
Thomas Haynes	ijs vjd
George Toms	ijs
Widdow Swayne	ijs
Widdow Penne	ijs
Robert Toms	js iijd
George Winckles	viijd
John Williams	vjd
Thomas Haynes for little mill	iiijd
Richard Hanley	xijd
Charles Butcher	xijd
Edward Williams	xd
ffrancis Davis	vijd
John Jenings	vjd
William Bricknill	vjd
John Upston	vjd
William Peedle	vjd
John Sworder	vjd
John Clements	vjd
John Rawlins	vjd
ffrancis Whitby	iijd
William Parrish	3iij
Katherin Jenings	vjd
Simon Watts	vjd
Widdow Darby	vjd
Thomas Bett	vjd
John Warner	vjd
William Whittwell	vjd
Thomas Watson	vjd
Richard Arlatch	vjd
Widow Castill	vjd
Henry Heritage	vjd
George Jenings	vjd
Robert Bricknill	iiijd
Roger Jarvis	iiijd
Michaell Upston	iiijd
William Owers	iiijd
Thomas Wyatt	iiijd

George Maule	iiijd
Widdow Price	iiijd
William Bett	iiijd
John Whitaker	iiijd
Thomas Harris	iiijd
Widdow Longe	iiijd
ffrancis Bigge	iijd
Edward Upston	iijd
George Andrews	iijd
Thomas Darby	iijd
William ffathers	ijd
William Cooper	ijd
Richard Yates	ijd
John Clemens	ijd
Mathew Stacie	ijd
Simon Dumbleton	ijd
Richard Nevill	ijd
Alexander Smith	ijd
Henry Paynter	ijd
John Williams	ijd
Simon Wheeler	ijd
William Hawes	ijd
William Pillie	ijd
William Peedle	ijd

Mr Cartwrights land	viijs
Thomas Warner	vs
John Wyatt	ijs
Mr Chambers	iijs
Mr Crews land	ijs
John Newman	ijs
George Toms	ijs
Mr Piggott	js
John Kirby	vjs
John Wyatt	vjd
Thomas Wyatt	vjd
Thomas Durman	vjd
Widdo Penn	vjd
William Wyat	ijs
William Smith	ijd

Purston

| Mr Crasswell | iijs iiijd |

Charlton

Mathew Haddon	ijs iiijd ob
John Phipps	ijs iijd
Widdo Lucas	ijd
Denis Emberly	vijd
Mr Marshall	xd ob
Alce Yeomans	iijd
Thomas Hobcraft	jd
John Garner	jd
Willia fflecnole	jd
Robertt Glaze	jd

Decimo sexto die Aprilis
anno dnj 1639

Churchwardens chosen by the minister
and maior part of the parrish present
the day and yeare aforsaid vzt

Churchwardens   { George Toms
                {Thomas Taylor

Sidsmen   { Robert Toms
           { John Pargiter

Overseeres for the   { John Jeninges
poore   { John Quatermaine

Overseeres for   { William Parrish
the highway   {William Peedle iun:

By us   John Creeke vic
Thomas Bodicott
John Pargiter
Thomas Tailer
ffrancis Davies

Richard Harries
Thomas Harries
John Kirby
Alexander Smith
William Bett
Richard Rawlins
William Whitwell
Robt Bricknell

The Receipts of George Toms & Thomas Tailer Churchwardens
for the parish Church of King Sutton for this yeare 1639

Inprimis Received of a former levie made in Mathew Neale & Edward Toms there time uppon the xvth day of Aprill 1639	£4 4s 4d
Item Received of a latter levie made in our time the eighth day of March 1639	£10 6s 9d
Item Received of John Wyatt for a levie wch was behinde in Mathew Neale & Edward Toms theire time the twentieth of October 1638	4d
Item Received of Katherin Jenings for Alce Hanley her buriall in ye Church	6s 8d
Item Received of the Communicants at Easter in halfe pence	10s 6d
Item Received of John Pargiter and Edmund Carpenter wch was behinde & due to the Church at the deliveringe of theire accoumpts	8s 4d
Item received of Thomas Tayler for his mother hir buriall in the Church	6s 8d
Item received of a Levy made the 16th of May in the yeare 1640	£4 12s 2d
All these our receipts	£20 15s 9d

The Layings out of George Toms & Thomas Tayler Churchwardens
for the parish Church of King Sutton for this yeare 1639

Inprimis payd to the old Churchwardens wch was due unto them at the deliveringe up of their accoumpts the sume of	2s 10d
Item to the roaper for a Bell roape	2s 6d
Item for Bread & Wyne at Michaellmas	16s 10d
Item to John Sworder for helpinge to fetch the wyne from Banbury at ye same time	4d
Item for grease for the Bells	6d
Item given to the Bookbinder in change betweene the old Common prayer booke and a booke for the Clarke to answere in	4s
Item for washinge the Church cloathes	6d
Item for a prayer booke for the fift day of November appoynted for ye same	6d
Item for a Parchmente booke to write the Registers in, of Christeninge Marryinge and Buryinge the sume of	6s 6d
Item for oyle for the Clocke	2d
Item for dismisinge the Court kept at Layton the fourteenth day of December the Apparrators fees delivinge in our presentments and all other Charges	£1 10s 6d
Item for Bread & Wyne at Christmas	15s 1d
Item for Oyle to liquor the bells	4d
Item to the Roaper for two Bell Roapes	5s
Item to Michaell Upston for mendinge the Church grate	6d
Item to the plummer for soder to mende the Leads and for himselfe & his mans worke about the same	7s
Item to Edward Rowsam for helpinge the Plummer one day	8d
Item for a table Cloath for the Communion table	5s 7d
Item for Bread & Wyne on Palme Sunday on Easter even and on Easter day	£2 2s 7d
Item to John Whittakers his whole yeares wages for mending the Church windowes	8s
Item to Edward Rowsam his yeares wages for keeping the Clocke & ye Bells	3s 4d
Item to the Gaole and Lame Souldiers	4s 4d
Item to Simon Watts for Poyntinge the Leads Sweepeinge the Church & plasteringe up pieces wch were broaken downe in the Church	10s
Item for Grease for the Bells	2d
Item to Widdow Pillie for Oyle for the Clocke	2d

Item to John Carpenter for the Pewter wyne Bottles for the Communion wch was more then hee had to bestow uppon them from Astrup youth	2s 10d
Item payd for the timber to make the gate at the grate the boards the Iron worke and the workmanship about ye same in all comes to	6s 6d
Item to John Quatermaine for two Strike of Lime	1s 4d
Ite for a hundred and a halfe and thirty foote of boards	£1 1s 9d
Item for a Strike of Lime	6d
Item to the Plumer for casting the old lead of the North Portch for five hundred fourescore & tenn Pounds of new lead for soder to mende the Leads and for the workmanship about the same in all is	£7 4s 5d
Item to William Dolton for his worke about the north Portch and the gate	5s
Ite to Simon Watts for slattinge plasteringe & poyntinge the Portch for mosse & for nayles in all is	3s 2d
Item to John Upston for nayles	2d
Ite to William Needle for ridding under the Church grate	2d
Ite to Francis Daves for a packe of Lime	2d
Item to Richard Tibbs for foure transoms to make lineings for ye Rafters of the North Portch	2s 8d
Item to Georg Toms for carrying the Lead to Brackley to be cast and for bringing the same wth some more new Lead home again	5s
Ite for washing the Church Cloathes three times	1s 6d
Item for three hundred of nayles for the North Portch	2s 6d
Item for writeing the registers	4s
Item to Edward Upston for his keepinge the Clocke this last yeare	1s
Item to Edward Upston for his worke about the bells and other worke	10d

Octavo die Martii Anno 1639

A levie made by the minister and maior part of the parish present for
necessary uses and repaires of our parish of KingSutton vzt

Kingsutton levied at ijs the yard land
Astrup at xijd the yard land
Charlton at vjd the yard land
Cottages of the Lords hold vjd a peece
Cottages of the Parsonage hold iiijd
Walton   53s 4d
Purston levie   26s 8d

Richard Kenwricke

       Jo: Creeke vic

       George Toms }
       Thomas Tayler} Churchwardens
       John Pargiter
       John Jeninges
       Edward Toms
       Francis Davies
       John Kirby
       Robert Bricknill
       Thomas Warner

King Sutton levy

	s	d
Richard Kenwricke Esq	9	0
Mris ffrankes	4	6
Mr Chambers	1	6
Thomas Bodicutt	3	3
John Pargiter	3	0
Thomas Rawlins	2	0
Richard Haynes	2	3
Thomas Haynes	2	6
Thomas Tayler	3	0
Edward Toms	1	6
George Toms	2	0
Thomas Toms his land	2	0
Widdow Swayne	2	0

Widdow Penn	2	0
Robert Toms	1	3
George Winkles	1	1
John Williams	0	6
Charles Butcher	1	0
Thomas Haynes for little mill	0	4
Richard Hanley	0	4
John Waters	0	2
George Grime	0	6
Jeromie Parrish	0	6
Edward Williams	0	10
ffrancis Davis	0	7
Richard Rawlins	0	9
Widdow Colegrave	0	6
John Jenings	0	6
William Bricknill	0	6
John Upston	0	6
William Peedle	0	6
John Sworder	0	6
John Clemence	0	6
John Rawlins	0	6
ffrancis Whitbie	0	3
William Parrish	0	3
Katherin Jenings	0	6
Simon Watts	0	6
Elizabeth Darby	0	6
Thomas Bett	0	6
John Warner	0	6
William Whitwell	0	6
Thomas Watson	0	6
Richard Arlatch	0	6
Henry Heritage	0	6
George Jenings	0	6
Robert Bricknill	0	4
Roger Jarvis	0	4
John & Thomas Wyatt	0	4
Michaell Upston	0	4
William Owers	0	4
George Maule	0	4
Widdow Price	0	4
William Bett	0	4
John Whittakers	0	4
Thomas Harris	0	4

Widdow Longue	0	4
ffrancis Bigge	0	3
Edward Upston	0	3
George Andrewes	0	3
Alce Darby	0	3
William ffathers	0	2
William Cooper	0	2
Richard Yates	0	2
John Clemence	0	2
Robert Longue	0	2
Simon Dumbleton	0	2
Richard Nevill	0	2
Alexander Smith	0	2
Henry Paynter	0	2
Henry Hobcraft	0	2
Simon Wheeler	0	2
William Hawes	0	2
William Pillie	0	2
William Peedle	0	2

Astrup Levy

Mr Steward his land		
{ John Quatermaine	12	0
{ John Kirby	6	0
Mr Cartwright his land		
{ John Wyatt	2	0
{ Thomas Haynes	2	0
{ Thomas Rawlins	1	0
{ Edmund Carpenter	1	0
{ Roger Jarvis	1	0
{ Edward Crasse	1	6
{ Robert Sergeant	0	6
Mr Crews land		
{ John Carpenter	1	0
{ Thomas Warner	1	0
Thomas Warner	5	0
Edmund Carpenter	4	0
John Carpenter	4	6
Thomas Bodicott	2	0
John Wyatt	2	0
Mr Chambers	3	0
Mr Piggott	1	0
John Newman	2	0
George Toms	2	0

Thomas Taylor	2 4
Edward Toms	1 0
William Wyatt	2 0
John & Thomas Wyatt	0 6
Thomas Wyatt	0 6
Thomas Durman	0 6
Widdow Penn	0 6
William Smith	0 2

Walton Levie

Sir Thomas Pope	53 4

Purston Levie

Mr Croswell	3 4
Mr Blinkow	13 4
Mr Walker	10 0

Charlton Levie

Mr Croswell his land	3 3
William Haddon his land	3 7 ob
George fflowers	2 4 ob
Mathew Haddon	2 4 ob
John Phipps	2 3
Widdow Lucas	1 0
Mr Marshall	0 10 ob
Dennise Emberly	0 10
Alce Yeomans	0 5
Thomas Hobcraft	0 1
John Garner	0 1
William Flecknole	0 1
Robert Glaze	0 1

Whole Levie comes to   £11 4s 8d

George Toms & Thomas Taylor have received of this levy
    the sume of   £20 6s 9d ob
And there is left of the saide levy to be gathered up by
    Richard Haynes and Robert Toms the
    summe of   17s 10d ob

Septimo die Aprilis
Anno 1640

Churchwardens chosen by the minister
and maior part of the parrish present
the day and yeare aforsaid vzt

Churchwardens   { Robert Toms
                { Richard Haines

Sidsmen   { Richard Tibbs
            { Thomas Warner

Overseeres for the   { Thomas Haynes
poore   { Robert Bricknell

Overseeres for   { John Warner
the highwayes   {John Clemence iun:

Richard Kenwricke

John Creeke vic
Edward Toms
George Toms
John Jenings
Thomas Tayler
Thomas Haynes
Robert Bricknell
John Warner
Thomas Warner

The rest of the Layings out of George Toms & Tayler
for their yeare beginning in the yeare of our Lord
1639 & ending 1640

Inprimis our Court expences that is to say our dinners the delivering
the presentments the writeing the presentments the Old Churchwardens
oathes the new Churchwardens oathes the apparators fees in all is
                                       £1 8s 10d

The whole sume of our layings out comes to   £19 17s 11d

Decimo sexto die Maij
Anno dnj 1640

A levie made by the minister and maior part of the parish present for
necesary uses and repayres about our parish Church of Kingsutton vzt

Kingsutton at ijs ye yardland
Astrup levied at xijd ye yardland
Charlton at vjd ye yardland
Cottages of the Lords hold vjd a peece
Cottage of the Parsonage hold 4d a peece
       Walton   53s 4d
       Purston   26s 8d

Richard Kenwricke   John Creeke vic
       George Toms }
       Thomas Taylor} Churchwardens

       John Pargiter
       Robert Bricknell
       Thomas Heynes
       Edward Toms
       John Carpenter
       John Upston

King Sutton levie

	s	d
Richard Kenwricke Esq	9	0
Mris ffrankes	4	6
Mr Chambers	1	6
Thomas Bodicott	4	0
John Pargiter	3	0
Thomas Rawlins	2	0
Richard Haynes	2	3
Thomas Haynes	2	6
Thomas Tayler	3	0
George Toms	2	0
Thomas Toms his land	2	0
Widdow Swayne	2	0
Edward Toms	1	6
Widdow Penn	2	0

Robert Toms	1	3
George Winckles	1	1
John Williams	0	6
Charles Butcher	1	0
Richard Hanley	0	4
John Waters	0	2
Thomas Haynes for little mill	0	4
George Grime	0	6
Jeromie Parrish	0	6
Edward Williams	0	10
ffrancis Davis	0	7
Widdow Colegrave	0	6
John Jenings	0	6
Simon Watts	0	6
John Upston	0	6
William Bricknill	0	6
John Rawlins	0	6
Widdow Darby	0	6
William Whitwell	0	6
William Peedle	0	6
John Clemence	0	6
Katherin Jenings	0	6
George Jenings	0	6
Thomas Bett	0	6
John Sworder	0	6
John Warner	0	6
Richard Arlatch	1	0
Henry Heritage	0	6
Thomas Watson	0	6
Robert Bricknill	0	4
Roger Jarvis	0	4
John & Thomas Wyatt	0	4
Thomas Harris	0	4
Michaell Upston	0	4
William Bett	0	4
William Owers	0	4
John Whittakers	0	4
Widdow Price	0	4
George Maule	0	4
Widdow Longe	0	4
ffrancis Whitbie	0	3
William Parrish	0	3
William Pillie	0	3

Edward Upston	0 3
George Andrewes	0 3
George Toms	0 3
William ffathers	0 2
William Cooper	0 2
Richard Yates	0 2
John Clemence	0 2
Robert Longe	0 2
Simon Dumbleton	0 2
Richard Nevill	0 2
Alexander Smith	0 2
Henry Paynter	0 2
ffrancis Bigge	0 2
Henry Habcraft	0 2
Simon Wheeler	0 2
William Peedle	0 2
William Hawes	0 2

Astrup Levie

Mr Steward his land	
{ John Quatermaine	12 0
{ John Kirby	6 0
Mr Cartwright his land	
{ John Wyatt	2 0
{ Thomas Haynes	2 0
{ Thomas Rawlins	1 0
{ Edmund Carpenter	1 0
{ Roger Jarvis	1 0
{ Edward Crasse	1 6
{ Robert Sergeant	0 6
Mr Crew his land	
{ John Carpenter	1 0
{ Thomas Warner	1 0
Mr Chamber his land	
{ William Haddon	1 0
{ Edmund Carpenter	1 0
{ Edward ffoane	1 0
Mr Piggott his land	1 0
Thomas Warner	5 0
John Carpenter	4 6
Edmund Carpenter	4 0
Thomas Bodicott	2 0
John Wyatt	2 0
John Newman	2 0

George Toms	2 0
Thomas Tayler	2 4
William Wyatt	2 0
Edward Toms	1 0
John & Thomas Wyatt	0 6
Thomas Wyatt	0 6
Thomas Durman	0 6
Widdow Penn	0 6
William Smith	0 2

Walton Levie

Sir Thomas Pope	53 4

Purston Levie

Mr Cresswell	3 4
Mr Blinkow	13 4
Mr Walker	10 0

Charlton Levie

Mr Cresswell his land	3 3
William Haddon his land	3 7 ob
George fflowers	2 4 ob
Mathew Haddon	2 4 ob
John Phipps	2 3
Widdow Lucas	1 0
Mr Marshall	0 10 ob
Dennise Emberly	0 10
Widdow Yeomans	0 5
Thomas Habcraft	0 1
John Garner	0 1
William Flecknole	0 1
Robert Glaze	0 1

The whole levy comes to   £11 4s 8d

Wee George Toms & Thomas Tayler have received of this levy
      the summe of   £4 12 2d
And their is left of the said Levy to be gathered up by Richard Haynes &
Robert Toms the sume of   £6 12s 6d

The accoumpts of George Toms and Thomas Tayler given to the parish
the eighth day of July 1640

All our receipts are   £20 15s 9d ob
All our layings out are   £19 17s 11d

Soe there is remayninge in our hands to bee payd to the next
Churchwardens Richard Haynes and Robert Toms
         the sume of   17s 10d ob
which we have now payde
Also we have delivered to the new Churchwardens Richard Haynes and
Robert Toms all the Church goods that is to say the Church Bookes a
surplis a table Cloath a Carpet the pulpit Cloath and the Cushion wth
other necessaries belonging to the Church
                       Robert Toms his marke }
                     Richard Haynes his marke}
                         Churchwardens

                       John Quatermaine
                       John Jenynges
                       Robert Bricknell
                       Thomas Haynes
                       Thomas Warner

                     Vicesimo sexto die Aprilis
                          anno dni 1641

A levie made by the minister and maior part of the parish present for
necessary uses and repaires about our parrish Church of Kingsutton vzt

Kingsutton at ijs the yardland
Astrup levied at xijd ye yardland
Charlton at vjd the yardland
Cottages of the Lords hold sixpence a peece
Cottage of Parsonage hold iiijd a peece
         Walton   53s 4d
         Purston   26s 8d

Richard Kenwricke   John Creeke vic
         Robt Toms }
         Richard Haines} Churchwardens
         Thomas Bodicott
         John Pargiter
         Mathew Haddon
         Edward Toms
         John Phipps
         John Warner
         Tho   [sic]

KingSuton levie

Richard Kenwricke Esq	9 0
Mris ffrankes	4 6
Mr Chambers	1 6
Thomas Bodicot	4 0
John Pargiter	3 0
Thomas Rawlins	2 0
Richard Haines	2 3
Thomas Heynes	2 6
Thomas Taylor	3 0
George Toms	2 0
Thomas Toms his land	2 0
Widdow Swayne	2 0
Edward Toms	1 6
Widdowe Penne	2 0
Robert Toms	1 3
George Winckles	1 1
John Williams	0 6
Charles Butcher	1 0
Richard Hanley	0 4
John Waters	0 2
Thomas Haines for little mill	0 4
George Grime	0 6
Jeromy Parish	0 6
Edward Williams	0 10
ffrances Daves	0 7
Widdowe Colgrave	0 6
John Jenings	0 6
Simon Watts	0 6
John Upston	0 6
William Bricknell	0 6
Richard Williams	0 6
Widdow Darby	0 6
William Whittwell	0 6
William Peedle	0 6
John Clemens	0 6
George Jenings	0 6
Katherine Jenings	0 6
Thomas Bett	0 6
John Sworder	0 6
John Warner	0 6
Richard Arlatch	0 6

Henry Heritage	0 6
Thomas Wattson	0 6
Robt Bricknill	0 4
Roger Jarvis	0 4
John & Thomas Wyatt	0 4
Thomas Harris	0 4
Michaell Upston	0 4
William Bett	0 4
William Owars	0 4
John Whittakers	0 4
Widdow Price	0 4
George Maule	0 4
Widdow Longue	0 4
ffrancis Whitby	0 3
William Parish	0 3
John Maule	0 3
William Pillie	0 3
George Andrews	0 3
George Toms	0 3
William ffathers	0 2
Will: Cooper	0 2
John Clemens	0 2
Richard Yeates	0 2
Robert Longue	0 2
Alexander Smith	0 2
Henry Painter	0 2
ffrances Bigge	0 2
Henry Hobcraft	0 2
Simon Wheeler	0 2
Simon Dumbleton	0 2
William Rawlins	0 2
William Peedle	0 2
William Hawse	0 2

Astrup Levie

Mr Steward his land	
{ John Quatermaine	12 0
{ John Kirby	6 0

Mr Cartwright his land	
{ John Wyatt	2 0
{ Thomas Haines	2 0
{ Thomas Rawlins	1 0
{ Edmund Carpenter	1 0
{ Edward Crosse	1 6
{ Robert Sergeant	0 6
{ Roger Jarvis	1 0
Mr Crew his land	
{ John Carpenter	1 0
{ Thomas Warner	1 0
Mr Chambers his land	
{ William Haddon	1 0
{ Edmund Carpenter	1 0
{ Edward ffoane	1 0
Mr Piggott his land	1 0
Thomas Warner	5 0
John Carpenter	4 6
Edmund Carpenter	4 0
Thomas Bodicott	2 0
John Wyat	2 0
John Newman	2 0
George Toms	2 0
Thomas Taylor	2 4
William Wyat	2 0
Edward Toms	1 0
John and Thomas Wyatt	0 6
Tho: Wyatt	0 6
Tho: Durman	0 6
Wid Pen	0 6
William Smith	0 2

Walton Levie

Sir Thomas Pope	53 4

Purston Levie

Mr Cresswell	3 4
Mr Blincoe	13 4
Mr Walker	10 0

Charlton Levie

Mr Cresswell his land	3 9
William Haddon his land	3 7 ob
William Haddon	2 4 ob
Mathew Haddon	2 4 ob
John Phipps	2 3

Widdow Lucas	1 0
Mr Marshall	0 10 ob
Dennice Emberly	0 10
Widdo Yeomans	0 5
Thomas Hobcraft	0 1
John Garner	0 1
Edward Snelson	0 1
Robert Glaze	0 1

The layings out of Robert Toms and Richard Haines for this theire yeare

In primis layd out for bread and wine for Midsomer Communion	14 6
Item for our Court dinner	15 0
Item for a booke for the fast	1 0
Item for John Phipps his oath	0 4
Item to Rowsame the apparitore	0 4
Item payd for the Registers carriinge	3 4
Item to two travailers	0 6
Item to the Geoyle & lame souldiers	4 4
Item for laying down Katherine Macocks grave	1 0
Item for our dinners on the court day	3 0
Item for Stones to pave the Church	0 10
Item our Visitation dinner the 2d of October	8 10
Item our oathes at ye Visitaton	1 6
Item our bill of presentmts	0 6
Item to the apparitore	0 4
Item bread & wine at Michaellmas Communion	15 8
Item oyle for the bells	0 5
Item to John Stratford for worke	0 4
Item for a prayer for ore Kinge	0 6
Item oyle for the Clocke	0 2
Item leather for the bells	0 6
Item for mending the bell claper	2 0
Item for mending another bell claper	1 8
Item bread and wyne at Christmas communion	16 0 ob
Item oyle for the bells	0 3
Item spent at Brackley when we delivered in a bill concerning Recusants	1 4
Item in going to Ketteringe to deliver in the Recusants bill	7 3
Item oyle for the Clock	0 2

Item to Dolton for worke about the Church and bells	6 0
Item to the Smith	0 6
Item for nayles	0 5
Item payd for two bellropes	5 6
Item for washing the surplis three times	1 6
Item for mending the Church gate	0 6
Item for mending the Church cloaths	0 6
Item for mending a bell clapper	2 0
Item for bread and wyne on Palme Sonday and on Easter Day	47 5 ob
Item to Rousam the Clerks wages	3 4
Item wasshing the surplis twise	1 0
Item to the Geoyle and lame souldirs	4 4
Item for writinge and casting up accounts	3 0
Item to Thomas Alibone for works	1 0

All our receipts this our yeare are
In primis that we have gathered up of the old levies   £8 8s 3d
Item received of the Easter comunicants   xs
In all received   £8 18s 3d
All our layings out are   £8 19s 2d
Soe that there is due to us for that we have layd out more
        than we have received   xjd
        which is payd to us this 7th of May 1641 by Richard Taylor &
        Thomas Rawlins the new Churchwardens
Memorand we have left them one whole levie to gather up made the sixt
and twentieth of Aprill last 1641 as aforesaid

                        Robert Toms
                        Richard Haines

Received of the old Churchwardens that was payd for theire
dinners and not allowed by the parish   3 0
Item that was given to some travailers and not allowd of 0 6

These are part of the Layings out of Thomas Rawlins and Richard Taylor

In primis our dinners at the visitation	17 0
Item paid to ffrancis Davies for lyme	0 3
Item to the apparitor for warninge the Court	0 8
Item for the diall making uppon the Church	4 6
Item payd John Whittakers his wages due to him for the yeare 1640	8 0
Item to John Upston for nayles	0 1
Item for writing the Registers	4 0

This was due in theire yeare Robt Toms and Richard Haines but payd by the Churchwardens Thomas Rawlins and Richard Taylor

Allsoe there is layd out by the Churchwardens Thomas Rawlins and Richard Taylor for this theire yeare 1641 as followeth

In prim to the old Churchwardens	0 11
Item to Simon Watts for slatts lathes nayles pinns and for a rafter and three dayes work about the Vestry	6 4
Item one strike of lime	0 8
Item half a pound of grease for the Bells	0 3
Ite for washing the surplis	0 6
Ite mending the Churchyard wall and other work about the Churchyard don by Tho: Sparkes	0 9
ffor bread and wyne at Midsomer Communion	14 10
ffor mending the surplis	0 6
ffor oyle for the Clocke	0 2
ffor three bellropes	7 6
Item our charges at the Visitation at Brickhill	25 7
Item payd for three horse hire	9 6
ffor bread and wyne at Michaelmas Communion	15 4
To the Geoyle and lame Souldiers	4 4
for washing the surplis	0 6
ffor oyle for the bells	0 3
To Tho: Allibone for mending the Church wall	1 0
To Edward Upston for mending the Churchyard Gate	1 0
Item for a Proclamation and confirmation concerning the takeing away the Rayles in the Chancell commanded to be read in the Church	0 3
Ite for taking up the said Rayles	0 4
Item to Tho Allibone for worke about the Church	0 6

ffor a strike of lime	0	8
To William Dolton for work about the bells	2	6
To Edward Upston for mending the great bell Clapper and other work about the bells	5	3

Churchwardens chosen by the minister
and maior part of the parrish present
whose names are subscribed

Churchwardens   { Thomas Rawlins
                    { Richard Taylor

Sidsmen   { John Warner
             { Mathew Haddon

Overseers for the { John Pargiter
poore   { Thomas Warner

Overseers for   { William Wyatt
ye highways   {Thomas Wyatt:

Richard Kenwricke

John Creeke vic
John Pargiter
Edward Toms
Richard Haines
Robt Toms
Thomas Warner
Robt Bricknell
ffrancis Davies

Here follow the rest of the layings out of Richard Taylor and Thomas
Rawlins for theire yeare aforsaid 1641 Sct

In prim for bread and wyne for Christmas Communion	15	10
Oyle for the bells	0	11
washinge the surplis and table cloath twise	1	0
Item for washing the table cloath	0	2

to Bowers the Plummer for ten pounds and halfe of soder and two dayes work for his man and himselfe	13 0
to the Clarks wyfe for attending the Plummer	0 6
Item for bread and wine on Palme Sonday and Easter day and at other Communions	£2 5 3
Ite to Edward Upston for worke about the bells	1 0
Item to John Upston for nayles	0 2
More Receipts	
Received of the Easter Comunicants	10 0
Received of William Hadon	£2 3 4
Received of Edmund Carpenter the sum of being part of the monyes which he is to count for	1 0
Item we have received more of Edmund Carpenter	£1 0 0
Item received of William Haddon	£1 0 0
Item received more of Edmund Carpenter by Mr Creeke the summe of	£1 5 0
Item received of the Easter Communicants 1643	10 0
Item received of the Easter Communicants 1644	10 0
Ite received for Mers Pargiters grave	6 8
Ite received for William Rawlins wifes grave	6 8
Ite for Elizabeth the daughter of Mr Leake her grave	6 8
Ite received of Ed Taylor for hay in Lady meade	22 4
Ite received of John Pargiter for ye wet ham	10 0
Ite received of Jo: Clemens for the hay in Lake mead	10 0

Vicesimo quarto Aprilis 1642

Churchwardens chosen by the minister
and maior part of the parish present
whose names are subscribed vz

Churchwardens   { John Jenings
                   {   .

Sidsmen   { George Jenings
              {   .

Overseers for the   { ffrancis Davies
      poore   { John Wyatt

Overseeres for   { ffrancis   [sic]
   the highwayes   {   .

Vicesimo die Martij
Anno dnj 1642

A levie made by the minister and maior part of the parish for the providinge for a Communion this next Easter and for other necesary uses and repayres about our parish Church of KingSutton vzt

Kingsutton at ijs ye yardland
Astrup at xijd ye yardland
Charlton at vjd ye yeardland
Cottages of the Lords hold vjd a peece
Cottage of ye Parsonage hold iiijd a peece
Walton   53s 4d
Purston   26s 8d

John Creeke vicar

George Toms
Thomas Rawlins

Kingsutton levie

Richard Kenwricke Esq	9	0
Mris ffrankes	4	6
Mr Chambers	1	6
Thomas Bodicott	4	0
John Pargiter	3	0
Thomas Rawlins	2	0
John Haynes	2	3
Thomas Haynes	2	6
Thomas Taylor	3	0
George Toms	2	0
Thomas Toms his land	2	0
Widdow Swayne	2	0
Edward Toms	1	6
Widdow Penne	2	0
Robert Toms	1	3
George Winckles	1	1
John Williams	0	6
Charles Butcher	1	0
Richard Hanley	0	4

John Waters	0 2
Thomas Haynes iunior	0 4
George Grime	0 6
Tymothy Parish	0 6
Edward Williams	0 10
ffrancis Davis	0 7
Edmund Carpenter	0 6
John Jenings	0 6
Symon Watts	0 6
John Upston	0 6
William Bricknell	0 6
Richard Williams	0 6
Jonathan Kinge	0 6
William Whitwell	0 6
William Peedle	0 6
John Clemens	0 6
George Jenings	0 6
Katherine Jenings	0 6
Thomas Bett	0 6
Edward Sworder	0 6
John Warner	0 6
Richard Arlatch	0 6
Henry Heritage	0 6
Thomas Wattson	0 6
Robert Bricknell	0 4
Roger Jarvice	0 4
Jo: & Tho: Wyatt	0 4
Thomas Harris	0 4
Michaell Upston	0 4
William Bett	0 4
William Oares	0 4
John Whittaker	0 4
Widdow Price	0 4
George Maule	0 4
Widdow Longue	0 4
ffrancis Whittby	0 3
William Parish	0 3
John Maule	0 3
William Pillie	0 3
George Andrewes	0 3
George Toms	0 3
William ffathers	0 2
William Cooper	0 2

John Clemence	0 2
Richard Yeates	0 2
Robert Longue	0 2
Alexander Smith	0 2
Henry Painter	0 2
Humphry Jenings	0 2
Henry Hobcraft	0 2
John Sanders	0 2
Simon Dumbleton	0 2
William Rawlins	0 2
William Peedle	0 2
William Hawes	0 2

Astrup Levie

Mr Steward his land	
{ Jo: Quatermaine	12 0
{ John Kirby	6 0
Mr Cartwright his land	
{ John Wyatt	2 0
{ Thomas Haines	2 0
{ Tho: Rawlins	1 0
{ Edmund Carpenter	1 0
{ Edward Crasse	1 6
{ Robert Sergeant	0 6
{ Roger Jarvis	1 0
Mr Crew his land	
{ John Carpenter	1 0
{ Thomas Warner	1 0
Mr Cartwrights land	
{ Charles Butcher	1 0
{ George Toms	1 0
{ Will House	1 0
Mr Piggott his land	1 0
Thomas Warner	5 0
Edmund Carpenter	4 0
John Carpenter	4 6
Thomas Bodicott	2 0
John Wyatt	2 0
Widdow Newman	2 0
George Toms	2 0
Thomas Taylor	2 4
William Wyatt	2 0
Edward Toms	1 0
John & Tho Wyat	0 6

Thomas Wyat	0 6
Thomas Durman	0 6
Widdow Pen	0 6
William Smith	0 2

Walton Levie

| Sir Thomas Pope | 53 4 |

Purston Levie

Mr Cresswell	3 4
Mr Blincoe	13 4
Mr Walker	10 0

Charlton Levie

Mr Cresswell his land	3 9
William Haddon	3 7 ob
William Haddon	2 4 ob
Mathew Haddon	2 4 ob
John Phipps	2 3
Widdow Lucas	1 0
Mr Marshall	0 10 ob
Dionisse Emberly	0 10
Widdow Yeomans	0 3
Tho: Hobcraft	0 1
John Garner	0 1
Edward Snelson	0 1
Robert Glaze	0 1

Memorandum this levie was written and made in the time of Warre and never gathered

Item here follow the rest of the layings out of Thomas Rawlins and Richard Taylor Anno 1642 and anno 1643 as followeth vzt

In prim to Rowsom his wages 1643	3 4
Ite to John Whittakers his wages	8 0
Ite to the Geoyle and lame souldiers	4 4
Ite to Edward Upston for mending the second bell Clepper	3 4
Ite payd for 3 bell ropes	8 0
Ite for writing the registers 1642	4 0
Ite for bread and wine at midsomr Communion	15 2
Ite for oyle for the Clocke	0 2
Ite for bread and wyne at Michaelmas Communion	15 5

Ite to Edward Upston for mending the Churchgate and worke about the bells	2 11
Ite payd for wine at Buckingham on Palm Sonday 1643	14 0
Ite to Ned Upston for fetching the said wyne	1 6
Ite to Thomas Sumner for more bred & wine the Easter day following	30 0
Ite for fetching the wine from Aynho	0 6
Ite for washinge the surplis and tablecloath	1 0
Ite to Besse Harrisse for washinge and mendinge the surplis before it was taken away	1 0
Ite to Taylor of Banbury for wine at Midsomr Comunion 1643	12 3
Ite for bread at the same communion	0 5
Ite for writing the Registers Anno 1643	4 0
Ite for paviours to stop up the Churchgate way when the gate was burned by the souldiers	1 0
Ite for setting up the said paviours	0 3
Ite to Humphry Jenings for fetching the wine aforsaid	0 4
Ite to William Paynter for two loads of stone	1 0
Ite to John Clemens for fetching the said paviours stones	2 6
Ite to John Clemens for a load of his owne stones	1 0
Item payd for making the Churchyard stile	1 0
Ite for iron worke about the stile and gate	0 3
Item to Thomas Allibone for all his worke about the Churchyard walles	2 0
Ite for bread and wine on Palme sonday and Easter day this yeare 1644	35 3
Ite to Rowsam his wages for keeping the clock and the bells for two yeares last past	6 8
Ite for one old rope for a bell	1 6
Ite for nayles to mend the bell wheeles	0 8
Ite for fetching wyne fro Banbury 4 sevrall times	1 4
Ite oyle for the clocke	0 4
Ite Grese for the bells	0 10
Ite for writing the Registers anno dnj 1644	4 0
Item for more wyne for som more Communicants	1 6
Item for fetching the said wine	0 4
Item given to poore Widdow Clarke being in great distress	1 0
Ite more to Widdow Clarke	1 0
Ite for carriing her to Astrup	0 6
Ite for mowinge & makinge Lady mede	6 0
Ite for mowing & making ye Nothings in the Lake meade	4 0

Ite for bread & wine this Palme sonday 1645 and Easter day & some other needfull communions to poore people diseased	41 5
Memorand since I tendred my account I provided a load of paviors to lay upon three graves	3 0
and layd out for the laying them downe	3 0
Memorand we have left of ye Levie made ye 26th of Aprill Anno Dnj 1641 ungathered	5 2

All our receipts for our time from the yeare 1641 untell the yeare 1648
are   £22 4s 2d
All our layings out for the time aforsaid are   £23 3s 9d
Compared together there remaines due to the old Church Churchwardens
Thomas Rawlins and Richard Tayler the summe of 19s & 7d

Churchwardens chosen by the parish of King Sutton the 4th day of Aprill
anno dnj 1648

Churchwardens   { John Heynes
                { John Phipps

Overseeres for the   { John Clemence
Poore   { Thomas Durman

Survayers for   { John Jenings
ye Highwayes   {Edmund Carpenter

Jo: Blincow   Jo: Creeke minister
William Haddon   John Kirby
          Richard Taylor
          John Carpenter
          John Quatermaine

Vicesimo die Aprilis
Anno dnj 1648

A levie made by the Minister and others of the parish whose names are
subscribed for necesary uses and repayres about the Church and
Churchyard mounds vzt

Kingsutton at ijs ye yardland
Astrup at xijd ye yardland
Charlton at vjd ye yardland
Cottages of ye Lords hold vjd a peece
Cottages of ye Parsonage hold iiijd a peece
        Walton   53s 4d
        Purston   26s 8d

            John Creeke minister

            John Phipps   }
            John Heynes } Churchwardens

            Kingsutton levie

Richard Kenwricke Esq and Mris Kenwricke	9	0
Mr Chambers & Mris Chambers	5	0
Thomas Bodicott	4	0
Richard Pargiter	3	0
George Toms	3	0
Thomas Taylor	3	0
John Kirbie	2	0
John Heynes	2	3
Thomas Heynes	2	6
Thomas Toms	2	0
John Swayne	2	0
Thomas Penne	2	0
Edward Toms	1	6
Robert Toms	1	3
George Winkles	1	1
Charles Butcher	1	0
Widdow Williams	0	6
Richard Hanley		
John Waters		

John Burford for little mill	0 4
George Grime	0 6
Tymothy Parish	0 6
Edward Williams	1 2
ffrancis Davies	0 7
Edmund Carpenter	
John Jenings	0 6
Thomas Watts	0 6
John Upston	0 6
William Bricknell	0 6
Richard Williams	0 6
Jonathan Kinge	0 6
William Whitwell	0 7 ob
William Peedle	0 6
John Clemence	0 7 ob
George Jenings	0 6
Katherine Jenings	0 6
Thomas Bet	0 6
Edward Sworder	0 6
John Warner	0 4
Edward Cosby	0 6
Henry Heritage	0 6
Simon Wattson	0 6
Twyford mill meade	2 0
Robert Bricknell	0 4
Roger Jarvice	0 2
John & Tho: Wyatt	0 4
Charles Butcher for one Cottage at ye mill	0 6
Richard Chambers his acre lands	0 6
Thomas Harrise	0 4
Michaell Upston	0 4
Samuell Green	0 4
John Whittaker	0 4
Widdow Price	0 4
John Maule	0 4
Edward Upston	0 4
Whittbyes house	0 3
William Parish	0 3
Thomas Jenings	0 3
Widdow Pilly	0 3
Widdow Andrewes	0 3
George Toms	0 3
William ffathers	0 2

William Cooper	0 2
Thomas Clemence	0 2
Richard Yates	0 2
Stacies house	0 2
Alexander Smith	0 2
Henry Painter	0 2
Humphry Jenings	0 2
John Heynes sen	0 2
John Sanders	0 2
William Heynes	0 2
Thomas Blincowe	0 2
William Peedle	0 2

Astrup Levie

Mr Steward	18 0
Mr Cartwright	12 0
Mr Crew	2 0
Mr Crew	2 0
My Hyerns	5 0
Mr Piggott	1 0
Edmund Carpenter	4 0
John Carpenter	4 6
Thomas Bodicott	2 0
John Wyatt	2 0
Widdow Numans land	2 0
George Toms	2 0
Thomas Taylor	2 4
William Wyatt	1 0
Widdow Wyatt	1 0
Edward Toms	1 0
John & Thomas Wyatt	0 6
Thomas Wyatt sen	0 6
Thomas Durman	0 6
Thomas Pe [sic]	0 6
William Smith	0 2

Sir Thomas Pope for Walton	53 4

Purston Levie

Mr Cresswell	3 4
Mr Blincowe	13 4
John ffreeman	10 0

Charlton Levie

Mr Cresswell his land	3 9
William Haddon	3 7 ob

William Haddon	2 4 ob
Mathew Hadon	2 4 ob
John Phipps	
John Lucas	1 0
John Marshall	0 10 ob
Dennice Emberly	
[entry incomplete]	

The recepts of John Phipps and John Heynes beginning Anno 1648

	£ s d
Memorand we have received of William Haddon for halfe the Xch grass being in ye Ladie mead and the Nothings in both meades (belonging to our Church of Sutton) ye summe of	1 16 8
Ite received of Alexander Smith for the other halfe of the above named Church grasse wch said grasse was set in June Anno 1647 (being the last yeare) the like summe of	1 16 8
Ite received the Easter Communicants half yeare 1648	0 10 0
Ite received of Thomas Bodicott for the Church barne	1 0 0
Ite received for the Church grass Anno dnj 1648 June 8th	4 3 4
Ite received for the Xch grass of Thomas Toms Anno dnj 1649 the summe of	5 7 8
Ite received for Mr Chambers his grave	0 5 8
Ite for Gabriell Chambers his grave	0 5 8
Ite for Mris Chambers her grave They had bin a noble a peece but they layd them downe at their owne charges	0 5 8
Ite for John Pargiters and An Pargiters grave received	0 11 4
Item Widdow Carpenters grave	0 5 8
Ite for John Quatermaine his wifes grave	0 5 8
Ite received of John Lucas for his mothers grave They pd for the laying ym down	0 5 8
Ite received of John Maule for ye Xch barne Anno 1648 He payd noe more for ys yere because he bestowed cost to repayre it	0 13 4
Ite received of William Hodges for ye yeare 1648 & for ye yeare 1649 7s a yeare in regard twas out of repayre; received but	0 14 0
Ite of Henry Hobcroft for ye yeare 1648	0 7 0

Ite of Richard Andrewes 1648	0 6 0
Ite of Anthony Parkins for ye Xch land Anno 1648	0 10 0
Ite received of William Whitwell for a fortnights grass in Lake mead 1649	0 4 8

Here follow the rest of the Receipts of John Phipps and John Heynes

In prim received the Communicants halfe pence 1649	
Item received the Communicants halfe pence 1650	
Ite received of William Haddon for the Church Grasse Anno dnj 1650	5 7 8
Item received of Anthony Perkins for the land in Breach	0 4 6
Ite received of Hodges his rent this yeare 1650	0 7 0
Ite of Richard Andrewes his rent for 2 yeares last past at Michaelmas 1650	0 12 0
Ite of Henry Hobcroft his rent 1649	0 5 0
Ite Easter Communicants half pence Anno 1651	

13 Junii 1648

Memorand the Church grasse was sold ye yeare aforsaid to
William Haddon and John Heynes for £4 3s 4d

Here begin the layings out of John Phippes and John Heynes for this
theire yeare Anno Dnj Dej 1648

In primis to Richard Maule for wine this Palme sonday and Easter day 1648	2 4 0
Item to the baker for bread for ye Communions on Palme sond: Easter eve Easter day and twelve private Communions to diseased people ye Easter 1648 aforsaid	0 1 10
Item to John Stratford for fetching ye wine from Aynhoe	0 0 8
Item paid for rajking ye Ladie meade ditch	0 5 0
Item paid Rowsam for keeping the bells & Clock in ye yeare 1646 behind	0 3 4
Ite to Rowsame yt he layd out in the yeare aforsaid for oyle for ye clocke & mending ye clocke bell wheeles &c	0 2 11

Ite to Rowsame for keepinge ye bells & Clock in ye yeare 1647	0	3	4
Ite paid him yt he layd out for ye yeare aforsaid for oyle for ye clock washing the table cloath and nayles to mend the bellwheele	0	1	2
Ite Ed Upston for wood for ye plummer and to round the Church lader	0	3	4
Ite to him for mending the Church gate	0	0	3
Ite to him for roddes for ye bell:wheeles	0	0	6
Ite to him for a Cromp for the Spoute & a key	0	1	4
Ite for a bellrope and a tag for ye great bell	0	3	4
Ite for oyle for ye bells	0	0	4
Ite stones to mend the Xch yard wall and ye carriage	0	2	6
Ite to Allibone for making the wall	0	0	10
Ite to ye plummer for ye worke he did about ye church in ys our yeare 1648 and for ye soder	0	15	9
Ite to Rowsam for serving him	0	1	4
Ite to Thomas Toms his work to round ye Xch ladder	0	1	0
Ite our expenses upon the Plummers	0	1	6
Ite nayles	0	0	1
Ite payd to ye Joyle amd maimed Souldiers	0	4	6
Ite given to travellers	0	0	6
Item for bread & wine at Easter 1649 wh Easter day was on our Ladie day having many privat communions	0	45	4
Ite to John Whittaker for glazing all the Church windowes in ye yeare 1648 the summe of	7	3	4
Item to Ned Upston for barres for the Xch windowes 1648	0	7	0
Ite for mending the bells and some iron work about ye seats	0	2	6
Ite to ffrancis Davies for a quarter of Lime	0	8	0
Ite to William Whitwell for 3 strikes of lime more all spent about ye Xch & Xch windows	0	3	0
Ite to George Whitwell for plastering	0	5	0
Ite to Henry Upston for making up the Xchyard wall	0	1	0
Ite to Thomas Toms for mending the Xchyard stile	0	0	6
Ite to Locke for making ye Dyall on the Xch	0	3	4
Ite for a bellrope bought of Mr Creeke	0	1	6
Ite for two bellropes more	0	6	10
Ite to Goale and maymed souldiers for 3 paymts more in our time being 4s 4d a time the summe is	0	13	0

Ite pd Rowsam since our time for gresse for ye bells, oyle for ye clocke and wyer for ye clock	0	4	0
Ite pd Rowsam his wages for looking to the clock & bells anno 1648	0	3	4
Ite for washing the table cloath & fetching wine 1649	0	3	7
Ite payd for hayre and sand spent about the Xch	0	1	0
Ite to Alex: Smith for trussing the bells	0	1	6
Ite the new Xchyard gate the iron worke the post and workmanshipp coms to	0	10	0
Ite payd to Rowsam Anno 1649	0	5	0
Ite payd Thomas Rawlins towards his 19s 7d due to him	0	5	0
Item bread and wine on Easter day Anno 1650	2	7	0
Ite to the plummer this Michaelmas 1650	1	9	0
Ite serving the plummer	0	2	0
Ite spent on the plummer	0	0	6
Ite to Dolton for trussing the bells	0	9	0
Ite to Rowsam to help him	0	1	0
Ite pd for two bell ropes	0	7	0
Ite Rowsame for keeping the bells and clocke this yeare 1650	0	3	4
Ite Grease oyle & nailes for the bells when they were new trust	0	4	0
Ite to Rowsame fetching ye wine ye Easter 1650 aforsd and washing the tablecloath	0	1	0
Ite to Allibone for a dayes work in the Church	0	1	2
Ite to Rowsam serving him	0	0	6
Ite to Lod: Upston for work about the clock weight wheels	0	1	4
Ite to Robert Bricknell for washing out ye Kings armes	0	0	9
Ite for a planke to make a seat bottome	0	0	6
Ite to Jo: Clemens the Constable for ye Goale and maimed souldiers	0	4	4
Ite to him againe for ye Goale and maimed souldiers	0	4	4
Ite to Robert Bricknell ye Constable for ye Goale and maimed souldiers	0	4	6
Ite work and stones about the Xch wall	0	1	2
Ite payd for an iron plate and cramp for ye fore bell wheels	0	3	8
Ite for more nayles	0	0	4
Ite payd for wine Easter 1651	2	4	6
Ite payd for comunion bread	0	1	8

Ite payd to Lod: Upston for a plate & nayles for one of ye bell wheeles	0 3 8	

August the 19th 1651

The Accompts of us John Phipps & John Haynes Churchwardens for the Parrish Church of Kingsutton for three yeares past were delivered the day aforesd to the new Churchwardens John Quatermaine & Thomas Toms

All the receipts of us John Phipps & John Haynes are   £26 17s 10d

All our layings out are   £27 8s 2d

Soe it appears that wee have layd out more
than wee have received   10s 4d

And there are three yeares halfe pence for the easter communicants in Mr Creekes hand

1651

Layed out by John Quatermaine and Thomas Toms

	s	d
for 1 pound of grease	0	4
for two roaps for the clock	7	8
for oyel for the clock	0	2
for trusing the bell	2	6
payed rowsam his wages	3	6
and oyel rowsam payed for	0	2
and for 4 pound of greas	1	4
to Ludawick Upston	3	6
for greas	1	0
to John Hityens that was du to him	10	4
for wien	£2 11	0
for fetching the wine	1	0
for bred	1	7
for washing the cloeth	1	0
to the Cunstabel for the Jayel and maymed sollders	5	0

for oyel for the clock	0 2
for our cargis to Culworth	0 8
for a warant	0 6
for a bell rope	2 6
for greas 1 pound	0 4
for oyel for the clock	0 3
for greas 1 pound	0 4

£4 14 10

receaved
of goodman hadon   £2 15s
of Tho Tayelar   £2 15s
for the grase

the recaits of John Quatermaine   £5 10s

the layings out of John Quatermaine is   £4 14s 10d

remaine due   15s 2d

1652

Churchwardens chosen the 20th day of Aprill 1652 according to
the accustomary manner by the Minister & the maior pt of the parish then
present whose names are subscribed

Churchwardens   { John Quatermaine
                { Tho: Tomes

Sidsmen   {
              {

Overseers for ye   { Edward Tomes
     poore   { Tho: Heines

Overseeres for   { Edward Willies
   ye highwayes   {Ed: Spittle:

receved of richard **
receved for the Church grase   £9 3s 4d

willyam hoyg his rent due   7s
receved of iustis the lick sum of   7s

reseved by Thomas Toms   £2 17s 4d

layed out by John Quaterman and Thomas Tomes

for haing the belles	13 0
for the smiathe	15 6
for a pies of wooad	3 0
payed to rowsuam his waiges	3 6
for the joare and lame shoulder	4 6
for lathes and nailes	2 8
for Thomas [beat]	6 4
for the cloaketh makir	13 0
for rowsuam	2 6
for on pound of greas	0 4
for yoall	0 3
for bealles roapes	7 0
for woad	1 0
for yoall	0 2
for nayeales	0 2
to the houes of corection	5 10
for wine at yeaster	£2 11 0
and	2 0
for bread	1 0

£8 10 xi

spent at moreton pinkary   0 8
for [illegible]   0 6

signed out by Thomas Toms   £6 * 11
remaien due   £3 5 5

remains due up to this ***   £6 16 *

payed to Georg Whittill for worke aboweat the chearch	5 0
payed to rowsam for washing the surpelis and feching the wien	2 6
for 2 pound of greas	0 10

The resaites of John Quatermaine and Thomas Toms
for thayer too years is   £15 7s 4d

Thayer layings out for the saied time is   £11 17s 1d

the remaindar is   £3 10s 3d

The receipts of us John Quatermaine & Thomas Tayler
Church wardens for the parish of Kingsutton for the yeare 1653

	£	s	d
Inprimis there was received from the Church wardens for the last yeare	3	10	3
Ite for the Lady meade & the nothings & the ley	6	14	4
Ite received of Richard Andrewes in part of rent	0	4	1
Ite received of George Toms John Wyatt & Thomas Tayler for a yeares rent for the Church barne due from the executrix of Tho Boddicott[1]	0	18	0
for a yeares rent for the two lands	0	4	0
	£11	10	8

all those following are unpayd

Mris Chambers for two graves	0	11	4
Richard Pargiter for three graves	0	17	0
Mr Blinckow for two graves	0	11	4
John Carpenter for one grave wch was Mr Marshalls	0	5	8
Richard Tayler for one grave	0	5	8
Thomas Wyatt for the Church barne – two yeares	1	12	0
Alexander Smith & Richard Smith for the Church barne – one yeare	0	16	0

The Layings out of John Quatermaine & Thomas Tayler Churchwardens
for the parish of Kingsutton for the yeare 1653

Inprimis payd for scoureing of Lady meade ditch	0	2	8
Ite for mending the Beere & for wood for the same	0	0	10
for oyle for the Clock	0	0	8

---

[1] Thomas Bodicote's memorial tablet is now fixed to the vestry wall on the north side of the chancel.

for Greasse for the bells	0	1	0
to the Constable for the Goale & lame souldiers	0	5	0
to Rowsam for his wages	0	3	4
to widdow Pilly for nayles	0	1	2
to the Clock maker his pay for keepeing the Clock	0	1	0
to widdow Pilly for oyle	0	0	4
to Thomas Allibone for a dayes worke about the church window	0	1	4
to John Stratford for serving him	0	0	8
to Lod Upston for plates & for mending the for bell wheele [sic]	0	2	8
to William Borton & his son for five dayes worke about the gudgings & Brasses & trussing the bells	0	10	0
to Rowsam for helping of Borton about them	0	1	8
to Lod Upston for brobbs & nayles & wedges about the same for six keyes & foure ferre[l]s	0	3	4
for mending a wheele staple make two staples for the copses & mending the Clock hammer	0	1	0
for Greasse for the bells	0	0	9
to widdow Pilly for nayles	0	1	0
to William Dolton for two dayes worke of himselfe	0	4	4
to William Dolton & his sonne for one daye about wedging the beames in the steeple & putting Corbitts under them	0	2	2
for timber to brace & loyne the foure lower frames	1	0	0
to William Dolton & his sonne for 12 dayes worke about braceing & loyneing the lower frames	1	6	0
to John Sutton for two dayes worke about the lower frames	0	2	4
to Lod Upston for making six pinns for the sayd frames	0	4	0
for five new bell wheeles	3	0	0
for five new bell roapes	0	17	6
to Will: Borton & his sonne for nine dayes worke about trussing & hanging the five bells	0	18	0
to Richard Mott for foure daye helping of them	0	4	8
to Lod Upston for mending the Irons for the five bells & for keyes & nayles for them	0	7	5
for five new wheele staples	0	2	6
for mending six wheele staples & for keyes	0	2	0
for three pound of brobbs use about the frames	0	1	3
for making & mending tenn staples for the copses	0	2	0
for six new rodds for the bells	0	6	6
for mending the old rodds	0	1	0

for mending two clapers	0	4	0
for a hocke key & ferrell to hang the Clocke weight on	0	0	4
hookes to fasten the clocke	0	0	4
mending the clocke	0	1	6
mending two lockes on the church dores	0	1	0
a staple for the steeple dore	0	3	0
bread & wine on Palme Sunday & Easter day	1	18	9

£13 6 3

All the receipts of us John Quatermaine & Thomas Tayler
   comes to   £11 10s 8d

Our laying out comes to   £13 6s 3d

soe it appears that we have layd out more than we have
   receved   £1 15s 7d

seene & allowed   29 Mar 54
John: briden Jo. Cartwright

for two warrants at the sitting	0	1	6
spent at the sitting	0	0	6
for washing the table cloath and fetching the wine	0	1	3

Wee nominate for Churchwardens for the yeare next ensuing
Thomas Taylor of Sutton and John Carpenter of Astropp

The receipts of us John Carpenter and Thomas Tayler Churchwardens for
the yeare 1654 are as followeth

Inprimis received for the nothings and Lady meade	6	0	0
Item received for the two lands belonging to the Church	0	4	0
Item received of John Swayne for the Church barne for this yeare 1654	0	14	6

Item received of William Justice for rent for his house for two yeares ending at Michaellmas 1653 as appears by the Accompts of John Phipps and John Haynes and also by the Accompts of John Quatermaine and Thomas Toms	0 14 0
Item received of John Carpenter for Mr Marshall his Grave	0 5 8
Item received of Richard Taylor for one Grave [wch w]as behinde	0 5 8

£8 3 10

Aprill the 17th 1655

there is two yeares and a halfe behinde of rent due from William Hodges to the Church at our Lady day last past

there is one yeare and a halfe behinde of rent due to the Church from William Justice and two shillings wch were due in old hobcraft his life time

there hath bin but 4s and 1d received of Richard Andrewes for these three yeares and a halfe last past as appeares by the booke

William Hodges the younger never payd any to the Church as yett

there hath not any bin received for ffreebodyes and Mary Chapmans Houses as we can find by this booke

there is behinde for the Church barne we know not what, and there wilbe a true Accompt made of all particulers wee know not when

all the Graves are still unpayd wch are specified at the later end of the receipts of John Quatermaine except those wch are expressed above in our receipts

The layings out of us John Carpenter and Thomas Tayler
are as followeth

Inprimis payd to the old Church wardens wch they layd out more than they received as appears in their Accompts	1 18 10
Item to John Whittaker for worke done about the Church	0 19 0
Item to Lod: Upston for worke about the barrs for the Church windows foe mending the Clock hammer and spring for makeing two keyes and for shutting rodds	0 4 8
Item for a peece of timber wch was cutt to make the upper floure in the steeple and to mend the seates behind the south doore	1 6 8
Item to William Dolton for sawing the peece of timber for worke about the floure and seates and two dayes about the fourth bell and first trebell	2 1 0
for nayles used about the seats	0 0 9
for two bell roapes	0 6 2
for oyle for the clock	0 0 10
for Grease for the bells	0 1 10
to the Goale and maimed souldiers	0 10 10
to William Poynter for slatts to mend the North portch and for stones for the north window	0 1 0
to George Whittwell for gathering mosse and mending the portch	0 1 0
to Thomas Allibon for walling the window and mending of broaken places in the pavements	0 2 10
for carrying the slatts & stones	0 0 9
for mending the Church bucketts and some leather for the baldriggs	0 3 0
to Rowsam for his wages	0 3 4
for washing the table Cloath	0 0 6
for wyer for the Clock	0 0 2
to Sim Hodges for goeing to Westbury & Brackly for the schoolmaster Mr Gibbs to officiate here one sabbath	0 0 4

£8 3 6

All the receipts of us John Carpenter and Thomas Tayler for
this yeare 1654 comes to £8 3 10
Our layings out comes to 8 3 6
Soe there is in our handes wch we received more
than we layd out 0 0 4

there is due from William Wyatt for his unckle John Wyatt			
his Grave	0	6	8
spent at the sitting at Daintree	0	0	10
for a warrant	0	0	6
Soe it appears that we John Carpenter and Thomas Tayler			
have layd out more than we received	0	1	0

Churchwardens Chosen by the Major part of the parish present
Aprill the 17th 1655 for the yeare ensuing

Churchwardens   { Richard Pargiter
                     { William Haddon

Alexander Dig[by] Apr 1655
Edw ffarmer
Hen Barkelry

The receipts of us Richard Pargiter and William Haddon Church
wardens for the parish Church of KingSutton for the yeare 1655. I say
received by me Will: Haddon as followeth

Inprimis received for John Wyatt his Grave	0 6 8
It received for part of ye Church grasse	2 12 6
It received of Mr willowby mony yt was in arrerayes for ye Church land being ye some of nine pounds 6 shilling 8 pence I say received by mee	5 6 8
Received for ye tow lands	0 4 0
Received for ye Church Barne for ye yeare 1655 ye some of	0 14 6

Received by me Richard Pargiter as followeth vid

of Mr Willoby in part of ye arrares above expressed ye some of	4 0 0
received for part of ye Church gras ye some of	2 10 6
received of Mr Blincow for 3 graves	0 17 0
for 4 graves for himself to pay	1 2 8

The layings out of Richard Pargiter and William Haddon for the yeare
1655

Inprimis payd to the old Church wardens	0	1	0
Item to the Goale and maimed souldiers	0	6	0
Ite pd to William Dolton for mendinge ye bellwhele	0	2	6
Ite pd to Ladvike Upston	0	1	0
Ite pd to Henry Heritage for scouringe the dish of ye lady mead	0	1	4
Ite pd to Will Smith for menddinge the buckets	0	0	4
It paid to William Dolton for eight dayes worke about mending ye beame of ye church yt was broken and for his sonne seaven dayes	0	19	0
It for ye Gayle and maimed sould:	0	4	9
It to lad Upston for making wedges for ye therd bell	0	1	0
It to Rousom for keeping ye clock	0	3	4
It to Rowsom for a dayes worke	0	0	8
It to Thomas Alibonn and his man for 3 dayes work apeece about ye Church	0	6	6
Paid to Nathaniell Chester for five dayes worke there	0	7	6
paid to Timothy Chester for on dayes worke	0	1	6
Paid to John Stradford for 3 dayes for serving ye mason	0	2	6
Paid to Tho: Robinson for one dayes worke	0	0	10
Paid to Ladd Upston for mending a ladder yt was broken which was Mr Kenwrickes	0	3	0
paid ladd Upston for mending ye Church ladder	0	3	5
to him for mending ye great bell claper	0	10	0
to Upston for making tow pinns for ye beame	0	2	8
for making of 8 keyes 3 wedges 2 stables and mending of another staple and for nayles	0	7	0
for 3 more wedges for ye bells: for shutting 2 rods and for 2 pinnes	0	1	10
It paid to ye Glazier for 48 quarryes of new Glasse putt in	0	3	6
It for leading, sodering, banding and poynting ye old glasse	0	4	0
It to John Maule for wood to mend ye Church	xjs		
for Beare to make ye workme Drinke	0	1	2
It to Tho: Robinson for going twise to Adderbury for a minister	0	0	6
It for oyle for ye clock	0	6	0
It for grease for ye clock	0	0	6
It to Dolton for I know not what	0	0	2

It to Dolton for mending ye Church stile	0	1 0
It to Dolton for mending of ye forth bell wheele and for mending a pully about ye Clocke	0	1 4
ffor sendinge mony to Daventree yt was collected for ye protestants	0	1 0
It for a bar to willi: Upston for Church use	0	0 6
Spent at Culworth when wee went to give in a certificate concerning parsonages and vicarages donatine	0	1 6
It to John Swaine for carring stonnes and morter and timber for ye Church use	0	4 0
It ffor Bread and wine on Easter day Easter Even and Palm Sunday	1	18 0
ffor fetching of ye wine	0	0 4
to Austin Smalbonn for mending the balriggs	0	0 10
for wood to John Maule for the Saintes	0	2 6
It ffor five Bellropes	0	16 6
It for washing ye tablecloth	0	0 6

Soe it apeareth ye receipts and layings forth compared together ther remaines to ye Church the som of eight pounds seventeen shillings five pence halpenny as is hearunder expressed

vid[ite] In ye hands of Richard Pargiter eight pounds tenn shillings tow pence
and In ye hands of Willia Haddon ye younger seven shillings three penc halpenny

laid forth more since this account as follows
To Rousam for Grease and nayles   1s
spent at ye sitting att Brackly   8d
paid for a warrant   6d
Soe ther remaines In ye hand of Will Haddon   5s 1d ob
wh is paid to ye new Churchwardens

there remaines upon this Acompt and the former those particular funds unpayd
first Mris Chambers for two Graves   £0 11 4
Thomas Wyatt for the Church barne for two yeares   1 12 0
Alexander Smith & Rich Smith for the
        Church barne for a yeare   0 16 0
there is three yeares and halfe behinde for rent from
        Will Hodges the elder at our lady day last
there is two yeares and halfe behinde from Will Justice
        at our lady day last besides two shillings

there hath bin but 4s 1d received of Rich Andrews for foure yeares and
halfe last past   as apeares by the last accompt and this
Will Hodges the younger never payd any rent as yett
there hath not any bin received for ffreebodyes house and mary Chapman
hir house as   we can finde by this booke
there is behinde for the Church barne from Tho Boddicot we know not
whatt

remaines   7s 3d

Aprill the eigth 1656

Church-wardens chosen or nominated by the minister & the maior part
present at the parish church of Kingsutton are as follows

Robert Bricknell }   Church
Edmund Carpenter }   wardens

Seene & allowed 11 Apr 1656
Jo. Cartwright   Hen Barkelry

The receipts of us Edmund Carpenter & Robert Bricknell Churchwardens
for the parish of Kingsutton for the yeare 1656

Inprimis received of Richard Pargitor	8 10 2
Item received of William Haddon	0 5 1 ob
Item of Mr Blincow for Lady meade and the Nothings	5 15 0
Item of William Hogges the elder for a yeares rent due at Michaelmas	0 8 0
Item of William Justis for two yeares rent att Michaelmas	0 14 0

Item receved for two pewter bottles which were solde	0 6 6
Item of Richard Andrewes for one yeares rent due att Michaelmas	0 6 0
Item of Thomas Taylor for one yeares rent for the two Church lands	0 4 0
Item of John Haynes for wood which grewe in Lady meade	0 10 8
Item of Allexander Smith for a halfe yeares rent for the Church barne	0 8 0
Item received of William Marcombe and Thomas Winkels for one yeares rent for the Church barne	0 8 0
Item received of Richard Smith for a halfe years rent for the Church barne which was formerly due	0 8 0

The layings out of us Edmund Carpenter and Robeart Bricknell beinge Churchwardens for this yeare — 1656

Inprimis laide out for the Goayle and maimed souldiers	0 5 10
Item paid for a pound of grease	0 0 4
Item paide to the glazier for worke	0 5 2
Item paide to William Borton for his worke about the bells	0 7 0
Item paide to the clockmaker for three yeares	0 3 0
Item payde to the Glazier for new glase and new leading of glase and worke	0 4 3
Item payde to the plummer for sixteene pounds of soder	0 26 0
Item payd to the plummer for a spout of leade	0 4 0
Item payd to the plummer for a dayes worke	0 2 0
Item paid to the Goayle and maimed souldiers	0 5 0
Item paid to Allexander Smith for wood for the plummer	0 1 0
Item paid to Rowsom for serveing the plummer	0 0 6
Item to Robert Bricknell for a dayes worke about the vestry and Church with slatts and mose	0 1 6
Item paid to the workmen for scowering of the river	0 2 1
Item paid to Lodawicke Upstone for worke about the Church	0 8 0
Item paid to Rowsom for his yeares wagges	0 3 4
Item paide to Margaret Pilly for oyle and nayles	0 1 1
Item paid to the Goayle and maimed souldiers	0 6 0
Item paid to Evins for two belropes	0 6 0
Item paid for fower pounds of grease	0 1 4

Item paid to little Jude for washing the cloath and for feching of the wyne	0 0 10
Item paid for breade and wine for palme sundaye ester even and ester daye	1 14 10
Item spent at Northamton upon the towns behalfe	0 10 6
Item spent at Brackly	0 1 2

Our receipts and layings out compared together are as followeth

Our receipts are   £18 1 11 ob

Our layings out are   6 5 9

soe there remaynes due to the towne   11 16 2 ob

                          Allowed by us
                          Hen Barkelry
                          Edw ffarmar

Layd out at Daventry since the accompt   1s 9d

The eight shillings which was receved of Richard Smith was received since the account

Soe there remaines due to the Towne   £12 2 5 ob

In the yeare 1657

Richard Carpenter was elected church-warden by Robt Mansell
Vicar of Kings-Sutton for the yeare above written:
And to remaine in that office untill the next election

                          Robt. Mansell
                          Vicar of Kings-sutton

Churchwardens Chosen by the
maior part of the parish
then present
                      Churchwardens
                      Richard Carpenter
                      Thomas Durman

Thomas [th]iorne
Edm: Carpenter
Robert Bricknell
Jo: Carpenter
George Toms
John Watters
John Kerby
John Quatermaine
Thomas Pen
Richard Pargiter

The receipts of us Richard Carpenter and Thomas Durman
Churchwardens
for the parish of Kingsutton for the yeare 1657

Item received of Robert Bricknill   £5 18s 6d

August ye 24
Received of William Haddon and ffrancis Wyatt seven pounds one
shilling and eight pence for ye Church grasse and there remaineth five
shillings which they keepe in theire hands untill they are satisfied for ye
grasse which Edward Toms and William Marckrom tooke away

	s	d
Item received of Tymothy Chester for a peece of wood wch grew in ffrebodies yeard	4	6
Item received of Tho: Tayler for ye two Church Lands on yeares rent	4	0
Item received of William Marckrome and Thomas Winckells one yeares rent for the Church Barne	14	6
Item received of Rich: Andrews on yeares rent due at Mychaelmas	6	0
Item received of William Justice on yeares rent due at Mychaellmas	7	0
Item received the five shillings of Will: Haddon and ffrancis Wyatt which they stopt for the grasse that Edward Toms and Will: Marcombe tooke away from ye Church grasse		
Ite received of William Hodges the elder in part of payment of his rent	5	0
and there is in his hand unpayd	3	0
Received of William Wyatt for stones yt covered his uncle Jo: Wyatts grave	1	4

Received of Edmund Carpenter and there is fifty three shillings and eleven pence halfe peny which the towne is content to be stopt for old arreares	£3 10 0

The layings out of us Rich: Carpenter and Tho: Durman being
Churchwardens for this yeare 1657 are as followeth

Inprimis payd to George Whittwall for a peece of wood which mended ye fift bell	5 0
Item payd to Ladwick Upston for shuting the fore bell claper	4 6
Item payd to Lad: Upston for making of staples and other iron worke about the fift bell stock	9 11
Item payd to William Dolton for to days worke about ye fift bell stock and wheelle	3 4
Item payd to Rich: Hanly for helping of William Dolton a day and halfe about ye bells	1 3
Item payd to Edmund Peedle for scouring of the Lady meade ditch	1 4
Item payd to William Pointer for a loade of paviers	3 0
Item payd for the fetching of them	1 0
Item payd to Thomas Alibone for worke yt he did about ffreebodys house	4 6
Item payd to John Stratford for serving the Mason	0 10
Item payd to Will: Hodges for serving the mason	0 8
Item payd to Tho: Toms for on days worke	0 4
Item payd to Nathyaniell Chester for a peece of wood which mended the bell wheelles and for his worke	0 9
Item payd for beere for the workmen to drinke	0 4
Item payd to widdow Pilly for nayles	0 4
Item payd to Will: Hodges for straw which was layd upon ye gabell stelch on ffreebodys house	0 4
Item payd to John Clemence for bords to make Richard Chapman a doore	2 2
Item payd to ye ropier for ropes	£1 3 0
Payd Rowsam his wages	3 4

Payd Rowsam for mending ye gate at ye Church grate	0	3
Payd unto Robert Bricknill for stones which were layd upon Jo: Wyatts grave	1	4
payd unto Tho: Alibone for laying down John Wyatts grave and other worke about the Church	2	0
Item payd unto Will: Dolton for mending the bell wheeles	0	8
Item payd unto Lad: Upston for worke which he did about ye bells and pulpitt	6	6
Item payd for three pounds of grease for the bells	1	0
payd unto Widdow Pilly for oyle and nayles	1	9
payd for a booke which was anact for ye sabbath	0	6
payd for fetchinge of ye booke	0	4
Item payd unto the glasier for new glasse and new leading of glasse	1	6
Item to Will: Dolton for mending the pullpitt	0	4
Item payd for bread and wine for Palme Sunday and Easter even and Easter day	£1 16	0
Item payd unto Littil Jude for fetching ye bread and wine and washing the Table cloath twice	1	3
Payd unto Nathanyell Chester for a peece of wood which mended the bell wheeles and for his worke	1	6
Payd to ye goale and maimed soldiers	6	0
Payd unto Astill Smallbone for lether for ye bathering of ye bells	1	0
Payd for ye Goale and maimed soldiers ye 13th day of Aprill	6	0

Our receites is   £18 12 6
Our layinges out is   £6 14 10
There remains due to the Church in our hands   £11 17 8

Seene & allowed 14 April 1658
        John Briden
        Jo: Cartwright

April 13 1658

According to the custome used in Kings-sutton in this county
of Northampton I Robt Mansell vicar thereof doe elect Christopher North
to be churchwarden for this yeare ensuing

Ro: Mansell. vicar
of Kings-sutton

Christopher North}
John Waters}   Church wardens

George Whittwell }   Surveiours for the
William Wyatt iunior }   highwayes

Richard Carpenter
Thomas Durman
Robert Johnson
Edm: Carpenter
John Quatermaine
Tho: Tayler
Robert Bricknell
Richard Pargiter
John Whittaker

Received since ye acount
of William Hodges three
shillings which was left
behind of his Michaelmas rent

Laid out since ye acompt as followeth

Layd out at Brackly at the sitting	6d
Payd for a warrant	6d

The receites of us Christopher north and John Waters church Wardens for the yeare 1658

Receved of Richard Carpenter and Thomas Durman the sume of	11 19 8
Receved of master Kendricke for on years rent of the church barne	0 14 6
Receved of Richard Andrues for on yeares renetes	0 6 0
Receved of John Henes for the church gras	6 10 0
Receved of Thomas Tayler for the church land	0 4 0
Receved of William hodg senner for on yeare	0 5 0
Receved of William Justis	0 5 0

our Receite is   £20 4 2

The layeinges out of us Christopher North and John Waters eares as folueth being church wardens for this yeare 1658

Item given to a poore traveler	0 1 0
Item payd to nathaniell chester for mending the pulpit and the pewe	0 1 6
Item payd to Alecsander Smith for bordes to mende the pulpit and piew	0 1 2
Item paid for nailes for the same	0 0 5
Item payd for oyle for the clocke	0 0 4
Item payd to John Upston for thetching of the church barne	0 3 0
Item paid to Richard Hanly for serving thetching	0 2 0
Item paid to gooddie gervise for youllming	0 1 6
Item paid to John Waters for stretcheres and binders	0 0 4
Item for three pound of greas for the belles	0 1 0
Item for nayles for mending som that were amis	0 0 6
Item for oyle for the clocke	0 0 4
Item to Rousame for wages	0 3 4
Item paid to William Dolton for taking up the belles and weedging of them	0 9 9
Item payd to William Upston for the weedges	0 1 6
Item payd to Rousom for helping them	0 0 6
Item payd to William Dolton for a lader for the steeple	0 3 0
Item paid to Thomas Clemence for lether for the belles	0 1 2

Item paid to John Wateres for three mates for the pulpit and pue and seate	0	1	2
Item paid to to Lad Upstone for mending of the vestrie dore and for nayles	0	0	9
Item for carying the mony to the shrefe [*sheriff*] witch gathered for poland and bohemy and for aquitance and for sending of the noate to London all is	0	1	8
Item for strawe to thetch the church barne	0	5	4
Item to John Witacer for mending on wind[2]	0	1	8
Item for oyele fo the clocke	0	0	4
Item for on pound of greas for the belles	0	0	4
Item for wier for the clocke	0	0	4
Item payd to Littiol Jude for washing the tabell cloth	0	0	6
Item paid to nathaniell chester for mending of seates and the yeat [*gate*]	0	0	3
Item paid to Alesander Smith for wood for the plumer	0	2	4
Item payd to the plummer for soder and for thre days worke	1	7	6
Item payd to rousum for helping of the plummer	0	2	0
Item payd to lad upston for mending of the great bell cleaper	0	6	6
Item for bread and wine for Ester day and palme sunday and ester wefe	1	19	8
Item payd to the goale and mame soilders	0	11	9

our layings out eare   £6 14 11
There remaineth to the nexte   £13 9 3

Seene and allowed 7 Aprill 1659 by us
        Jo. Cartwright   George Benson

April the fifth 1659

According to the custome used in Kings-Sutton in the County of
Northampton
I Rob. Mansell vicar thereof doe elect William Kerby
to be Church-warden for this yeare ensuing
                 Rob. Mansell Vicar
                 of Kingsutton

---

[2] one window

Geor[g]e Toms & }
William Kerby } Churchwardens

Mr Hiorns and}   Surveyors for
Jonathan King } the Highwayes

Cristopher North
John Wateres
Edm: Carpenter   John Quatermaine
Edward Toms
the mark of John Heynes
John Whittaker

Layd out since the acount as faloeth

Layd out at brackly at the sitting	1s
paid for a warrante	6d

William hodg the younger is behind for on yeares rent   three shillinges

The receites of us gorg tomes and William Kerby Church Wardans
as faloeth for this yeare 1659

Receved of Cristopher North and John Waters the sum   £3 7s 9d

There is put out upon land with the consent of the parishe tenn pound witch doath belong to the church

Collected in the Parish of Kings-sutton in the county of Northampton the last day of July one thousand six hundred fifety and nine the sume of eight shillings and nine pence for Blunham in the County of Bedford
Rob. Mansell minister
Willia Kerby Church-warden

Received for ye church la [*sic*]	£0	4	0
Received by me Georg Toms for this present yeare 1659			
Ite for ye church grasse		4 0 0	
Ite for parte of the mony received of the ould church wardens			
		1 14 3	
ssome is		5 18 3	

The receits of Willia Kerby

Recvd of Mr Kenwricke the sume of	£0	14	6
due for a yeares rent for the church barne			
Received of William Justis for one yeares rent	0	7	0
Received for ye church grase	4	0	0
Received of the mony payd by ye			
ould church wardens	1	13	6
ssome is	6	15	0
	12	13	3

Received due upon bond from Christopher North	10	12	0
Our whole receipts is	23	5	3
our layings out is	8	9	5
Remaining in our hands	14	15	10

     whereof there is tenn pounds delivered into Mr Mansells hand and
     a bond is taken for the same

[*Crossed out* Memorandum that wee George tomes and william Kerby
dide in the yeare 1659 delivered upon our acounte unto Mr Robart
Kendwrich and to thomas tayler to william Haddon & to Richard
Carpenter the summe of tenne pounds whoe are trustes to the parish for
the sume and they dide put it out to use & wee receved one yeares use
being twelfe shilings]

    The layings out of Georg Toms and William Kerby churchwardens for
             this present yeare 1659 are as followeth

[*Crossed out* Imprimis payd to my brother Edward Toms	£2	10	0]
[*Crossed out* Ite pd to me Georg Toms	0	16	8]
Ite pd to John Whitaker for glassing ye church wendoes	0	9	6
Ite pd to Edward Rowsome	0	3	6
Ite pd for worke done about ye Bell wheles	1	9	0
Ite pd to the Jayle and lame soldiers	0	4	4
[*Crossed out* ssome is £5 13 9]			
ssome is £2 6 8			

Inprimis pd to William Kerby for scowering ye lady mead dich	0	1	4
Ite pd to ye clockmaker	0	3	0
Ite pd to ye plumer	0	7	0
Ite pd to Allexsander Smith for wode for the plumer	0	1	6
Ite pd to Nataniell Chester for mending 2 bellwheles and making a new logger	0	1	0
Ite pd for 3 pound of grease for the Bells	0	1	3
Ite pd to Margarit Pellye for nayles & oyle for ye clocke	0	1	6
Ite pd for Bell Ropes	1	4	0
Ite pd for the bellwheles	1	16	0
Ite pd to Judith Rowsome for feching the bred & wine & washing ye table cloath	0	1	6
Ite pd for bread & wine for palme Sunday Easter Eve and Easter day	1	19	0
Ite pd to William Poyntter one days work for ye vestry	0	1	2
Ite pd to John Waters for six mattes for the Ringinge flower	0	4	0
Ite given to poore people	0	0	6

ssome is   £6 2 9

The whole ssom of the layings out is   £8 9 5

April 24th 1660

[*Crossed out* According to the custome used in Kings-sutton in the County of Northampton for the Vicar to elect one Church-warden I Robert Mansell Vicar of the sayd parish church doe elect John Pargitter for this yeare ensuing]

Robt Mansell

The parrish nominateth to be Churchwarden Thomas Penn

Overseers for the   { Thomas Toms
poore   { William Wyatt senior

Surveiors for the { William Parrish
high wayes   { Edward Wyatt

By us whose names are subscribed
George Toms
William Kirby

Edm: Carpenter
John Quatermaine
Jo: Carpenter
Rich: Carpenter
Tho Tayler
Richard Phillips

Receipts of us George Toms & William Kirby for the yeare 1660

Remaining in our handes upon the last yeares acount	£4 15 10
Item received for the Church Grase of Edward Wyatt	£8 2 0
Item received of Thomas Tayler for the two lands	£0 4 0
Item received of Richard Pargiter & Thomas winckles for the Church barne	£0 14 6
The receipts is	£13 16 4
The layings out is	£17 8 0
Soe there is due to George Toms & Will: Kirby from the Church which they have layd out more than they have received	£3 11 8
Aprill the 16 1661 received of Mr Mansell for the use of Tenn pounds by me – George Toms	£0 12 0
Soe then there is now due to George Toms & william Kyrbie	£2 19 8

[*Crossed out* The Resaites of George tomes & willaim Kerby
for this yeare 1660 are as followeth   £12 11 10]
         meorandom

heare begineth the layings out of George Tomes & Willaim Kirby for this
yeare 1660 Aprill th 15 as followeth

Inprimos payd to Willaim Poynter	0	10	10
Item payd to the payntter	2	10	6
Item payd to Nathaniell Chester for making the pullpite staares	0	8	0
payd to Alexsander Smith for timber	0	2	0
payd to William Ponter	2	3	0
payd for glovers sseeds	0	1	6
payd to John Maull for boar[d]es als to make syse	0	4	6
for milke to make sise	0	1	6
payd to Robart Jenings for nayls	0	1	0
Item given to poore people that had a pase	0	1	6
Item given to poore people	0	0	10
payd to Allexsander Smith for yew wode	0	1	6
payd for foure Hundred of Coles for the paynter	0	6	0
payd for grease	0	1	0
payd for the Church bucketes	0	6	6
Item payd for bread & wine on Palme Sunday & Ester day	2	1	0
Item payd to the painter	2	16	0
payd to the man that mended the Church bucketes	0	10	6
payd to the gaile & mained soulders	0	4	4
payd to the paynter	3	6	0
payd to the paynter	0	15	8
payd to the Clarkes wife for feching the bread & wine & washing the tabel cloath	0	1	6
Item payd to the smith for work doune about the beles	0	7	1
Item payd to John Whittaker for righting the acounts to yeare	0	2	0
payd to a boy for going to banbury of anarand	0	0	3

The layings out of George Toms & Willaim Kerby are   £17 8 0

According to the custome used in Kings-Sutton in the county of
Northampton for the Vicar to elect one Church-warden I Robert Mansell
Vicar of the sayd place doe elect John Pargiter to be Church-warden this
next yeare: being 1661

April 16 1661

Rober Mansell vicar
of Kings-Sutton

Wee whose names are subscribed doe nominate Thomas Penn
to be Church warden for this ensuing yeare

Overseers for { Thomas Tayler
the poore   { Thomas Winckells

Surveiors for { Richard Williams
the highways {Thomas Blinckoe

The accounts of the Church-wardens are found just by us whose names
are underwritten

Edm: Carpenter
John Carpenter
Robert Bricknell
Richard Phillips
Richard Carpenter
Thomas Penn his marke
Thomas Tomes
John Whittaker

a levey made the 22 day of ffebuary 1661 for the Repares of the parish
Church
of Kingsutton by us whose names are subscribed

Kingsutton att 2s the yardland
Astrop att 12d the yardland
Charlton att 6d the yardland
Cottages of the lords holde 6d
Cottages of the parsonage holde four pence
Walton levey att £2 13s 4d
Purston levey att £1 6s 8d

Kingsutton levey

Richard Kenwrick Esq & Robart Kenwrick gent	9	0
Richard Carpenter	2	8
John Tibbots	4	7
Richard Pargater	2	0
Mr Cartwright his mill & mill mead garith akers and to yeardland	8	0
gorge Tomes	3	3
Thomas Tayler	3	4
Thomas Toms	4	6
Thomas Penne	2	0
John Haynes	2	3
Thomas Haynes	2	6
Edward Tomes	1	9
Edward Willaims	0	10
Thomas Winckels	1	1
Edward Thomas & Thomas Toms	0	6
John Whittaker for Parishes land	0	6
Edward Carpenter	0	10
Richard Mathews	1	0
Robart Jenings junor	0	3
Richard Pargiter	0	3
Charles bucher	1	6
John Bett	0	4
John Waters	0	10
Richard Phillips	0	6
Willaim Parish	0	3
John Burford	0	8
georg Whitwell	0	8
Thoms Wyatt	0	9
Richard Willaims	1	0
John Clemanes	0	8
Robart Jenings	0	6
George Jenings	0	4
Thomas Bett	0	4
Robart Bricknell	0	3
Simon Wates	0	6
Willaim Bricknell	0	6
Jonathan King	0	6
Willaim Upston	0	6
John Pargiter	0	3
Willaim Poynter	0	3

Willaim Parish junor	0	3
nicko Bricknell	0	1 ob
John Warner	0	4
Simon Watson	0	6
Jarves house	0	2
Charels Butcher for one Cotag att mill	0	6
Thomas Watson	0	4
John Upston	0	4
Wido: Jenings	0	4
Wido: Price	0	4
John Maule	0	4
Allexsander Smith	0	4
ffrances Whitby	0	3
[*Crossed out* Lennerd Bideford	0	3]
John Basley	0	3
[*Crossed out* Wido] Pilleys House	0	3
George Thomes Junor	0	3
Willaim ffathers	0	2
Thomas Clemans	0	2
Edw: Price	0	2
Mathew Stacei	0	2
Heniry Paynter	0	2
Humpfrey Jenings	0	2
Ladwecke Upston	0	2
Robart Smith	0	2
Richard Peddel	0	2

Sur Thomas Pope   53   4

Asstrop levey

Sur Nicklos stewards	18	0
Mr Cartwright	12	0
Mr Hiornes	5	0
Mr Crews land	2	0
Edmund Carpenter	4	0
John Carpenter	4	6
John Tibbets	4	0
Willaim Wyatt	2	9
George tomes	2	0
Thomas tayler	1	6
Edward tomes	1	0
wido wyatt	1	0
ffrances wyatt for Mr Picgots land	1	0

Thomas Penne	0	6
Thomas Durman	0	6
Thomas wyatt of Newbotel	0	6
willaim wyatt junor	0	6
Thomas wyatt	0	3
willaim Smith	0	2
Purston		
John Willoby gent	4	0
Mr blincke	13	0
Mr anslor	9	0
Charlton		
Mr Willoby	3	9
Richard Haddon	2	4 ob
Willaim Haddon	3	7 ob
Mathew Haddon	2	4 ob
John Phippes	2	10
Richard Mathews	0	10 ob
John Lucas	1	0
Wido Emberly	0	3 ob
John Lapworth	0	3

This levy before written was consented unto by us whose names are subscribed

Rob. Mansell Vicar
George Tomes } Church-
Willm Kirby } wardens

The marke of Thomas Penne

[*Crossed out* Memorandu that Mr Mansell and John Pargiter is endebted to the Church by bond for ** the summe of ten pounds twelve shillings this twenty fourth of April One thousand six hundred sixtie two]

[*Crossed out* Rob: Mansell Vicar
Geo: Toms   } Church-
Willm Kirby } wardens]

Mem this twentie first of April 1662 Receid then of Mr Kenwrick and John Maul the sume of four pounds seaventeen shilling for ye next sumers crops of all and singular the grass grounds that belongs to the Church of KingSutton in ye County of Northampt by us

Geo: Toms } Church-
Will Kerby } Wardens

Memorandu that this twenty eighth day of Aprill 1662:
Received then of Mr Robert Mansell vicar the summe of ten pounds due
to the Church upon bond　　　　　　　　　By us
　　　　　　　　　The marke of George Tomes
　　　　　　　　　　William Kerby　　Church-wardens
Witnesses hereunto are
Edm: Carpenter
Rich: Carpenter
Rich: Phillips

The Receipts of us George Tomes and Willaim Keirby for the yeare 1661

Inprimis Receved for the Churchgrase that is to say for Lady med & for
the nothings in lack med & whet ham & a lay on Rye Hille the summe of
　　　　　　　　　　　　　　　　　　　　　£1　0　2
Received of Thomas Tayler for his wives Grave　　　　　£0　5　8
Received of Thomas Tayler for the Rent of the two landes March
　　　the five and twentieth 1662　　　　　　　　　　£0　4　0

The Layings out of George Tomes & William Keirby for the yeare 1661
as followeth

Item payd to the Plomer	1 2 0
Item payd to Alexsander Smith for woode for the Plomer & for a prop for the Vestry	0 4 6
Item payd for bread & wine	1 18 8
Item spent att banbury att the visitation	0 2 0
Item payd to the gaile & mained soldurs	0 4 4
payd to Nathanell Chester	0 0 6
Item given to poore peopel	0 0 9
Item payd to Rousham his waiges	0 3 4
Item payd to the Clarkes wife for fecthing the bread & wine & for for washing th tabel clothe	0 1 6
Item payd for grese for the Bels	0 1 4
Item for nayles & oyle	0 2 6

　　　　　　　　　　　　　　　Summe is　　£4　1　5
The layings out of George Tomes & Willaim Keirby for the yeare 1661
are four pounds & one shilling & five pence

payd more to Edward Rowsam towards his wages　　　　9s　4d
Also payd to Thomas Tayler for a ponde of Grese　　　　0s　4d

Accordinge to the custome used in the parish of Kings-sutton in the
County of Northampton (but in the Diocesse of Lincolne) for the Vicar to
Elect one Church-warden, I Robert Mansell Vicar of ye sayd place doe
appoint John Pargitter to be one Church-warden for this ensuing yeare:
Being in the yeare of our Lord 1662

         Aprill 2 1662   Rob: Mansell.
                                               Vicar

wee the majior pt of the parish then present doe nominate Thomas Penn
to be the other Church warden wth John Pargiter

and overseers for the Hiways
Thomas bett and Richard Smith

the layings out of George Tomes & Willaim Kerby from aprill th 1 1662
untell July the 28 1662

In primes payd to thomas holding of Sisham [*Syresham*]for timber & lime	2 7 0
Item for the Carig of the timber & lime	0 7 0
payd to willaim dolton & his sunne & to Nathanell Chester for worke	1 11 0
Item payd to Thomas Alliboun & to Thomas Kerby for worke doune	3 16 6
Item payd to John Stratford	1 0 0
Item payd to John Whittaker for glasing worke doune about the Church	4 14 6
Item payd to Mr Kendwrick for timber	0 7 6
Item payd for a sett of bell ropes	1 7 0
Item payd to Robart Jenings for nayles and oyle	0 6 3 ob
Item payd to the aturny	0 1 0
Item payd to poore people	0 0 6
Item spent att the Vissitation	1 10 4
for the hiere of Willaims Upstons House	0 3 0
Item payd to Willaim Poynter	0 5 0
Item payd to George Jenings for caring of stones & morter	0 3 0
Item payd to the Gaile & mained solders	0 4 4
Item spent one the workemen att severall times att the Church	0 2 0
Item payd for to yeares Righting	0 3 0

A Levey made the 8 day of november 1662 for the Repares of the Parish Church of Kingsutton by us whose names are heare subscribed

Kingsutton levey november 8th 1662

Richard Kenwrick Esq & Robart Kenwrick gent	9	0
Richard Carpenter	2	8
John Tibbits	4	7
Richard Pargiter	2	0
Mr Cartwright his mill & mill med & garith akers & to yardland	8	0
George Toms	3	7 ob
Thomas Tayler	3	4
Thomas Toms	4	6
Thomas Penne	2	0
John Haynes	2	3
Thomas Haynes	2	6
Edward Toms	2	1 ob
Edward Willaims	0	10
Thomas Winckels	1	1
Edward Toms & Thomas Toms	0	6
John Whittaker for Parishes land	0	6
Edward Carpenter	0	10
Richard Mathews	1	0
Robart Jening junor	0	3
Richard Pargiter	0	3
Charls Butcher	1	6
John Bett	0	4
John Watters	0	10
Richard Phillips	0	6
Willaim Parish	0	3
John Burford	0	8
George Wittwell	0	10
Thomas Wyatt	0	9
Richard Willaims	1	0
John Clemanes	0	8
Robart Jenings	0	6
George Jenings	0	4
Thomas Bett	0	4
Robart Bricknell	0	3
Simon Watts	0	6
Nicklos Bricknell	0	7 ob
Dannelle Smith & Jonathan King	0	6

Willaim Upston	0	6
John Pargiter	0	3
Willaim Poynter	0	3
Willaim Parish junor	0	3
John Warner	0	4
Simon Wattson	0	6
Charls Butcher for one Cotag att mill	0	6
Thomas Wattson	0	4
John Upston	0	4
Wido: Jenings	0	4
Wido: Price	0	4
John Mall	0	4
Allexsander Smith	0	4
ffrances Whidbey	0	3
John Basley	0	3
Willaim Wyatt junor	0	3
George Toms Junor	0	3
Thomas Clemanes	0	2
Dianne Price	0	2
Mathew Stacy	0	2
Ladwecke Upston	0	2

The Lord of Dounes for Walton   53   4

Astrop levey

Sur Nicklos stewards tennants Willam Haris & Willaim Markham	18	0
Mr Cartwright his tennants Richard Haynes & Charles Butcher Arter Battle & Richard Tayler	12	0
Mr Hiornes	5	0
Mr Crews land	2	0
Edmund Carpenter	4	0
John Carpenter	4	6
John Tibbtes	4	0
Willaim Wyatt	2	9
George Toms	2	0
Thomas Tayler	1	6
Edward toms	1	0
wido wyatt	1	0
ffrances wyatt for Mr Piggits land	1	0
Thomas Penne	0	6
Thomas Durman	0	6

Thomas wyatt of Newbotell	0	6
Willaim wyatt junor	0	6
Thomas wyatt	0	3
Willaim Smith	0	2
Purston levey		
John Willobe gent	4	0
Mr Blincko	13	0
Mr Anslow	9	0
Charlton Levey		
John Willoby gent	3	9
Willaim Haddon	3	7 ob
Richard Haddon	2	4 ob
Mathew Haddon	2	4 ob
John Phipes	2	10
Richard Mathews	0	10 ob
John Lucas	1	0
Wido Emberly	0	3 ob
John Lapath	0	3

£7 17 2 ob
£3 5 1 ob

£11 2 4

This levy before written was consented unto by us whose names are subscribed

Ro: Mansell Vicar

John Pargitter } Church-
Tho: Penne } wardens
Georg Tomes
Richard Carpenter

April 20th 1663

Church-wardens chosen for the yeare ensuing are these following, elected by the minr and major part of ye Parish

Thomas Haynes jun.

the 6 day of december 1662 the Layngs out of Thomas Penn &
John Pargieter Church wardens

In Primos payd to allexsander Smih for wodde & for a littell bord	0	9	4
Item spent att the vissitacyon att Buckinggame	0	4	6
payd for greese	0	0	4
payd to Rowsham for 6 days of worke for helping the plommer	0	3	0
Item payd for a surpless	3	10	0
Item payd for a Common Prayer Book & the Booke of Cannanes & a table of marriges	0	10	0
Item payd to the man that Brout the Bookes	0	1	0
payd for caring the surpless from Oxford & for caring a letter to have it mad	0	0	8
Item payd to the plumer	3	0	0
Item payd to Rowsham for wages Behind	0	0	8
payd to him for wages due	0	3	4
payd to the gayle & mained soldurs	0	4	4
payd to Edward Willames for Bread for the Communon att Estour	0	1	0
payd to Rowsam for faching of wine fron ayno	0	1	0
payd to Edward ffathers his wife for washing ye surplis & ye communion cloth	0	1	0
payd for gres for the Beles	0	0	4
payd to Edward Rousham his wages	0	3	4
payd to Willaim Poynter for to dayes [work]	0	2	4
payd to Rowsham his wages	0	3	4
payd to antony Parkines for to mates	0	0	8
payd to Georg Tomes for lime & strick	0	2	0
payd to Robart Jenings for nayles & oyle	0	2	0
payd to Laddwick Upston for worke done att severall times in georg tomes his time & Willaim Kerbys	1	15	6
payd to Thomas Norriss for wine for the communion of Palme Sunday & Easter daye	2	2	0
Item payd to the glasuer	0	1	8
Item payd to Thomas Turbite for seven dayes worke about the vestery	0	8	2
Item payd for slattes Lathes & pine	0	6	2
payd to Nedeles boyes for 3 dayes worke for sarving the slattur	0	1	0

payd to Willaim Poynter for one hend[red] of slattes	0 5 10
for the Charige	0 2 0
payd to Willaim Dolton for worke about the Vestery	0 2 8
payd for two pound of grese for the beles	0 0 8
payd to the tanner for Lime	0 1 0
payd to John Malle for woode	0 1 0
payd to the glasuer for worke doune	0 2 0
paid in expenses at Jo: Maule when the Suragat was here & to the parator	0 4 2
paid in expenses at Banbury the last Vissitation	0 4 0
Given to a poore widdo whose house was burnt	0 0 6
payd to dolton for worke about the belles	0 3 10
Item payd to John Whittaker for Righting for to yeare	0 3 0
Item payd Robart Jenings for nayles & oyle	0 3 0
Item payd for bred for the communion	0 1 1
Item payd wine for the communion unto Thomas Norris of ayno	2 5 0
Item payd to Judy fathers for washing the surples & the table cloth three severall times	0 2 0
payd for feching the wine att tow severall times	0 0 6

The summe is   £18 9 3

Item payd more to John Haynes for
to pay for trenching the nothings   6d

aprill the 12: 1664

The Recaits of John Pargiter & Thomas Penn Churchwardens for thare time is as followeth

Item Received of the Levy `	10 17 5
gathered up of george Tomes & Willaim Kerbys levey	0 12 4
Receved with the Booke	0 15 0
Receved of John Haynes for the Church grase	3 17 0
Received of Ladwecke Upston for one yeares Rent for the Church Barne due in Georg Tomes & Willaim Kerbys time	0 18 0
Received of Mr Cartwright & John Pargiter for to yeares Rent for the said Barne	1 16 0

the summe is   £18 15 9

There Remaines in the Churchwardens hands   6s
Item received more of Thomas Tayler for the
two Church lands for two yeares to this yeare 1664   8s

Aprill 20 1664

Whe whouse names are subscrbed doe nominate
Thomas Winkels and Robart Jenings the younger
the Churchwardens this insuin year

Thomas Pen his marke
John Pargiter his marke
Thomas Toms   John Haines
John Clemenes   Willim marcom
Richard Phillips
overseares for the hiways
John Waters seneur
Lodwick Upston

Receipts & payments by Jo: Pargiter & Tho: Penn Churchwardens
after Easter 1664 as followeth

Remayning in their hands the last amount	14s
Recd of John Warner for the Church grass	£6 1 0
Totall of Receipts	£6 15 0

Disbursements by Tho: Penn & Jo: Pargiter

Paid in expenses at the Court kepte at Sutton last & to the Parator twenty five sh:	1	5	0
Paid Robert Kirby for minitt Cords for ye Clerk	0	0	4
Paid Sym: Watson & Roger Jarvis for scouring of Lady mead ditch five shillings eight pence	0	5	8
Paid Lodowick Upston for mending the Clock	0	7	0
Paid Robert Lucas for mending the Clock	0	5	0
Paid Rowsam in part of his wages	0	3	4
Paid in expenses at the vissitation at Stony Stratford & for horse hyre twenty one shill nine pence	1	1	9
Given to a poore woman that had a pass	0	0	6
Paid Rowsam for keeping the Register book for one yeare ending Easter 64 tenn groats	0	3	4
Paid for grease & oyle for the Bells	0	0	6
Paid Natt:Chester & Tho: Williams for work done about the Bells two shillings	0	2	0

Total of Disbursements   £3 14 5

Md that the totall of their Receipts with the remaine that was in their hands upon the last account date amount to six pounds ffifteene shillings & that their disbursemts since the same account date amount to three pounds fourteene shillings five pence And soe their is now in their hands three pounds seaven pence which £3 0s 7d is paid to Tho: Winkles & Robert Jenings the ensuing Churchwardens

Receipts of Robert Jenings & Thomas Winckles Churchwardens for the yeare 1664 are as followeth

Inprimis received of the old Churchwardens		
Thomas Penn & John Pargiter ye sume of	£3	0 7
Item received of Thomas Tayler for the two landes	0	4 0
Receivd of Jo: Waters for Church Grasse	7	10 0
Sume tot	10	14 7

Layings out of Robert Jenings & Thomas Winckles for the yeare 1664

Inprimis for three new bell roapes	0 13 6
Item to Tho: Williams for worke about the bells	0 4 6
Item to Thomas Turbitt for worke about the vestry	0 2 6
Item to Nath: Chester for worke about the bells	0 1 6
Item to the Clarke for his wages	0 6 8
Item for writeing the Register	0 3 4
Item to Robert Kirby for Leather to mend the Gable & for minute Coards	0 0 5
Item to Tho Allibone for mendeing the vestry wall	0 0 8
Item to Sparkes his wife for giving notice to parte of the Parrish to meete about the choyce of new Churchwardens	0 0 3
Item for nayles & oyle	0 3 1
Item to William Warde for his horse goeing to Stonny Stratford	0 3 0
Item oyle	0 0 2
Item for trenching Lady Mead	0 5 6
Item pd to Old Rossham for a bord to mend the Vestry dore	0 0 4
Item pd to Old Hodge for mending the Church Wall	0 1 4
Item for Wier about the Clocke	0 0 6

Item for Oyle	0	0	2
Item for Whasing the Surplis & table Clothe & Mending	0	2	0
Item to Tho: Williams for Worke	0	1	0
Item to Nath: Chester for Worke	0	1	0
Item to Ladwick Upston for mending the bell Claper	0	2	0
Item Charges & expenses at the Court at John Maule	1	8	4

Sume tot   £4 1 9

The Receipts of Tho: Winckles & Robt Jenings   £10 14 7
The disbursemts of them are   £4 1 9
The remainder   £6 12 10

Wch sume of six pounds twelve shillings & ten pence was this 9 Octob
1665 payd unto John Clemts and Willia Wyat jun now Church Wardens

    £6 12 10
Item they have received for church grasse   £8 0 0
Item rent of the widdow Andrewes for her house   £0 6 0
Item of the farmer Taylor for church land   £0 4 0
    £15 2 10

March the 28th 1665

We whose names are subscribed doe nominate & Appointe to be
Churchwardens for the ensueing yeare John Clemence &
William Wyatt Junior

Thomas Winckles   Surveiors for
Robeart Jeninges   the highwayes
Tho: Tayler
Thomas Tomes   Edward Toms
Edward Toms   & Richard Phillips
Tho: Toms
Richard Phillips
Thomas Penn
John Watters
Thomas Haynes

The charges for the necessary repaires of the Church barne disbursed by Mr Kenwricke are as follows

Inprs to Hodges for his worke and his wifes	6	6
To Milicent Westley for her worke	2	6
To Lad. Upstone for boards	3	0
for a sill and other wood	1	1
To Nat: Chester for his worke	1	2
To Edw: Peedle for his worke	6	0
for Rushes and strawe	23	0
Summe tot	£2 3	3

ffor wch Charges Mr Kenwricke is to enjoy the Church barne until Michal 1669 paying 4s 9d and keeping the said barne in good repaire; and afterwards to pay 12s by ye yeare and keep it in repaire

Layings out of John Clemmence & william wiat for
the yeare 1665

Inprimis payd to John Whitakor for glasing the Church windows	2 5 10
Item payd to Ludiwik Uopston	0 18 0
Item payd for bred and wine	0 15 5
Item payd for 3 belropes	0 9 6
Item payd to the Clarke for his waiges	0 10 0
Item payd to the paritor	0 4 0
Item payd to the Carpenter for work aboute the Chirch	0 4 6
Item payd for flurshing the diall	0 3 0
Item payd for wshing the sorples	0 1 9
Item payd to Robord genines for oyle and nails	0 1 10
Item payd to Richard Chiners at 5 seferall times for goinge for Mr gartnor	0 1 6
Item payd to one Timothi crone	0 1 0
Item payd for woud and grease used about the belles	0 0 6
Item payd for a nue booke	0 0 10
Item payd to Robard Kirby for minute strin[gs]	0 0 2
Item payd to Thomas williams for mending the belles	0 1 6
Item payd to Richard [Hugh] for mendin the cloke	0 2 8
Item payd to william Upston	0 0 6
Item payd to a pore womon	0 0 3
Item payd to william hodges for mending the churchyard wall	0 3 0

Item payd for 3 bellropes	0 11 0
Item Charges and Expenses for the Corte at John Maules and other Expenses	1 7 0

	£8 5 5
Receaved	£15 2 10
Disbursed	£8 5 5
	£6 17 5

Mr Shackerly Cartwright and John Pargiter behind for rent
for the Church barn   £0 18 0

Aprill the 17th 1666

We whose names are subscribed doe nominate to be Churchwardens
for the ensueing yeare

John Phips   } Church
Thomas Haynes Junior } wardens

Surveiors for   { Thomas Tayler
the highwayes   { George Toms Junior

Edward Toms
Willam Wiat
the marke of John Clemence
[the marke of] Thomas Pen
Jhon Haynes
John Carpenter

The Recepts of Thomas Haynes and John Phipes Churchwardens for the
yeare 1666 are as followeth

Receved of the other Churchwardens that was of John Clemans & william Wyatt the sume of	£6 17 5
Receved of John Pargiter for the Rent of the Church barne	£0 18 0
Receved of William Haddon for breking the ground in the Church for a grave	£0 5 8
Receved halfe the mony for the church grase being	£3 6 6
sume is	£11 7 7

Receved by us   £11 7 7
Payd out of that   £9 18 7
due to the new Churchwardens   £1 9 0

Heare begineth the layings out of John Phipps and Thomas Haynes
Churchwardens for this present yeare 1666

Ite for mending the church yarde walle	0 0 10	
Ite for 3 loads of stones	0 1 0	
Ite for ye carrage of 3 loades of stones	0 2 6	
Item for mending ye Church yeard gate	0 1 0	
Item payd to Edward Rowsam in parte of his wagges	0 5 0	
Item spent at the cashing upp of the last accounts	0 1 0	
Item payd to the plummer for his worke and other expenses	0 14 8	
Item payd to the Smith for a Staple for the Church yeard gate	0 0 2	
Item payd for a booke	0 1 0	
Item payd & spent att Banbury att the visitation	0 8 0	
Ite for mendding the surplis	0 0 4	
Ite for washing ye suplis & and ye communion cloath	0 2 0	
Ite for washing the surplis & and the communion cloath	0 1 6	
Ite one pound of grease for the belles	0 0 4	
Ite pd to Laddicke Upston for worke [wch] he did	0 11 0	
Ite paid to ye carpenters for worke done to the Belles	0 6 0	
Ite pd to ye baker for bread for ye communions	0 0 9	
Ite payd to Thomas Norris for winne for ye communion palme Sunday Easter eve and Easter daye	1 19 3	
pd to Robert Kerby for lether for the Bells	0 0 5	
Ite pd to John Whittaker for mendding ye church wendoes	0 16 0	
Ite for castinge of the gt bell & for mettell as was put in	1 13 10	
pd for other charges for ye bell carrying & bringing of it home	0 2 2	
Pd to John Strafford for lime	0 0 3	
Ite spent at ye courte	1 0 0	
Ite pd to the parritter	0 2 6	
Ite for one load of stones and ye carrage and for layeing them up	0 1 4	
Ite pd to Laddicke Upston for the greate bell claper & for Iorne worke done on the gte belle & a hing for ye church yarde gate	0 14 6	
Ite for nayles for ye church yarde gate	0 0 3	

Ite for [spottin] ye bell Ropes	0 0 2	
Ite pd to the minister for Ritting the Regester	0 3 4	
Ite pd to Rowsome for his wagges	0 5 0	
Ite given to poore people	0 0 6	
Item payd to John Whittaker for wrighting & making our acounts	0 1 6	

sume is	£9 18 7
Iten reseved of wido Andrs	£0 5 10

wee doue nominat Robart Jenings senur to be Church warden

Thomas Haynes
John Phipes
John Tebbetts
Edmd Carpenter
Willaim Kerby
John Watters
Thomas Tomes

The Receipts of Edmund Carpenter & Robert Jennings

Recd of the Old Church wardens	£1 14 0
Recd of Rich: Williams for the Church grass	£3 6 6
Recd of William Justice being part of his rent	£0 9 0
Reseved of John Turland and Richard Mathews for part of the Church grase	£1 5 0
Reseved of John Warner for part of the Church grase	£2 10 0

The disbursmts of Edm: Carpenter & Robert Jennings

Payd for Oyle & Nayles	0 1 3	
Payd Edw: ffathers for the Bell Ropes	0 0 8	
Payd to Edw: Rowsham	0 5 0	
Payd for Poles	0 5 0	
Payd to Nath: Chester & Tho: Williams	0 4 4	
Payd for a tree to make a Ladder	0 7 0	
Payd for Wyer	0 0 2	

Payd for a Gabell Rope	0	15	0
Pd to Lodw: Upston	0	4	6
Payd to Nath: Chester & Tho: Williams	0	17	0
Payd to Tho: Kyrbye	0	1	0
Payd for a [stick] of Oake	0	8	0
Payd for Grease	0	1	0
Payd for Oyle & Nayles	0	1	0
Payd for Nayles	0	0	4
Payd to a Breefe	0	2	0
Payd for three Bell-Ropes	0	11	0
Payd to John Wittakers for Glasing	0	8	0
Payd to Mr Haddon	0	3	4
Payd for mending & washing the Surplis	0	2	0
Payd to Edw: Williams for Bread	0	0	10
Payd to Th: Williams for mending the little Bell	0	0	6
Payd to Rob: Kyrbye for [shred] of Lether	0	0	3
paid to Willm pointer for stones	0	0	8
Paid to John Pargiter for carriage	0	1	0
Paid to Mr Horseman	0	1	4
paid to ye Apparitor for warng the Court	0	2	0
paid to Thomas Williams for making ye Church gate	0	8	0
paid for a Rope for ye bells	0	4	4
paid for bread & wine at Easter	1	15	3
paid to John Upston for mending the Church wall	0	1	0
payd to Evins for a rope for the Clock	0	7	6
payd to John Maule for bread & beare & meate at the Vissitation	1	1	0
payd for greese	0	0	8
payd for a payre of bras garners for the Church gate	0	2	10

wee whose names are subscribed doe nominate to be Churchwardens for the ensuing yeare and surveyours for the highwayes

William Haddon   } churchwardens
Edward Williams }

Edward Carpenter   } Surveyour for the
Robert Jennings junior } highwayes

wee whose names are subscribed doe nominate to be Churchwardens for the ensuing yeare and surveyours for the highwayes [*sic*]

Tho: Heydon minister
Will Cottesford
Edm: Carpenter
Robert Jenings
Edward Toms
John Whittaker
Georg Tomes junior
John Waters
William Kerby

Receved of Richard Phillips and John Haddon for halfe the Church grase[3]	2	1	0
payde to thomas Willaims foe mending the the [*sic*] beles and for thre plankes	0	5	6
payde to nathaniel Chester	0	4	0
paid to John Stratford for mending the Church yard walles	0	1	0
woode for the plomer youse	0	1	6
Item payde to Judy fathers for washing the surplis	0	3	0
Item paid to Robert Corby for leather	0	0	6
Item paid to John Stratford for mending the Church yeard walls	0	1	3
Recved of John haddon and Richard phillipes for the Church Grase	2	1	0
payed for oyle and nailes	0	1	3
Item paid for bread and wine	1	16	2
Item paid to the Clarke for his waiges	0	10	0
Item paid to the Clarke for greas and oyle for the bells	0	1	0
Item paid to Judy fathers for washing the surplis	0	1	10
Item paid to thomas allebon for mend of the Church	0	1	0
Item layd out att the visitaiton att Stony Stratford	1	6	6
Item payd to the plomer	0	16	0
Item payd t[h]o the Smith for mending the Clock	0	2	6

---

[3] These 18 items are duplicated , with small variations, below at p. 110

Aprill 13th 1669

Wee whose names are here subscribed doe nominate and appoynt

Richard Mathewes
Edward Wyatt
Church Wardens
for the yeare ensuing

Will Cottsford
Jo: Tebbetts
Edmund Carpenter
Edward Williames
William Haddon

A singel
Levey

A levey made the 5 day of June 1669
for the Repares of the Parish Church of
King Sutton by us whose names are
here subscribed

Richard Kenwrick Esq }	4	6
Robert Kenwrick gent }		
Mr Tibbites	2	8 ob
John Pargiter	1	1 ob
Lodweck Upston	0	9
Willaim Kerby	2	0
Mr Cartwright his mill millmed & garits akers	2	0
George Toms	1	0
Thomas Taylor	1	7
Tho: Toms farms	2	3
Tho: Penne	1	0
John Haynes	1	2
Thomas Haynes	1	4
Tho: Toms	0	9
Edmund willaims	0	5
Tho: winckels	0	6 ob
Edward Toms	0	9
Thomas Toms and Thomas Toms sons of George Tomes & George Toms junor	*[4]	

[4] The right hand margin of the book appears to have been cut for the next 22 items

John Whittaker	*
Edmund Carpenter	*
Robart Jenings	*
Charles Butcher	*
Richard Mathewes	*
John Bett	*
John Watters	*
Richard Phillepes	*
William Parish	*
Little Milles	*
Wido Whittwell	*
Tho: Wyatt	*
Richard Willaims	*
Edward Wyatt	*
John Clemans	*
Robart Jenings	*
Robart brickenell	*
Thomas Bett	*
Tho: Jenings	*
Johnathan King	*
Tho: blincko	*
Nicklos bricknell	0 3 ob
Willaim bricknell	0 [8] ob
Daniell Smith	0 1 ob
Willaim Parish junor	0 1 ob
Willaim Poynter	0 1 ob
Willaim Uston	0 3
John Warner	0 2
Simon wattson	0 3
Charles butcher for his cottag att mill	0 3
Thomas Wattson	0 2
John Upston	0 2
Wido Jenings	0 2
Willaim Harries	0 2
John Maulle	0 2
Lenerd beadforde	0 1 ob
Edmund Chandler	0 1 ob
Willaim wyatt	0 1 ob
Tho: Clemanes	0 1
Ladwick Upston for his house	0 1
Mathew Stacye	0 1
Walton Levey is	£1 6 8

Astrop		
Sur Nichlos Steward for Eighten yard Land	9	0
Mr Cartwright 12 yard land	6	0
Mr Hirens	2	0
Mr Crewes land	1	0
Edmund Carpenter	2	0
John Carpenter	2	3
Mr Tebbetes	2	0
Mr bushe	2	4 ob
George Toms	1	0
Richard Haddon	0	6
John Carpenter for a halfe yard land & one cottage in Sutton	0	7
Tho: Toms	0	6
Tho: Penne	0	3
Tho: Durman	0	3
Tho: Wyatt of newbotel	0	3
Willaim Wyatt	0	3
Tho: Wyatt	0	1 ob
Willaim Smith	0	2
Purston		
John Willoughby Esqr	1	8
Mr blincko	6	6
Mr anslow	4	6
John wlloughby Esqr	1	10 ob
Willaim Haddon	1	9 ob
Wido Haddon	0	7
Richard Haddon	1	9
John Phipes	1	5
Richard Mathewes	0	5
John Luckes	0	6
Wido: Emberly	0	1 ob
John Lapworth	0	1 ob

William Haddon } Church
Edmund Willaims } wardens

The Receptes of Edward Willaims and Willaim Haddon Churchwardens
for the yeare 1668

In Primis Receved of Richard Phillepes and John Haddon
    for the Church grase   £4 2 0
Receved of Thomas Taylor for three yeares rent for the
    Curche Land the sume of   £0 12 0
Receved of John Turland and Richard Mathewes for part
    of the Church grase   £1 5 0

The layings out of William Haddon and Edmund Williams Church
wardens for the yeare 1668 are as followeth

Paid to Nathaniell Chester	0	4	0
Paide to Thomas Williams for mending of the belles and for plankes	0	5	6
paid to John Stratford for mending of the Church walle	0	1	0
paid for wood for the plomer	0	1	6
piad to Judy fathers for mending of the Surplis	0	3	0
Paid to Robert Kerby for lether	0	0	6
paid to John Stratford for mending of the Church walle	0	1	3
paide for bread and wine	1	16	2
paide to the Clarke his wages	0	10	0
paide for grease and oyle	0	1	0
paid to Judy fathers for washing the Surplis	0	1	10
Paid to Thomas Alibon for worke	0	1	0
paide to the plomer	0	16	0
Payd out att the Visitation att Stony Stratford	1	6	6
Paide to Robert Luckes for mending of the Cloke	0	2	6
Paid to Ladweck Upston for Iorneworke for the belles	0	16	0
Paid for six bellropes	1	2	6
Paid to Ladweck Upston for Iorneworke for the belles	0	1	6
the charges at the visitason at bunbury	0	10	6
Paid to Wido Rowsom that was be hind of wages	0	5	0
Item payd to the ould Churchwardens that thay ware out of pay	0	5	2
payd to watsones sune for helping the plumer	0	0	10
payd for a peck of lime	0	0	3

Item payd to the parieter att severall tines	0 4 0
Item spent by us when we made up our acounte	0 1 0
to John Whittaker for Righting of our levey & acounts	0 2 0

Receved in all	£11 12 1 ob
Layd out	£9 0 6
payd to the next Churchwardens the sume of	£1 19 4 ob
to gather of the levey	£0 12 3

1669
the Receits of Richard Mathewes and Edward Wyatt Churchwardens

In Primis Receved of Mr Kenwrick for the Rent of the Church barne due att mickelmas	£0 4 9
Receved for the Church grase	£4 15 0
Recevd of John Carpenter for his fathers grave	£0 5 0
Receved with the book	£1 19 4 ob
gathered up of the levy	£0 5 10

the Recaits are £7 9 11

wee whose nams are heare subscribed doe nominate
John Watter & John Maule to be Chirchwardens
for this yeare enshuing
and [thomas toms *struck through*] and
nicklos bricknell survayers for the Hiwayes

Jo Tebbetts
Edward Wyatt and } Church
Richard Mathews } wardens
John Carpenter
Thomas Haynes

the Layings out of Edward wyatt and Richard mathewes
Churchwardens for this yeare 1669

Inprimis payd to the pariter	0	3 6
Payd to Judy ffathers for washing the surples	0	1 6
Payd to John Stratford for mending the Churchyard walle	0	0 6
Payd for a locke for the Churchyard gatte	0	0 6
Payd for Righting of the Returnes	0	0 2
Payd to the glasner for worke doune about the Church	0	15 0
Item layd out att the visitation att Banbury	0	11 4
Item payd for nayles & workemanshep for mending the belles	0	4 9
Item payd for glasing worke doune about the church	0	4 0
Item payd to the Ploumer for worke doune att the Church	1	0 6
Item payd the Clarke his waiges	0	10 0
Item payd for grease for the beles & oyle for the Clocke	0	1 8
Item payd for lether	0	0 6
payd for nayles	0	0 4
payd to John w[at]son for to dayes worke for helping the Ploumer & the carpenter	0	1 4
Paid to Thomas Willaims & nathanell Chester for mending the bells & for tombes & for taking doune the grate House	0	4 10
Paid to Judy ffather for washing & mending the surples & washing the tabel cloath	0	1 10
Paid for wine for the sacrement att Easter	2	0 0
Paid for Righting our acounts	0	1 9
Itm spent att the making our acounts	0	0 6
Item payd to Mr Hadon for Righting the Regester	0	3 4

Sume £6 7 10

1670
Layd out by us Edward Wyatt & Richard Mathewes
sinas wee made our acounts

Paid to the smith for worke doune about the belles	0	4 2
Payd to Richard Chimes for puling doune the gratte house walles	0	1 4
Paid to the Clarke for oyle	0	0 2 ob
Paid to Edward Willaims for bread	0	1 0

Paid to Mr Haidon	0	3	4
Paid to a poore traveler	0	0	6
Paid to Thomas Allibonn for worke	0	3	0
Paid to Thomas Turbit & his man for worke donne att the Church	0	5	6
Item paid to John Whittaker for glasing worke doune att the Church	1	1	6
Paid for sixe bell Ropes	1	3	6
Paid for bread & wine	0	17	0
Paid to Judy fathers for washe the surples & the tabel cloath	0	1	10
Item given to a poore mane of [Kedelington] that had a lose by fiere	0	2	6
given to a poore traveler	0	0	2
Paid to John Stratford for mending the Churchyard walle	0	0	10
Paid to the tanner for Lime & heare [*hair*]	0	4	6
Paid to Thomas Willaims for worke done about the bells	0	0	6
Paid to robart Kerby for theed for the Clocke	0	0	4
to nathanell Chester	0	0	8
and for mending of the Churchyard gate	0	0	8
Item our expenses at the Courte kept att John Mauls	1	5	0
Item paid to the Clarke his waiges	0	10	0
Paid to the Clarke for greese & oyle & Lining for the belles	0	3	0
Item paid to Thomas Willaims & Nathanell Chester for worke donne about the belles	0	3	6
Item given to tom brookes	0	1	0
Paid for Righting the Leveys & our acounts	0	2	6
Spent when our acounts ware made	0	0	7

Sume is   £6 18 7 ob

The Receits of Edw: Wyat and Richard Mathewes sence
their last accounts

Inps of Mr Kenwricke for a yeares rent of the Church barne due
     at St Michael one thousand six hundred and seaventie   £0 12 0
     the sume of twelve shillings
Receved of Mr Willoughby for A Levey that was behind   £0 3 6 ob
It: Rcd of Blencow for his childs grave   £0 5 0
Received of John Carpenter for his mothers Grave   £0 5 0

Item received of Thomas Tayler for two yeares rent for
  the Church land   £0 8 0
Item the Church grase was sold for   £6 2 6

             £7 16 0 ob

The Recaits of Edward Wyatt & Richard Mathewes Churchwardens
for the yeare 1669
& for the yeare 1670
& part of the yeare 1671
the acounte for the yeare 1669 being made
thair wase due to the booke £1 2 1
Received since £7 16 0 ob
gathered of the levey £4 12 11 ob
Sume is £13 11 1
Layd out £6 18 1 ob
due & paid to the next Churchwardens £6 12 [5]ob

to gather in the booke of this Levy made the 20 daye of January 1670
the sume   £0 19 1 ob

A Singl Levey made the 20 day January 1670
for the Repares of the Parish Church of
King Sutton by us whose names are
heare subscribed

Richard Kenwrick Esq }	4	6
Robert Kenwrick gent } payd his part being	3	6
Mr Tebbetes	2	8 ob
John Pargitter	1	1 ob
Wido Pargitter	0	10 ob
Mr Cartwright his mille & millmeade & garriotts akers	2	0
Willaim Kerby	2	0
Thomas Toms	1	1 ob
Thomas Taylor	1	7
Thomas Toms farmer	2	3

Thomas Penn	1	0
John Haynes	1	2
Thomas Haynes	1	4
Thomas Toms	0	10 ob
Edmund Willaims	0	8
Thomas winckels	0	4 ob
Edward Toms	0	9
John Whittaker	0	3
Edmund Carpenter	0	5
Richard Mathewes	0	6
Robart Jenings	0	3
Charles Butcher	0	9
John Bett	0	2
John Watters	0	5
William Parish	0	1 ob
Wido Whittwell	0	5
Edward Wyatt	0	5 ob
Thomas Wyatt	0	1 ob
Richard Willaims	0	6
John Clemanes	0	4
Robart Jenings senior	0	3
Wido Bricknell	0	3 ob
Thomas Jenings	0	3
Nicklos bricknell	0	3 ob
Jonathan King	0	2 ob
Thomas blincko	0	0 ob
Willaim bricknell	0	0 ob
Daniell Smith	0	1 ob
Willaim Parish junor	0	1 ob
Willaim Upston	0	3
Willaim Poynter	0	1 ob
John Warner	0	2
Charles Buttchere cottag att mille	0	3
Simon Wattson	0	3
Thomas Wattson	0	2
John Upston	0	2
Thomas Bett	0	2
Wido Jenings	0	2
Willaim Haries	0	2
John Maulle	0	2
Lenerd bratford	0	1 ob
Ed Chandler	0	1 ob
Willaim Wyatt	0	1 ob

Thomas Clemanes		0	1
Ladwecke Upston for his House		0	1
Mathew Stacye		0	1
Waltton The Countes of Doune for walton		£1	6 8
Astrope			
Sur Nicklos Stewards 18 yrd land		9	0
Mr Cartwright 12 yard land		6	0
Mr Hiornes his land		2	0
Mr Crewes land		1	0
Edmund Carpenter		2	0
John Carpenter		2	3
Mr Tebbetes		2	0
Mr bushe		2	4 ob
Wido Toms		1	0
Richard Haddon		0	6
John Carpenter a halfe yard land & a cottag in Sutton		0	7
Thomas Toms		0	6
Thomas Penn		0	3
Willaim Durman		0	3
Thomas Wyatt of newbottel		0	3
Willaim Wyatt		0	3
Tho: Wyatt		0	1 ob
Willaim Smith		0	1
Purston			
Mr Willoughby		1	8
Mr blincko		6	6
Mr anslow		4	6
Charlton			
Mr Willoughby		1	10 ob
Willaim Haddon		1	9 ob
Wido Haddon		0	7
Richard Haddon		1	9
John Phipes		1	5
Richard Mathewes		0	5
John Luckus		0	6
Wido Emberly		0	1 ob
John Lapworth		0	1 ob

Edward Wyatt } Church
Richard Mathewes } wardens

1671

Laid out upon the church account by John watrs an John Maule

paid to wiliam upston for irnwork for repars for the bels	0	11	0
paid to Thomas Wiliams	0	5	6
paid to nathanil Chester	0	3	4
paid for wood and oyl	0	3	3
laid out for chargis at buckingham at the Biships cort	0	13	0
paid to a letor of request	0	3	4
paid to John Stratford for mending the church wall	0	1	6
for oul an nails	0	0	4
paid for lime and mending the hols in the church to John Stratford	0	1	0
paid to thomas wiliams for making the seet in the pulpit	0	0	6
paid to thomas wiliams an nathanil chester an ladwick upston for the church grats an reparing the sets in the church and a bout the bels	0	18	6
paid to John stratford for mending the church wall	0	1	3
paid to John pargter for a lod of pafers caring to the church	0	1	6
paid to Robard Kerbey for lether	0	0	8
paid to Robard Jenings for nails	0	0	6
paid to Thomas alibon for work doon in the church and at both the gats	0	19	2
paid for the communin wine an breed	1	0	4
paid to Daritey Jenings for feching the win	0	0	7
paid to Thomas watson his waiges	0	10	0
paid Judy fathers for washing the surplis an tablcloth	0	1	9
1672			
paid to Thomas wiliams for mending a seat	0	1	0
paid to Thomas Wiliams for bords	0	2	2
paid to nathanil chester and to Richard Wiliams for work	0	1	6
paid Robard Jenings for nails	0	0	3
paid to Thomas wiliams for putting up the iolepice in the church	0	2	6
paid to Thomas watsin his waidges	0	10	0
paid to him for gres for the bels	0	2	0
for oyle for the clock	0	1	0
paid to Robard Jenings for nails	0	1	3
paid to Ladwick upston for nails and mending a claper	0	5	0
paid for mats in the church	0	5	0
paid to Edward pidle for mending the churchyeard wall	0	1	0
for the cort chargis			

paid to the Doctor	0	2	6
paid to the pariter	0	1	0
Item our chargis at the cort cast	1	0	0
paid for lether	0	0	3
paid to nathanil chester for mending the sets and the gats	0	1	0
paid to Thomas Robsin for caring in the timbr an cliving the spouts	0	1	4
paid to wiliam Hoges for caring in timber	0	0	4
paid to Daniel smith for work doon at the churchyard wall and for the stons	0	16	9
paid to him more for worck an stons theare	0	4	6
paid to Thomas wiliams for mending the bels	0	1	4
paid for six new bell rops	1	2	6
to Wiliam Kerbey for carig of stons to the church yard wall	0	5	0
for chargis at brackley caring in the setificate	0	2	0
to mile whitaker for worck donn at the church			
paid for glasing att thre severall times	0	8	2
paid to Thomas Wattson	0	12	0

Layd out the sume of   £12 8 4

1673

Item gave to a leter of request	0	1	0
paid to Richard wiliams for mending the bels	0	0	9
paid for comunin bread an winne	0	15	0
paid to John Whitker for glasing don at the church	0	6	6
paid to Thomas Wiliams for nu geering the great bell	0	6	8
paid to wiliam upston for irn worck doon a bout the bels an clock	0	2	6
paid to Thomas wiliams for mending the bels	0	5	4
paid to Mickel Whitaker for mending the windos	0	8	0
paid for a lock for the steeple dore	0	1	2
1674			
paid to Ladwick upston an thomas wiliams for worck doon to the tenor	0	4	6
paid for 6 bell rops	1	4	6
chargis a banbury cort	0	1	0
paid to Judy fathers for whing the surplice an tablcloth an mending the surplis	0	1	10
paid for comunin breed an wine	0	5	3
paid to Robard Jenings for nails an oyle	0	1	6
paid to Thomas Wiliams for half a days worck dun a bout the bels	0	0	8

paid to Thomas watson for grese an linings for the bels	0 3 0
paid to thomas watson his waiges	0 10 0

the laings out of John Maule in the yeare 1673 is the sum of £4 19 2

1671	receved when we took the boock	£5 13 3 ob
	receved of Mr Kenwrick for the rent of the barn	0 12 0
	receved of Thomas Taylor for the rent of the church land on yeare	0 4 0
	receved of Mr blinko of porsin for childs grave in the church	0 6 8
	receved of John fips of charlton for a grave in the church	0 6 8
1672	receved for the church gras	5 9 0
	receved of Mr Kenwrick for the church barn	0 12 0
	Receved of Wiliam Jestis for rent for his hous	0 4 0
	Receved of farmer Taylor for on yeares rent for the church land	0 4 0
	Recepts is	£13 6 11 ob
1673	receved for the church gras	£5 5 0
	receved of farmer Taylor for on yers rent for the church land	0 4 0
	receved of Mr Kenwrick for the church barn and yard	1 0 0

the recets of John Maule for yeare 1673 is the sum of   £6 9 0
april 20th day 1674

Soe remains in the hand of John Maule this 20th day
of april 1674 the som of   £2 8 5 ob

Laid out more

paid for a hook for the church yard gate	0 0 6
paid to a brife for St catrns aspitall	0 2 0
paid to a brif thatt came out of stafordshearr to on waters	0 2 0
paid to Thomas wiliams for mending the bels	0 3 0
paid to wiliam upston for worck	0 2 4

1674			
the chargis at the cort for mansmet and horsmeat[5] came to	1	1	6
disburst in mony for thare feese	0	8	0
paid to Thomas Alibon for making up the churchyard wall in severl places	0	4	0
paid to wiliam Kerbey for caring the stons	0	1	0
paid to roger Jarvies for ditching Lady mead	0	9	4
paid to Robard Jenings for nails	0	0	2
paid to George Clarke for grease for the bels 3 pounds	0	1	0
paid to wiliam Hodges for kiling heghoges	0	0	6
paid to a man for kiling 7 dosen of sparos	0	0	4
paid to the hayward for making knone the siling of the church grace[6]	0	0	2

the disbostments more is   £2 16 1

receved for the church grace for the yeare 1674
the sum of   £4 12 0

Soe due and paid to the next Church wardens by me John Maule
the som of   £4 4 1 ob

We whose names are here subscribed this 8th day of Aprill 1672 doe nominate John Maule and John Carpenter to be Church wardens for the yeare ensueing

Tho: Tomms
William Durman
George Tomms
Will Kirby

We also nominate Tho: Heynes and William Paynter to be Supervisirs for the high ways for the yeare ensueing

---

[5] food for men and horses
[6] selling of the Church grass

Wee whose names are here Subscribed doe nominate and appoint Tho
Tomes the sone of Edward Tomes and John Carpenter to bee Church
wardens for the yeare ensuing this 20th of April 1674

Edward Toms

Thomas Tomes

Thomas Penn

Wee also nominate and appointe ffarmer Tomes and Willi: Durman
to be oversers for the high wayes for the yeare ensueing

Item received of Mr Kenwricke for the Church barne and yard	£1	0	0
Item receved of Tho: Taylor for the to lands		0 4 0
Item received of the Old Churchwardens		4 4 7ob
Item received of Mr Kenwricke for the Church barne and yard	£1	0	0
Item Received of William Parish for the Church grasse		4 14 0
It Recd of a Leavy for ye Church		10 8 1 ob
It Rcd part of ye old leavy wch was laft ungathered		0 12 5 ob

our Receits for the two yeares was   £22 3 2 ob

The Laings forth of us John Carpenter and Thomas Toms for this our
yeare 1675

Inprimis to John Witakars for menden the Church windows	0	6	0
Geven and spent to a paratar	0	2	0
Item to a leater of request	0	1	0
Item to Will: Houge for kilil a hege houge	0	0	4
Item to Gorge Clarke for waiges	0	6	0
Item to Thomas Williams for menden the belles and other worke	0	6	0
Item to Will: Upston for worke	0	1	0
Item to a leter of request	0	0	6
Item to Thomas Toms for Caring Pavarse and mortor to pave the Church	0	1	0

Item to Robart Lukecus for menden to belles Clapars	0	5	9
Item to Thomas Turbit for ston	0	1	4
Item to Thomas Williams for menden the belles	0	1	6
Item to brefes	0	2	0
Item to Robard Lukecos for menden a bell Clapar	0	2	8
Item to John Evenes for 6 belleropes	1	2	0
Item to Tho: Allibon for worke don about the Church	0	8	0
Item to a letar of request	0	0	6
Item to Robart Lucos for mending the clock	0	0	6
Item to Thomas Tombes for Carring of Stones	0	1	0
Item payd to Mikell Whittaker for glasing the windos	1	0	6
Iem ot [sic] Gorge Clarke for waiges	0	4	*
Item payd to Thomas Alibon for making the wall	0	2	0
Item payd to Georg Clarke for grese & [oyle]	0	3	*
Item payd to George Clarke for washing the surplies & table cloth	0	1	9
Item payd to George Clarke for fetchin the wine	0	0	6
Item to Tho: Williams for the Church gate	0	7	0
Item for the Comuinon bred and wine on palm Sunday and Ester day	0	12	4
Item to a leter of request	0	0	6
Item payd at Banbury at the cort	0	9	9
Item payd to Thomas Williams for mending the trebel gugines & oter thinges	0	5	0
Item payd when G spake to Barnes to mend the leds	0	0	6
Item payd to Thomas Williames for mending the bel frames & garters & the ringin flore	0	5	0
Item payd at banbry when the led was cast	0	5	0
Item payd at Clarks for ale	0	1	6
Item spent at John maules	0	1	0
Item payd to a leter of request	0	1	9
Item payd to John Maulle for ale	0	1	6
Item payd to Richard Philips	0	2	8
Item payd at Clarks for ale	0	1	8
Item payd to Thomas Williams for mending the bels	0	10	9
Item payd to Robert Lucurce for mending the bels clapers	0	5	0
Item payd to Robert Lucurce for mending the bel Claper and the clock	0	4	0
Item payd to a leter of request	0	0	6
Item payd to William Barnes for casting the leads & mending	11	2	11
Item payd to letter of request	0	0	6
Item payd to Thomas Williams for mending the Beles	0	3	0

Item payd to Thomas Turbet for poynting the leads & lime & hare	0	8	6
Item payd to a letter of request	0	1	0
Item payd to Robart Kerbey	0	1	4
Item payd for carring the Lead and fatchen	0	6	0
Item payd to Hu Giles for helping about the lead	0	1	0
Item payd to the parriter	0	2	0
Item payd to Mr Roads	0	2	6
Item paid to John Maule for part of ye charge of ye Court	0	14	6

Our Layings out cometh to   £22 3 2 ob

We hose names are here subscribed doe nominate

Mr John Tebbets[7] } to be Church
and John Haris   } wardens
John Bricknell

Tho: Toms   John Carpenter
Edward Toms
Thomas Toms
Richard Phillips   Tho: Tayler
William Kerby   Richard Haddon
Thomas Haynes   Thomas Winkles
Thomas Toms

---

[7] John Tibbets died in 1675 before he could take up his appointment; his memorial is on the south wall of the nave. As a result Thomas Toms and John Carpenter appear to have acted as churchwardens for 1675, and John Harris was appointed in 1676.

A dubel Levey made the 2 day of August 1675 for the Repares of the
Parish Church of Kingsutton by us whose names are subscribed

Robart Kenwrick Esq	0	9	0
Mrs Tebbets one yardland 3 qurt & [co]wnham 5 halfe akers to layes 3 cottags and little mill	0	5	10
John Pargeter one yardland & half qt	0	2	3
Wido Pargiter 3 qurt & a halfe	0	1	9
Willaim Kerby 2 yardland	0	4	0
Mr Cartwright his mill mill md and gariets akers	0	4	0
Thomas Toms 2 yardland & aleven akers	0	4	6
Thomas Toms one yardland & sume od land	0	2	3 ob
Thomas Taylor one yardland & 3 Cottages	0	3	2
Thomas Penn one yardland	0	2	0
John Haynes 3 qurt & a halfe one Cottag [harp] layes his land in astrop	0	2	4
Thomas Haynes one ydland tow cottages	0	2	8
Thomas Toms a halfe yadland one Cottage & sume od land	0	1	9 ob
John Willaims allmost 3 qurtrs	0	1	4
Thomas Winckels a qut & halfe	0	0	9
Edward Toms 3 qurt	0	1	6
Gorge Toms	0	0	1 ob
Edmund Carpenter	0	0	10
Robart Jenings junor	0	0	3
Charles Butcher 3 cottages	0	1	6
Richard Phillepes	0	1	6
John Bett	0	0	8
John Watters	0	0	10
Willaim Parish senio	0	0	2
Richard Willaims	0	1	0
Wido Whittwell	0	0	10
Willaim & Allexander Wyatt	0	0	3
John Whittaker	0	0	6
Edward Wyatt	0	0	6
John Clemans	0	0	8
Robart Jenings senio	0	0	6
Thomas Bett	0	0	4
Wido Bricknell	0	0	7
Thomas Jenings	0	0	6
Jonathan King	0	0	6
Mathew Stacy	0	2	0 ob
Nicholos bricknell	0	0	7 ob

willaim bricknell	0	0	1 ob
Daniell Smith	0	0	2
Willaim Upston	0	0	6
Willaim Parish	0	0	3
Willaim Poynter	0	0	3
John Warner	0	0	4
Wido Wattson one Cottage	0	0	6
Thomas Wattson	0	0	4
Charles Butcher one cottag att the mille	0	0	6
John Upston & Samuel Mecocke	0	0	4
Wido Jenings	0	0	4
Willaim Haries	0	0	4
John Maule	0	0	4
Alexsander Smith	0	0	4
Lenord Brattford	0	0	2
Edmund Chandler	0	0	3
Thomas Clemans	0	0	2
Lodwecke Upston	0	0	2
Robart Kerby	0	0	2
Walton Levey			
The Counts of doune for walton	2	13	4
Astrop Levey			
John Haries 12 yardland	0	12	0
Thomas Lovell 6 yardland	0	6	0
Danill Kinche 7 yardland	0	7	0
Richard Taylor	0	0	6
antony toms one yardland & halfe	0	1	6
Charles Butcher 3 yardlands	0	3	0
Mr Hiorne 5 yardlands	0	5	0
Edmund Carpenter 4 yardlands	0	4	0
John Carpenter 4 ya & a halfe tow yardland of Mr Crewes & halfe a yardland & one cottage	0	7	2
Mr bush 4 yardland & 3 qurt	0	4	9
Mrs Tebbets 4 yardland	0	4	0
Edward Toms 2 yardland	0	2	0
Richard Haddon 1 yrdland	0	1	0
Thomas Toms one yrdland	0	1	0
Willaim Wyatt a half yardland	0	0	6
Thomas Penn a half yardland	0	0	6
Will Durman a halfe yardland	0	0	6
Thomas Wyatt a half yardland	0	0	6

John Wyatt a qurt land	0 0 3	
Willaim Smith	0 0 3	
Purston Levey		
Mr Willoughby	0 4 0	
Mr Bincko	0 13 0	
Mr Overs	0 9 0	
Mr Wodhall	0 0 6	
Thomas Taylor of midelton	0 0 1 ob	
Charlton Levey		
Mr Willoughby for his farme	0 3 9	
Willaim Haddon	0 3 11	
Richard Haddon	0 3 6 ob	
Wido Haddon	0 1 2	
John Phipes	0 2 10	
Richard Mathewes	0 0 10	
John Lucus	0 1 0	
John Lapworth	0 0 3	
Willam Phipes	0 0 3 ob	

Wm Bradley Curate
Thomas Toms } Church
John Carpenter } wardens

left in the booke of this leavy to gather   £0 19 2

Mar 28th 1676
Wee whose names are here subscribed doe nominate

Mr John Blincoe of Purston
John Harris Church=Wardens

Wm Bradley Curate
John Carpenter }
Tho: Toms }
Thomas Toms } overseers
and William Kerby }
Edward Toms
Georg Toms

Wee whose names are heare subscribed doe nominate

Daniell: Kinche

1676

The Receivings of John Blencow & John Harris for this yeare

Received of John Warner for the Church grasse	£4	5	0
Recd of Mr Kenwreick for ye Church Barne	1	0	0
Red of ye old leavy	0	11	1 ob
Rd of Samuel Macocke	0	4	0
Red of will Hadon of ye old leavy	0	3	11
Rcd for ye breaking the church for ye widdow Pargiter	0	6	8
for ye church grasse	5	5	0

£11 15 11 ob

left pd to ye new Churchwardens	£0	18	4
Recevd of Richard Phillips and Richard Mathews for the Church houses rent	0	2	0
Recd of John Carpenter	0	4	0
Resvd of Mr Kinreck	1	0	0
Resvd of Samull Mekock	0	4	0

The Layings out of John Blencow & John Harris 1676

ffor the Charges of the Court to John Maule	0	12	6
Nathaniel Chester for mending the Churchgate & vastry dore	0	3	0
Will Cotman for iron worke	0	2	11
Will Upston for mending ye Claper	0	2	3
John Maule for ale for ye Ringers one 5 of Nov: 1675	0	2	6
Tho Alibon for Mason worke	0	2	6
Tho Williams	0	2	6
George Clarke	1	3	11
Tho Burnard for eight heghogs	0	2	0

Rob Lucas	0	1	6
John Maule for ale for ye ringers one ye 5 of Nov 1676	0	2	6
To edward Peedle for scouring ye River in Lake Meade & hugh Giles for scouring ye brooke	0	6	0
Michael Whitaker in part of his one pound eight shillings & four pence for glasing ye church windows	0	18	4
Paid to John Maule for ale	0	2	7
Pd to Mr Horsiman	0	2	6
pd to the pariter	0	1	0
Nathaniel Chester [for laying] a grave	0	1	6
John Maule for the charges of ye court	1	4	0
Rob. Jenings for oyle & nayles	0	2	10
pd George Clarke	0	17	3
pd to Tho Norris	0	16	4
pd Joyce Maull	0	6	0
Rob Kirby	0	1	8
pd John Every	1	2	6
Michel Whittiker	0	19	0
pd to three letters of request	0	3	6
pd Tho Willeams for work	0	5	0
pd Lod Upston	0	7	0
To Joyce Maule	0	2	6

£10 17 7

Wee whose Names are here subscribed doe nominate
Tho: Phipps of Charlton } Church
George Jenings } wardens

W Bradley Curate
John Blencowe
John Harris
John Carpenter
Edward Toms
Will: Kerby

A single Levy made the 1th day of November 1677 for the Repares of the Parrish Church of Kingsutton by us whose names are heare subscribed

Robart Kenwrick Esq	0 4 6
Mrs Tebbets	0 2 11
John Pargeter	0 1 1 ob
Thomas Pargeter	0 0 10 ob
Twiford mill mill mead and garrits Akers	0 2 0
William Kerby	0 2 0
Thomas Toms farmer	0 2 3
Thomas Toms	0 1 1 ob q[8]
Thomas Taylor	0 1 7
Thomas Penn	0 1 0
John Haynes	0 1 2
Thomas Haynes	0 1 5 ob
Thomas Toms	0 0 10 ob q
John Williams	0 0 8
Thomas Winckels	0 0 4 ob
Edward Toms	0 0 9
George Toms	0 0 3 ob q
Edmund Carpenter	0 0 5
Robert Jenings	0 0 1 ob
Charles Butcher	0 0 6
Richard Phillips	0 0 4
John Bett	0 0 2
John Waters	0 0 5
Willaim Parrish	0 0 2
Richard Williams	0 0 6
Wido Whitwell	0 0 5
Will and Alexander Wyat	0 0 1 ob
John Whittaker	0 0 3
Edward Wyatt	0 0 3
John Clemans	0 0 4
Robert Jenings sen	0 0 3
Thomas Bett	0 0 2
Wido Bricknell	0 0 3 ob
Wido: Jenings	0 0 3
Jonathan King	0 0 2 ob
Mathew Stacy	0 0 1 ob
Nicholas Bricknell	0 0 3
William Bricknell	0 0 0 ob q

---

[8] ob q signifies three-farthings; q alone signifies one farthing (or quarter)

Daniell Smith	0	0	1 ob q
William Upston	0	0	2
John Warner	0	0	2
William Wyatt [ ]	0	0	1 ob
Thomas Watson	0	0	2
Charles Butcher at the mill	0	0	3
John Upston and Samuell Maycok	0	0	2
Wido: Jenings	0	0	2
William Harris	0	0	2
John Maull	0	0	2
Alexander Smith	0	0	2
Lenard Bradford	0	0	1
Edmund Chandler	0	0	1 ob
Thomas Clemans	0	0	1
Ladweck Upston	0	0	1
Robert Kerby	0	0	1
The Countes of downe for Walton	1	6	8
Astroppe			
John Harris	0	6	0
Thomas Lovell	0	3	0
Daniell Kinch	0	3	6
Richard Taylor	0	0	3
Antony Toms	0	0	9
Charles Butcher	0	1	6
Mr Hiorn	0	2	0
Edmund Carpenter	0	2	0
John Carpenter	0	3	7
Mr Bush	0	2	4 ob
Mrs Tebbets	0	2	0
Edward Toms	0	1	0
Richard Haddon	0	0	6
Thomas Toms	0	0	6
George Toms	0	0	3
Thomas Penn	0	0	3
William Durman	0	0	3
Thomas Wyatt	0	0	3
John Wyatt	0	0	1 ob
William Smith	0	0	1 ob
Purston			
John Craswell Esqr	0	1	8
Mr Bincko	0	5	6

Mr Overs	0 4 6
Mr Wodhall	0 0 3
Thomas Taylor of Midellton	0 0 0 ob q
Charleton	
John Craswell Esqr	0 1 10 ob
William Haddon	0 1 11 ob
Wido Haddon	0 0 7
Richard Haddon	0 1 9 q
John Phippes	0 1 5
Richard Mathewes	0 0 5 q
John Luckos	0 0 6
Joh Lapworth	0 0 1 ob
William Phipps	0 0 1 ob q

Thomas Phipps } Church
George Jenings } wardens

The recepts of Thomas Phipps and George Jenings Churchwardens for
the yeare 1677

Recd of the old Churchwardens	£0 18 4
Recd of Richard Phillips and Richard Mathewes overseres of the poore for the Church houses rent	0 2 0
Recd of John Carpenter	0 4 0
Recd of Mr Kenwrick for rent	1 0 0
Recd of Samuell Maycoke	0 4 0
Recvd of the Levy	5 9 9
in all	7 18 1
Laid out	7 0 11
in hand	0 17 2

The Laings out of Thomas Phippes and George Jenings Churchwardens
for the yeare 1677

It: paid for a sett of bell Ropes	1 2 6
It: paid to George Clark	0 8 0
It: paid for glasing	1 0 0
It spent att Clarkes	0 0 4
It paid to Nathaniell Chester for worke	0 7 0
It paid to John Maull for beare for the Riners the 5 of November	0 2 6
It paid to Richard Haddons Steward for a heg hoge	0 0 2

It: paid to Will: Larans for 3 heghogs	0	0	6
It paid for paper	0	0	1
It paid to Will: Sawyer for 5 heghogs	0	1	8
It paid to Lenard Bradford for 5 heghogs	0	1	3
It paid to Huge Giles for 12 heghogs	0	2	0
It spent att Clarkes	0	1	0
for mending the windos	1	14	0
It spent at Jo: Mawles	0	0	8
It spent at Aynoho	0	1	0
It: paid to Robert Kerby for Linings and thred	0	1	2
paid for glasing	0	4	0
It to a breffe for fier	0	1	0
It paid for mending the windos	0	4	6
It pad for a booke	0	1	4
It paid to Nathaniel Chester for worke	0	1	6
It: spent at John Mauels	0	1	0
It: paid for glasing	0	7	0
It paid to George Clarke for washing the surplis	0	1	9
It paid for oyle	0	2	0
It paid to George Clarke for halfe a yeare for the cloke	0	5	0
It paid for fetching of wine	0	0	9
It paid for lime and sand	0	0	6
It paid to Nicholas Bricknell for a heghog	0	0	3
It paid to the parrator	0	1	0
It paid for the trancescript	0	2	6

Wee whose names are here subscribed doe nominate

Thomas Toms junar
and William Kerby to be
Churchwardens

Richard Phillips
Richard Mathewes
George Toms
Tho: Tayler
John Carpenter

Maye the 27 1678

Received by us Thomas Toms and William Kerby of Thomas Phillipes
and George Jenings the sume of   £0 17 2
Recd: of Mr Kenwrick for the Church barne the sume of   £1 0 0

A levey made 6 daye of September 1678 by us
Thomas Toms and William Kerby
Churchwardens of Kingsutton

Robert Kenwrick Esq	0	9	0
Mrs Tebbets	0	5	10
John Pargeter	0	2	3
Thomas Pargeter	0	1	9
Twiford mill mill mead and garrits Akers	0	4	0
William Kerby	0	4	0
Thomas Toms farmer	0	4	6
Thomas Toms	0	2	3 ob
Thomas Taylor	0	3	2
Thomas Penn	0	2	0
John Haynes	0	2	4
Thomas Haynes	0	2	8
Thomas Toms	0	1	9 ob
John Williams	0	1	4
Thomas Winckels	0	0	9
Edward Toms	0	1	6
George Toms	0	0	1 ob
Robert Jenings	0	0	3
Charles Butcher	0	1	6
Richard Phillips	0	0	9
Wido Bett	0	0	4
John Waters	0	0	10
William Parish	0	0	5
Richard Williams	0	1	0
Wido Whittwell	0	0	10
William Wyatt	0	0	3
John Whittaker	0	0	6
Edward Wyatt	0	0	6
John Clemans	0	0	4
Robert Jenings senr	0	0	6
Thomas Bett	0	0	4
Wido: Bricknell	0	0	7
Wido: Jenings	0	0	6
Jonathan King	0	0	5
Mathew Stacey	0	0	2
Nicholas Bricknell	0	0	6
William Bricknell	0	0	1 ob
Daniell Smith	0	0	3 ob

William Upston	0	0	4
John Warner	0	0	4
William Wyatt [on cottage]	0	0	6
Thomas Watson	0	0	4
Charles Butcher for the mill	0	0	6
John Upston & Samuel Maycok	0	0	4
Wido Jenings	0	0	4
Willaim Harris	0	0	4
John Maull	0	0	10
Alexander Smith	0	0	4
Lenord Bradford	0	0	2
Edmund Chandler	0	0	3
Thomas Clemans	0	0	2
Robert Kerby	0	0	2
Walton	2	13	4
Astrop			
John Harris	0	12	0
Thomas Lovell	0	6	0
Danell Kinch	0	7	0
Richard Taylor	0	0	6
Antony Toms	0	1	6
Charles Butcher	0	3	0
Mr Hiorne	0	5	0
Edmund Carpenter	0	4	0
John Carpenter	0	7	2
Mr Bush	0	4	9
Mrs Tebbets	0	4	0
Edward Toms	0	2	0
Richard Haddon	0	1	0
Thomas Toms	0	1	0
William Wyatt	0	0	6
Thomas Penn	0	0	6
Will Durman	0	0	6
Thomas Wyatt	0	0	6
John Wyatt	0	0	3
William Smith	0	0	3
	5	14	9
Purston			
John Cerswell Esqr	0	3	4
Mr Blincko	0	13	0
Mr Overs	0	9	0

Mr Woodhull	0 0 6
Thomas Taylor of midelton	0 0 1 ob
	1 5 11 ob
Charlton	
John Creswell Esqr	*
William Haddon	*
Richard Haddon	*
Wido Haddon	0 1 *
John Phippes	0 2 10
Richard Mathewes	0 0 10
John Luckes	0 1 0
John Lapworth	0 0 3
William Phippes	0 0 3 ob
	0 17 7 ob

in Tho: tom his hand   £2 13 9

1678

Receved by us thomas toms and willaim Kerby Churchwardens
of John Warner for the Church grass   £4   14s

May the [27] 1678

The Layings out of Thomas Toms and Will Kerby are as ffolloweth being
Churchwardens [for] Kingsutton for the yeare 1678

It: paid to Thomas Williams for worke	0 5 8
It: paid to Robert Jenings for knayles	0 1 4
It paid to Ladweck Upston for work	0 9 *
It paid for wine	1 1 *
It paid for one that had a Letter of request	*
It for a sett of Ropes	1 2 *
It for the wollon Acte[9] and a regester	0 2 *
It to a Letter of request	0 1 *
It to a Letter of request	0 0 *
Item spent att John Maules att the Corte	1 5 0

---

[9] By an Act of 1678 (30 CII c.3), an affidavit had to be made within 8 days of a funeral that the corpse had been buried in a woollen shroud, and there were a variety of £5 penalties for non-compliance

paid to the Clarke his waiges	0	5	0
It to 14 that had a Letter of request	0	1	*
Spent att Brackley at the [siting]	0	2	*
	4	17	9
It paid to Robert Lucas for a bell claper and other worke	0	12	0
It paid to Daniell Smith for Stones and worke	0	7	11
It paid to Nathanell Chester for bordes and worke	0	8	0
It given to the ringers the 5 day of November	0	3	0
for 4 Lodes of Ston carrag	0	4	0
to 1 that had a pas	0	0	6
It paid to Robert Kerby springs for the Cloke and Linings	0	1	2
It paid to Thomas Williams for worke	0	7	6
It paid to George Clarke as followeth			
for a booke	0	0	4
for a booke	0	1	0
for a dore locke	0	1	2
for oyle for the Cloke	0	1	0
for knayles	0	0	4
for oyle and grese	0	2	6
for knayles	0	0	6
for one years wages	0	10	0
	3	0	11
for oyle	0	0	6
for washing the surplis and mending the tabell Clothe	0	2	6
for fetching wine	0	1	0
It paid for bred and wine	1	0	2
It paid to Ladweck Upston for worke	0	9	2
for a sum for parkers child	0	1	8
to Thomas Williams for worke	0	1	6
paid for glasing worke donne by michell whittaker	1	15	0
paid tow John maule for the Charges of the Corte	1	10	0
paid to thomas blincko killing of urchines	0	0	4
paid to nicholas bricknell for killing urchins	0	0	6
paid for killing of one urchin	0	0	4
paid to nicholas bricknell for killing of urchines	0	0	6
paid for Righ[t]ing our leveys & making our acounts	0	3	0
sum	5	6	2

We whose names are heare subscribed doe nominat and apoynt
William Ward of Charlton and William Parrish of Kingsutton
to be Church Wardens for the yeare 1679

Tho: Toms
Willi: Kerby
Rich: Philips
George Toms   John Blinco
John Jeninges   Tho Toms
John Waters   Tho: Heynes

November 5th 1679
the acounts of thomas toms & William Kerby air as followeth

ourr Receptes are   £17 11 1
our layings out arr   £13 4 10
and we have in our hands   £ 4 6 3

November 5th 1679
Receved by me william parish Churchwarden
of thomas toms and william Kerby   £ 4   6   3

We whose Names are here subscr doe Nominate:

John Jenings }   Church
Edward Toms   }   wardens

W Bradley   vic
Willaim Parish
John Whittaker
Willaim Kerby
Edward Wyatte
thomas toms
Gorge toms
thomas Lovelle
thomas haynes

and for overseeres for the hiwayes
thomas butcher
and John Pargiter

tho toms
Thomas Haynes
Edward Wyatte
Willaim Parish
Willaim Kerby
John Bricknell

The Receptes of Willaim Parish and Willaim Ward Churchwardenes for
the yeare 1679

In primos Received with the book	£4 6	*
Received for the Churchgrase	5 11	*
Received of Samuell Mecoke for tow years Rent for the Churchland	0 8	*
Received of Mr Kenwricke for one years Rent for the Churchebarne	1 0	*
sume	£11 5	*

the layinges out of Willaim Parish and Willaim Warde
Churchwardens for the yeare 1679

Item payed to John Whittaker for glasing worke donne att siverall times about the Church	2 1	*
Item payed att the visitaton att Buckingham	0 18 4	
given to a letter of Request	0 1 0	
payed to Gorge Clark for his yeares waiges	0 10 0	
Item spent of the Ringers the fifte of november	0 3 6	
payd to nicokles [sic] bricknell for Killing of a yurching	0 0 2	
Item spent att taking the ould Churchwardens acounts	0 2 0	
Item payed to thomas Shackeles man for four yurchines	0 1 0	
Item payed to Mr Yomanes for preching one tim	0 8 0	
payed for a lock for the Church gate	0 0 6	
for a sett of bell Ropes and for a pese Rope	1 6 0	
sume	£5 12 0	
Item payd to thomas Kerby for work	0 0 7	

Payd to a Letter of Request	0	0	6
Item to John Pargiter for carig of one load of Stones	0	1	0
Payd to a letter of request from Wopnaham [*Wappenham*]	0	2	0
Payd to danill Smith for Stones and work	0	3	0
Paye to a letter of request	0	1	0
Paye to thomas Willaimes for Worke	0	1	6
Payd to Gorge Whittwell for lime sande hair and worke	0	18	0
Item for a horse to feche the Lime and sand	0	1	0
Payed to the Pariter of buckingham	0	9	0
Item payd to Gorge Clarck his bill			
for nayles	0	0	10
for oyle for the Clock	0	1	0
for oyle and grees	0	3	0
for washing the surples and the tabell clouth	0	1	9
for feching of the wine	0	1	0
Payed for brede and wine	1	1	10
for mending the surples	0	0	6
for 3 lininges	0	0	9
Payd for a threed	0	0	2
Payd for nayeles	0	0	8
Payd to Lodweck Upston for worke donne at severall times	0	4	1
Payd to thomas willaims for worke for woode	0	1	6
for lether to line the Claper	0	1	6
Payd to him for worke	0	7	6
Payd to John Whittaker for Righting and making our acountes	0	1	6
Item spent att John Maules att the Cort	1	0	0
Paid for a transcript	0	2	6
Paid to the Pariter of Banbury	0	1	0

the Layings out are   £11 0 8
the Receptes are   £11 5 3
In hande thair is   £0 4 7

The Receptes of John Jeninges and Edward Tommes Churchwarden
ffor the yeare 1680

In primos   Receved for the Chu[r]ch grase   £1 15 0
Receved with the boocke   0 4 7

Receved of Richard Pargiter for his ffather and motheres graves	0 13 4	
Receved of thomas taylor for his daughters grave	0 6 8	
Receved of John Pipes for his fathers grave[10]	0 6 8	
Recd of Mr Kenwricke for one years rent for ye Church Barne	1 0 0	
Received for one yeares Rent for the Church land	0 4 0	
Iteme the church grase solde to John Carpenter Maye 16th 1681 for	5 2 0	

sum   £9 12 3

due to be paid by John Jeninges to
     the next Churchwardens   £1 13 2

The Layinges out of John Jeninges and Edward Tommes Churchwardens
for the year 1680

Inprimis paid to Thomas Shackel for killing of sixe urchinges	0	1	*
paid for bred and wine	0	0	*
given to the Ringers the 5 of november	0	4	*
for brede and wine	0	4	*
to a letter of Request	0	1	*
paid to Danill Smith for laying doune the graves in the Church	0	7	*
paid for mending th clocke	3	0	*
paid for the caring the clocke and bringing it backe againe	0	2	*
Item spent att severall times with the Clock-maker	0	3	*
Item for bread & wine att Easter	0	14	*
paid for the Messenger	0	0	*
Given to a ltre of request	0	2	*
paid to Robart Luckes	0	0	*
paid to Edward wyattes boye for going fratwell [to Fritwell]	0	0	*

[10] The will of John Phipps senior, a yeoman from Charlton, provided that his body should be buried "within the great Alley of King Sutton church at my own seat's end" (PEC 49/1/9, Oxon Rec Off).

paid to Lodweck Upston for worke doune att severall times	0	8	*
paid to Danill Smith for worke doune att the Churchyard wall	0	1	*
paid to Gorge Clarke for killing of a urching	0	0	*
paid to one of Charlton for killing of a urching	0	0	*
paid to Gorge Clarke for washing & mending the surples and tabele Clouth	0	6	*
for his waiges	0	1	*
for oyle and grese for the Clocke and belles	0	*	*
paid for lininges & oyle and nayles	0	3	*
to Thomas Burford for work	0	*	*
to Thomas Willaims for work	0	*	*
paid for Righting of a levey	0	*	*
Item spent att the Cort	0	18	*
Item given to the pariter	0	*	*

sum is   £* *s *d

Wee whose names are here subscribed doe nominate for
the yeare ensuing 1681

John Williams   }   Church
Thomas Tomms farmer } wardens

Richard Haddon
Jo: Carpenter
Jo Jennings
Willm Kerby
George Tomms

John Harris } overseers
} of ye poore

Received with the book	£1	13	2
of Mr Kenwrick for a grave	0	5	0
Received of Thomas Taylor for a grave	0	5	0
Received of wido: Carpenter for a grave	0	5	0
Received of Mr Kenwricke for on yeares Rent for the Church barne	1	0	0
Received of Samouell mecock for on yeares Rent of the Church land	0	4	0

The layings out of Thomas Toms and John Williams Church wardens
for the yeare 1681

Item for a set of b[e]ll rops	1	2	6
Item paid to the ringers the 5 of november	0	4	0
Item paid to William hoge for 4 urchins	0	1	4
Item paid to nicklis bricknill for 7 urchins	0	1	8
Item given to a leter of request	0	0	8
Item Laid out about the Cloock	0	1	6
Item for a pound of gres	0	0	3
Item given to 3 leters of Requests	0	1	0
Item paid to Nicklos Bricknill To urchins	0	0	8
Item paid to John Whitaker for Glasing the Church windos	1	9	0
Item given to a leter of Request	0	0	4
Item given to a leter of Request	0	0	2
Item paid to the plomer for Casting of 4 sheets Of lead and sodring	12	17	6
Item paid for bords to lay under the lead	0	5	0
Item paid to Thomas williams for making A new wheal and Other work	1	12	6
Item paid to the clark for his waiges	0	10	0
Item paid for washing the surplis	0	1	9
Item paid for halfe A hundred of coeals	0	0	9
Item paid for washing the surplis & tab cloth	0	1	9
Item george Clark for helping the plomer & thomas williams	0	6	0
Item paid for oyl & grese	0	4	0
Item paid to ladawick upston	0	9	*
Item paid to Roberd Lucos to george Clark	0	4	0
Item for 3 linins for the bells	0	0	9
Item for candels	0	0	2
Item for wyer	0	0	4
Item for bred & wine	1	1	4
Item for lime	0	0	6
Item for A bord for the c[h]urch windo	0	0	6
Item for A leter of request	0	1	0
Item for to urchins	0	0	8
Item for A leter of request	0	0	4
Item for expencis	0	3	10
Item for writing the Leveys And Acounts	0	3	0
Item for caring the lead And bring it A gain	0	6	0

Item paid to George Mall ffor the Charges at the Cooart	1	7	0
Item paid to the pariter	0	2	6
It for A letter of reqest	0	1	6
It for A letter of Reqest	0	1	1
It for A locke for the Steepledore	0	1	0

The Layins out is   £23 7 8

The Receites is   £25 14 10 ob

Due to the new Church wardens the sum of   £2 7 2 ob
Theier is to Receive of Mikell Coalle for
     the Church grase   £2 13 0

Thomas Tomes   John Williams
A Dubell Leveye made 8th daye of September 1681 for the Reparaiton of
the Parish Church of Kingsutton

Robert Kenwricke Esq	0	9	0
Mrs Tebbetes	0	5	10
Richard Pargiter	0	0	3
Thomas Pargitter	0	1	9
Twiford mille mille meade & gariets ackers	0	4	0
William Kerby	0	4	0
Tho: Tomes farmer	0	4	6
Tho: Tomes jun	0	2	3 ob
Thomas Taylor	0	3	2
Thomas Penn	0	2	0
John Haynes	0	2	4
Tho: Haynes	0	2	11
Tho: Tomes senior	0	1	9 ob
John Willaims	0	1	4
Thomas Winckeles	0	0	9 ob
Edward Tomes	0	1	6
George Tomes	0	1	0 ob
Robart Jninges	0	0	3
Charles buttcher	0	0	6
Thomas buttcher	0	0	6
Henry buttcher	0	0	6
Richard Phillipes	0	0	9

Wido Bett	0	0	4
John Watters	0	0	10
William Parish	0	0	5
the lande that wase gunnes	0	1	0
Wido Whitwell	0	0	10
Willaim Wyatt	0	0	3
John Whitaker & his mother	0	0	6
Edward Wyatt	0	0	6
John Clemanes	0	0	4
Robart Jninges senor	0	0	6
Tho Bett	0	0	4
Wido bricknell	0	0	7
Wido Jeninges	0	0	6
Jonathane King	0	0	5
Mathew Stacey	0	0	2
Nicholos bricknell	0	0	6
Willaim bricknell	0	0	1 ob
Daniell Smith	0	0	3 ob
Willaim Upston	0	0	4
John Warner	0	0	4
Willaim Wyatt for a cottage	0	0	6
Tho: Wattson	0	0	2
Charles buttcher – a cottag att mille	0	0	6
John Upston & Samuell Mecoke	0	0	4
Wido Jninges	0	0	4
Willaim Haries	0	0	4
Charles Wheeler	0	2	0
John mauell	0	0	10
allexsander Smith	0	0	4
Leonard Bradford	0	0	2
Edmund Chandler	0	0	3
Thomas Clemanes	0	0	2
Robart Kerby	0	0	2
	3	6	2
Waltton Levye is	2	13	4
Astrop			
John Harries	0	12	0
Thomas Lovell	0	6	0
Daniell Kenche	0	7	0
Richard Taylore	0	0	6
Henry Linnett	0	1	6
Charles buttcher	0	3	0

Mrs Hiorne	0	5	0
Edmund Carpenter	0	2	0
Thomas Haynes	0	2	0
John Carpenter	0	7	2
Mr Bushe	0	4	9
Mrs Tebbetes	0	4	0
Edward Tomes	0	2	0
Richard Haddon	0	1	0
Thomas Tomes	0	1	0
Gorge Tomes	0	0	6
Thomas Penne	0	0	6
Willaim Durmane	0	0	6
Thomas Wyatt	0	0	6
John Wyatt	0	0	3
Willaim Smith	0	0	3
	5	14	9
Purston			
John Creswell Esq	0	3	4
Mr John blincko	0	13	0
The Lorde Crewes Lande	0	9	0
Mr Woodhall	0	0	6
Thomas Taylor of midelton	0	0	1 ob
	1	5	11 ob
Charlton			
John Creweswell Esq	0	3	9
Willaim Haddon	0	3	11
Richard Haddon	0	3	6 ob q[11]
Wido Haddon	0	1	2 q
Thomas Phipes	0	2	10
Richard Mathewes	0	0	10
John Luckes	0	1	0
John Lapworth	0	0	3
Willaim Phippes	0	0	3 ob
	£0	17	10 ob

---

[11] ob q signifies three-farthings; q alone signifies one farthing (or quarter).

A Dubell Levey made the 8 day of may in the yeare 1682 for the Church of Kingsutton by us Thomas Tomes and John Williams Church wardens

Robert Kenwrick Esq	0	9	0
Mrs Tebbetes	0	5	10
Richard Pargitar	0	0	3
Thomas Pargitter	0	1	6
Twiford mill mill mead and garites akers	0	4	0
William Kerby	0	4	0
Tho Tomes farmer	0	4	6
Tho Tomes jun	0	2	3 ob
Tho Taylor	0	3	2
Tho Penn	0	2	0
John Haynes	0	2	4
Tho Haynes	0	2	1
Tho Toms senior	0	1	9
John Williams	0	1	4
Tho Winckes	0	0	9
Edward Toms	0	1	6
Geo Toms	0	1	0
Robt Jenings	0	0	3
Charles Butcher	0	0	6
Tho Butcher	0	0	6
Henry Butcher	0	0	6
Richard Phillipps	0	0	5
Widow Bett	0	0	4
John Watters	0	0	10
William Parrish	0	0	5
those lands that were Gunns	0	1	0
Widdow Whitwell	0	0	10
Will Wyatt	0	0	3
John Whittaker& his mother	0	0	6
Edward Wyatt	0	0	6
John Clemens	0	0	4
Robt Jenings senior	0	0	6
Tho Bett	0	0	4
Widdow Bricknell	0	0	7
Widdow Jenings	0	0	6
Jonathan King	0	0	5
Mathew Stacey	0	0	2
Nicholas Bricknell	0	0	6
William Bricknell	0	0	1 ob
Daniell Smith	0	0	3 ob

William Upstone	0	0	4
John Warner	0	0	4
Will Wyatt for a cottage	0	0	6
Thomas Watson	0	0	2
John Upston & Samuel Meacocke	0	0	4
Widdow Jenings	0	0	4
Will Harris	0	0	4
Charles Wheeler	0	2	0
Butchers Cottage att mill	0	0	6
George Maule	0	1	2
Alexander Smith	0	0	4
Leonard Bradford	0	0	2
Edmund Chandler	0	0	3
Thomas Clemens	0	0	2
Robert Kerby	0	0	2
Richard Pargiter	0	0	3
Walton Levy	2	13	4
Astrope			
John Harrys	0	12	0
Michael Cole	0	6	0
Daniell Kynch	0	7	0
Richard Taylor	0	0	6
Henry Linnett	0	1	6
Charles Butcher	0	3	0
Mr Hyhorn	0	5	0
Edmund Carpenter	0	2	0
Tho Haynes	0	2	0
John Carpenter	0	7	2
Mr Bush	0	4	9
Mrs Tebbets	0	4	0
Edward Toms	0	2	0
Richard Haddon	0	1	0
Tho: Toms	0	1	0
Geo: Toms	0	0	6
Tho: Penn	0	0	6
Will Durman	0	0	6
Tho: Wyatt	0	0	6
John Wyatt	0	0	3
William Smith	0	0	3

Purston	
John Creswell Esq	0 3 4
Mr John Blincko	0 13 0
The Lord Crews land	0 9 0
Mr Woodhall	0 0 6
Tho: Taylor of Middleton	0 0 1 ob
Charlton	
John Creswell Esq	0 3 9
Tho: Wyatt	0 3 11
Rich: Haddon	0 3 6 ob
Widdow Haddon	0 1 2
Tho: Phipps	0 2 0
Will & John Phipps	0 0 10
Richard Mathews	0 0 10
John Lucas	0 1 0
John Lapworth	0 0 3
William Phipps	0 0 3 ob

Sum is

W Bradley

Thomas Toms   Will: Kerby

John Williams   Jonathan King

John Carpenter   Tho: Penn

Tho Toms

Paid for Mr Bu[sh] by Tho: Toms & John Williams   9s 6d

We whose names are subscribed doe nominate for the yeare ensuing 1682

Robert Jenings jun }   Church

John Blencoe   }   Wardens

W Bradley. C.

Thomas Tomes

John Williams

Tho Margatts

John Haris X his marke

Edward Wiat X his marke

Tho: Tayler

Tho Toms

Tho: Hains X his marke

Jo: Carpenter
Richard Haddon
Will: Kerby X his marke
John Bricknell

A Levey made by the Minister and maior part of the Parish present for necessary uses & repaires of our Parish Church of Kings Sutton this Tenth day of March 1683

By us
W Bradley Cur
Robert Jeninges C.warden
Thomas Penn
John Blencoe C.warden

A double Levy made the 10th day of March 1683 for the Church of Kingsutton by us Robt Jenings Jun and John Blencoe Church wardens

Robert Kenwrick Esq	0	9	0
Mrs Tebbets	0	5	10
Richard Pargiter	0	0	3
Thomas Pargiter	0	1	6
Twiford mill mill mead and garritts acres	0	4	0
William Kerby	0	4	0
Thomas Toms farmer	0	4	6
Thomas Toms jun	0	2	3 ob
Thomas Taylor	0	3	2
Thomas Penn	0	2	0
John Haynes	0	2	4
Thomas Haynes	0	2	1
Thomas Toms senior	0	1	9
John Williams	0	1	4
Thomas Winckles	0	0	9
Edward Toms	0	1	6
George Toms	0	1	0
Robt Jenings	0	0	3
Charles Butcher	0	0	6
Thomas Butcher	0	0	6
Henry Butcher	0	0	6
Richard Phillipps	0	0	5
Widdow Bett	0	0	4

John Watters	0 0 10
William Parrish	0 0 5
those lands that were Guns	0 1 0
Widdow Whitwell	0 0 10
William Wyatt	0 0 3
John Whittaker& his mother	0 0 6
Edward Wyatt	0 0 6
John Clemens	0 0 4
Robt Jenings sen	0 0 6
Thomas Bett	0 0 4
Widdow Bricknell	0 0 7
Widdow Jenings	0 0 6
Jonathan King	0 0 5
Mathew Stacey	0 0 2
Nicholas Bricknell	0 0 6
William Bricknell	0 0 1 ob
Daniell Smith	0 0 3 ob
William Upstone	0 0 4
John Warner	0 0 4
William Wyatt for a cottage	0 0 6
Thomas Watson	0 0 2
John Upston & Samuel Meacock	0 0 4
Widdow Jenings	0 0 4
William Harris	0 0 4
Charles Wheeler	0 2 0
Charles Butchers Cottage att mill	0 0 6
George Maule	0 1 2
Alexander Smith	0 0 4
Leonard Bradford	0 0 2
Edmund Chandler	0 0 3
Thomas Clemens	0 0 2
Robt Kerby	0 0 2
Richard Pargiter	0 0 3
Walton Levy	2 13 4
Astrope	
John Harris	0 12 0
Michael Cole	0 6 0
Daniell Kinch	0 7 0
Richard Taylor	0 0 6
Henry Linnett	0 1 6
Charles Butcher	0 3 0

Mrs Hyornes	0	5	0
Edmund Carpenter	0	2	0
Thomas Haynes	0	2	0
John Carpenter	0	7	2
Mr Bush	0	4	9
Mrs Tibbets	0	4	0
Edward Toms	0	2	0
Richard Haddon	0	1	0
Thomas Toms	0	1	0
George Toms	0	0	6
Thomas Penn	0	0	6
William Durman	0	0	6
Thomas Wyatt	0	0	6
John Wyatt	0	0	3
William Smith	0	0	3
Purston			
John Creswell Esq	0	3	4
Mr John Blincoe	0	13	0
The Lord Crews land	0	9	0
Mr Woodhall	0	0	6
Thomas Taylor of Middleton	0	0	1 ob
Charleton			
John Creswell Esq	0	3	9
Thomas Wyatt	0	3	11
Richard Haddon	0	3	6 ob
Widdow Haddon	0	1	2
Thomas Phipps	0	2	0
William & John Phipps	0	0	10
Richard Mathewes	0	0	10
John Lucas	0	1	0
John Lapworth	0	0	3
William Phipps	0	0	3 ob

Recevings of of [*sic*] Mr John Blencowe & Robert Genings
Churchwardens

Recd with the Book	2	7	2 ob
It of Mile Coale for the church Grase	1	13	0
It for Lady mead	0	1	8
It ffor wett ham lake mead & ryehill	0	14	0

Rcd of Mr Kenwrick for a years rent	1	0	0
It of Sam Meakock for ye church lands	0	4	0
It Rcd of Mr Kenwrick for ye church barne & yard	1	0	0
It Rcd of Daniel Kinch for breaking up the ground in the Church for his wifes buriall	0	5	0
Recd of Samuel Meakuk for ye Church lands	0	4	0
Recd of Mr Blincow for breaking the ground in ye Church for his Childe	0	5	0

The Receveng of Mr John Blincow and Robert Jennings is £19 13 6 ½
The Layings out is   £19 1 10 ½
There Remaines due to ye Churchwardens   11 8

The Layings out of John Blencowe & Robert Genings Churchwardens

The clarks wages half a yeare	0	5	0
Given to a letter of of [sic] request to Hanwell	0	2	6
for bread & wine	0	4	8
Given to ye Ringers of Gunpowder treason day	0	6	0
Tho Ward carpenter	0	0	4
Tho Kerby for worke & boords	0	5	8
for mending a locke	0	1	0
to Rob: Lucas	0	10	0
for a common prayer book	0	11	0
nayles	0	1	1
Mending the clocke	0	0	6
for bread & wine	0	15	0
for scowering Lady mead	0	4	0
Tho Williams for worke	0	15	0
Clarke for halfe a yeare	0	5	0
for washing ye sirplis & table cloath	0	5	0
The charge for ye court	1	4	6
for oyle & Grease	0	4	0
for 3 lynings to the bells	0	0	9
payd to nicolas Bricknill for 5 hedge hogs	0	1	8
ffor a sett of Bell rops	1	2	6
to Rich Jakeman 4 hedgehogs	0	1	4
to tho Robinson & tho Needle for bringing ye beer	0	0	8
Given to a leter of request	0	0	6
1 hegehog	0	0	4
Nayles	0	1	6
Nailes	0	0	8

Given to the Ringers of Gunpowder treason day	0	6	0
ffor bread & wine	0	4	10
a locke ffor the steeple dore	0	1	6
ffor wyer	0	0	2
Nayles	0	0	1 ob
Given to a leter of request	0	1	0
one old urchin and 5 great younge ones	0	1	2
a leter of request	0	0	6
a letter of request	0	1	0
payd to thomas Shackel for 3 heghog	0	1	0
payd to niclis Bricklin for 1 heghog	0	0	4
payd to Robert Watson for 1 hegehog	0	0	4
payd for bilding the Church yarde walles	0	9	6
Nailes	0	0	1
for expences	0	0	8
Given to Nikolas Golby	0	1	0
Paid the Parritor for a book	0	2	0
Paid Wm Upstone & Tho: Williams for ye great bell	0	4	0
Paid John Whittaker	2	13	6
Paid to the Parritor the Court day	0	4	6
paid to Geo: Maule for the Court dinner	1	3	0
Given to a letter of request	0	1	0
Payd to Tho: Turbitt and George Wittell ffor worke and lime and sa[n]de	1	6	8
Given to ye paritor ffor comenoues about ye ch:	0	1	0
payd to william nidle for slates and Lath and nailes and worke	0	16	0
payd to william upston for mend: ye great bell	0	1	0
payd for winde [sic] & bred	0	19	10
payd to Ri: Jackman for heghog	0	0	4
payd to Tho: Kerby for worke and bordes	0	4	6
Payd to the Clarke	1	2	0
Daniel Holyfield a heghog	0	0	4
for oyle	0	0	1
for writteing ye leavy & accounts	0	3	0
Payd to Ladwick Upston ffor worke	0	9	0
Nickolis Bricklin 2 heghogs	0	0	8
Richard Chimes a heghog	0	0	4
payd to Robert bricklin 2 heghoges	0	0	8
payd to thomas williams for mending ye great bell whele	0	0	8
for Nailes	0	0	4
Given to a letter of request	0	1	0

Wee whose names are herewith subscribed doe nominate for the yeare
ensuing

John Bett }
Tho Grantham   } C.Wardens

W Bradley Cur.
Willm Kerbey
Tho: Tomes
Henry Clemence
John Blencowe
Robert Jeninges
John Whittaker
Edward Wyatt
John Carpenter

Receivings of Thomas Grantham and John Bett Churchwardens 1684

Received of William ffield and ffoulk Harris for ye Church Grass	£7 17 0
Received of Mr Kenwrick	1 0 0
Received of Samuell mecock	0 4 0
Received of ffrances wyatt for the Church Grase	6 14 0
Received of Mr Kenwrick	1 0 0
Received of Samuell mecock	0 4 0
the sume is so much	£16 19 0

The Layings out

Paid to Mr Harris for mending the Clock	0 6 0
Paid to thom: Williams f A Bell Whele	1 0 0
Spent in ale	0 0 6
Given to a Letter of request	0 2 6
Given to ye ringers ye 5 of November	0 6 0
paid to Rob: Lucus for mending a lock	0 1 0
Given to a letter of request	0 2 0
paid for wine	0 6 0

paid for Nayles	0	0	1 ob
paid to Danill Valintine for to hurchings	0	0	8
Given to a Letter of request	0	2	6
paid to Rob: Lucus for shiers keys and feriles	0	4	0
The Clark one years wages	0	10	0
ffor three times washing ye surples	0	4	6
twise the table Cloth	0	0	6
ffor Grese and oyl	0	4	0
ffor mending the surples	0	0	6
paid for Bread	0	1	1
ffor riding the Leads	0	1	0
for fetching the wine	0	0	6
paid for wine	0	18	0
paid to ye parriter for a book & a paper	0	3	0
paid for mending ye Church winders	0	3	0
Given to a Letter of request	0	1	0
Given to a Letter of request	0	2	6
Given to ye parriter for a book of thanksguion and a procklimation	0	2	0
paid to walken shepard for hurchings	0	1	0
Given to a Letter of request	0	0	6
paid to Samuell mecock for hurchings	0	0	8
Given to a Letter of request	0	1	0
paid to thomas williams for a new stock for ye Saints bell	0	2	6
paid to Rob: Lucus for work for the Saints bell	0	4	0
Given to a Letter of request	0	2	6
paid to Rob: Lucus for A baldige for the Great bell	0	1	0
paid to Edw:Watson for a Lying	0	0	4
Given to a Letter of request	0	1	0
paid to the parriter for two book	0	2	6
paid to will: Watson for hurchings	0	1	2
paid to Thomas williams for the Great bell whele	1	0	0
paid to Tho: Williams for mending the bells fore severall times and for Bourds to mend them	0	12	0
paid for ale	0	1	0
Given to a Letter of request	0	2	2
Given to a Letter of request	0	1	0
Given to a Letter of request	0	1	0
The Charge of the Cort	1	8	0
ffor a sett of bell Rops	1	2	6
Given to the ringers on the 5 of november	0	6	0
paid to Rob: Lucus for mending [a] lock and work	0	1	4
Given to the parriter att the Court	0	4	6

spent in ale	0	1	0
The Clark bill halfe a years wages	0	5	0
ffor Grese and oyle	0	4	0
Washing ye surples and tableclath	0	1	9
Washing ye surples and tableclath [sic]	0	1	9
Riding the leads	0	1	0
for bread	0	1	0
paid to Coales Shepard for one hurching	0	0	4
paid to Rich: prat for one hurching	0	0	4
Given to a Letter of request	0	1	0
Given to a Letter of request	0	1	0
Given to a Letter of request	0	1	0
Given to a Letter of request	0	1	0
Given to a Letter of request	0	1	0
The Clark bill halfe a years wages	0	5	0
for washing the surples	0	1	6
for Clath and threed and mending the table Cloth	0	1	6
Given to the haywards	0	0	6
The Charge at the Court	1	1	6
Given to Mr Grenaway	0	1	0
Given to the parriter	0	4	6
paid for wine	1	14	0
paid to petter Jarvis for boards to mend ye gate	0	1	10 ob
paid to Joseph Bett	0	0	6
paid to will: upston for work	0	2	0

The Layings out is £15 10 1

The Receivings is	£16 19 0
The Layings out is	£15 10 1
Remaine in our hands	£1 9 11

These accounts allowed this 1st of June 1686 by us
W· Bradley Cur.
Jo: Carpenter
Willm Kerby
Tho: Heynes
Tho: Penn
John Whittaker

We whose names are hereunto subscribed doe nominate Church-wardens
for the yeare ensuinge 1686

George Tomes
Michael Cole

W Bradley. Cur

Thomas Tomes
John Whittaker
Willaim Kerby
Jo: Carpenter
George Maule
John Brinkcell

decimo Tertio Septs 1686

Foure Double Levies made by the Minister & major pte of
the Parish present for necessary uses & repairs of our Parish Church
of King Sutton

By us

W Bradley Cur
Geo: Kenwrick
Jo: Bett X his marke
Edward Wyatt

George Tomes } Church
Michaell Coales } wardens

The Receipts of George Toms & Michael Cole
Church=wardens for the yeare 1686

Imps. Recvd. of Mr Blencow & Robert Jenings	£0	11	8
Recd for ye church grasse	4	6	0
Recd of ye old churchwardens	1	9	11
may ye 13th 1687 received then of Mr Kenwrick for			
ye use of ye church barne for one yeares rent	1	0	0
Received of William Harris	0	0	11
Received of Richard Phillipps	0	0	5
Recd of Samuell mecock for ye church land for one yeare	0	4	0

our receivings for ye yeare 1687

recd for ye church grasse	£6	3	0
recd of the overseers of ye poore for goody Justces house	0	5	0
& for goody heritages hous	0	4	0

iune ye 8th 1688

Recd then of Mr Kenwrick for the use of the church barne for one yeare	£1	0	0
and fore shillins of Samuell mecock for ye church land	0	4	0

* * * * * * * *

November ye 6: 1686

the disbursments of george tomes and Michaell Coales Churchwardens
as foloweth

paid to Richard Watts for work about ye leads	24	19	8
I say Receved ye a bufe Named Sume of twenty foure poundes Ninteen Shilins and Eight pence I say Received p me Rich: Watts			
Receved by me John Whittaker of george tomes and Michell Cole Church-wardens for glasing worke donne about the Church the summe of	3	11	0
paid to Thomas Williams for wood and workmanship about ye Church porch	4	19	9
paid for wine at crismas	0	6	0
paid to Chas Ward for helping ye plumer	0	9	4
paid to Richard Williams for helping ye plumer too dayes	0	2	8
pd to John Fathers for mending the church porch	0	2	8
paid the pariter for 4 boocks	0	4	6
and for his fitching us to stony stratford	0	1	2
and for fetching us 3 times to alsbery	0	4	3
for ritting our bill at stony stratford	0	1	0
pd for our charges at stony stratford	0	3	0
and for our horses	0	3	0
paid to Robert Luckus for spickes for the leads & mending ye bell	0	8	6

spent at brackly when wee brought ye spade	0	1	6
spent at [ye] widdo Smithes when wee pd ye plumer	0	1	0
pd to goerge maul for ye plumers diat and coales for to heat his iorns	0	19	0
spent with ye plumers and other worke men that workt at ye church at george mauls	0	4	2
paid to Robard watson for urchins	0	0	4
for ye caring of 19 hundred & 9n of old lead & bringing of new from brackley	0	8	6

four double Levyes made the 13th of September 1686 for the Repaireing of the Church of Kingsutton by us George Toms & Michael Coales Cwardens

Robt Kenwrick Esq	0	18	0
Mrs Tibbetts	1	3	4
Richard Pargiter	0	1	0
Thomas Pargiter	0	6	0
Twiford Mill Mill mead & garritts acres	0	16	0
William Kerby	0	16	0
Thomas Toms farmer	0	18	0
Thomas Toms jun	0	9	3
Thomas Tayler	0	12	8
Thomas Penn	0	8	0
John Haynes	0	9	4
Thomas Haynes	0	11	8
Thomas Toms sen	0	7	3
John Williams	0	5	4
Tho: Winckles Land	0	3	0
Edward Toms Land	0	6	0
George Toms	0	4	2
Robt Jenings	0	1	0
John Butcher	0	2	0
Thomas Butcher	0	2	0
Henry Butcher	0	2	0
Richard Phillipes	0	1	8
Widdow Bett	0	1	4
John Waters	0	3	4
William Parrish	0	1	8
The Land that was Guns	0	4	0

George Whitwell	0	3	4
[Widow Wyatt] [*scored through*]			
John Whittaker & his mother	0	2	0
Edward Wyatt	0	2	0
Henry Clemens	0	1	4
John Jenings	0	2	0
Thomas Bett	0	0	8
John Bricknill	0	2	4
The heirs of Tho: Jenings	0	2	0
Jonathan King	0	1	8
John Stacey	0	0	8
Nicholas Bricknill	0	2	0
William Bricknill	0	0	6
Daniell Smith	0	1	2
William Upstone	0	2	0
John Warner	0	1	4
Widdow Wyatt for a cottage	0	2	0
Thomas Watson	0	0	8
Samuel Meacock	0	1	4
Widdow Jenings	0	1	4
Edward Watson	0	1	4
William Harris	0	1	4
[Charles Wheeler] [*scored through*]	0	8	0
John Butchers Cottage at ye Mill	0	2	0
George Maule	0	5	4
Alexander Smith	0	0	8
John Bradford	0	0	8
Edmund Chandler	0	1	0
Thomas Clemens	0	0	8
Robt Kerby	0	0	8
Richard Pargiter	0	1	0
Walton Levy	10	13	4
Astrope Levy			
Tho Heines [*added later*]	0	8	0
John Harris	1	16	0
Michael Coale	1	16	0
Daniel Kinch	1	8	0
Richard Taylors Land	0	2	0
Henry Linnett	0	6	0
John Butcher	0	12	0
[Mr Thomas Hester] [*scored through*]			

Edmund Carpenters Land	0	8	0
John Carpenter	1	8	8
Mr Bush	0	19	0
Mrs Tibbetts	0	16	0
Edw: Toms Land	0	8	0
Rich: Haddon	0	4	0
Thomas Toms	0	4	0
George Toms	0	2	0
Thomas Penn	0	2	0
William Durman	0	2	0
Thomas Wyatt	0	2	0
John Wyatt	0	1	0
Widdow Smith	0	1	0
Georg Jenings	0	15	0
Richard Pargiter	0	5	0
Purston Levy			
John Creswell Esq	0	13	4
Mr John Blincowe	2	12	0
Lord Crew Land	1	16	0
Mr Wodhull	0	2	0
Thomas Tayler of Middleton	0	0	6
Charleton Levy			
John Creswell Esq	0	15	0
Thomas Wyatt	0	15	8
Richard Haddon	0	14	3
Widdow Haddon	0	4	9
Widdow Phipps	0	8	0
William & John Phipps	0	3	4
Richard Mathewes	0	3	4
John Lucas	0	4	0
John Lapworth	0	1	0
William Phipps	0	1	2

Kingsuton parish
December ye 28th 1686
coleted then ye summe of thre shillings & eight pence
for the township of merriton in ye county of Salop

January the 16th 1686

Colected and gathered for the towne of Staunton in the County of Suffolk
five shillings

January ye 30 1686

Colected and gathered for parish Church of Eynsbury in ye County of
huntingdon
four shillings & one peny

ffebruary ye 13th 1686

Colected & gathered then for ye city of hereford fore shill

May ye 4th 1687

Colected and gathered then in our parish of kingsutton for white chapel in
ye parish of Stepnie in the County of Midlsex six shillings & four pence

Received by me Tho Banfeild for to Redeem his father and
two more Machants out of turkey
Received by me Tho Banfeild

may ye 20th 1688

Colected and gathred then in our parish of King Sutton towards the releife
of the
french pradistants six shillins six pence

1686
the layings of George Toms and Michael Coales

paid for 7 bottles of wine	0	14	0
pd for five quarter & one strike of lyme	1	0	6
spent when I fetcht ye lime	0	0	6
paid for loading ye lime	0	0	4
for fetching ye lyme from Sysom [*Syresham*]	0	7	0

pd the clarke 1 years wages	0	10	0
for washing ye surplis 3 times	0	4	0
for grease and oyle	0	2	0
for bread	0	1	1
for 3 linings for the bels	0	0	9
for wier for ye clock	0	0	6
for mending ye surplis and washing	0	0	10
our charges at brackly when wee caried in ye afe davies [*affidavits*] concerning ye burials[12]	0	2	0
pd for 5o strik of lime to wash the church	0	2	6
for fetching ye lime from brackly	0	1	0
for fetching 2 load of sand from aynho	0	4	0
for fetching one load of sand from ye ryhil	0	1	0
for fetching one load of stone at newbottle hill	0	2	0
for caring 2 load of stone from george whitals	0	1	0
paid to george whital for work and stufe to white ye church	1	19	8
paid for the court charges	1	1	6
paid to John Fathers for worke and stone and other matterials for ye church	3	11	9
I say Received by me John Fathers ye some of thre pound eleven shilins & nin pence 4th of June 1687			
paid to John Jameson for painting the church	9	5	0
I say received the sum of nine pounds & five shillings of the church wardens of King Sutton for painting the Church by me	John Jameson		
paid for Ale for the painter	0	2	10
paid for fier for the painter	0	1	0
paid to Jameson for ye [dyall]	0	5	0
pd for a lock for ye steeple dore	0	1	6
pd for 4 strike of haire	0	2	0
pd for a bord done up betwixt ye church and ye chancel[13]	**		

1687
George tombs and Michael Coales their disbersments

paid ye smith for mending ye wether cock	0	5	2
and for painting ye wether cock	0	5	0
paid to Valintine Quins for making ye bellrops	1	2	6

[12] For affidavits for burials in woollen, see p. 135
[13] The "board", a beam bearing the names of the churchwardens, the carpenter Thomas Williams and the date 1686, now hangs in the west porch

paid for mending and washing ye surplis	0 1 0
paid to Richard Jackman for a urchin	0 0 4
pd to Robert bricknel for 3 old ones and 6 yong ones	0 2 0
pd to georg clark for his halfe yeares wages	0 5 0
pd to henry franklin for caring a load of morter	0 1 0
pd to John Fathers & Dainel Smith for pointing ye steeple	16 5 0
wee say recd by us John fathers and Dainel Smith the above mentioned summe of sixteene pounds and five shillins by us	John Fathers Daniell Smith
pd to Charlton Smith for worke done about ye wether cock cross and other	0 4 9
pd to John fathers & dainel Smith for new stone work done about the spire	1 0 0
wee say recd the summe of one pound for work done about ye spire by us	John fathers & Daniell Smith
given to Tho banfeild for to redeeme his father & too other merchants out of turky	0 7 0
having a letter of request signed & alowed by ye cominitioners of our county	*
given to too gentlewomen that had a letter of request sined by Mr garner	*
pd for too bools for thanksgiving for ye queene being with child	0 2 0
given to a letter of request to Ric Marshal & Tho Smith of thetham [*Thatcham*] in ye County of barks	0 2 6
pd to Tho williams for ye church gats & mending ye pulpit stars	0 14 *
given to Tho Jones of dadly	0 1 *
paid to Roberd Lucus for making a key and mending the bell free [*belfry*] lock	0 1 *
paid goody watson for washing ye surplis	0 1 *
paid for seven bottles of wine for this ester communion and palme Sunday	0 14 *
for bread	0 6 *
paid Richard Smith for fetching 2 bottles of wine from banbury	*
paid for writing the Levyes this since ye acounts	0 3 0
******	*
pd for ale to george Maule that John fathers & daniel Smith and ye painter set us on the score	0 2 8
pd for ye diner & ale at ye court	1 1 0
pd for transcript	0 2 6

pd for ye pariters fees	0	2	0
given to Richard Metcalfe in ye county of lincoun	0	0	6

when the boock is cleard theire is remaining to the boock
eighteene shillins and six pence   18s 6d

Two double Levyes made the 13th day of June 1687 for the repaireing of the Church of King Sutton by us George Toms & Michael Coales Church Wardens

Robt Kenwrick Esq [14]	0	18	0
Mrs Tibbetts	0	11	8
Richard Pargiter	0	0	6
Thomas Pargiter	0	3	0
Twiford Mill	0	2	0
Mill mead	0	4	0
Garritts Acres	0	2	0
William Kerby	0	8	0
Thomas Toms farm	0	9	0
Thomas Toms jun	0	4	7 ob
Thomas Tayler	0	6	4
Thomas Penn	0	4	0
John Haynes	0	4	8
Thomas Haynes	0	5	10
Thomas Toms sen unpaid	0	3	7 ob
John Williams	0	2	8
Thomas Winckles Land	0	1	6
Edward Toms Land	0	3	0
George Toms	0	2	1
Robert Jenings	0	0	6
John Butcher	0	1	0
Thomas Butcher	0	1	0
Henry Butcher	0	1	0
Richard Phillipps	0	0	10
John Bett	0	0	8
John Waters	0	1	8
William Parrish	0	0	10
The Land that was Guns	0	2	0
George Whitwell	0	1	8

[14] A memorial brass to Robert Kenwrick, who died in 1689, is placed in the floor of the chancel.

John Whittaker & his mother	0	1	0
Edward Wyatt	0	1	0
Henry Clemens	0	0	8
John Jenings	0	1	0
Thomas Bett	0	0	4
John Bricknill	0	1	2
The heirs of Tho: Jenings	0	1	0
Jonathan King	0	0	10
John Stacey	0	0	4
Nicholas Bricknill	0	1	0
William Bricknill	0	0	3
Daniell Smith	0	0	7
William Upstone	0	1	0
John Warner	0	0	8
Widdow Wyatt for a cottage	0	1	0
Thomas Watson	0	0	4
Samuel Meacock	0	0	8
Widdow Jenings	0	0	8
Edward Watson	0	1	0
William Harris	0	0	8
Charles Wheeler	0	4	0
John Butchers Cottage Mill	0	1	0
George Maule	0	2	8
[Alexander Smith]	0	0	4
John Bradford	0	0	4
Edmund Chandler	0	0	6
John Stratford	0	0	4
Robt Kerby	0	0	4
Richard Pargiter	0	0	6
Walton Levy	5	6	8
Astrope Levy			
John Harris	0	18	0
Michael Coales	0	18	0
Daniel Kinch	0	14	0
Richard Taylers Land	0	1	0
Henry Linnitt	0	3	0
John Butcher	0	6	0
[Mr Hester Land *in margin*]George Jenings	0	7	6
Richard Pargiter	0	2	6
Edmund Carpenters Land	0	4	0
Thomas Haynes	0	4	0

John Carpenter	0 14 4
Mr Bush	0 9 6
Mrs Tibbetts	0 8 0
Edward Toms Land	0 4 0
Richard Haddon	0 2 0
Thomas Toms	0 2 0
George Toms	0 1 0
Thomas Penn	0 1 0
William Durman	0 1 0
Thomas Wyatt	0 1 0
John Wyatt	0 0 6
Widdow Smith	0 0 6
Purston Levy	
John Creswell Esq	0 6 8
Mr John Blincowe	1 6 0
Lord Crew Land	1 18 0
Mr Wodhull	0 1 0
Thomas Tayler of Middleton	0 0 3
Charleton Levy	
John Creswell Esq	0 7 6
Thomas Wyatt	0 7 10
Richard Haddon	0 7 1 ob
Widdow Haddon	0 2 4 ob
Widdow Phipps	0 4 0
William & John Phipps	0 1 8
Richard Mathewes	0 1 8
John Lucas	0 2 0
John Lapworth	0 0 6
William Phipps	0 0 7

This Levey allowed by us

George Toms   W Bradley vic

Michaell Coales   Geo: Kenwrick

Church Wardens   Tho: Tomes

The accounts of George Toms & Michael Coales Cwardens

Receiveing cometh to	£81	10	5
Disbursemts	79	17	4
Remains	1	13	1

These accounts allowed this 18th of Aprill 1688 by us

W Bradley Cur
John Blencowe
Tho: Hester
Geo: Kenwrick
Richard Haddon
Tho Grantham
John Tomes
Henry Clemmens

Wee whose names are hereunto subscribed doe nominate Churchwardens for
the yeare ensuinge 1687[15]

Tho: Penn
John Carpenter

W Bradley
Georg Toms
Michaell Coales
Tho: Hester
Richard Haddon
Henry Clemmenes
Wm: Kerby

---

[15] The accounts for 1687 appear in the names of George Toms and Michael Coales, not Thomas Penn and John Carpenter.

Wee whose names are hereunto subscribed doe nominate
Church-wardens for the yeare ensuinge 1688[16]

Tho: Penn
John Bricknell

W Bradley Cur.
John Blencowe
Tho: Hester
Geo Kenwrick
Richard Haddon
Tho Grantham
John Toms

Wee whose Names are hereunto subscribed doe nominate Churchwardens for
the yeare ensuinge 1689

Henry Clements
Richard Haddon   Cwardens

W Bradley
Tho: Hester
Geo Kenwrick
John Bricknell
Tho: Penn
Geo:Toms
Michaell Coales

Wee whose Names are hereunto subscribed doe nominate for
the yeare ensuinge 1690

Richard Pargiter }
Jeremiah Tibbetts } Cwardens

W Bradley
George Kenwrick
Tho: Hester

---

[16] The accounts for 1688 –1690, except for a levy in 1689, are missing.

Richard Haddon
John Phipps:
Henry Clemmens
Jo. Carpenter
Thomas Pargiter
Geo: Jenings:

Wee whose Names are hereunto subscribed doe nominate for
the yeare ensuinge 1691

Edward Wyatt:
Rich: Mathews   CWardens

W Bradley
Geo Kenwrick
Tho: Hester
Tho Grantham
Tho Toms
Richard Pargiter
John Tomes
Thomas Pargittur
Jeremiah Tibbetts
Thomas Penn

Receved of ye old Church wardens   £0   2   6
Receved of Mr Kenwrick ffor ye Church Barne the sum on Pound
Receved of Samuell Macocke ffor ye Church Lands   0   4   0
Receved of George Clarke for ye Church Grase
                              the sum six pound 19 shillings

ffebruary 11th 1689 a single Levey for the Reparation of the parish Church of Kingsutton

Mr George Kenwrick	4	6
Mrs Tebetts	2	10
Thomas Pargiter	0	9
The mill mill med & gariets ackers	2	0
Willaim Kerby	2	0
Thomas & John Tomes	2	9
Henry ffrancknell	1	0
Gorge Toms juner	0	1 ob
Thomas Taylor	1	7
Thomas Penne	1	0
John Haynes	1	2
Thomas Haynes	1	5 ob
Thomas Toms senr	0	10 ob
John Willaims	0	8
Winckels Land	0	4 ob
Georg Tomes junr	0	6
Robart Jenings	0	1 ob
Charles Butcher	0	3
Thomas Butcher	0	3
Henry Butcher	0	3
Richard Pargiter	0	1 ob
Richard Phillips	0	2 ob
Thomas Haynes and Edward Wattson for betts land	0	2
John Watters	0	5
Willaim Parish	0	2 ob
Whitwells Land	0	5
Allexander Wyatt	0	1 ob
John Whittaker & his mother	0	3
Edward Wyatt	0	3
Henry Clemans	0	2
John Willaims for a cottag	0	3
Wido Bett	0	1
John Bricknell	0	3 ob
Wido Jenings	0	3
Jonathan King	0	2 ob
John Stacy	0	1
Robart bricknell & his mother	0	3
Thomas Bricknell	0	0 ob
Daniell Smith	0	1 ob
Willaim Upston	0	2

John Warner	0	2
the miller att twiford mill for to Cottages	0	6
Thomas Wattson	0	1
Samuel Macocke	0	2
Wido Jenings	0	2
Willaim Haries	0	2
Charles Wheller	1	0
George Maule	0	8
Allexandr Smith	0	1
Chandlers House	0	1 ob
Robart Kerby	0	* ob
Astrop Levy		
John Harris & Mr lines	6	0
Michell Coale	3	0
Daniell Kinch	3	9
Henry linell	0	9
John Buttcher	1	6
Mr Hester	2	6
Thomas grantham	1	0
Thomas haynes	1	0
John Carpenter	3	7
M Bushe	2	4 ob
Mrs Tebetts	1	0
Jeremiah Tebetts	1	0
George tomes juner	1	9
Thomas Penn	0	3
Willaim Durman	0	3
Thomas Wyatt	0	3
John Wyatt	0	1 ob
Willaim Smith	0	1 ob
Walton Levey is	£1	6 8
Purston		
John Cresswell Esq	1	8
Mr Blincko	6	6
The Lord Crewes land	4	6
Mr Woodhull	0	3
Thomas Taylor of midelton	0	0 ob
Charlton		
John Cresswell Esq	0	10 ob

Thomas Wyatt	1 11 ob
Richard Haddon and Wido Haddon	2 4 ob
Wido Phipes	1 0
Richard Mathewes	0 5
Willaim Phipes	0 5
John Lucus	0 6
John lapworth	0 1 ob
John Phipes	0 1 ob
Thomas Tomes sener Kinguton	1 0
Richard Pargiter	0 1 ob
George tomes senur for a halfe yardland att astrup	0 3

Two duble Leveyes made the 15 day of March 1691 for the Repares of
the Church of Kingsutton By us Edward Wyatt & Richard Mathewes
Church Wardens

Mr Kenwrick	18 0
Mrs Tebbets	11 8
Richard Pargiter	0 6
Thomas Pargiter	3 0
Twiford mille	4 0
The mill mede	4 0
Grietes ackres	2 0
Willaim Kerby	8 0
Thomas Tomes & John Tomes	9 0
Heniry ffrancknell	4 0
George Tomes juner	0 7 ob
Thomas Taylor	4 0
Thomas Penne	5 0
John Haynes	4 8
Thomas Tomes senur	7 7 ob
Thomas Haynes	10 4
John Willaims	3 8
Winckeles Land	1 6
George Tomes	3 1
Robart Jeninges	0 6
John Buttcher	1 0

Thomas Buttcher	1	0
Heniry Buttcher	1	0
Richard Phillipes	0	10
John Watters	1	8
Willaim Parish	0	10
George and Wido Whitwell	1	8
John Whittaker & his mother	1	0
Edward Wyatt	1	0
Henry Clemanes	0	8
John Swaine	2	0
Wido Jeninges	1	0
Wido Bett	0	4
John Bricknell	1	2
Jonathan King	0	10
John Stacy	0	4
Robart bricknell	1	0
Thomas Bricknell	0	3
Daniell Smith	0	7
Willaim Upston	1	0
John Warner	0	8
Allexander Wyatt	0	6
John Wattson	0	4
Samuell Macoke	0	8
Thomas Jeninges	0	8
Willaim Harries	0	8
Charles Wheller	4	0
George Maule	2	8
Allexander Smith	0	4
Jerimiah Tebbets	0	4
George Tomes for the Hous that was Chadlers	0	6
Edward Wattson	0	2
Robart Kerby	0	4
George Jeninges	0	6
Mr Margrietts for his Hous	0	4
Wallton Levey	£5 6	8
Astrop Levy		
John Harries	18	0
Michell Coale	18	0
Daniell Kinche	15	0
Heniry Linell	3	0
John Buttcher	6	0

Mr Hester	12 0
Thomas Grantham	4 0
John Carpenter	14 4
Mr bushe	9 6
John taylor	4 0
George tomes	4 0
Willaim durman	1 0
Thomas Wyatt	1 0
John Wyatt	0 6
Wido Smith	0 6
	£5 10 10
Purston levey	
John Creswell Esq	6 8
Mr blincko	£1 6 0
The lord Crewes land	18 0
Mr Woodhull	1 0
Thomas taylor of midelton	0 3
	£2 11 11
Charlton levey	
John Creswell Esq	7 6
John Garner	7 10
Richard Haddon and Wido Haddon	7 6
Willaim Mathewes	1 0
Willaim Peckofer	1 0
Wido Phipes	4 0
Willaim Phipes	1 8
Richard Mathewes	1 8
John lucus	2 0
John Phipes	0 7
John Lapworth	0 6
	£1 15 3

Sum dubel Leves is   £22 18 10

[on reverse of King Sutton levy]

Georg Jenings[17]	0 1
old daniell Smith	0 1
yung daniell Smith	0 1

---

[17] There is no explanation of the entry of these three names in the accounts

	s	d
Thomas Warde[18]	0	2
Robart Wattson	0	2
Willaim Peddel	0	1
Samuell Bett	0	2
Thomas Jeninges senor	0	2
Edward ffathers	0	2
George Coles	0	2
George Clarke	0	2
Dannell Peckofer	0	2
Thomas Turbite	0	2
Wido Mauelle	0	2
Wido Kerby	0	2

a doubell Levey made the 25 day of May 1692 for the Reparing of the parish Church of Kingsutton By us Edward Wyatt & Richard Mathewes Church Wardenes

Mr Kenwrick	9	0
Mrs Tebbets	5	10
Thomas Pargiter	1	5
Richard Pargiter	0	3
Twiford mill	2	0
The mill mede	2	0
gariets ackers	1	0
Willaim Kerby	4	0
Thomas Tomes and John Tomes	4	6
Heniry ffrancknell	2	0
George Tomes juner	0	3 ob
Thomas Taylor	2	0
Thomas Penne	2	6
John Haynes	2	4
Thomas Tomes senur	3	9 ob
Thomas Haynes	4	11

[18] It is not clear whether these entries are part of a levy, and if so which one. They include the parish clerk, George Clarke, who seems to have been exempt from each levy. The names are not those which normally appear in the lists, suggesting that they were not property owners liable to the levy; and the list lacks any of the marks (X) which normally suggest that money had been received by the churchwardens. Whether the entry records payments made by them, or payments made to them, is impossible to say.

John Willaims	1	10
Winckles Land	0	9
George Tomes	1	0
Robart Jeninges	0	3
John Buttcher	0	6
Thomas buttcher	0	6
Heniry Buttcher	0	6
Richard Phillipes	0	5
John Watters	0	10
Willaim Parish	0	11
George Whittwell	0	10
Widow Whittwell	0	*
John Whittaker	0	6
Edward Wyatt	0	6
Heniry Clemanes	0	4
Wido Jeninges	0	6
Wido Bett	0	2
John Bricknell	0	7
Jonathan King	0	5
John Stacy	0	2
Robart bricknell	0	6
Thomas Bricknell	0	1 ob
Daniell Smith	0	3
Willaim Upston	0	6
John Warner	0	4
allexsander Wyatt	0	3
John Wattson	0	2
Sanuell Macoke	0	4
Thomas Jeninges	0	4
Willaim Harries	0	4
Charles Wheller	2	0
George Mauell	1	4
Kathren Maule	0	3
Dannell Smith Junr	0	1 ob
Allexsander Smith	0	2
George Tomes for Chandlers Houese	0	3
Edward Wattson	0	1
Robart Kerby	0	2
George Jeninges	0	5
Mr Margriets for his Hous	0	2
Wallton Levey	£2	13 4

Astrop Levy		
John Harries	9	0
Michell Cole	9	0
Daniell Kinch	7	6
Heniry linell	1	6
John Buttcher	3	0
Mr Hester	5	0
Thomas Grantham	2	0
John Carpenter	7	2
Mr bush	4	6
Jerimiah Tebbets	3	2
John Taylor	2	0
George Tomes and Wido Tomes	3	0
Willaim durman	0	6
Thomas Wyatt	0	6
John Wyatt	0	3
Wido Smith	0	3
George Tomes	0	6
Mr Hester for Skillmansmede	1	0
Edward Wyatt junr	0	2
Thomas Lenell	0	2
Purston levey		
John Crosswell Esq	3	4
Mr John Blincko	13	0
The Lorde Crewes land	9	0
Mr Wodhull	0	6
Thomas Taylor of midelton	0	1
Charlton		
John Crsswell Esq	3	9
John Garner	3	11
Richard Haddon and Wido Haddon	3	9
Willaim Mathewes	0	6
Willaim Peckofer	0	6
Wido Phipes	2	0
Willaim Phipes	0	10
Richard Mathewes	0	10
John lucus	1	6
John Phipes	0	3 ob
John Lapworth	0	3

sum is   £11   4   4

1691 & 1692

the Receptes of Edward Wyatt and Richard Mathewes Church wardens
for the parish of Kingsutton

Inprimos Receved for the Church grase in the yeare 1691 the sume of	£6	1	0
Receved of Thomas Haynes for the oulde thech that came ofe the Church houses	0	4	0
Receved of Samuell meccok for a yeares Rent for the Church land	0	4	0
Receved of Edward Hodges for wood	0	1	0
Receved of George Clarcke for wood	0	7	6
Receved of Thomas Buttcher for wood	0	13	0
Received or Mr Kenwrick for ye Church barne	1	0	0
Received of Tho: Ward for Chippes yt was [left] at C	0	1	6
Receved of the ould Churchwardens	0	14	4
Receved of Willaim Kerby for oulde timber	0	6	0
Received for the Church grasse in parte the sume of	4	0	0
Received of Mr Kenwrick for ye Church barne	1	0	0
Receved of Samuell Mecoke for the Rent of the Church land	0	4	0

14	16	4

The Layings out of Edward Wyatt and Richard Mathewes Churchwardens
for the yeares 1691 & 1692

In primos our expences when wee gave band for the wido Justes	3 0
given to onn that hade a pase	1 6
given to a woman that had a pase that dide lye in the towne wth 3 chidren	0 10
to a woman & children with a pas	0 4
to thomas Hodges for 5 urtchings	1 0
to daniell Vallantine for 5 urtching	1 8
to willaim Hodges for 2 urtchings	0 8
given to the Ringers th 5 of November	6 0
given to Collines boye for urtchings att sixe severall times	3 4
to Richard Buttcher for 2 urtchings	0 8
to thomas Grantham for one urtching	0 4

given to two that had a letter of Request	2 0
to John Whittaker for a urtching	0 2
to daniell Peckofer for a urtching	0 4
paid to the Pariter for a boock	1 6
given to 9 that had a pase	0 3
paid for new bellRopes	£1 2 6
spent att the same time	1 0
paid for wine att Crismas	5 0
paid for yer [wire] for the Clock	0 4
our expences when the Church was propd	2 6
to 4 that hade a pase	0 6
to 5 that hade a pase	0 4
to 7 that hade a pase	0 4
payed to Richard Haynes for work	7 8
spent when the ploumer came to see the work	1 0
spent when the towensmen dide mett abut the Repares of the Church	10 0
spent att brackly in bying timber for the church	1 0
spent att Charlton in bying timbr of wido Jàrves	1 0
given to a woman that had a letter of Request for sume that ware taken by the turck	5 0
given to 9 that hade a pase	1 0
given to a woman that hade a pase & 4 children	0 6
given to one that hade a pase	0 2
spent when wee mesuarde the mew tembr	2 6
spent when we bargned with watts for his woke about the Church	1 0
spent upon sum men that hop the greet timbr to the Church	
given to the carpenters in ye tim thay worked att the Church	0 6
given to 5 that hade a pase	0 7
paid to mr lines for wine att Estr	15 0
paid to the pariter for a boock	2 0
paid for 12 bushell of lime	6 0
spent att brackly a caring the ledes & bringing it	1 6
paid for the bringing a letter from a plomer	0 2
paid for halfe a pound of greese	0 2
pai to a letter of Request	0 2
Spent onn the ploumers att sevrall times	2 6
paid to the Clarke his waiges	10 0
for oyle and greese	4 0

for washing the surplis and tabell cloath	3	6
Item paid to Willaim Jarves for timbr & bordes for the use of the Church	£6 19	0

sum is   £13 12 0

the layinges out of Edward Wyatt and Richard Mathewes Churchwardens
1692

to to letteres of Request	0	1	0
to the backer for breade	0	0	9
to one that hade a pase	0	0	2
to one that hade a pase	0	0	2
paid to Thos Kerby for worke & timber	7	4	6
paid to Tho: Ward for worke & timber	3	1	6
paid charls whittall for worck dun at the church the same time 5 days	0	7	6
paid to George maule when ye workmen was paid for ye Church work	0	1	0
paid to George Clarke for cuting of a stick to prope the Church	0	2	0
paid to Robert Jenings for nailes	0	6	11
paid to Richard Haynes	0	10	8
paid to George ffathers for 3 days worke	0	1	6
paid to the tanner for 3 strick of hare	0	1	0
paid to Henry Clemans for the caring of a lode of morter	0	1	0
paid to Robart Kerby linenges for the belles	0	0	8
paid to George Whittwell for 4 dayes worke	0	6	0
paid to Willaim Kerby for caring a lode of ledde to brackly & bringing a lode of ledde from brackly	0	8	0
paid to him for feching a lode of lime from brackly	0	4	0
paid to him for feching a lode of sande	0	2	0
paid to Collines boye for a urching	0	0	4
paid to Collins boye for a urching	0	0	4
paid to gorge maule for a hondred of colls for the plomers yuse	0	1	6
paid to my sonne John Wyat for worke att the Church --- seven dayes worke	0	5	10
19th May 1692			
paid ye dinner yt Jer Tibbetts & Rich: Pargiter Left unpaid Last yeare	1	3	10
paid for this yeares dinner	1	3	10

paid to ye parriter	0	4	6
given to the Ringers for the victory against the ffrench	0	2	0
Item paid to the ploumer for worke donne about the Church	12	9	1
Item given to three women that had a pas	0	0	6
to a man & a wman that had a pas	0	0	6
given to two that had a pas	0	0	6
given to one that had a leter of Request	0	2	6
sume is	28	18	7
paid to John Whittaker for Righting our leveys & setting down our layings out	0	3	0
paid to John Whittaker for glasing worke done about the Church	1	18	0
paid & spent with the pariter when he gave notes of the Corte & for sighting [*citing*] of Mr John blincko to the Corte for Refusing to pay his levey	0	2	0
paid to Thomas Willaims for worke done about the belles	0	2	6
paid to Willaim Hodges for 5 urchings	0	0	10
paid to Richard Parker for Killing of urchings	0	0	4
paid to Edward Wyatt of astrop for 2 ould urchines & 5 young ones	0	1	6
to Willaim Hodges for foure urchines	0	0	10
to Richard Jackman for 1 urchine	0	0	4
to 4 that had a pase	0	0	8
to 3 that had a pase	0	0	6
to one that had a pase	0	0	2
octob: 11th 1692			
paid to one Harries a linckenshare [*Lincolnshire*] man that had a letter of Request for the see breecking in	0	5	0
to Collines boye for a urching	0	0	4
spent one the 5: of november	0	6	0
paid to the parieter for a booke & a procklenton [*proclamation*]	0	1	6
to a woman that hade a pase & did ly in the town one night	0	0	4
to 3 that had a pas	0	0	6
to 2 that hade a pas	0	0	4
paid to George Clarke	0	5	0
given to a poore man	0	0	3
given to a letter of Request	0	0	6
sum is	£3	10	5

1692

Laynges out of Edward Wyatt and Richard Mathewes Churchwardenes

paid to the Smith for worke doune about the Church	0	8	0
paid for wine	0	5	0
to one that had a letter of Request	0	0	2
spent one the carpenter	0	0	6
paid to Thomas Kerby and Thomas Warde for worke	0	3	0
given to one that had a leter of Request	0	0	6
to a woman that had a pas	0	0	6
to to other that had a pas	0	0	4
to a man that had a Letter of Request that had a lose by fior att glinton in this County	0	2	6
paid to the painter	1	12	6
for wood for the painter	0	1	9
paid to Robart Kirby for to lining for the belles	0	0	8
paid for a letter	0	0	2
paid to Thomas Nedell	0	0	6
to a woman that had a pas	0	0	2
paid for a uching mi[ ] hoges	0	0	4
paid to Willaim nedell for work done att the Church	0	5	2
paid to Georg Clark his half year waigs	0	5	0
for washing the surples 3 tines	0	4	6
for washing the tabel clouth	0	0	6
for oyle & grees for the bells	0	2	6
for oyle for the Clocke	0	1	0
paid to Richard Jackman for a urching	0	0	4
paid to the backer for bred	0	0	10
paid to Mr Lines for wine att Ester	0	17	6
for a prockimation	0	1	6
paid to gurmans daughter for a urching	0	0	4
paid to Willaim Hodges for a urching	0	0	4
payd to george Smith for a urching	0	0	4
payde to Thomas Kearby for a days worke for his man for mening the setes	0	0	8
payd to Thomas Kearby for mending the [Rales]	0	0	6

febr. 13th 1692

We whose names are underwritten doe agree that the Church-wardens
doe make a double Levey for the necessary uses & repaires of our parish
Church of King Sutton
Geo: Kenwrick
John Phipps
W Bradley
Jo: Carpenter
George Maule
John Tomes
Wm. Upstone Constable

We whose names are hereunto subscribed doe nominate Church-Wardens
for the yeare 1693

Edward Wyatt
George Maule

Geo: Kenwrick
W Bradley
Jo: Carpenter
Tho: Heynes
Tho: Hester

1693
The layngs out of Edward Wyatt & Richard Mathewes Church-wardenes

paid & spent with the pariator for sighting us to the Bicshops Corte	0 3 8
to a woman of newman [*Newnham?*] in this County that had a Lettr of Request	0 0 6
to Richard Jackman for a urchin	0 0 4
spent one the paritor	0 2 0

june 9			
paid the cort chareg	1	4	10
paid the regstor	0	1	0
paid the paritor his feese	0	4	6
paid to Willaim Mosly for a urchg	0	0	4
paid for mending the Churchyard wall	0	1	6
paid for Righting our levys and making our aCounts	0	3	0
paid for glasing the windos	0	18	2
paid to Roger Jarvis for [s]couring the lady mead dich	0	0	6

£3   2   4

a dubel Levey made 25th day of ffebruary 1692 for the Repares of the parish Church of Kingsutton by us Edward Wyatt and Richard Mathewes Churchwardenes

George Kenwrick Esq	9	0
Mrs Tebbets	5	10
Thomas Pargiter	1	5
Richard Pargiter	0	3
Twiford mille	2	0
gariets ackers	1	0
The mill mede	2	0
Willaim Kerby	4	0
Thomas Tomes and John Tomes	4	6
Heniry ffrancknell	2	0
George Tomes juner	0	3 ob
Thomas Taylor	2	0
Thomas Penne	2	6
John Haynes	2	4
Thomas Tomes senur	3	9
Thomas Haynes	4	11
John Willaims	1	1
Winckles Land	0	9
George Tomes	1	3
Robart Jenings	0	3
John buttcher	0	6
Thomas Buttcher	0	6
Heniry Buttcher	0	6
Allexander Daves	0	8

John Watters	0	10
Willaim Parish	0	11
George Whittwell	0	5
Wido Whittwell	0	5
John Whittaker & his mother	0	6
Edward Wyatt	0	6
Heniry Clemanes	0	4
Wido Jeninges	0	6
Wido bett	0	2
John Bricknell	0	7
Jonathan King	0	5
John Stacy	0	2
Robart bricknell	0	6
Thomas Bricknell	0	1 ob
Daniell Smith	0	1 ob
Willaim Upston	0	6
John Warner	0	4
Allexander Wyatt	0	3
John Wattson	0	2
Samuell Macoke	0	4
Thomas Jenings	0	4
Willaim Haries	0	4
Charles Weller	2	0
George Maule	1	4
Kathiren Maule	0	3
George Smith	0	1 ob
Allexander Smith	0	2
George Tomes for Chandlers Houses	0	3
Edward Wattson	0	1
Robart Kerby	0	2
George Jenings	0	5
Mr Margrietes for his House	0	2
Walton Levey	£2 13	4
Astrop		
John Harries	9	0
Michell Cole	9	0
Daniell Kinch	7	6
Heniry Linell	1	6
John Buttcher	3	0
Mr Hester	5	0
Thomas Grantham	2	0

John Carpenter	7	2
Mr bush	4	9
Jerimiah Tebbetts	3	2
John Taylor	2	0
George Tomes and Wido Tomes	3	0
Willaim Durman	0	6
Thomas Wyatt	0	6
John Wyatt	0	3
Wido Smith	0	3
George Tomes	0	6
Mr Hester for Skillmansmede	1	0
Edward Wyatt	0	2
Thomas Lenell	0	2
Purston		
John Cresswell Esq	3	4
Mr John blincko	13	0
The Lorde Crewes land	9	0
Mr Wodhull	0	6
Thomas Taylor of midelton	0	1 ob
Charlton		
John Cresswell Esq	3	9
Thomas Garner	3	11
Richard Haddon	3	9
Willaim Mathewes	0	6
Willaim Peckofer	0	6
Wido Phipes	2	0
Willaim Phipes	0	1 ob
Richard Mathewes	0	10
John Lucus	1	0
John Phipes	0	3 ob
John Lapworth	0	3

Edward Wyatt   }
Richard Mathews }
Churchwardens
The sum of this levey is   £11   4   4

The Receptes of Edward Wyatt & Richard Mathewes Church wardenes
iff all the Leveyes ware paid are   £59   13   8
and thare Layngs out are   £53   14 11

and thare is in all the leveyes that will not be payd the sumes under written

Mr Hester for Skillmans mead	2	0
Wido Smith	0	6
Wido bett	0	4
Wido bett	0	2
allexander Smith	0	2
Mr Hester for Skillmans mead	1	0
Wido Smith	0	3
Edward Wyatt jun	0	2
Thomas Lovell	0	2
Wido bett	0	2
allexander Smith	0	2
Wido Smith	0	3
Skillmans mede	1	0
Edward Wyatt junr	0	2
Thomas Lovell	0	2
Daniell Kinch	1	0

sum is   7   8

So thare Remaines in thair handes   £5   12   1

1693
the laings out of Edward wiatt and George Maule churchwardns

iune	
Item paid for a bible for the church	3 0 0
for a comin praire boock	0 10 0
paid for binding the chened boock[19]	0 4 0
the charg of the biships cort at buckingham	0 10 0
paid the pariter for a boock and procklamaishon	0 2 0
paid to a leter of request	0 1 0
paid to a letr of request	0 1 0
gave the carpntors in beere	0 0 6
spent when thay gave up thare accounts	0 0 6
paid Jumson for neu dooing the deyall	0 5 0

---

[19] The chained book – a reference to securing the church's bible, or other book, with a chain.

iuley 26		
paid the pariter for sumons and feese of the cort at Ailsbery	0 7 4
spent upon him	0 0 6
gave to a letr of request	0 2 0
septmbr 18		
paid to a letr of request that came from colworth	0 6 6
octobr 10		
paid for wier for the clock	0 1 6
paid for a cheen [*chain*] for the book	0 0 6
paid to Mr John Kenwrick for 4 heghogs he toock out of the muny for the church gras	0 1 4
novembr 20		
gave the ringers the 5 novembre	0 6 0
paid George Clark his half years waiges	0 5 0
paid to a letter of request fron Hanbrow [*Hanborough*]	0 2 0
26		
paid John fathers an George for mending the top of the tower window	0 2 6
Gave the Ringers the thanks giving day for king Wiliams safe return	0 3 0
January 2		
Gave sum that had a lose by watter by reson of the see banks brecking doun ar Whitlse [*Whittlesey*] with in [the Soke?] of pitorborah [*Peterborough*]	0 2 6
gave a woman that had a letr of request from stony stratford	0 1 6
paid to a letr of request from winterbun in Kent	0 0 2
paid Daniel falentin for to heghogs	0 0 8
aprill		
gave a man to a leter of request from bradford in yorkshere	0 0 6
paid Robrd kerby for to linings for the bels	0 0 8
paid to a letr of request	0 2 0
paid Richard hayns for severill things dun about the church	
paid George Clarke half years waiges	
for fier wood had to the church to melt led to run up a new belfree window	0 0 2
paid Tho: Kerby on days worck at the church gatts and mending the desk for the boock and mending the bels	0 2 2
spent on beere	0 0 6

aprill 10			
paid George Clarke half years waiges	0	5	0
for washing the surples 3 tims	0	4	6
for washing the tablecloth once	0	0	3
for gres an oyle for the bels	0	3	0
for oyle for the clock	0	1	0
for breed	0	1	0
paid George Clark feching the wine	0	0	4
for wine in all the yeare for the sacraments	0	16	0
paid John Whitaker for glasing ** church	0	15	0
aprill 17			
paid to moreton jarvis of charlton for a hedghog taken on this sid twiford	0	0	4
gave to a letr of request from cowbury in glostersheere	0	2	0
gave to a letr of request from fillstow [Felixstowe] in the county of suffolk	0	0	6
Gave to a letr of Request to a woman from the seese shiprack	0	0	6
gave to sum that had a pase from the seese	0	0	6
paid Robard watson for caching a heghog	0	0	4
paid to a leter of request to a woman came from about wisley wood thare house burned down	0	3	0
paid Richard Jackman a urching	0	1	0
paid Richard Hayns for macking a catg [catch] for church gate	0	1	0
paid Robard Kerby for a lining for the greet bell	0	0	4
for writing	0	3	0
paid to a leter of request cam out of warwicksheere	0	3	0

The Recpts of Edward wiatt and George maule for the yeare 1693

Receved of mickle coll [Michael Cole] for the church gras	£4 10 0
Receved of Richard pargtor for Mrs Cotsfords grave in the church	0 5 0
Receved of Thomasin & Ssarah Taylor for grave in the church	0 5 0
Receved of Mr Kenrick rent for the church barn	1 0 0
Receved of Samuell meckock for to church lands	0 4 0
our Repts in all this yeare is	6 4 0
and in hand last yeare	5 12 1

Wee whose Names are hereunto subscribed doe nominate Churchwardens for the yeare 1694

John Phipps   }
Thomas Heynes } C.wardens

W Bradley vic.
Geo: Kenwrick
Tho Hester
John Carpenter
Michaell Coales
John Tomes
Jeremiah Tibbetts

1694

The disbustments of Edward wiatt and George Maule sinc the other acount

Item to pay the pariter for a boock an procklamaishon	£0	1 6
iune 1 the charge of the cort	1	4 6
paid the pariter his feese	0	4 6
the Receps of Edward Wiat and George Maule is	11	16 1
there disbustments is	12	1 1
Remains due to me George Maule iune 1th 1694	0	5 7

we whose names are under written doe agre that the Church wardens doe make a singel Levey for the necessary use and repares of the parish Church of Kingsutton

George Tomes
John Tomes
Tho Toms
John Haynes
John Whittaker
John Willaims

a single Levey made 11th day of March 1694 for the Repares of
the parish Church of Kingsutton by us whous names are subscribed

Mr Kenwrick	4	6
Mrs Tebetts	2	11
Thomas Pargiter	0	8 ob
Richard Pargiter	0	1 ob
Twiford Mill	1	0
Gariets ackers	0	4 ob
The mill mede	1	0
Willaim Kerby	2	0
Thomas Tomes & John Tomes	2	3
Heniry ffrancknel	1	0
George Tomes juner	0	1 ob
The land that was Thomas Taylors	1	0
Thomas Penne	1	3
John Haynes	1	2
Thomas Tomes senur	1	10 ob
Thomas Haynes	3	5 ob
John Willaims	0	11
Winckles Land	0	4 ob
George Tomes senur	0	7 ob
Robart Jenings	0	1 ob
John buttcher	0	3
Thomas buttcher	0	3
Heniry buttcher	0	3
the Wido Daves	0	2 ob
John Watters	0	5
Willaim Parish	0	5 ob
George Whitwell	0	5 ob
Wido Whitwell	0	2 ob
John Whittaker	0	3
Edward Wyatt	0	3
Heniry Clemans	0	2
Wido Jenings	0	3
Wido bett	0	1
John bricknell	0	3 ob
Jonathan King	0	2 ob
John Stacy	0	1
Robart bricknell	0	3
Thomas bricknell	0	0 ob
George Smith	0	0 ob
Willaim Upston	0	3

John Warner	0 2
Allexsander Wyatt	0 1 ob
John Wattson	0 1
Samuel Macoke	0 2
Thomas Jening	0 2
Edward Wyatt for his hous	0 2
Thomas Tomes farm fo the land that was Gunes	0 6
Charles Wheller	1 0
George Maule	0 8
Charles buttcher	0 1 ob
Robart Kerby	0 1 ob
Allexand Smith	0 1
Edward Wattson	0 0 ob
George Jenings	0 2 ob
Mr Margriets for his hous	0 1
Walton Levey	£1 6 8
Astrop	
John Harries	4 6
Michell Cole	4 6
Daniell Kinch	3 9
Heniry linell	0 9
John buttcher	1 6
Mr Hester	2 6
Thomas Grantham	1 0
John Carpenter	3 7
Willaim Gouff	2 4 ob
Jerimiah Tebetts	1 7
George tomes & his mother	1 6
Willaim durman	0 3
Thomas Wyatt	0 3
John Wyatt	0 1 ob
Wido Smith	0 1 ob
Georg Tomes senur	0 3
Edward Wyatt	0 1
Thomas lovell	0 1
Purston	
John Cresswell Esq	1 8
Mr John blincko	6 6
The Lord Crwes land	4 6

Mr Wodhull	0 3
Thomas Taylor of mideton	0 0 ob
Charlton	
John Cresswell Esq	1 10 ob
Thomas Garner	1 11 ob
Richard Haddon	1 10 ob
Willaim Mathewes	0 3
Willaim Peckifer	0 3
Wido Phipes	1 0
Willaim Phipes	0 5
Richard Mathewes	0 5
John lucus	0 6
John Phipes	0 1 ob
John lapworth	0 1 ob

£10 4 4

The disbursmts of Thomas Heynes & John Phipps Church: Wardens 1694

paid to the Apparitor for a Booke & proclamacon	0 2 4
paid to a lter of request	0 0 8
paid to the Apparitor uppon the accounts of Geo: Maule	0 1 6
paid to a lter of request to greatr: Swell	0 0 6
paid to a lter of request	0 0 6
paid to a lter of request from Morton Pinkeney	0 2 0
paid to a lter of request out of Shropsheire	0 2 0
paid to a lter of request out of Wiltsheire	0 1 0
paid to a lter of request	0 1 0
paid to a lter of request	0 1 6
paid to a lter of request out of Devonshire	0 1 6
paid to a lter of request	0 1 0
paid to a lter of request	0 0 6
paid to Willm Westly for urchins	0 1 6
paid to Thomas Needle for urchins	0 1 0
pd Willm Pratt Richard Heynes Man for urchins	0 1 0
pd for a sheet of Stampt paper for Mrs Heynes accquit & for Geo: Clarks horse & John Clarks two iourneys	0 1 11
spent upon the Neighbrs about disposing Mr Heynes money	0 5 6
pd to John ffathers for laying two graves	0 3 0
pd for Oyle grease & nailes for the Bells	0 0 5

pd to Geo: Maule due to him when he was Church: warden	0	4	11
pd the Apparitor for a paper of alteratons in the prayers after the Queens death	0	1	3
pd to Rich: Heynes for the Clock & other things	0	4	6
pd to Tho: Williams for worke about the Bells	0	4	6
pd the Clarke his halfe yeares wages	0	5	0
Spent on the 5th day of November	0	6	0
ffor the Smiths worke aboute the Bells & 8d in beere	0	12	8
Given John Clarke to call the Overseers	0	0	2
Given to 6 Souldiers yt came from the Hospitall in Ostend	0	1	6
Given to a lter of request to 2 men of Abington	0	1	0
Given to a lter of request to a man of Wolverhampton	0	1	0
Given to a lter of request to Woolworth in Rutland	0	1	0
Given to a lter out of ffenns	0	1	0
pd for 2 bottles of Wine at Xstmas	0	4	0
Spent att Geo: Maules making the Levey	0	1	0
Given to a lter of request from Atlow in Darby sh	0	1	0
Spent amongst the Neighbrs att Geo: Maules	0	3	0
Given to two yt came from fflanders wth a lter of request	0	0	6
pd to Tho: Williams for the Bell wheele	0	15	6
Given to a lter of request aboute Tring in Bucks	0	1	0
pd for [14] load of Morter carrying	0	4	8
pd to Geo: ffathers for 8 days worke	0	10	8
pd to Dan: Smith for 5 days worke	0	6	8
pd to Geo: Smith for 5 days worke	0	6	8
pd to John Lett for 5 days worke	0	6	8
Given to Simon plester for serving ym	0	2	0
pd for Wine & Bread att Easter	0	12	10
Given to a lter of request out of Barksh	0	1	0
Given to two Women	0	0	2
pd for a Box for the surpellise to lye in	0	1	6
pd to Tho: Ward for worke aboute the Churchyard	0	1	0
pd to the Register & Apparitor att the Court	0	5	6
pd the Court Charges	1	3	6
pd John Whittaker for glazings	0	13	8
pd for a new sett of Ropes	1	2	6
pd for a new Surpellise	2	9	6
pd for wine att Charleton	0	1	3
spent att receiving money for the Ch grass	0	0	2
pd to Rich: Heynes slatting the Clapper & othr things about the Bells	0	6	8

pd to Geo: Clarke for wages to his bill	0	1	4
pd for writing our accounts	0	3	0
sum is	14	13	7
pd to a lter of request	0	0	6
pd to a lter of request	0	0	6
pd to a lter of request	0	1	0
in all	14	15	7
1695			
payd to Richard Heynes	0	8	6
payd to Tho Kerby for worke	0	3	6
payd for nailes about the Bell wheele & barne dooers	0	1	1
payd to John Williams for worke aboute the Bells	0	4	0
psyd to Geo: Smith for a Stone	0	0	6
pd to a lter of request	0	1	0
pd to a lter of request	0	1	0
pd to a lter of request	0	1	0
pd to a lter of request	0	1	0
pd to a lter of request	0	1	0
pd to a lter of request	0	0	6
pd to a [sic] 7 lters of request at severall tymes	0	3	3
pd to John Whittaker for glazing	0	6	6
pd for 2 bottles of Wine att Xstmas	0	4	0
pd to Geo: Maule Spent No: 5th	0	6	0
Spent upon Geo Smith & Tho: Kerbey	0	0	6
paid to the Apparitor for booke & proclamn	0	5	6
payd to a lter of request	0	0	6
payd to a lter of request	0	0	6
Spent among the neighbrs att Geo: Maules	0	1	0
pd to Willm Goff for urchins	0	1	0
pd to ffulke Harris for one urchins	0	0	4
pd to Rich: Collins for one urchins	0	0	4
pd to Dan: Smith for 4 days & halfe worke att the Church-Barne	0	4	8
pd to the Server	0	2	4
pd to Thomas Ward for 2 lintells	0	2	0
pd to John Williams for bread	0	0	11
pd for Wine att Easter	0	14	0
	£3	16	5
sum is	18	12	0

paid mr Bradley for righting   0   3   0

The Receipts of Tho: Heynes & John Phipps C.Wardens
1694

Recd for the Church Grass		£5 1 0
Recd for the Church-barne		1 0 0
Recd for the Church land		0 4 0
Recd of the Wid Pargiter for a grave		0 5 0
Recd of Mr Blencowe for breaking ye ground in the Church		0 6 6
Recd for the old Surplise		0 3 6
Recd of Alexander Wyatt for wood		0 15 8
Recd by Levey		5 12 4
	sum is	13 8 0
Recd for the Church Grass		3 6 0
	in all	16 14 0
Recd of Tho: Heynes for wood		0 10 7
Recd for the Church land		0 4 0
Recd of John Carpenter for breaking the ground in the Church	0 5 0
The receipts of Thomas Heynes & John Phipps is		17 13 7
soe Remains due to Tho: Hayns from the next church wardns	1 1 5

Wee whose names are hereunto subscribed doe nominate Churchwardens
for the yeare 1696

John Heynes   } Cwardens
Charles Wheeler }

W Bradley Cur
Thomas Heines
John Bricknell
Thomas Toms
George Toms
George Maule
Jo: Carpeneter
Michaell Coales

The 26th day of March 1695
Church=Wardens chosen by the Minister & major pt of the Parish present
the day & yeare abovesd

[*struck through*] Churchwardens   { John Carpenter   [*struck through*]
[*struck through*]   {George Kenwrick Esq [*struck through*]

W Bradley vicr
Michaell Coales
John Phips
Tho: Penn
Willm Goff
Jeremiah Tibbetts
Geo: Toms
Charles Wheeler

The laings out of John Hayns & Charles Whiler churchwardns 1696

paid George Clark his waidgis an his bill	0	16 10
paid spent macking a bargin for the clocke	0	6 2
paid at George Mauls at severall tims with the plomer and other worckmen & bargning	0	5 4
paid mr Parish being in arnist towards the clocke	1	0 0
paid for a boock an pricklashen [*proclamation*]	0	2 0
paid to a letter of request from Harergate [*Harrogate*]	0	1 0
paid Richard Jackman for urchins	0	3 0
paid for a pint of wine	0	1 0
paid the backer for bread	0	0 1
paid the cort dinor an chardg	1	2 8
paid to John Willams for bread	0	0 4
Pd to John Carpenter for a Lather pooh [*?pouch*]	0	3 0
paid mr paris for the neu clock, being the residu of our bargin	9	0 0
and the old clock belongeth to him		
paid at George Maules what was spent when we paid mr paris for the neu clock	0	4 0
pd to ye Parriter for a booke & proclamation	0	2 4
pd to a letter of request	0	3 0
pd to a letter of request	0	1 6

pd to a letter of request	0	1	0
pd to a letter of request	0	0	6
pd to a letter of request	0	1	0
pd to a letter of request	0	1	0
pd to a letter of request	0	1	0
pd to a letter of request	0	0	2
pd to a letter of request	0	2	0
pd to a letter of request	0	1	0
pd to a letter of request	0	1	0
pd to a letter of request	0	1	0
pd to a letter of request	0	1	0
pd to a letter of request	0	0	6
pd to a letter of request	0	1	0
pd to a letter of request	0	0	3
pd to John Harris for urchins	0	0	4
pd for wine for ye Communion	1	0	0
pd for bread	0	0	10
pd for scowering lady mead ditch	0	6	6
pd for Ale given ye workmen	0	0	6
pd for trencheing in lake meadow	0	0	4
pd to a letter of request	0	2	0
pd to a letter of request	0	1	6
pd to a letter of request	0	0	6
pd to a letter of request	0	3	0
pd to a letter of request	0	0	6
pd to a letter of request	0	0	6
pd to ye parriter at George Maules	0	4	6
pd for ye wett ham burge [*bridge?*]	0	3	6
pd for Expenses & Warneing into ye visitation	0	4	0
sum is	16	13	2
It pd for hedge hogs	0	1	0
It pd for a letter of request	0	1	0
It pd for a letter of request	0	1	0
It pd for a letter of request	0	1	0
It pd for a letter of request	0	1	0
It pd for a letter of request	0	1	0
It pd for a letter of request	0	1	6
It pd for a letter of request	0	1	0
It pd for a letter of request	0	1	0
It pd Thomas Jennings for bringing ye clocke from Banbury	0	2	0
It pd for a letter of request	0	0	6
It pd for a letter of request	0	0	6

It pd for a letter of request	0	0	6
It pd ye fees & Expenses at ye visitation at Stoney Stratford	0	12	4
It pd for a hedgehog	0	0	4
It pd for Expenses at Alsebury [o] parriters fees & other fees	0	11	10
It pd for a letter of request	0	3	0
It pd for a letter of request	0	1	6
It pd for a letter of request	0	1	0
It pd for a letter of request	0	0	6
It pd for a letter of request	0	1	0
It pd for a letter of request	0	1	0
It pd for a letter of request	0	1	0
It pd for a letter of request	0	0	2
It pd for a letter of request	0	1	6
It pd for a letter of request	0	1	0
It pd for a letter of request	0	1	6
It pd Upstones boay for cleanseing ye church & fetching soder for ye plumer	0	1	0
It pd for a letter of request	0	1	0
It pd for Expenses at Banbury when ye gabell rope was carried home	0	0	6
It pd for a letter of request	0	1	0
It pd for a letter of request	0	1	0
It pd for a letter of request	0	1	0
It pd Thomas Ward for Expenses when he fetch ye Gabell rope from Banbury	0	1	0
It pd Richd Jakeman for hedgehogs	0	2	0
It pd for a letter of request	0	2	0
It pd for a letter of request	0	1	6
It spent at Brackley wth ye plumers	0	3	0
It spent at George Maules	0	2	6
It spent at George Maules	0	0	6
It spent at George Maules	0	1	0
It spent at George Maules	0	0	10

3   *   *

One double Levie made the 23d of Octbr 1696 for the necessary uses &
Repaires of the Parish Church of King Sutton by us John Heynes and
Charles Wheeler Church Wardens

Imps George Kenwrick Esq	0	9	0	
It Mrs Tibbets	0	5	10	
It Thomas Pargiter	0	1	2	
It Richard Pargiter	0	0	3	
It Twyford mill	0	2	0	
It Gargets Acre	0	0	9	
It Mill mead	0	2	0	
Itm Will Kerby	0	4	6	
Itm Thomas Toms and John Toms	0	5	6	
Itm Geo Toms Junior	0	0	3	2[20]
Itm Thomas Tayler	0	2	0	
Itm Thomas Penn	0	2	6	
Itm John Heyns	0	2	4	
Itm Thomas Toms Senior	0	3	9	2
Itm Tho Heyns	0	4	11	
Itm John Williams	0	1	10	
Itm Winkles Land	0	0	9	
Itm George Toms	0	1	3	2
Itm Robert Jenning	0	0	3	
Itm John Butcher	0	0	6	
Itm Thomas Butcher	0	0	6	
Itm Henry Butcher	0	0	6	
Itm the Widdow Phillips	0	0	5	
Itm John Waters	0	0	10	
Itm William Parrish	0	0	11	
Itm George Whittall[21]	0	0	5	
Itm the Widdow Whittall	0	0	5	
Itm the Widdow Pargiter	0	0	3	
Itm John Whittaker	0	0	6	
Itm Edward Wyatt	0	0	10	
Itm Henry Clemence	0	0	4	
Itm the Widdow Jennings	0	0	6	
Itm the Widdow Bett	0	0	2	
Itm John Bricknill	0	0	7	

[20] The payments are recorded in four columns, with the fourth column for quarters (farthings). The figure 2 therefore represents a halfpenny

[21] The spelling of the Whitwell family's name has changed to Whittall. They later gave their name to Whittall Street

Itm Jonathan King	0	0	5
Itm John Stacy	0	0	2
Itm Robert Bricknill	0	0	6
Itm William Upstone	0	0	6
Itm Alexandar Wyatt	0	0	3
Itm John Watsone	0	0	2
Itm Samuell Meacock	0	0	4
Itm Thomas Jenning	0	0	4
Itm Charles Wheeler	0	2	0
Itm George Maule	0	1	4
Itm Charles Butcher	0	0	3
Itm George Smith	0	0	2 2
Itm Alexander Smith	0	0	2
Itm George Toms for Chandlers house	0	0	3
Itm Edward Wyat	0	0	1
Itm Robert Kerby	0	0	2
Itm Thomas Margretts house	0	0	2
Itm Walton Leavy	2	13	4
Itm John Harris	0	9	0
Itm Michaell Cole	0	9	0
Itm Dainell Kinch	0	7	6
Itm Henry Linnett	0	1	6
Itm John Butcher	0	3	0
Itm Mr Hester	0	5	0
Itm Thomas Grantham	0	2	0
Itm John Carpenter	0	7	2
Itm Mr Goffe	0	4	9
Itm Jeremiah Tibbets	0	3	2
Itm Thomas Heyns	0	2	0
Itm George Toms & the Widdow Toms	0	3	0
Itm Isabell Goosron	0	0	6
Itm Thomas Wyatt	0	0	6
Itm Widdow Smith	0	0	3
Itm John Wyatt	0	0	3
Itm George Toms	0	0	6
Itm Mr Hester for Skillmansmead	0	1	0
Itm Edward Wyatt	0	0	2
Itm Thomas Lovell	0	0	2
Itm Itm [sic] John Craswell Esq	0	3	4
Itm the Lord Crews Land	0	9	0
Itm Mr Woodhill	0	0	6
Itm Thomas Tayler of Middleton	0	0	1 2

Itm John Craswell Esq	0	3	9
Itm Thomas Garner	0	3	11
Itm Richard Hadden	0	3	9
Itm William Mathews	0	0	6
Itm William Peckofer	0	0	6
Itm Widdow Phips	0	2	0
Itm William Phips	0	0	10
Itm Richard Mathews	0	0	10
Itm John Lucas	0	1	0
Itm John Phips	0	0	3 2
Itm John Lapwoth	0	0	3

W Bradley vic
George Maule
Jo Heynes} C.wardens
Cha: Wheeler}

Given to Streatham Breife in the Isle of Ely foure shillings and
    six=pence:
Given to Holbeach in the County of Lincoln three=shillings:
Given to Warwicke Breife the sum Three=pounds Two-pence farthing

It pd for grease	0	0	2
It pd for nailes	0	0	2
It pd for a hedgehoge	0	0	4
It pd for a letter of request	0	1	6
It pd for a letter of request	0	1	0
It pd Richd Jakeman for 14 hedgehogs	0	4	8
It pd Tho Gurman for a hedgehoge	0	0	4
It pd John Harris for 4 hedgehoges	0	1	4
It pd Richd Collings for 7 hedgehogs	0	2	4
It pd John Summerton for 5 hedgehogs	0	1	4
It pd for a hedgehoge	0	0	4
It pd for a letter of request	0	1	6
It pd for a letter of request	0	1	0
It pd for a letter of request	0	1	0
It pd for a letter of request	0	1	0
It pd for a letter of request	0	1	0
It pd for a letter of request	0	0	6
It pd for a letter of request	0	0	6
It pd for a letter of request	0	1	0
It pd for a letter of request	0	1	0

It pd for a letter of request	0 0 6
It pd for a letter of request	0 1 0
It pd for a letter of request	0 0 2
It pd for a letter of request	0 3 0
It pd for a letter of request	0 1 6
It pd for 3 hedgehoges	0 1 0
It pd for a hedgehoge	0 0 4
It pd for a letter of request	0 1 0
It pd for a letter of request	0 1 0
It pd for a letter of request	0 0 6
It pd for a letter of request	0 0 6
It pd for a letter of request	0 0 6
It pd Robt Collings for a hedgehoge	0 0 4
It pd to John Harris for 2 hedgehoges	0 0 8
It pd to John Harris for 4 hedgehoges	0 1 4
It pd to Richd Jakeman 3 hedgehoges	0 1 0
It pd to Richd Hyornes one hedgehoge	0 0 4
It pd for a letter of request	0 1 6
It pd for a letter of request	0 0 8
It pd for a letter of request	0 0 4
It pd for a letter of request	0 1 0
It pd for a letter of request	0 1 0
It pd for a letter of request	0 1 0
It pd ye parriter for a booke	0 1 6

£2 3 6

Three Double Leavys made ye 13th day February Anno Domini 1696/7 for ye necessary uses and Repaires of ye parish Church of Kingsutton By us John Heyns and Charles Wheeler Church Wardens

Geo: Kendwrick Esq	1 7 0
Mrs Tibbets	0 17 3
Tho. Pargiter	0 3 6
Richard Pargiter	0 0 9
Twiford mill	0 6 0
Gariots acre	0 2 3
Mill mead	0 6 0
Willm Kerby	0 12 0

Thomas Toms	0	11	4 2[22]
Henry ffranknill	0	6	0
George Toms junr	0	0	10 2
Tho: Tayler	0	6	0
John Toms	0	16	6
Tho: Penn	0	7	6
Charles Wheeler	0	6	0
Thomas Heyns	1	0	9
John Williams	0	5	6
Winkles Land	0	2	3
Geo: Toms	0	3	0
Rob: Jennings	0	0	9
John Bucher	0	1	6
Tho Bucher	0	1	6
Henry Bucher	0	1	6
Widdow Davis	0	1	3
John Watters	0	2	6
Willm Parrish	0	2	9
Geo: Whittall	0	2	6
Thomas Pargeter	0	0	9
John Whittaker	0	1	6
Edward Wyatt	0	2	6
Henry Clemence	0	1	0
Widdow Jennings	0	1	6
Widdow Bet	0	0	6
John Bricknill	0	1	9
Jonathan King	0	1	3
John Stacy	0	0	6
Robert Bricknill	0	1	6
Willm Upstone	0	1	6
John Warner	0	1	0
Alexander Wyatt	0	0	9
John Watsone	0	0	6
Sam meacock	0	1	0
Thomas Jennings	0	1	0
Geo Maul	0	4	0
Charles Bucher	0	0	9
Geo: Smith	0	0	7 2
Geo: Toms for Chandlers House	0	0	9
Edward Wattson	0	0	3
Robert Kerby	0	0	6

---

[22] see footnote 20

Geo: Jenning	0	1	6
Tho Margrets	0	0	6
Walton Leavy	8	0	0
John Harris	1	7	0
Michaell Coales	1	7	0
Daniell Kinch	1	2	6
H Linnet	0	4	6
John Bucher	0	9	0
Mr: Hester	0	15	0
Thomas Grantham	0	6	0
John Creswell Esq	0	10	0
John Carpenter	1	1	6
Mr Goffe	0	14	3
Jerimiah Tibbets	0	9	6
Geo Toms senior [added in different hand:]& ye Widdow	0	9	0
Isabell Gooson	0	1	6
Tho Wyatt	0	1	6
Widdow Smith	0	0	9
Jo. Wyatt	0	0	9
Geo Toms	0	1	6
Mr Hester for Skilmans [added in different hand:]mead	0	3	0
Edward Wyatt	0	0	6
Thomas Lovell	0	0	6
Mr John Blinkow	1	19	0
The Lord Crews Land	1	7	0
Mr Woodhill	0	1	6
Tho Tayler of midleton	0	0	4 2
John Creswell	0	11	3
Thomas Gardner	0	11	9
Richard Hadden	0	11	3
Willm Mathews	0	1	6
Will Pekover	0	1	6
Widdow Phips	0	6	0
William Phips	0	2	6
Richard Mathews	0	2	6
Hugh Elms	0	3	0
John Phips	0	0	10 2
John Lapworth	0	0	9

April 26

paid for to letters of Request which Mr Bradley laid down for	0	3	0
It pd to George ffathers for mendeing ye Church yard ground Walls	0	3	0
It pd for Expenses when Recd Walton levie	0	1	4
It pd for bread for ye Communion	0	1	0
It pd for Ale given to ye Workemen when they ware at worke at ye Church	0	3	0
It pd for Writeing ye leavies for one yeare	0	3	0
It pd for a letter of request	0	1	0
It pd for a letter of request	0	0	6
It pd for a letter of request	0	1	6
It pd for a letter of request	0	0	10
It pd for a letter of request	0	0	6
It pd to John Harris for a hedgehoge	0	0	4
It pd to John Harris for a hedgehoge	0	0	4
It pd to Tho: Kerby for mending ye church Gates	0	3	0
It pd for Nailes	0	0	3
It pd for a letter of request	0	1	0
It pd for a letter of request	0	0	6
It pd for a letter of request	0	1	0
It pd for a letter of request	0	2	6
It pd for a letter of request	0	1	0
It pd for a letter of request	0	1	0
It pd for a letter of request	0	0	6
It pd to John Harris for hedgehoges	0	0	4
It pd for a letter of request	0	1	6
It pd George Maule for ye Expenses at the Spirituall Court	1	11	6
It paid to ye Parriter	0	4	6
It paid to ye Parriter for a pEsentmt	0	1	0
It pd for Expenses at ye vissitation at Banbury	0	17	0
It pd to ye deanes parriter & Expenses	0	2	6
It pd to Joseph Bett for hedgehoges	0	2	8
It pd to Richd Collings & Joseph Bett for hedgehogs	0	3	0
It pd to Richd Collings & Joseph Bett for hedgehogs	0	1	8
It pd to Tho: draper for hedgehoges	0	0	4
It pd to Anthoney harris for on hedgehoge	0	0	4
It pd for a letter of request	0	1	0
It pd for a letter of request	0	1	0
It pd for a letter of request	0	0	6
It pd for a letter of request	0	0	6

It pd John Harris for hedgehogs	0	1	8
It pd to John Stacy for hedgehoges	0	0	8
It pd for a letter of request	0	0	6

sume is 5 1 *

July ye 12th 1697[23]

It pd to Thomas Ward for timber and worke done at the Church	8	13	0
It pd to John Warner for timber	1	13	4
It pd for fetching & carrying two loads of lead to Brackley	0	16	0
It pd for carryeing a parcell of lead more to Brackley	0	1	0
It pd for Carriage of a lode of timbr to ye Church	0	1	0
It pd Thomas Williams for his owne & his sone Richards worke done at ye Church	5	2	9
It pd John Whitaker for glass & worke	3	5	2
It pd Willaim Kerby for boards	6	5	0
It pd to John Williams for Worke done at ye Church	1	17	3
It pd to John ffathers for Worke done at ye Church	0	9	4
It pd Tho: Haynes & John Phips ould churchwardens	1	1	5
It pd Wm. Peedle for ****	0	5	8
It pd Richd Williams & his sone **** for forty five dayes worke done at ye Church	3	7	6
pd ye charge at George Maules at ye Doctors Court	1	9	4
It pd for Expenses when we bargained for ye Work	0	6	8
It pd for Expenses ye fifth of Novembr	0	*	4
It pd for Expenses when ye clocke came home	0	3	4
It pd for Expenses when ye clocke was dunn	0	3	5
It pd ye plumers Charges	1	7	11
It pd for beere when they agreed for a house for Ladwicke Upston	0	4	10
for beere when ye plumers gave in their bill	0	3	0
It pd ye Clarkes bill a yere & ½ Wages & Washing ye surplis & tablecloth & grease & Oyle for ye clock & ye bells	1	5	3
It pd Mr Bradleys Charges when ye children were bushoped at Banbury	0	13	6
It pd Richard Watts & Benjamin Bull for Lead Exchainged new soder & worke	34	1	1
It pd George Toms for boards	3	5	7
It pd Thomas Kerby for Timber & Worke	5	14	0
It pd Thomas Margetts for boards	2	8	0

[23] These major expenses were entered separately from the rest, at a later page of the book.

It pd Thomas Kerby for bords	0	9	7
It pd Richard Haynes for worke done	1	9	0
It pd for Wine at Chrismas for ye Cumnion	0	5	0
It pd Robt Jennings for Nailes	0	11	4
It pd to George Jennings for Nailes	0	10	2
It pd Thomas Turbett for Nailes	0	8	4
It pd for Writing ye levies for one yeare	0	3	0
It pd for Wine for ye Communion against Easter	0	12	0
It pd to John Evans for ye bell ropes	1	2	6
It gave Robt Willmeads man for bringing ye wine	0	0	2

sume is   £84   1   7

Three double Leavyes made ye 25th day of November Anno Dom 1697 for ye necessary uses and Repaires of ye parish Church of Kingsutton By us John Haynes and Charles Wheeler Church Wardens

George Kenwrick Esq	1	7	0	
Mrs Tibbetts	0	17	6	
Thomas Pargiter Senr	0	3	6	
Richard Pargiter	0	0	9	
Twiford mill	0	6	0	
Garrett Acres	0	2	3	
Mill Mead	0	6	0	
William Kerby	0	12	0	
Thomas Tomes	0	11	4 2[24]	
Charles Wheeler	0	6	0	
George Toms jun	0	0	10 2	
Thomas Carpenter & ffran: Goodwine	0	6	0	
John Tomes	0	16	6	
Thomas Penn	0	7	6	
John Haynes	0	7	0	
Thomas Jennings & Edwrd. Watson & Jeremiah Tibbetts for Mrs. Tibbettses land	0	6	0	
Thomas Heynes	1	0	9	
John Williams	0	5	6	
Winkleses Land	0	2	3	
George Toms Senr	0	3	0	3ob[25]
Robert Jennings	0	0	9	

[24] see footnote 20

[25] This entry includes both 3 farthings and "ob", which in earlier times signified a halfpenny

John Butcher	0 1 6 .
Charles Butcher	0 1 6
Henry Butcher	0 1 6
Widdow Davis	0 1 3
John Watters	0 2 6
William Parish	0 2 9
George Whittwell	0 2 6
Thomas Pargiter Junr	0 0 9
John Whittaker	0 1 6
Edward Wyatt	0 2 6
Henry Clemence	0 1 0
Widdow Jennings	0 1 6
John Betts	0 0 6
Widdow Bricknell	0 1 9
Edward King	0 1 3
John Stacy	0 0 6
Robert Bricknell	0 1 6
Wm. Upstone	0 1 6
John Warner	0 1 0
Alexander Wyatt	0 0 9
John Watson	0 0 6
Samuell Meacockes	0 1 0
Thomas Jennings	0 1 0
George Maule	0 4 0
Charles Butcher	0 0 9
George Smith	0 0 7 2
Alexander Smith	0 0 6
George Toms for Chandlers House	0 0 9
Edward Watson	0 0 3
Robert Kerby	0 0 6
George Jennings	0 1 6
Thomas Margetts	0 0 6
Walton Leavy	8 0 0
Astrope	
Mr Hester	0 15 0
Mr Hester for Skillmans Mead	0 3 0
John Harris	1 7 0
Michaell Coale	1 7 0
John Carpenter	1 1 6
John Butcher	0 9 0
Daniell Kinch	1 2 6
Henry Linnett	0 4 6
William Goffe	0 14 3

Thomas Grantham	0 6 0
Jeremiah Tibbets	0 9 6
George Tomes Junr	0 9 0
Humphrey Bloxham	0 1 6
Thomas Wyatt	0 1 6
William Smith	0 0 9
John Wyatt	0 0 9
George Toms Senr	0 1 6
Edward Wyatt	0 0 6
Thomas Lovell	0 0 6
Purson	
John Creswell Esq	0 10 0
Mr John Blincoe	1 19 0
The Lord Crews Land	1 7 0
Mr Woodhill	0 1 0
Tho: Tayler of Midleton	0 0 4 2
Charwelton	
John Creswell	0 11 3
Thomas Gardner	0 11 9
Richard Haddon	0 11 3
William Mathews	0 1 6
Will Peckover	0 1 6
Widdow Phips	0 6 0
William Phips	0 2 6
Richard Mathews	0 2 6
Hugh Elbmes	0 3 0
John Phips	0 0 10 2
John Lapworth	0 0 9

Two double leavies made ye 25th day of Aprill Anno Dom 1698 for ye necessary uses & Repaires of ye parish Church of Kingsutton By us John Haynes and Charles Wheeler Church Wardens

George Kenwricke Esq	0 18 0
Mrs Tibbetts	0 11 8
Thomas Pargiter Senr	0 2 4
Richard Pargiter	0 0 6
Twiford mill	0 4 0
Garrett Acres	0 1 6
Mill Mead	0 4 0

William Kerby	0	8	0
Thomas Tomes	0	7	7
Charles Wheeler	0	4	0
George Toms junr	0	0	7
Thomas Carpenter & ffran: Goodwine	0	4	0
John Tomes	0	11	0
Thomas Penn	0	5	0
John Haynes	0	4	8
Thomas Jennings & Edwd.Watson & Jeremiah Tibbetts for Mrs. Tibbettses land	0	4	0
Thomas Heynes	0	13	10
John Williams	0	3	8
Wincleses Land	0	1	6
George Tomes Senr	0	2	1
Robert Jennings	0	0	6
John Butcher	0	1	0
Charles Butcher	0	1	0
Henry Butcher	0	1	0
Widdow Davis	0	0	10
John Watters	0	1	8
William Parish	0	1	10
George Whittwall	0	1	8
Thomas Pargiter Junr	0	0	6
John Whittaker	0	1	0
Edward Wyatt	0	1	8
Henry Clemence	0	0	8
Widdow Jennings	0	1	0
John Betts	0	0	4
Widdow Bricknell	0	1	2
Edward King	0	0	10
John Stacy	0	0	4
Robert Bricknell	0	1	0
William Upstone	0	1	0
John Warner	0	0	8
Alexander Wyatt	0	0	6
John Watson	0	0	4
Samuell Meacocke	0	0	8
Thomas Jennings	0	0	8
George Maule	0	2	8
Charles Butcher	0	0	6
George Smith	0	0	5
Alexander Smith	0	0	4
George Tomes for Chandlers House	0	0	6

Edward Watson	0	0	2
Robert Kerby	0	0	4
George Jennings	0	1	0
Thomas Margetts	0	0	4
Walton Leavie	5	6	8
Astrope			
Mr Hester	0	10	0
Mr Hester	0	2	0
John Harris	0	18	0
Michaell Coale	0	18	0
John Carpenter	0	14	4
John Butcher	0	6	0
Daniell Kinch	0	15	0
Widdow Linnett	0	3	0
William Goffe	0	9	6
Thomas Grantham	0	4	0
Jeremiah Tibbets	0	6	4
George Tomes Junr	0	6	0
Humphery Bloxham	0	1	0
Thomas Wyatt	0	1	0
William Smith	0	0	6
John Wyatt	0	0	6
George Tomes Senr	0	1	0
Edward Wyatt	0	0	4
Thomas Lovell	0	0	4
Purson			
John Creswell Esq	0	6	8
Mr John Blincoe	1	6	0
The Lord Crews Land	0	18	0
Mr Woodhill	0	1	0
Thomas Tayler of Midleton	0	0	3
Charwelton			
John Creswell Esq	0	7	6
Thomas Gardner	0	7	10
Richard Haddon	0	7	6
William Mathews	0	1	0
William Peckover	0	1	0
Widdow Phips	0	4	0
William Phips	0	1	8
Richard Mathews	0	1	8
Hugh Elbmes	0	2	0
John Phips	0	0	7
John Lapworth	0	0	6

It pd to John Whittaker for glazeing ye Church Windows	0	16	0
It pd for a letter of request	0	1	0
It pd for a letter of request	0	1	0
It pd for two letters of request	0	1	0
It pd to John Whittaker for glazeing at ye Church	1	0	0
It pd for 3 letters of request	0	3	0
It pd for a letter of request	0	1	0
It pd Tho: Williams for mending ye clocke Wire	0	1	0
It pd for a letter of request	0	0	6
It pd for 3 letters of request	0	1	6
It pd for lime	0	0	4
It pd for Expenses when ye great Bell was mended	0	0	2
It pd for a letter of request	0	1	0
It pd for a letter of request	0	1	0
It pd for a letter of request	0	0	6
It pd for 4 letters of request	0	2	0
It pd for a letter of request	0	0	6
It pd Henry ffarrin for a letter from Ailsebury	0	0	8
It pd for 3 letters of request	0	3	0
It pd for a letter goeing to Warwicke	0	0	2
It pd Mr Paris for scowering ye clocke	0	5	0
It pd to John ffathers for mending ye Church Walls	0	5	6
It pd to Mr Cave of Banbury for brasses for the great bell	0	8	0
It pd to John [Toms] for mending the bells	0	4	0
Ipd for carring in ye Church barne doores	0	0	6
It pd for 4 letters of request	0	4	0
It pd for 3 letters of request	0	1	6
It pd for 4 letters of request	0	4	0
It pd for 5 letters of request	0	5	0
It pd for expenses one the fifth of November	0	6	0
It pd for a letter of request	0	0	6
It pd for expenses when ye Church grass was sold	0	1	0
It pd for Wine for the Communion at Christmass & for this Easter in the yeare 1699	1	3	9
It pd for brasses for the second bell	0	8	0
It pd for bread for the Communion	0	1	2
It pd Richard Williams for mending ye bells	0	3	0
It pd for 3 letters of request	0	4	6
It for writeing & casting up the booke	0	3	0
It pd for 4 letters of request	0	2	2
It pd the parriter for a booke & proclamacon	0	2	10
It pd Richard Hayneses bill	2	0	2
It pd John Whittakers bill	0	11	*

Sume £10 0 5

One dobble Levie made ye 20th day of ffebruary 1698 for ye necessary uses and repaires of ye parish Church of Kingsutton By us John Haynes & Charles Wheeler Church Wardens

George Kenwricke Esq	0	9	0
Mrs Tibbetts	0	5	9
Thomas Pargiter Senr	0	1	2
Richard Pargiter	0	0	3
Twiford Mill	0	2	0
Garrett Acres	0	0	9
Mill Meadow	0	2	0
William Kearby	0	4	0
John Tomes	0	5	6
Thomas Tomes	0	3	9 ob
Charles Wheeler	0	2	0
George Toms Junr	0	0	3 ob
Tho: Carpenter & ffran: Goodwine	0	2	0
Thomas Penn	0	2	6
John Haynes	0	2	4
Thomas Haynes	0	6	11
Tho: Jennings & Edwd. Watson & Jeremiah Tibbetts for Mrs. Tibbettses land	0	2	0
Edward Williams	0	1	4
George Tomes Senr	0	1	0 ob
Robert Jennings Senr	0	0	3
And for John Winkleses land	0	0	6
John Butcher	0	0	6
Charles Butcher	0	0	9
Henry Butcher	0	0	6
Widdow Davis	0	0	5
John Watters	0	0	10
William Parish	0	0	11
George Whittwall	0	0	10
Thomas Pargiter Junr	0	0	3
John Whittaker	0	0	6
Henry Clemence	0	0	4
Edward Wyatt	0	0	10
[struck through Widdow Jennings] John Meacocke & John Jen.	0	0	6
John Bett	0	0	2
John Parish for Robert Bricknills land	0	0	7
Edward King	0	0	5
John Stacy	0	0	2

Robert Bricknill	0	0	6
William Upstone	0	0	6
William Dobbins	0	0	0
John Warner	0	0	4
Alexander Wyatt	0	0	*
John Watson	0	0	2
Samuell Meacocke	0	0	4
Thomas Jennings	0	0	4
George Maule	0	1	4
George Smith	0	0	2 ob
George Armett	0	0	1
Edward Watson	0	0	2
Robt. Kearby Senr	0	0	2
Robert Jennings Junr	0	0	7
Robert Kearby Junr	0	0	3
Elizabeth Jennings	0	0	3
Thomas Margetts	0	0	2
Richd. Joynes for Tho: Winckleses land	0	0	3
George Tomes for Chandlers house	0	0	3
Walton levie	2	13	4
Astrope levie			
Mr Hester	0	2	0
Mr Hester for Skillmans Meadow	0	1	0
Thomaas Hester & George Tomes Junr	0	3	0
Michaell Coales	0	9	0
John Harris	0	9	0
John Carpenter	0	7	2
John Butcher	0	3	0
Daniell Kinch	0	7	6
Widdow Linnett	0	1	6
William Goffe	0	4	9
Widdow Grantham	0	2	0
Jeremiah Tibbetts	0	3	2
George Tomes Junr	0	3	0
Humphery Bloxham	0	0	6
Thomas Wyatt	0	0	6
William Smith	0	0	3
John Wyatt	0	0	3
George Toms Senr	0	0	6
Edward Wyatt	0	0	2
Thomas Lovell	0	0	2
Purson leavie			
John Creswell Esq	0	3	4

Mr John Blencow	0 13 0
The Lord Crews Land	0 9 0
Mr Woodhull	0 0 6
Mr Wise of Midleton	0 0 1 ob
Charwelton leavie	
John Creswell Esq	0 3 9
Thomas Gardner	0 3 11
Richard Haddon	0 3 9
William Mathews	0 0 6
William Peckover	0 0 6
Widdow Phipps	0 2 0
William Phipps	0 0 10
Richard Mathews	0 0 10
Hugh Elbmes	0 1 0
John Phipps	0 0 3 ob
John Lapworth	0 0 3

The Receivings of John Haynes & Charles Wheeler Church Wardens
April the 11th 1699

Recd for the Church grass for ye yeare 1696	4 12 0
Recd of Samll. Meacocke for ye Church land	0 4 0
Recd of Charles Butcher for Chips	0 15 0
Recd for ye Church grass for ye yeare 1697	4 0 0
Recd of Samll. Meacocke for ye Church land	0 4 0
Recd of Tho: Haynes for ye straw of ye Church barne	0 5 0
Recd for ye Church grass for ye yeare 1698	6 11 0
Recd of Samll. Meacocke for ye Church land	0 4 0
Recd tenn dubble levies w.ch amounts to	112 3 4
Sume is	128 18 4
Recd since Ester of Tho Carpenter Richd Haddon Mr Taylor & the Widdow Grantham	1 0 0
The disburstments are	124 6 10
the disburstments since Ester	10 4 0
pd Richard Haynes	0 5 0
pd Thomas Turbutt for Candles & Nailes	0 5 4
pd to Edward Watson for lether for the bells	0 * 2
pd to John ffathers	0 3 6

pd to Robert Watson for scowering the ditch in lady mead & scoweing the trench	0 3 0
	135 8 10
	9 6
	129 18 4

Disburstmts since the Accounts

It. for carrying a load of pavemt. to the Church	0 1 0
It. for a letter of request	0 0 3
It. for a hundred of Nailes	0 0 6
It. pd George Clarke his bill for his wages for one yeare & ½ till the 25th day of March 1699	1 7 4
It. pd the Parriter at the visitation	0 5 6
It. pd to the Kings parriter for books & proclamaton	0 3 6
It. pd for Expenses when the pavem. was carryed to the Church	0 0 6
It. pd for a letter of request	0 3 0
It. pd for 3 letters of request	0 2 6
It pd for a hedgehoge	0 0 4
It. pd Henry ffrankline for carrying of stones	0 4 0
It. pd to George Smith for paveing of the Church & mending of the mound walls	1 17 9
It. pd to Daniell Smith for stones	0 1 6
It. pd to George Tomes for 3 bushells of lime	0 3 0
pd to George Maule for the Expenses at ye Spirituall Court	1 16 0
pd to Thomas Ward for mending the bell Wheeles	3 7 6
It. pd to Richard Haynes for mending ye Church gate	0 0 10
It. pd to Thomas Kearby for making ye Church gate	0 4 0
It. spent w.th the Workemen at George Maules	0 2 0
It. pd to foure letters of request	0 3 0

Sume is   10 * 0

Remaines due to John Haynes & Charles Wheeler   5 10 6

Wee whose names are hereunto subscribed nominate
Churchwardenes for the yeare 1699

John Meacocke & } Church
John Blencowe   } Wardens

W Bradley vic
Tho: Hester
Jo Carpenter
Michael Coales
Tho: Penn
George Tomes
Thomas Haynes

Wee whose names are hereunto subscribed doe nominate
Church wardens for ye yeare 1700

Robt Jennings son of George Jenings
William Goffe   Church wardens

John Blencowe
John Macocke
George Tomes Senr
Jo: Harris
William Kearby
Michael Coales

Receved of the old Churchwardens	£2	4	4
Receved of John Warner for the Church grass	7	1	0
Received of Samuell macocke ffor the Church Land	0	4	0
ffor the Church grass	6	19	0
Received of Samuel macocke for the Church Land	0	4	0
receved of mr bradly for an old bible	0	4	0
Received of Gorge clark	0	3	0
Received of neley wyatt for the church gras	4	18	0
Sume is	21	17	4
Recd of Samuell Macocke for the Church land	0	4	0
Recd of John Bett for house Rent	0	2	0
Recd five dobble levies	55	17	1
Sume is	78	0	5

one shilin to the paretr	0	1	0
Spent Spent [*sic*] upon him at males	0	6	8
Spent in Ale and met at nopot [*Newport Pagnell?*]	0	5	6
ffor my hoas [*horse*]	0	3	0
ffor 8 heg hogs	0	1	0
one Church Lock	0	0	6
John fathers worke	0	3	3
Spent Recnem [*reckoning?*]the mony for the Church grase	0	1	0
for 9 duson of sparos	0	1	6
Spent of gunpoder Treason	0	6	0
spent in Alle	0	0	6
ffor hoocks & hinges	0	5	6
ffor the spicks	0	17	3
ffor wine	0	5	0
payd george Clarke whasin the Church Linnin	0	1	11
payd george Clarke	0	1	9
ffor 12 duson of sparos	0	2	0
ffor 6 hed [*sic*] hogs	0	1	4
for 8 duson of sparos	0	1	4
one Lock	0	0	7
ffor 3 duson of sparos	0	0	6
Willam nedle had for riedin [*reeding?*] the vestry	0	10	6
Richard hearis for worke	0	3	0
for Line and hare [*lime and hair*]	0	2	9
for 4 heg hogs	0	1	0
Jhn walms one day worke	0	1	6
for 6 dusen of sparos	0	1	0
Richard wilms 5 days worke and halfe	0	12	9
the pareter booke for the fast	0	4	0
for the Smith worke	0	3	6
John fathers worke	0	3	3
one pecke of sand	0	0	3
Thomas Kurby worke 4 day worke	0	6	6
for 10 dusen of sparos	0	1	8
for glasen the windows	0	17	4
Thomas warde had for the Church gate	0	3	3
Richard Hearis worke	0	5	0
ffor nayls for the Church hose [*house*]	0	5	5
0ne shilin to the paretr	0	1	0
spent upon him at molls	0	2	0

Charges of the bushop of Linkorn quort[26]	0	3	4
ffor the penchol [penitential?]	0	4	10
ffor Charges	0	2	0
gave to A man that came out of Korby	0	0	6
gave to A woman of [sawod]	0	2	0
gave to the parsen of kilnnoth	0	1	6
ffor 2 heg hogs	0	0	8
ffor hge [sic] hogs	0	1	0
gave to the paretr	0	1	0
hoas hier to nupot [horse hire to Newport]	0	3	0
John fathers 6 days worke & halfe	0	8	6
ffor 7 heg hogs	0	1	6
ffor the Church booke	0	2	10
payd george Clarke halfe year wagges	0	5	0
payd for 12 duson of sparos	0	2	0
payd george Clarke halfe years wagges & yashing the Church Linnige	0	8	6
ffor 7 bottles of wine	0	14	6
spent in ale	0	0	6
Rafters for the Church housen	0	8	4
ffor bred	0	0	7

Sume is   £11 5 0

Gentlman that had Ale at se*	0	2	6
ffor 2 lode of straw for the Church hosen [houses]	0	12	0
ffor A honderd and halfe of bords	0	12	0
ffor lase and binders	0	4	0
heanry flors [Flowers?] for 2 day worke	0	1	0
Gdman grantom [Grantham] 5 dosn & halfe sparos	0	0	11
Thomas goof [Goff] ffor half duson of sparos	0	0	1
willam bucher [Butcher] for 6 duson of sparos and halfe	0	1	1
Charls nedle one duson of sparos	0	0	2
willam bucher for 3 duson of sparos	0	0	6
Jerimaya Carpentr 3 duson pf sparos	0	0	6
ffor fechin A lode of odde [lead?]	0	2	0
willam bucher 3 duson of sparos	0	0	6
Jerimaya Carpenter one duson & halfe of sparos	0	0	3
ffor Charges At the qurt [court] at malls [Maules]	1	9	10
for the paretr	0	4	6
ffor presenting the Chancel	0	1	0
Spent upon the paretr	0	1	8

[26] The visitation at the Peculiar Court of Banbury, which was the Bishop of Lincoln's jurisdiction

ffor pedle hose glason [*Peedle's house glasing*]the windows	0	9	2
willam gof for 4 heg hoges	0	1	4
ffor 3 duson of sparos	0	0	6
ffor 3 Lode of hame[27] At nedle hose	1	1	0
ffor 5 beroes [*barrows?*] of Lath	0	5	6
ffor 12 paire of Rafters	0	5	6
ffor 4 peces of rodde	0	7	0
John fathers 4 days worke	0	5	4
ffor 2 Lode of stons & Charegs	0	2	10
payd Eward watson for 4 days worke	0	3	4
willam dumtlon for 3 days & halfe	0	3	6
willam pedle for 3 days worke	0	2	0
payd willam pedle for thising & yoling [*teasing and oiling?*]	0	3	5
ffor A pece of oke	0	2	0
ffor 2 lod of stons & 2 lode of mortor	0	3	0
ffor 5 heg hogs	0	1	0
John wiot [*Wyatt*]for 3 heg hogs	0	1	0
John wiot for 1 heg hogs	0	0	4
John wiot for 4 heg hogs	0	1	4
John wiot for 1 heg hog	0	0	4
John wiot for 2 heg hogs	0	0	8
John wiot for 2 hegs hogs	0	0	8
ffor one heg hog	0	0	4
John wiot for 2 heg hogs	0	0	8
John wiot for 4 heg hogs	0	0	10
John poatrger [*Pargiter?*] for mendin the Clok	0	4	0
gave to A pore man that had A Lose bii ffoier [*loss by fire*]	0	1	6
John wiot for 2 heg hogs	0	0	6
John wiot for 6 heg hogs	0	1	2
ffor hinges & hoks for pedles hose	0	2	2

sume is £8 13 4

ffor logs & twigs for nedles hose	0	2	0
ffor making a dore for nedles hose	0	5	0
paid John wiot for one heg hogs	0	0	4
payd Thomas Rich for 2 doson & halfe of sparos	0	0	5
ffor 3 honderd & therty fott of bords	1	13	9
Thomas botler for one doson of sparos	0	0	2
moses Saryes for 6 duson of sparos	0	1	0

[27] This was haulm, the stalks of peas etc which were used as thatching straw.

ffor A boock	0	1	0
spend upon the pareter	0	0	8
spet upon the man that mended the Clok	0	0	8
spent of gonpor [*gunpowder*] Treson	0	3	0
payd george Clark for halfe year wages	0	5	0
ffor gres A bot the bels	0	1	5
ffor Ayoll [*oil*] for the Cloke	0	0	8
payd foll yeuegis [*full wages?*] for the bels Rops	1	2	6
gave to A pore man that had a Los At the fen	0	1	0
ffor Thomas kinc [*King*] for 3 doson of spars	0	0	6
John wotton for 3 douson of sparos	0	0	6
ffor 4 heg hogs	0	0	10
spent upon the plomer	0	1	0
spent upon the woman At the mill	0	1	0
Thomas ward work & Tember A bot the Church hosen	5	13	5
payd for the mason work of pedle hose	2	10	0
danel holfild one heg hog	0	0	4
gave A man with a Leter of Request	0	1	6
danel holfild one heg hog	0	0	4
danel holfild for 3 heg hogs	0	1	0
Smiths worke A bot the Church	0	2	4
ffor nue lether A bot the bels	0	1	6
John willams for mendin the bells	0	4	*
Smiths worke A bot the Church	0	7	3
Gonpoder Treson spent	0	3	0
spent upon the paretr	0	2	0
ffor 9 duson & A halfe of sparos	0	1	7
Eward willams for mendin the bels	0	2	6
Thomas ward for mendin the bels	0	1	0
ffor 3 duson & halfe of sparos	0	0	7
ffor ye whyer A bot the Clock	0	1	0
Thomas Jennings for 2 hondred of Coals	0	3	0
John Parish 2 days work at Church	0	1	4
to Richard hayns for menden the bel Claper and other worrk	0	13	10
ffor Caringe a load of Led to brackly	0	4	0
ffor bring a Load of Led back again	0	4	0
for caring som more Led to brackly	0	1	6
ffor expense at brackly	0	1	2
payd George Clarck half yare wages	0	5	0
illegible	0	5	0
Ester wine and bred	0	13	3

sume is   £*   8   *

INDEX OF NAMES

[Numbers in **bold** refer to pages in the Introduction]

INDEX OF SUBJECTS

[Figures in **bold** refer to pages in the Introduction]

INDEX OF PLACES
[Numbers in **bold** refer to pages in the Introduction]

I dedicate this book to my mother who encouraged me to read historical stories, my history teacher, Mabel Wooldridge, and my husband, John, for his support.

Doreen Rawsthorne

THE PRICE OF PEARLS

AUSTIN MACAULEY PUBLISHERS™

LONDON • CAMBRIDGE • NEW YORK • SHARJAH

A CIP catalogue record for this title is available from the British Library.

ISBN 9781528997386 (Paperback)
ISBN 9781528997393 (ePub e-book)

www.austinmacauley.com

First Published (2021)
Austin Macauley Publishers Ltd
25 Canada Square
Canary Wharf
London
E14 5LQ

Table of Contents

Chapter 1
Ravenwood

It was a beautiful September afternoon, the air warm but fresh, with a gentle breeze stirring the branches of the trees, and sending a ripple through the leaves. There was no sign of autumn that day when Felicity had decided to go for a walk. The strained atmosphere of the house disturbed her, and to avoid further encounters with her stepmother, she had suddenly decided to walk to the little copse at the end of the lane. She remembered it in bluebell time and thought longingly of the many spring days she had spent so happily there. She hadn't had much time last spring to enjoy it, as her father had written to say that he was bringing home a 'new mother' for her, and 'Would she see that everything was in order'. This meant that, together with Mrs Danvers and Cook, she had had the whole house spring-cleaned. Both Mrs Danvers and Cook knew what a new mistress would mean. Although the household was managed efficiently, a new mistress would be highly critical.

Ravenwood Manor was a comfortable establishment, and if they wanted to retain their positions, then the new mistress must be favourably impressed. Felicity had wondered what her 'new mother' would be like. Her own mother had died many years ago, and her father had seemed to accept the situation.

Last winter though, whilst in London seeing to family matters with his lawyer, he had met the Hon. Mrs Cecily Blake. To Felicity, it had seemed only a matter of weeks before her father had married this lady and changed his daughter's whole life. Felicity couldn't really resent this marriage, for she had never known her mother, but she knew that she would be unable to monopolise her father's attention as she had been used to doing, not that she imagined that the new Mrs Anderson would let her! Although she lived in the country, Felicity was no shy country girl. She had been well educated, and her father had insisted that she went to a very select finishing school for young ladies at Parkwood. The Misses Frobisher had certainly given her that 'finished' air, and she had been very disappointed that she too would not be staying in London for the season, but her father had promised her that she would have her debut next year. With this, Felicity was content for she realised that her father must have strained his finances in sending her to the Misses Frobisher. This select school for young ladies was indeed select, and most of the young ladies there had titles and took it for granted that they would be present at Court at the end of their stay. Felicity had been very happy there and had made many friends. She was a happy girl, and everyone enjoyed being with her. Her special friend was Lady Jane Douglas, and together they had made the year at Parkwood a time to remember with pleasure although they both knew that afterwards their lives would follow different paths. Lady Jane would be presented at Court and then return to her home in the North. Felicity would go home to Ravenwood, and perhaps be present at Court next season. They parted tearfully, Jane giving Felicity her London address, and insisting that she call on her if she were ever in London. As most girls of their age do, they pledged eternal friendship and promises were made never to forget each other. Felicity knew that in her case, she would always remember Jane, but knew, or thought she knew that they would rarely meet again. Jane was a truly beautiful young lady, almost regal in bearing, and with her sparkling personality, her golden hair and deep blue eyes, she was to break the hearts of many of the most eligible of young men she was to meet that season at Court.

With a sudden start, Felicity realised that she had dallied far too long and the sun had fallen low down in the sky. Suddenly a ray of sunshine broke through the clouds and picked up a sparrow-hawk just beginning to plummet down to seize its terrified victim from the ground. It was a startling, dramatic moment; the deadly, swift attack in a searchlight beam.

Instinctively she ran to the spot, but there was nothing there, yet miraculously, up above, a flying object still held in the moving beam against a darkening sky. It was an experience which she was to remember for a long time. The evening sky.

With a shudder, Felicity turned back along her path home. Climbing over the stile, she saw a fox slink along the hedgerow. Had the sparrow-hawk plucked the helpless victim from the fox's path? Perhaps if it was going to die, it was better to be the hawk's victim with instant death, rather than face the long moments of terror as the fox inexorably closed in.

Nature was cruel, but there was always a reason for everything.

Chapter 2
The Decision

Mrs Cecily Anderson had been in a fearful temper for the last few days. She had met Felicity's father, John Anderson, in London, and had taken the trouble to have a mutual friend introduce them, for he had the air of a wealthy, contented gentleman. She was the widow of the Hon. Robert Blake, who had not succeeded to his family's title or fortune, being the second son. Also, having poor health, he did not live long enough to succeed his elder brother, who succumbed to some fatal illness shortly after his brother, The Hon. Mrs Blake thus was foiled in her attempt to become the Countess of Lindsey.

There was no Countess of Lindsey at the moment, as her elder son, Jason, had inherited the title of *Earl of Lindsey* on his uncle's death, and he was not married. He had also declared that he had no intention of marrying yet, either! Therefore, the Hon, Mrs Blake had decided to look around and see if there were any eligible men around. Although John had told her that they would be living at Ravenwood, she had made him promise that they would come up to London at least once a year for the Season, and she was planning to find some reason to extend that season for as long as possible. Little did she know John Anderson!

He knew that one day Felicity would leave him to get married, and he would be alone in that large old manor house, so when he met Cecily, he decided that perhaps it would be better to provide for that day. He was obviously not marrying merely for companionship, for although Cecily was rather a chatterbox, she had a gracious air about her, and he was quite proud to be seen in her company. Therefore, John Anderson decided to take the plunge, not dreaming that she and Felicity would not like each other. To a man, the thought had not occurred that the two ladies – both used to being mistress of a household, for Felicity had certainly been that since her return from Parkwood – would not like the position. Felicity had done her best to agree to all her stepmother's ideas, but it had seemed as though her home was being altered out of all recognition. There had been the inevitable clash, and after two days of avoiding each other, Felicity decided that it could no longer remain a two-mistress household.

"Where can I go?" she cried in despair to her maid. "Meg."

"Your aunt in Gloucester would surely be pleased to see you, m'lady," said Meg, who had grown up with Felicity, being the daughter of Thomas, the gardener, who had been at Ravenwood for many, many years.

"No, she has enough to do with her family at the moment. I remember Father saying that she had written to him that the twins have the fever."

In vain, they both considered all the relatives who could possibly give Felicity a room, but one after one, they were crossed off the list.

"Meg, I've got it," exclaimed Felicity.

"I'll go to Jane. She will certainly help for a short time until she returns to the country. She will be in London now for the Season."

"Are you sure, m'lady, that Lady Jane will be in London, for didn't she say in her last note that she wasn't certain of going?" said Meg.

"Oh, Meg, don't spoil it! It's my only chance, as I cannot stay here a day longer." Desperately she clung to Meg. "I've got to take the risk, and if she isn't there, then I'll have to go to the Misses Frobisher and see if I can help out there."

With the decision made, Felicity knew immediately that she had to carry it through. If she didn't, then she would have to stay and allow her 'new mama' to change the home she loved into one which had no place for her. She immediately began to gather her thoughts and plan ahead. She knew that she couldn't really go for a few days as she had no means of getting to London by herself. In four days' time, there would be a chance to catch the coach from the next village, which was on the main coaching route to London.

Four days, how could she possibly keep out of her stepmother's way until then? Somehow she would have to avoid her and only speak to her when absolutely necessary. Meg would have to go to the village and find out the time of the coach and see if there would be a seat available. Perhaps it would be best to say that Meg would be travelling to see her sister who had been ill, and book it in her name. Then when it was discovered that she had run away, it would foil pursuit for a short time.

"But what will you do, Meg?" exclaimed Felicity, suddenly thinking of her maid who had been such a staunch ally in her lone fight.

"Well m' lady, it will perhaps turn out for the best, for you see Will the footman over at Sandshaw Lodge at Welksham asked me to marry him, and I've been keeping him waiting for his answer until I could tell you. I didn't rightly know how to tell you for I didn't want to leave you, my lady, whilst all this trouble was on."

"Meg! Oh, why didn't you tell me before," exclaimed Felicity.

"I couldn't have left you by yourself, m'lady," cried Meg. "We've been together for so long, and I don't like to see you so unhappy."

"I'm so very, very glad for you, Meg. I hope you'll both be so happy. You've been a good friend to me, and I know you'll make a wonderful wife for Will."

"Thank you, m'lady."

"Perhaps, then, we can work something out so that I can leave when you leave to go to Will," said Felicity.

"Oh, yes, m'lady," said Meg. "I'll send a note over to Will and let him know. I can leave here the same day as you, and we can get married by the parson in Welksham, so no one needs ever know in Stan Bourne. You can catch the coach at Stan Bourne and Will and I will be away at his sister's for our honeymoon. No one will ever know. Oh, m'lady, I'm so happy. I do hope you will be happy too. I'll be sorry to leave Ravenwood in one way, for I've had some happy times here – we've had some happy times, m'lady it doesn't seem the same anymore now, though."

"Now, Meg, don't make me cry, because if I think about it too much, I'll change my mind, and I mustn't do that. I can't; I won't stay with her! I won't ever come back here whilst she is at Ravenwood!"

"But what about your father, m'lady? You can't dislike him, now then, can you? You loved him before, so you must still love him! You won't stop coming here just because of her, surely? You must think of your father. He loves you, and I'm sure he'll be very distressed to hear you speak so," said Meg. "If he asks you to come back, you must come back to him."

"If Father is ill and really needs me," cried Felicity, "I'll come back to see him, but I'll not come back for her."

Happy that at least Felicity would come back to see her father, Meg gathered the cloak that was lying where Felicity had thrown it on returning from her walk, and put it away in the closet.

"I must decide what to take with me," said Felicity.

"Leave that to me, m'lady," said Meg. "I know just what you need, and you will not be able to take much – just a small trunk and a small bag to hold your jewellery and personal belongings."

With a sigh, Felicity drew her feet up under her on the comfortable chair in front of the warm fire which Meg had made in her room. The sky outside was black, and it looked as though there would be a storm soon.

Another storm, Felicity mused. Everywhere she went these days, there was stormy weather. Perhaps with Jane, she would find peace. She would certainly miss all this homely comfort of Ravenwood, but which was for the best? Only time could tell.

Chapter 3
Jason, Earl of Lindsey

Jason, Earl of Lindsey, approved of his mother's second marriage, not only because he liked John Anderson, but because he wanted her away from the London scene. Jason and his brother Claude knew their mother's failings, and whilst Jason did all he could to protect her from herself, Claude, the younger brother, played on her motherly feelings, and when he was in debt to fellow gamblers, which was often, she paid his debts and never chided him for the trouble he caused. Jason had inherited the Lindsey fortune with the earldom but gave his mother a comfortable allowance. Not too much because he knew Claude would just take it away from her once he knew how much she had and yet not too little because he was proud of his family name, and knew how his father had suffered through being the second son, and not always having enough for indulging his wife and children. Jason knew John Anderson would be a good steadying influence on his mother.

The estate of the former Earl of Lindsey, the Hon. Robert Blake's brother Charles, had been carefully restored by Charles and his father before him. Being Royalists, the family had suffered greatly many years ago at the hands of the

Cromwellian forces, and only on the Restoration of Charles II in 1660 had they had their estate restored to them. The property had been in very poor shape, and although Charles II had been generous, in those times, it had been difficult for the Lindsey family. However, over the following century, it had been carefully looked after, and Jason had inherited a beautiful manor house at Charnford and a very comfortable London home, where he stayed during the Season. He much preferred to be at Charnwood, but a London home was very convenient.

He was far away from both of those places at the moment. In fact, he was on the high seas! He was on His Majesty's ship 'Firefly', which had met him as arranged just off the coast of France that evening. Soon after he had gone aboard and they had got under sail, the wet sea mist had descended upon them and dogged them for most of the night, whilst they edged slowly up the channel. It was thicker than ever, and swirled around the black criss-cross of shrouds and rigging, and seemed to cling to the hull like dew. Beyond the nettings, with their neatly stowed hammocks, the sea was heaving in a deep offshore swell but was quite unbroken in the low breeze. It was dull, the colour of lead. Jason shivered and wondered what he was going to do for his mission in France had been a dismal failure.

As far as everyone knew, except a couple of his close friends, he had gone to Charnford for a couple of weeks.

However, as soon as they had gone a few miles along the road out of London, Jason and his two companions had split up. Patrick and Damian, or to be precise, the Hon. Patrick Lovelace and Damian, the Right Honourable Viscount Needham, had gone north to the Scottish capital whilst Jason had made his way to Falmouth to join the 'Firefly' as arranged by Castlereagh, the Tory Foreign Secretary.

Napoleon Bonaparte, Emperor of the French, had been devastating Europe and it was only a matter of time before he looked across the Channel at England. Jason had spent some years in France and could easily pass as a Frenchman. Therefore, a few years earlier, when Castlereagh had been in need of an agent who could slip backwards and forwards under the noses of the French, he had approached Jason one evening to seek his help in the matter.

Like most young men of that age, he had felt the need to do more than just spend the day and evening gambling, racing his horses and socialising with the ladies. What to do was a problem, and when approached by Castlereagh, he had jumped at the idea of doing something for his country, and also solve his problem of boredom by the spirit of adventure, excitement and secrecy, which the venture would obviously bring. Castlereagh had felt that for Jason by himself, it would be rather too risky, and he had asked him if he knew of any of his friends of a similar inclination. He had immediately thought of Damian, whom he had known since childhood and of Patrick, a friend from his days in France. Both these other young men could also speak French like natives, and were also capable of making split-second decisions. Castlereagh had made it a rule that the three of them would never be abroad at the same time, and only Castlereagh and the captain of the 'Firefly', Captain Thelwall, knew their identity. It was decided that when one was abroad, then the other two would make a journey somewhere in England, Scotland or Wales, and thereby provide an alibi for the other companion in France.

This time it had been Jason's turn to go to Brest in Brittany, but it had been an utter failure, for the agent he had been sent to meet and collect vital information from had not turned up at the assigned rendezvous.

He had, however, kept another appointment – with his Maker – and Jason was wondering exactly how much information had been passed to Napoleon's spies before Monsieur Richard had met his end.

Jason glanced towards the short, rotund shape of the ship's captain. His worn, heavy coat was buttoned up to his several chins so that in the strange light, he looked like a round blue ball. He was white-haired and had it tied at the nape of his neck in an old-fashioned queue. Jason knew that he could rely on Captain Thelwall for the captain had a deep-rooted hatred of the French. His only son had been killed in action with the French off Brest some years earlier. Michael had been his only son, his wife having died at Michael's birth, and when his son was killed, the captain had been ready to tackle any French vessel, whatever the size. One of the agents had heard of this revenge-seeking captain, and when he approached Captain Thelwall, he had an immediate ally for Castlereagh's projected venture for Jason and his friends.

Captain Thelwall knew every cove and inlet around Falmouth and for several miles in both directions. Even so, memory could play tricks, especially in such foul murky weather, and although Jason trusted the captain's memory, he preferred to stay on deck.

Jason swung round as a shaft of sunlight, pierced the swirling mist and touched the quarterdeck with gold. The big topsails flapped loudly, and the deck tilted to a sudden pressure of wind, and like an army of departing ghosts, the mist seeped through the shrouds and moved clear of the ship. He knew that Captain Thelwall would have managed to bring the ship as near to Falmouth as possible, but he was not prepared for the sudden sight of green fields stretching as far as eye could see, coming alive in the early morning sunlight. St. Anthony's beacon, usually the first sight of home to a returning sailor, was just where it should be, and slightly to larboard. With a silent sigh of relief, Jason went below to get his few belongings, for he knew that shortly a boat would put out to meet him, and he would begin his long ride back to London.

It was one of the annoyances of this whole scheme. He liked riding, but at the end of a sea voyage, which he rarely enjoyed, he was usually too tense to enjoy the hurried journey back to London. If his mission had been a success, it was sometimes a relief to be able to breathe in the fresh country air and get rid of the salt from his lips, but today, well, he knew that he did not have good news for Castlereagh.

That one of his French agents had been killed, and perhaps tortured to give away valuable secrets, was rather unnerving. Jason knew that the whole future of the operation was at stake. In a way, he wondered whether it was time he got out of it before he too was caught, but the thought of the London Season and the eternal round of debutantes and their grasping mothers was far worse to Jason than the thought of being captured and thrown in a French prison.

Down below in the small cabin, Jason paused to study himself in a mirror that hung on the bulkhead. The dark shadows under his eyes and the dark stubble just showing round his chin did nothing to detract from his rugged good looks. His dark-blue eyes and black wavy hair had caused many a young debutante and her mother to go weak at the knees, but he never deliberately got entangled with one of the debutantes. One smile too many and mothers would be talking, not that he didn't like the right female company, but to his way of thinking, it was rarely found at Court.

He had told his mother he had no intention of marrying, and at the time he had meant it, but during these lonely nights on the high seas, or in some remote French inn, he had occasionally wondered what it would be like to have a wife waiting at home for him. After these last two missions, he had taken more than his usual flippant once – over of his female acquaintances and had tried to see any of them in the role he was thinking of for them. None of them seemed to be right. Most of them were beautiful and rich, with fond Mamas dangling many enticements before him, but there was not that mystical something which created the magic that would make him want to come back to a wife. He flattered them, complimented them, teased them, and flirted with them, but never once could they say that he had said anything at all serious to them. He was accepted as one of the usual crowd of lordly young bucks who followed the Regent around, and aped his manners. Not that this was anything to recommend the young men of that time, but to Mamas trying to find husbands for spoilt, pretty daughters, to catch a member of the first ton for a husband was the aim of their season.

Just before Castlereagh had approached them the last time, which had sent Jason on this futile journey, Damian had broken the news that he had got himself engaged! Patrick and Jason were both amazed for Damian was a quiet, reserved person who rarely sought the ladies' attention. However, his grandfather had been close friends with the Marquess of

Queensdown, whose son was Lord James Douglas. Lord James had a daughter, Jane, and so when Lady Jane had been presented at Court last Season, the two grandfathers had conspired together with the result that a 'chance meeting' had brought Damian and Jane together. Damian's father had some years earlier, so there was a closeness between Damian and his grandfather. Damian needed no persuasion from his grandfather to marry Jane, and so both families were very happy when the young couple announced their news. To Jason and Patrick, though, it seemed the end of their venture, and on his ride through the Devon countryside, Jason was wondering if Castlereagh had managed to find another companion. Damien had gone to the country with Patrick, but he had been promised by Castlereagh that he would not be sent abroad again. For the time being, Patrick and Jason must share the trips to Europe. Neither of them minded this, for they both had no real reason to stay in England. Jason had his mother and his brother, and Patrick was the only child of elderly parents. He would one day inherit a fine estate in Norfolk, but he was not looking forward to this yet. He knew that when that happened, he would have to stay at home and get married to provide an heir for the future, so he lived for today and tomorrow looked after itself.

Chapter 4
Plans are Made

Felicity had made her plans and Meg had got in touch with Will, who had, in turn, arranged with the Minister that they should be married on the day the coach would take Felicity to London.

"Have we forgotten anything, Meg?" asked Felicity anxiously.

"No, m'lady, I've picked out the cloak and dresses you will be taking, and ordered the carriage to take us to Stan Bourne in time to catch the London coach. Have you decided which jewellery to take with you, m'lady?"

"I think I'll take the sapphire necklace, which was my mother's, and the diamond and ruby brooch Father gave me for my last birthday," said Felicity.

"What about your mother's pearls?" Meg asked.

"Father has those in his safe, and it will be too difficult to get them, although they are mine, and Father was going to give them to me for my eighteenth birthday. I should love to take them with me, but it is far too risky to ask Father for them. He would be suspicious because he told me only last week that I should have them for my 18th birthday."

"Never mind, m' lady, perhaps by your 18th birthday, you will be back here at Ravenwood, and your father will let you have them as planned."

"Do you think so, Meg?" said Felicity wistfully.

"I hope so, for I do not wish to be away from Father, but it is impossible to go on and on like this. It isn't as if I ever meet anyone eligible. Father keeps saying that someday I shall marry, but who do I ever meet who will marry me?"

"Not that odious Mr Richards, but my stepmother would like that because he has a fortune, and she will be rid of me. I hate him – he's so short and fat, with such terrible bad breath. He always smells of the port, and I'm sure he's got gout. Oh, Meg, can you possibly see me married to him?"

"No, m'lady, and it may be that in London with Lady Jane, you will meet one of those handsome beaus. I hear that there are some fine young lords in London these days, and that the Prince Regent encourages them to dress in such a magnificent manner."

Felicity smiled at this because she knew that Lady Jane would attract many of these young bucks, and she would just stay in the background. She did not know yet, of course, that Lady Jane was affianced. Whilst Lady Jane had golden hair, Felicity had dark curly hair, which often made her cry in rage for it just would not lie flat and lie smoothly round her face. She, therefore, found it best to let it fall freely to her shoulders, and she pinned it up for the evening. She had green eyes, which was unusual for a brunette, and the unusual combination resulted in many an admiring glance.

A couple of days later, her stepmother announced that both her sons would be coming to visit them and that they would both be arriving in time for dinner that evening.

Felicity had met Claude and disliked him immediately. She found his sickly compliments made her most uncomfortable, and she avoided his company as often as possible. Claude had been down quite often, usually to get his mother to pay his debts and keep the debt collectors away from his door. His mother adored him and as usual was completely blind to his faults. She was always pleased to see him and went to a great deal of trouble to make sure that Cook had his favourite dishes for him. She also insisted that Mrs Danvers had his room kept ready all the time and he didn't need to give any notice of his coming. Her other son, though, had never been to Ravenwood, and it was to her surprise that a message was received the same morning as Claude's, to say that he would be breaking his journey to call and see his Mama and her new husband.

Jason had, in fact, been in France when his mother had married Mr Anderson, and had only met him by accident when Mr Anderson had gone up to London for a few days a month or so after his marriage to finalise the details of his new will now that he had married. Jason liked Mr Anderson, and it was really to improve his acquaintance with him that he had accepted Mr Anderson's invitation to join them when next possible at Ravenwood.

He had no idea that his brother was also to be there, so it came as a shock to him to pass his brother's curricle at an inn a few miles outside Stan Bourne. Claude had, in fact, stayed at that inn overnight because he had left London in a hurry and didn't want to make it too obvious to his mother, from whom he anticipated getting enough funds to calm his debtors. Jason didn't normally encourage too close a friendship with Claude.

Their personalities were so very different, and Jason found it took him all his time to stop himself interfering in Claude's affairs. He felt that Claude was old enough to get himself out of the trouble he was old enough to get himself into. He thought the best way to rid Claude of his bad habits was to rescue him only from anything which would bring shame to the family, and it was up to Claude to sort out his own problems.

Claude, too, had no idea that his brother was on his way to his mother's new home, and it was, therefore, a shock to see Jason's well-cut figure standing in the doorway of the inn. At first, Jason couldn't see Claude in the dull light of the inn, and it gave Claude those few seconds to compose his features. When Jason's eyes became accustomed to the gloom, he could see Claude sitting at a round table with a jug of ale before him. The landlord could see immediately that Jason was a cut above his usual customer and immediately began to enquire of his visitor's requirements and offer the hospitality of his humble inn. However, Jason had no intention of staying much longer than necessary, and on finding that Claude had the same destination, they both immediately left and travelled the few remaining miles together.

Chapter 5
Claude Finds a Solution

Felicity decided on hearing that her stepmother's two sons were coming to stay at Ravenwood to plead a sick headache that evening. She had no intention of meeting Claude if she could help it. She also presumed that Jason would be just as odious as Claude and therefore thought that the two of them would be too much. Her father was very disappointed on hearing of Felicity's indisposition. He too, didn't hold a very good opinion of Claude, but liked Jason very much. He thought it would do Felicity good to meet such an interesting person. Of course, he did not know just how interesting Jason could be or the stories he could tell. Jason was dressed in the latest fashion and to all intents and purposes was a handsome buck and a man about town, and John Anderson thought that Felicity would be interested to hear of the gay adventures of the Regent's circle. However, that evening Felicity had her way and she was delighted that she could stay in her room. Tomorrow was the big day, and she needed plenty of sleep as she knew there was a long hazardous journey ahead of her. She had heard of highwaymen but never seen any. Stan Bourne was a delightful village tucked away in the depths of the country, and apart from a few places like Ravenwood

Manor, there was little to interest highwaymen. Never the less the journey to London would cross many of their haunts, and so Meg had sewn a hidden pocket into the gown Felicity would wear to keep her money and most precious jewels safe.

After a most successful dinner for which John Anderson sent his praises to his Cook, he and his two stepsons sat drinking their port. The conversation for some reason, turned to the remoteness of the area and the safety of Ravenwood and its contents. John Anderson chuckled and said that there was nothing of value to thieves in his house. There were one or two fine paintings and some silver, but he didn't think it worthwhile for thieves to come all the way to Ravenwood Manor for those few items.

"Of course, at the moment there are the pearls which Felicity will have on her 18th birthday. There are few pearls, even in London, to match these. My grandfather was a jeweller to Queen Anne, and she presented them to my grandmother on their wedding day. Felicity will get these on her 18th birthday, but I have them here at the moment. I brought them back with me from London on my last visit. They need a new clasp, unfortunately, so I shall have to take them back again. Fortunately, there is some time yet before her birthday."

"It would indeed be an honour to see these pearls," said Claude. "There is nothing finer than a good string of pearls to enhance a woman's beauty, eh, Mr Anderson?"

"Exactly, Claude," agreed John Anderson, "and I shall be delighted to show them to you. They are in my study. Would you like to come along and see them?"

These pearls were indeed a prize possession of the Anderson family, and John Anderson was very proud of them.

They all went along to his study, and he brought them out of his safe.

There was a beautiful luminous glow from the pearls, and Jason confirmed he had never seen their equal except in the Royal circle. John Anderson put them away carefully and safely and they joined his wife in the drawing room. The evening was spent quietly, and after a game of backgammon and some musical entertainment from their mother, the two sons retired to their rooms, both pleading fatigue from a long journey that day. This was not true for Claude, but Jason had travelled many miles over the past few days and he was beginning to feel the effect. Jason soon fell asleep, but Claude sat in his room and pondered over his many problems.

Ha had the usual debts, but last week he had succumbed to the charms of a young lady and had foolishly agreed to set her up in a quiet pied-a-terre. Where he was going to get the money from, he had no idea.

The pearls had given him an idea, but how could he possibly get hold of them and throw suspicion elsewhere. Perhaps he could just take them and hide them safely until the alarm had died down and then take his leave from his fond mama and slip away. That jeweller in Shaftesbury Road would certainly give him a good price for them if they were as good as John Anderson had led him to believe, for the time being.

That was something he would have to assume for having made his plans, he slipped quietly downstairs. John Anderson and his wife had also gone to bed and there was no light showing anywhere.

Claude slipped into the study and drawing back the curtains, he could see the safe in the moonlight. He had taken a mental note of how John Anderson had opened the safe and where they kept the key. Opening one of the desk drawers he found the safe key and stealthily turning it in the safe lock, he opened the door, and there were the pearls! The dark blue case was there before him, and all his problems were solved! Quickly, he checked that the pearls were in the case, and he put them in his pocket. He relocked the safe and put the key back. He reckoned the safe would not be opened again for a few hours, at least until the next day, and so he returned to his room. He then undressed and got into bed. One can imagine the thoughts churning over and over again in his head, but he finally managed to get some sleep.

The next morning, he was awakened by the maid, Lucy, drawing back his curtains.

He suddenly remembered his midnight visit to the study and hurriedly looked around the room. Were the pearls out of sight? Where had he put them? No sooner had these thoughts gone through his mind, than he remembered all what he had done. To cover his nervousness, he loudly exclaimed what a lovely morning it was and that he would go for a walk before his breakfast. He had planned to get up earlier and go for a walk, but perhaps it was as well not to do anything too unusual. He had often gone for a morning walk to get the fresh air before partaking of a hearty breakfast during his other visits. Dressing quickly, he hastened down the stairs and went out through the small side door into the small walled garden. Thomas, the gardener, greeted him, and Claude returned it – full of the joys of living, for he was continually thinking of how his problems were solved.

He intended to put the pearls, which he had wrapped in a piece of cloth, into a cavity, which he had found one morning when he had taken a similar walk. It was behind a loose stone in the stone wall running along the lane past the lodge. For the time being, he would have to leave them there whilst the hue and cry was on. It was certainly the best place he could think of away from the house and any search.

Returning to the house, he met Jason, who had also been for a walk, but in a different direction. Together they sat down for breakfast and planned what to do. Claude had no intention of being left in the house by himself that day, for when the theft was discovered, it would be as well if he had been with someone else for most of the time. Jason would be an excellent alibi; however, he managed better than that as Mr Anderson himself suggested that they all spend the day together. He thought they might like to ride around his small estate, perhaps calling for lunch at the 'Four Feathers' inn at Helmswick. This suited both Jason and Claude, and so off they all went. Everything was falling into place, and Felicity and Meg, too were keeping their eyes on the clock. At two o'clock, the carriage drew up at the side door. Mrs Anderson had retired for a nap following her lunch, the housekeeper, cook and the maids were all occupied, so Felicity and Meg slipped away quietly.

Chapter 6
The Theft Discovered

"An excellent day, sir," said Jason to Mr Anderson. "It was a pleasure to see such a well-kept estate, and I only hope that my place at Charnford will be as interesting to you when you come to visit."

"I am sure it will be, Jason," replied Mr Anderson. "I am looking forward very much to visiting Charnford, and I am sure Felicity, too, will be delighted to see it."

"I hope so, and perhaps we shall have the pleasure of meeting your daughter and our stepsister this evening, sir," Jason said politely.

"Yes, I expect she will be down this evening. I am sure her slight indisposition will have disappeared by now."

Claude was very quiet because he realised that very soon the storm would break, and that he must keep calm and not let anything ruffle him. He could quite easily let something slip when upset, so he must concentrate on being careful tonight. Perhaps it would be as well not to drink as much as usual.

Later that evening, when the gentlemen had gathered in the library for a sherry before dinner, Mrs Anderson burst into the room. Ladies, even the mistress of the household, were not expected to invade the sanctum prior to dinner at Ravenwood.

Mr Anderson had kept this small habit of his, and he had invited the young men to join him there.

"Mr Anderson, oh, something dreadful has happened!" she exclaimed.

"Madam, please, calm yourself! It surely cannot be that bad," Mr Anderson said soothingly.

"It's Felicity and her maid, Meg," she cried. "They have both gone!"

"Gone, both gone where?" Mr Anderson asked in a daze. "What can you mean?"

"Mother, now calm yourself and speak slowly," said Jason. "We cannot do anything until you tell us everything."

"Mrs Danvers found a note from Meg saying that she was leaving to get married. She went to see if Felicity knew anything of it, and found that Felicity had gone too. Felicity's travelling cloak, some of her dresses and her jewels have gone too. The sapphire necklace and the ruby and diamond brooch, in particular, seem to be missing. Oh, dear, where can she have gone?" she cried.

"Her jewels!" whispered her stunned father.

Mrs Anderson sobbed. "What about the pearls? Who knew of the forthcoming present? She hasn't taken those with her, has she?"

Claude, in the meantime, couldn't believe his ears. Here was a wonderful escape for him. Ever since he had entered the library, he had realised that he had made one serious mistake – he had not left any clues pointing to an outsider. He should have broken a windowpane or forced the window lock, but in the rush, he had forgotten to do this. *Now,* thought Claude, *Felicity would be blamed.* Heaven knows why she has run off, but the errant girl could take all the blame. At least until she was found, but by that time, Claude planned to be a long way away.

"Perhaps it would be as well to check if the pearls are still there, sir," he suggested to Mr Anderson.

"I'm sure she wouldn't take them. She knows how valuable they are. They are family heirlooms," said her father.

Mr Anderson just could not believe that his little Felicity could have run off just like that. *Why, why should she? They all got on well together, or so* he thought. Perhaps she didn't like living in the depth of the countryside after her stay in London. But no, that couldn't be so, because she would have said something to him. They could talk to each other on such matters, John Anderson knew. She had only said something last week about loving the country and hoping it never changed.

What was it that had made her leave home? He wasn't wealthy, but he was certainly comfortably well off, and if she had wanted to live in London, he would have done his utmost for her. Not necessarily live himself in London, because he didn't want to do that, but some solution could have been found. No, there must be something else!

In a daze, he found the key to the safe, and when he opened it and saw the empty case, he broke down.

"There must be some reason," he sobbed. "Felicity just would not do this to me. Where can she be?"

Jason and Claude both knew that there wasn't much that could be done that night. It was dark and if she had run away, she would be a long way away by now. Checking with the housekeeper, they discovered that she had heard a carriage and horses leave the place during the early afternoon.

She had been half asleep when she heard it, and until then had completely forgotten it. She had not missed Meg because Meg usually stayed in Felicity's room during the afternoon doing her sewing and repairs to Felicity's clothes.

Jason and Claude managed to get both Mr Anderson and his wife to take some nourishment, and promised them that they would both ride in search of the runaway girl at first light tomorrow morning.

The following morning saw an upset household. Meg had lived in the house since she was a child, and her father, the gardener, was upset that she had done off to get married without a word to him.

The horses of the two young men were saddled ready for them to ride in search of Felicity and Meg, and after a hurried breakfast, they both rode off. Jason went to Stan Bourne and Claude in the other direction.

Meg and Felicity had not intended to cover their tracks too well, as they felt it wiser that some indication was left of their general direction. They knew that Meg's marriage would soon be found out and also that Felicity was not with her. Felicity planned to write to her father when she reached Jane's, but until then, she didn't want to give too much cause for concern, but she wanted some time to get far enough away to avoid being brought back home.

When Jason enquired at the inn, the local farrier recollected seeing Felicity around the time of the London coach passing through. Further enquiries confirmed that a young lady had in fact, got on the coach, but at first, it was not possible to know whether it was Meg or Felicity.

Jason was used to making discreet enquiries, and on hearing that Meg had been keeping company with a footman from Sandshaw Lodge at Welksham, he rode over there. Will, the footman, had not kept secret the fact that he was marrying Meg, so Jason was soon able to establish what had happened. He was not able to find the happy couple, though, so when he returned to Ravenwood, he was quite confident that it was, in fact, Felicity who had taken the London coach and not Meg.

Claude fortunately for him had had no need to lie. He had gone the way, which was entirely opposite in direction to the escape route, and his enquiries had therefore met with no luck. Jason's findings were, therefore, as certain as could be.

"We must wait for a letter or some news perhaps from a relative," said Mr Anderson, who had revived a little. His colour was not very good, and the shock had hit him badly.

"Perhaps she has gone to her aunt. In which case, we will soon hear from her," said Mrs Anderson reassuringly. Her conscience was pricking her greatly. She knew that she had made Felicity's life rather uncomfortable over the past few months. She had not done it on purpose. She had been very disappointed that she would not be able to have her own way with Mr Anderson as she had hoped. He was not as rich as she thought. He was comfortably well off, but any extra expense, such as a house in London for the purpose of extending their stay there indefinitely, except for the summer when they would not be expected to stay in London, but go to Brighton with the Prince Regent's circle, was impossible.

Then really Ravenwood would be ideal to escape the uncomfortable heat which always seemed worse in London; that was, if they couldn't go to Brighton with the Court.

However, she had now come to realise that her dream would not come true, and she had been angry for a time. She knew that Mr Anderson loved the countryside and his thoughts all the time whilst in London was of Ravenwood.

She, too, had come to like Ravenwood eventually, and she was now thinking how it must have been for Felicity to see her changing everything around. She must have been upset. Mrs Anderson was not really a hard woman, and indeed she could be very compassionate. Down problems had pushed all other things into the background. She now regretted her earlier attitude to Felicity and promised herself that she would mend her ways when Felicity got back. She thought that Felicity would soon be back and that she had just gone to stay for a few days with her aunt following their recent disharmony, and taken the pearls in a fit of pique. Never in all her thoughts did she think that Felicity intended to stay away forever.

In fact, no one at Ravenwood expected that. They all knew how much she loved Ravenwood. It was, however, for that reason that Felicity had run away. She loved Ravenwood too much to bear seeing it changed.

Chapter 7
London

When Meg left Felicity to get on the coach, she rode off with Will to his sister's home and as planned, were married soon afterwards. They went off on their short honeymoon hoping that Felicity had got to her friend in London safely.

Felicity was rather apprehensive when she saw Meg going away, but she was determined not to go back to Ravenwood. The driver had put her small trunk with the rest of the baggage of the other passengers, and she had climbed into the small space waiting for her. She looked around at her companions and was relieved to see that no one else had got on the coach at Stan Bourne. That was one thing that had been worrying her, and she had planned to say that she was visiting a sick relative.

Thankfully, she relaxed as best she could and watched the countryside slipping by. None of the other passengers was very interesting, being mainly ordinary country folk going to the city. Meg had thoughtfully provided Felicity with some refreshment, and when some of the other passengers started to bring out some food, Felicity thought it best to follow suit, in case her difference was noticed.

When the coach finally reached London, it was going dusk, and Felicity looked around rather helplessly. She did not know where the coach had stopped or where Jane lived in relation to it, so when all her companions had disappeared into the fading light, the coach driver realised that Felicity was still there. Felicity asked him if he knew where Grosvenor Square was, but he didn't rightly know, so he, in turn, asked one of the young lads who had been unloading the passengers' baggage.

He gave directions, and when Felicity began to walk, struggling with her small trunk, they were all horrified.

"M'lady, you cannot walk there. It isn't safe for young ladies to be walking around London at night."

By her speech, the coach driver had guessed that she was no ordinary servant, and thought that perhaps she was a governess just arriving in London.

"Is there a carriage I can hire to take me there, please," asked Felicity timidly. She had a sinking feeling in her stomach, and she was thinking about all kinds of things.

The coach driver said something to one of the young boys, and he disappeared.

"Young Torn has just gone to get you one," he replied.

Within minutes, young Tom was back, and there was a small closed carriage, with a very fat man sitting on the box, holding the reins in one hand and lifting his hat with his other.

"Grosvenor Square, Milady. Certainly. Jacobs will get there in no time," he wheezed.

"Oh, thank you very much," Felicity said, putting a coin in the young lad's grubby hand.

She climbed into the carriage, and her small trunk was also put inside with her, and off they went at a most alarming rate. Felicity was quite worried but had to accept it, for she had no idea where she was going.

The carriage stopped suddenly, and with a rap on the roof, Jacobs said, "Grosvenor Square, m'lady. What number was he wanting?"

"Number seventeen, please."

The horse jogged a few steps and Jacobs announced their arrival at the number.

Felicity was relieved to see that lanterns were lit at the entrance to the house, and she paid Jacobs. She expected him to unload her small trunk, but it seemed that he was glued on his perch, so she dragged her trunk out of the carriage, which immediately moved off. She looked hesitantly at the door and plucked up her courage. There were six steps to climb, and so she left her trunk on the pavement.

She pulled the bell, and immediately a most haughty looking footman opened the door, and he had great difficulty in saying, "Servants' entrance round the back, young lady," and almost shut the door in Felicity's face.

"Stop," she cried, "I'm no servant. I wish to see Lady Jane Douglas. I'm a close friend of hers. Please!" she entreated.

"Please tell her that Miss Felicity Anderson is here and would like to speak to her."

The door was opened again much wider this time by the footman, who drew back uncertainly. He could see now that he looked properly that she didn't look like a maidservant, although she was dressed in quiet clothes. She knew she had arrived at a most unusual time and without any warning, so she took no notice of the footman's manner. However, the footman decided that rather than risk any trouble from his master and young mistress, he had better ask her inside.

"I do apologise, m'lady. Will you kindly come this way?" he said. "I shall inform Lady Jane that you are here. I expect she will be getting ready for dinner, but she will be informed immediately of your arrival."

He motioned to a servant to bring in her trunk, and he showed her into a small room just off the main hall.

She looked around her. Thankfully she sat down on a beautiful apple green satin-covered chair, and took in just how luxurious were her surroundings – glittering chandeliers, polished furniture, silver sconces and gilt-framed pictures. Jane did indeed live in comfort, and perhaps she would not want her to stay with her. No, that would not be, she said to herself. They had been good friends, and Jane had no need to be ashamed of her friend. She hadn't indeed, and as soon as Jane's maid passed her the message of Felicity's arrival, she brushed aside her maid's protestations and ran down the stairs to the small drawing room. "Felicity, how wonderful," she cried and threw her arms around her.

"Jane, thank goodness you are here. I just hoped you would still be in London. All the way here, I've been praying that you would be here."

"All the way to London! Goodness, you've not just arrived from Stan Bourne surely," exclaimed Jane. "Why you poor thing, you must be exhausted and famished. Come, you must go with my maid, and when you've rested and freshened yourself, you must tell me why you are here. I'll send some food on a tray to you, and when you are ready, Betsy will tell you where to find me."

Felicity could have cried with relief, but she held back her tears and clinging to Jane, they climbed the stairs and Betsy,

Jane's maid showed her into a room which was next door to Jane's.

Felicity woke with a start. She looked around her?

She sat up quickly and then realised where she was in a bedroom of the most unbelievable luxury. Her bed was hung with white and gold brocade against pale blue walls.

The carpet was eggshell blue, and the silver and blue hangings at the windows completed the picture.

Her trunk had been unpacked, and everything was laid ready for her to use. Her hairbrush had been put on the dressing table, and at that moment, intuitively, Betsy put her head around the door.

"Are you awake, my lady? Breakfast will be served in the dining room shortly. Shall I help you to dress?"

Felicity looked amazed.

"Breakfast! Good heavens, have I slept all night?"

She remembered feeling drowsy after eating her supper, which Betsy had brought to her, and in fact, Betsy had put her to bed soon after. The tension and the long journey had finally told their own story. Now she must get up and explain to Jane why she was here.

"Thank you, Betsy. If you would help me, I shall be down immediately for breakfast."

Quickly, Felicity dressed, and Betsy brushed her hair. She had a quick look to check that the jewels were still in the pocket, which Meg had made for her, and she was relieved to find them still there. She left them there for the time being, and when she knew whether Jane would allow her to stay with her, she would ask Jane's father to put them away safely for her. She followed Betsy down to the dining room, and Jane greeted her like a long-lost sister.

"Are you feeling better after your long sleep, Felicity?" she inquired, and with a laugh, they both slipped into that easy companionship they had enjoyed at the Misses Frobisher's.

Felicity explained to Jane why she had come to London and left Ravenwood. Jane was speechless. It was the last thing she expected of Felicity, but she knew how much Felicity loved Ravenwood and that to see things changed would upset her.

"You must stay here as long as you like, Felicity," said Jane. "I'm sure my parents will agree, when they return. Oh, how marvellous it will be for both of us to be together again. You will be here too for my wedding. Oh, how exciting. You can certainly be my bridesmaid now, and there is nothing to stop it."

Jane was so excited and Felicity too when she heard of Jane's marriage. Jane told her of how wonderful Damian was and how they had met, how they fell in love, where they were going to live, what dresses she had bought, and so many, many things which girls talk about at times like this.

Time went by quickly that morning, and Felicity was so relieved that Jane didn't mind her coming to stay with her. However, one thing that Jane thought Felicity should do, and that was to write to her father telling him where she was. Felicity agreed that perhaps it was wise to do this, and so it was settled that she would write to her father, explaining why she had left and that she would be staying with Jane for a time. No dates were given for a return, and both girls thought that perhaps this was the best way.

Jane had to go to Miss Tyson's, her milliner that afternoon. She had promised to visit her to see a new collection of bonnets which had been delivered to the Bruton

Street salon that morning. When Jane saw how few dresses Felicity had brought with her, she suggested that perhaps she would like to go to Jane's dressmaker.

"You must have a dress to go to the ball next week at the Marchioness of Queensdown's. Damian will insist on you going to it with us. It will be so exciting, and there will be every one of importance coming to it. Even the Regent has promised to come, so you must get a dress for it." Felicity agreed and was thankful that she had brought some money with her. Jane, though, was insistent that the ball gown was a present from her, and it was to no avail that Felicity tried to refuse it. Felicity realised, of course, that if she was to stay in London for a time in the same social circle as Jane, she would have to be careful with her money. Once her father knew where she was, she knew he would send her some money, but she didn't want to have to write asking him for more. She knew Jane was a very wealthy young lady in her own right, having been left a fortune by her aunt, so she didn't feel too badly at accepting the ball gown from her. At Miss Tyson's, Jane chose a beautiful Angouleme bonnet of white thread net, trimmed with tiny pink roses. There was also a most extravagant bonnet, which Jane insisted on buying for Felicity. It was of the palest sea-green satin, with a huge upstanding poke, with cascades of curled plumes in shades of green, from the palest and most delicate green to the deep green of pine needles. Jane saw immediately how it emphasised Felicity's beautiful green eyes. They arranged for the bonnets to be sent round to Grosvenor Square, and then they set off in their carriage to Jane's dressmaker, Miss Starkey in Conduit Street.

They were greeted with delight as Jane had been a very good customer, and especially since she announced engagement to Viscount Needham. When she heard that Felicity was going to be her bridesmaid and that she also wanted a dress for the grand ball being held by the Marchioness of Queensdown, she fluttered and exclaimed in delight. Instantly she knew just the thing for Felicity.

"I think this new gown will be just right for my lady!" she exclaimed with positive rapture. Both girls fell in love with it immediately, and when Felicity tried it on, she was transformed. Beautiful.

She knew then that she was in white silk, trimmed with delicate silver and gold lace, with pale pink roses round the hemline. The material was gathered into a tiny bustle, which then fell into folds to the floor. The neckline was quite low, and at first, Felicity demurred, but Miss Starkey insisted that it was all the rage and was quite the latest fashion.

They went on to choose many other things, including a fabulous ermine trimmed green velvet cloak for Felicity to wear over her dress to the ball.

The girls then returned home and excitedly opened the parcels which Miss Starkey had wrapped for them. A beautiful pair of delicate lilac kid gloves for Jane, with a matching parasol, and for Felicity a pale green walking dress trimmed with swansdown, and a matching muff, which she would be wearing with the beautiful bonnet from Miss Tyson's. There were many other ribbons and trimmings which they had chosen, and soon they were talking about Jane's wedding.

Jane had chosen a white satin dress with embroidered panels on the skirt and around the hem, of pearls and diamonds. The dress had long sleeves that were trimmed with lace with pearls entwined in it. Her veil was a family heirloom of Bruges lace.

Her excitement communicated itself to Felicity, and soon the two girls were engrossed in it. Lady Douglas had, in the meantime, arrived at her London home, and Jane introduced Felicity to her mama, who was delighted to meet her, but upset for her that it was under such circumstances. She knew how much their friendship had meant to her daughter, and she reiterated her daughter's invitation to Felicity to stay as long as she liked, and she approved the writing of the letter to Felicity's father. She intended to follow it up with one of her own, confirming that Felicity was in the care of their family.

Lady Douglas had been visiting some friends outside London and was delighted to tell Jane that she had met Damian returning to London and that he would be calling to see her tomorrow. Jane was so excited because she hadn't seen Damian for a few weeks, he having been away for Castlereagh in the country whilst Jason had been abroad, but of course, Jane didn't know all this.

"You will like Damian, Felicity; I'm sure you will," exclaimed Jane.

"I know I will," said Felicity, who had heard so much of this wonderful person from Jane. "If you like him so much and he sounds wonderful, then we shall be very good friends too."

They soon retired to change for dinner, and Felicity wondered how formal it would be as Lord Douglas had also returned with Lady Douglas, and she did not know what kind of a household was kept whilst his Lord and Ladyship were in residence. Betsy soon calmed her fears, though, as she said that unless there were visitors, and Felicity was now considered to be one of the family, that everyone would change for dinner, but formalities were kept to the minimum.

Betsy helped her to change to her pale blue silk dress, which enhanced her beautiful complexion, and she arrived downstairs with Jane just in time as dinner was announced by Hawkins, the butler.

Felicity was used to good simple country food, for although the cook at Ravenwood would have liked to experiment with lobsters and such things, John Anderson preferred simple food, and so Felicity was more used to that.

The Douglas's cook apparently was used to entertaining on an elaborate scale. Indeed the Prince of Wales had once dined at 17 Grosvenor Square before becoming Prince Regent – such was the fame of the Douglas's cook.

Now though, the meal was a simple repast of asparagus soup, followed by pheasant pie and cold meats, with apple pie and thick fresh cream.

Lord Douglas, being the only gentleman present, did not drink his port alone after dinner, and everyone withdrew to the drawing room.

A very pleasant evening followed, and Felicity once again had to tell her story – this time to Lord Douglas, who had had the gist of it from his wife.

"I can see we shall have to find a husband for Felicity," he said. "I think that is the only answer!" he said, laughing at her blushes.

"What a wonderful idea!" exclaimed Jane. "Who can there be? I'll ask Damian tomorrow which of his friends he would recommend!"

"No, for goodness sake, no, Jane," cried Felicity, who didn't like being teased. "I have no intention of being offered up just like at an auction!"

"Oh, no," Lady Douglas intervened. "That will not happen, Felicity. I can assure you I will not let anything like that happen in this house," she said severely to Jane. "Perhaps Damian will be able to introduce you to some of his friends, and if there is anyone you like, then let nature take its course. Don't worry, Felicity."

Quickly, to hide Felicity's confusion and to stifle the teasing which she knew from old would follow from her daughter and her husband, Lady Douglas suggested they either play 'Jackstraws' or 'Bilbocath', or perhaps Felicity would sing for them. Felicity declined tactfully, as she felt she had had enough attention for that evening, so the evening was spent playing games, and after such an exciting day, it was a couple of excited tired young ladies who finally retired for the evening.

Chapter 8
Surprises

Meanwhile, back at Ravenwood, Jason and Claude had both decided to make their farewells to their mother and stepfather. Jason actually left before Claude, as Claude wanted to take a final walk around the grounds, ostensibly to see it once more before returning to the turmoil of London life, but really to collect the pearls from their hiding place. Jason, however, knew he had an appointment to keep with Castlereagh, who had said he had a successor in mind for Damian. He was going to approach him whilst Jason was away, so Jason now hoped that all was settled. Claude had travelled down to Ravenwood in his curricle, but Jason preferred the freedom of his horse. Therefore, Jason was soon back at his London home, and very soon gone was the casual yet immaculate attire of his apparel, which he had worn at Ravenwood. In its place was a person 'of the first stare', one whom would be taken for granted as being a member of the closest circle of friends of the Regent. Indeed, he was very close to the Regent, who had been let into the secret by Castlereagh of the service which Jason was giving for his country! However, to allay any suspicions that could possibly arise, Jason was at pains to ape the latest fashions and be everything that he was expected to be by the aristocratic mamas. Now he was wearing a dark-blue coat which fitted him like a glove, with very pale pantaloons, highly polished hessian boots, and his snowy white neck cloth arranged to a nicety. His footman handed him his hat, cape and gloves and his phaeton had been brought round to the front door for him. He was proud of his horses, and the greys he was driving now had deep, broad chests, light necks, their hocks perfectly straight; quarters well let down. They were a well-matched team with their forward action. Just perfection!

Castlereagh was waiting for him. Not that Jason was late, hut the Tory Foreign Minister knew only too well how important a matter they had to discuss. Napoleon's 'Continental System' was designed to close Europe to England's commerce. Wellington had led his forces to the Pyrenees, and Napoleon had marched over Austria, Prussia and a large part of Russia. The objective was not to starve out England but to suffocate her. Deprived of her European markets, Napoleon Bonaparte argued that she would perish through over-production, unemployment and evolution on the part of her own workless multitudes. He envisaged himself as a liberator! Instead, he ended up outside Moscow in boots and blankets 'made in England', but that was still to come.

Great Britain, though, was nearer to capitulation in 1812 than at any time during the war. Castlereagh knew this. Spencer Perceval, the Tory Prime Minister, had been assassinated earlier in the year, and the King's recurrent illness had produced in him a condition indistinguishable from lunacy, culminating in the proclamation of a Regency. Exports were down by 331 and poor-law expenditure up by some six million. Prices were 87% above pre-war level, wheat standing at 160s. A quarter. Men were smashing machines wholesale in the islands and the North. 'Order in Council' in Napoleon's Berlin Decrees had produced Great Britain's solitary war with the United States.

All that was in the past, that is – a few months old. Wellington had stormed Badajoz in April, defeated Marshal Marmont at Salamanca in July and entered Madrid in August.

Castlereagh had to know Napoleon's plans and how England would be affected.

A trusted agent was a necessity these days, and the news which Jason had brought back from his last visit did not help matters. Richard had been a good man, and he had been able to trust the information the Frenchman sold.

Also, with Damian's disappearance from the scene, who could he trust to take his place? He had hoped to tell Jason today, but the gentleman he had thought of had incurred high debts recently at the gaming tables, and Castlereagh trusted no man who owed money, especially at London gaming tables?

Whilst Castlereagh was gathering his thoughts, Jason was being shown into the library, oak-panelled, full of books and pictures. Jason particularly liked one by a man called Turner. A beautiful sailing ship, glorious hues in the sky, full of colour. It reminded him of the 'Firefly', which brought him down to earth. He wondered what Castlereagh had worked out.

He knew that he and Patrick would have to visit France more often until the new man could take his full part.

Castlereagh entered the library at that moment. Silently they shook hands, and each knew the other's career or life was in the other's hands.

Castlereagh knows that if he couldn't outwit Bonaparte, he would be unable to face the other members of the party. He knew that to the British people, they wanted another Pitt – he only wished he was capable of handling the thunderbolts like Pitt? Jason also knew that he had to rely on Castlereagh to choose a successor to Damian; someone who would also hold their lives in his hand. He was startled; therefore, when Castlereagh said he had not been able to get the man he wanted. "How will we manage without the safeguard of an extra person," enquired Jason.

"It has been one of the reassuring things of the whole venture, that there were others who could be called upon. If anything happens to the first of us, then the second could follow to try and help. If the second disappears, there is no one else to send now."

"Very true," agreed Castlereagh. "And I've given it every thought. The safety of the whole mission and your safety and Patrick's is uppermost in my mind, but rather than risk letting someone else into the secret who may be open to blackmail, it is better not to take the risk."

"I am pleased to hear it, but there is always a time when one or two of us are not enough."

"I agree, and for that reason alone, if anything happens, the whole venture will be called off. This will be the last mission in any case. The net is tightening in France. The next visit will be to Paris."

"Paris," exclaimed Jason. "We shall have to be on our guard. Brest or other provincial towns are not so bad as their guards are not as bright nor as keen, and can be bribed easily enough."

"Napoleon is on the way to Moscow, and we hope that contact can be made in Paris to undermine his support, whilst the tie is away."

"Does Patrick know of this yet?" asked Jason.

"No, I wanted to know your opinion first," said Castlereagh. "Do you think you will be able to pierce the Napoleonic ring placed around Paris?"

"It will be difficult, and I think it may be better if we both go this time."

Two pairs of eyes and ears are better on an occasion like this. If anything goes wrong, it will be too late to get word to you by the usual method. In fact, impossible!

"Yes, perhaps you are right, will you discuss this with Patrick?"

"Yes, I expect he is back with Damian by now, and I'll call to see him immediately."

Rising, Castlereagh held out his hand to Jason, who clasped it. Both knew how much work lay ahead. To Jason, it seemed that there was an air of dejection around Castlereagh, and he was determined to do his best. He knew how much England owed to Castlereagh. A Foreign Minister's job was no sinecure!

Patrick had returned with Damian, and he was not surprised to see Jason. He was upset to hear about old Richard, who had been his contact for many months. When he heard about the Paris trip, though, he was as excited as Jason was quiet. To him, the excitement was all he lived for at that time; it was the salt on his meat, the clean clothes on his back and the money to buy everything meant nothing to him, compared with the thrill of the hunt. He enjoyed these trips to France more than Jason, and the more difficult, the better. Usually, being the youngest, he only got the easier jobs, and to hear that it was Paris this time was worth waiting for. He agreed with Jason that perhaps it was better that the two of them went together this time. He, too, knew that one slip would mean no head; Madame Guillotine preferred the heads of English spies, had had her fill by now of French aristos!

Patrick had been born in France but had been smuggled out safely when only a baby. His mother was French, and it had been touch and go whether or not they were discovered. However, with more than their share of luck and help from an English gentleman who thrived on trouble such as theirs, they managed to get to England. Patrick, though, had heard so much of Paris since the quick flight. Now he drew upon his memory, and together he and Jason planned their journey.

Castlereagh would meet them sometime next week and give them their final instructions, their contact and password, money to buy friendship all the faster and a sailing date. This time they would go from Dover not Falmouth, so Jason arranged for his servant, Robert, to ride to Falmouth to warn Captain Thelwall. He knows that it would take – at least seven days for Castlereagh to clear everything, so he arranged that the 'Firefly' should anchor off Dover until he could send word to the captain as to his definite movements. Robert was used to these extra rides and had occasionally accompanied Jason on these trips, but never landing in France. He didn't really know what Jason did, but it is expected he had a good idea. He was an honest and trusting servant, who had been with Jason for many, many years.

Patrick knew that Damian would be wondering what was happening. It was usual for Castlereagh to contact them soon after their return. It would seem very strange for Damian not to be involved. Therefore, Patrick suggested they call upon Damian and let him know what was going on.

Jason agreed, knowing full well that Damian would want to come along when he heard it was Paris, but Jason was as certain that he would not encourage him. Jason knew their chances of all returning safely were very slim indeed.

Damian greeted them with delight. He had certainly been wondering what was going on, but he was looking forward to seeing Jane far more.

He was in fact, just leaving for Grosvenor Square, and it was agreed that they should all make their way there. Jane called them 'The Three Cavaliers' and was so delighted to see her beloved Damian again. Jane, Felicity and Lady Douglas were in the drawing room, so when Hawkins announced the three young men, it was with surprise that Felicity heard the name of the Earl of Lindsey.

Surely it couldn't be her stepbrother! Of all the places to meet him.

Perhaps he wouldn't connect her with his stepfather! He had never met her or seen her likeness as far as she knew, not of course that he had been down to Ravenwood and seen her portrait from when she was but a child to the one her father had recently painted of her. In fact, Jason had wondered who was the pretty young girl whose portrait he saw smiling at him everywhere in the house at Ravenwood, and on making enquiries was surprised to hear it was his stepsister. However, the artist had not really done her justice, and he did not connect her at all with the lovely young lady he saw was with Lady Douglas and, her daughter.

Lady Douglas was delighted to see three young men and immediately introduced Miss Felicity Anderson to them in turn.

On hearing the name, Jason started and whilst trying to remember all those little girl faces, he had imagined Felicity to be, he enquired of Lady Douglas if Miss Anderson was from Ravenwood manor?

"Why, yes, Jason, Miss Anderson is from Ravenwood Manor. I didn't know you were acquainted with that district!"

Patrick and Damian, together with Jane and her mother, looked on in dismay when Jason haughtily refused the introduction.

"Jason, whatever is the matter?" exclaimed Damian.

Felicity was in tears. She thought immediately that her stepmother had poisoned his mind, and that the son was supporting his mother naturally. She ran across to Jane's mother, who put her arms around her and soothingly said:

"I'm sure there is some mistake here. Jason, please explain yourself."

"Ma'am, I am sorry to upset you. It is the last thing I would wish to do, but having just returned from visiting my stepfather, Miss Anderson's father, and my mother at Ravenwood, I am sure that Miss Anderson knows why I am acting like this. I see you are not wearing your pearls, Miss Anderson?" he haughtily enquired of Felicity.

"My pearls." She sobbed. "My father has them. What is it to do with you?" she cried.

"No, ma'am, please," Jason said.

"You know quite well that your father hasn't got them."

"I was there when he opened the safe after you left suddenly."

"My pearls are gone!" exclaimed Felicity. She could only stare at Jason as though he had uttered something outrageous.

"I do not know what you are talking about," she cried. "Jane will tell you that I only brought my sapphire necklace and a ruby and diamond brooch with me, apart from a few worthless trinkets."

Jason could not believe this. He had been so sure that she had taken the pearls. It would have been just the thing to sell to obtain some money to set herself up in London. He had been surprised to see her here with Damian's fiancée. If she knew the Douglases, then it also stood to reason that she would not necessarily have immediate need of money. He had also, of course, left Ravenwood before Felicity's letter had arrived, giving them the details of her whereabouts. To his own thoughts.

He then began to have serious doubts as Lady Douglas insisted that the introduction be formally completed, and Patrick and Damian also assured Felicity that they believed her utterly.

But how could the pearls have gone, Felicity wondered. *Father was always so careful. No one knew they were there. Only Father and your mother knew.*

"Claude and I knew too, as Mr Anderson showed them to us the night before," Jason explained.

"Then it could have been you who took them," Felicity spiritedly replied.

"Indeed, I suppose now it would seem that Claude and I are suspects, but I know that I didn't take them, and of course there is your maid. She left at the same time as you did!" retorted Jason.

Felicity was horrified that poor Meg, who had helped her so much, should be suspected of stealing her pearls, and she quickly told her story without mentioning Jason's mother to the young men. It was unanimously decided that Claude must be the culprit. How to prove it, though? Jason knew that Claude usually had gambling debts and so it was probable that he had already sold them for this reason.

Felicity found herself the centre of attention, a position which she was not used to holding, but unconsciously she accepted it and unsuspectingly made a conquest of at least one of the young men! She realised, however, that Damian and Jane would want to be alone, so she continued to hold the attention of Patrick and Jason, whilst the two lovers were lost in each other's attentions.

After a short time, Hawkins entered with the tea trolley, and whilst they were entreated to stay, the young men pleaded other matters needed their attention and left. Damian was to return for dinner, and so Jane did not mind the short farewell.

Patrick had done most of the talking to Felicity, and when they had gone, she realised that she could not really remember Jason – only his dark-blue eyes! Jason had been quiet as he realised that the Lindsey good name was threatened. He had silently vowed to see Claude and get back the pearls. It was not certain that it was Claude, but he knew that he, Jason, hadn't taken them. There had been no signs of forced entry, and as Felicity had said, so few of them had known of their existence. Claude had an apartment, and decided to go there as soon as possible. In the meantime, it had been decided that the three friends would turn over the problem of going to Paris, and all the extraneous matters that would need to be sorted out. Damian had mixed feelings about the mission. He knew it was dangerous, and that he now had other responsibilities, but he knew that all his life he would regret not going if either of his friends or both of them should lose their lives through him not being there to help. He had not mentioned this to Jane because she knew nothing of his other life, but he knew her enough to know that she would urge him not to desert his friends. She liked Jason and Patrick as much as Damian but in another way. She knew their friendship over the years had developed into a brotherly tie, and Damian was sure that if she had the choice, she would encourage him to go. After many arguments, therefore, Jason sent word to Castlereagh that the three of them would go for this, their final mission. Word came back immediately: "God has arranged this; he will be with you through your dangerous journey."

Chapter 9
Claude's Losses

At Ravenwood Felicity's letter had been received with mixed emotion. Her father was relieved that she was safe, but puzzled why she had gone.

Her stepmother thought she knew the reason – but had worried whether or not she would return. She knew Mr Anderson loved his daughter, and as Felicity made no mention of any return, she knew that a great deal depended upon her attitude to Felicity. She would have to make the overtures first, and on hearing that Mr Anderson intended to go to London to see his daughter, she pleaded to go with him too. Mr Anderson knew, though, that his daughter would talk to him if he was by himself as she had done when she was young, so he said it was best if she stayed at Ravenwood.

Before Mr Anderson set out for London as he could not leave immediately, a note arrived from Jason, addressed to Mr Anderson, which cleared his mind of one serious matter. Jason told Mr Anderson how he had met Felicity and that it had come out that she knew nothing of the disappearance of the pearls. Therefore, Jason concluded, "I must regretfully advise you that the culprit must be my brother. I suspect his debts have over forced him, and his temptation on seeing the pearls was too much for him. I intend visiting him as soon as possible and will attempt to exact full retribution for the terrible loss you have sustained."

Jason was being optimistic when he wrote that letter. He expected that Mr Anderson would come to London, and to save him confronting his daughter about the pearls, he could perhaps atone for his behaviour to her by saving both Mr Anderson and Felicity some embarrassment, so he despatched this quick note giving the fewest details possible. He had tried to find his brother, but he had moved from his apartment in Wimpole Street, and in spite of many enquiries had not yet found him. In fact, Claude had joined his new mistress in her apartment, which Claude had found for her in St. John's Street.

Claude had been amazed how quickly he had found a jeweller to take the pearls, and he knew that Mr Anderson had been speaking the truth, because he saw the gleam which came into the old jeweller's eyes, when he examined them. Claude got the price he asked for them, and immediately regretted he hadn't asked for more. The old man had agreed far too quickly to Claude's asking price. However, be that as it may, Claude had set up his Lucy in a sweet little apartment, not very fashionable, but enough for Lucy to think that Claude was her prince. Claude had been expecting Jason to search for him because he knew that his luck could not last forever. The errant daughter would be found and she would plead ignorance of the theft. Claude knew Jason well enough to realise that Jason would soon put two and two together. Love nest for his Lucy.

It had solved all problems then when he found this. So overjoyed was he, though, that he foolishly showed all the money to Lucy one night when she had been particularly delightful. True love may be blind, but Lucy wasn't and was old enough and wise enough to know that that amount of money would never come her way again and that it would be better in her pocket than his.

She sent him out the following day to please a capricious whim, and on his return she had gone with all his money except that which he had taken to buy the bottled perfume she had asked for. He just could not believe it?

His own darling Lucy had done this to him! All that money gone, just like that. He hadn't even settled his debts. She had come first with him! Broken, he knew that he couldn't turn to Jason or his mother this time. Somehow or other, he would have to get some money. show her the money. He had even thought of marrying her, although she was so below him. Ye gods, how could it happen to him!

In desperation, he staggered down the stairs and out to the tavern around the corner. He had a few pence left, and he knew that somehow he had to find more.

He had somewhere to sleep as the rent was paid, and there was some food left, but that would soon be gone. There wasn't even enough money to get drunk, so recklessly, he decided to take the plunge.

He returned to the apartment and dressed carefully. No one should see how matters stood. A brave face and no questions would be asked. He couldn't even afford a cab, so walking quickly, he finally arrived at a quietly lit house off St. James's square. From the outside, it was a rather modest house, and it was only on entering that one knew that it was far from that. The door was opened quietly by a liveried footman, and Claude was shown into the hall, which was dimly lit. However, a further door at the end of the hall opened, and a stout, bewigged gentleman came forward with arms outstretched.

"Welcome, Monsieur, welcome to my home," he kept repeating jovially. Claude handed his cloak gloves and hat to the footman, and the 'host' escorted Claude into the other room. Claude had heard of this place from 'friends', and he could see immediately that it was another world. Gaming tables and beautiful young 'ladies' escorting fashionable young and old gentlemen were everywhere. Claude knew that for the moment, his credit was good. No word could possibly have got out yet. Such rumours soon started, and no one knew how. Therefore, he intended to win enough tonight no matter what happened. Win! Far from it. He ended up owing £10,000 and knew he has finished. He could never repay that without Jason's help, and he knew that he would never get that!

When the croupier finally announced his defeat, Claude staggered away from the table. Reason had left him, and he was at first unaware of the helping hand, which guided him to a table in a quiet alcove. A drink appeared in front of him, and when the brandy took effect and calmed his nerves, his rescuer quietly spoke – Claude began to get up, but found it took far more effort than he thought it would, he sat down suddenly and looked around the brightly lit room as though he was really seeing it for the first time. To him, it looked like hell. It had put him in hell, and he could see no way clear.

"Is Mr James the brother of the Earl of Lindsey?" asked the slight figure sitting quietly beside him.

In dismay, Claude began to deny it as he thought that the man was threatening to let Jason know.

"No, no, Monsieur, sit down," he said quietly. "I only ask because I may be able to help you regain some of the money you have lost!"

Claude came out of his daze with a shock. It was as though someone had thrown cold water over him. Someone offering to help him! Through knowing Jason? Did Jason know. There must be some plot here to get him into Jason's hands. Perhaps Jason had set his spies looking for him. Quietly though, the stranger offered Claude an explanation.

"I am from the French embassy, Monsieur James, and I seek the help of a friend in these troubled times. It is very difficult for me in these dangerous days to help my country, and I rely on the help of those few brave people I can meet."

Claude couldn't believe his ears. He didn't like the French, and indeed had not enjoyed being in France. He too had had the chance of learning French when he had gone with Jason to France when he was young. However, he had soon come home and whilst Jason had stayed until he had been forced to leave because of the troubles prior to the revolution, Claude had been glad to get home. He could speak French but would never be mistaken for a Frenchman. What on earth could this man want? He didn't like the French, and he was no friend of France, but he needed the money.

He looked at the soberly clad Frenchman, so out of place in this gaudy cheap gambling den. Then he realised that the jovial 'host' had spoken with a French accent. He guessed then that the place was a rendezvous for sympathisers with the French cause, probably started many years ago by exiled Aristos, but now full of Boney's men.

He knew too that the gambling was a lure for men like him who gambled and lost. It was a sure way to trap

66

unsuspecting victims to help them. However, Claude knew he had no choice, and with Jason out of the way, perhaps for good, he would then inherit the Earldom. Claude had never really thought about it until then. He knew that that was another way out of his problems. Frightened, he turned and gave a long hard look at the Frenchman.

What on earth was he going to be asked to do Kill Jason – never! He couldn't do that perhaps someone else could do that, and he would only need to give information. Relieved at the thought, he turned to the Frenchman and shrugged his shoulders, and said, "Well, my friend, what do you have in mind?"

With a smile that seemed entirely out of place on his face, the Frenchman beckoned to one of the footmen standing around the room, and Claude knew his fate was sealed.

Chapter 10
Arrangements are Made

Time flew by For Felicity, and it was with delight that she welcomed her father. She was not surprised to see him, as she knew that he would want to see for himself if she was happy in her new surroundings. If that was what she wanted, then he would be happy too.

He had been searching his mind for reasons for her leaving, and he had realised that perhaps he had expected too much from Felicity in accepting a stepmother without any upsets. Now, though, he clasped her in his arms, and she knew that he had accepted the fact that she was happy here.

He had called earlier in the morning, but Felicity and Jane were out, and he had had a long talk with Jane's mother, Lady Douglas, who had assured him that Felicity could stay here at Grosvenor House for as long as she wanted. Even after Jane's wedding if she wanted.

Mr Anderson would not hear of this, as he explained that he was certainly willing to rent somewhere for them all to stay during the Season, and as he had planned that Felicity would be presented at Court next year, perhaps it would be as well if he made arrangements as soon as possible.

Anyway for the time being Felicity could stay with Jane until her wedding, and then other arrangements would be made.

Mr Anderson was also pleased to meet Jason shortly afterwards, as he wanted to thank him for his letter of explanation. Jason was surprised to see Mr Anderson, and was upset that they could not assure him that the culprit had been apprehended. Mr Anderson assured Jason that he knew that he was doing everything possible and that for the time being, he would leave it in his hands and not advise the authorities of the matter.

Jason was relieved about this as it gave him time to save the family name, once the theft was known, then it would take a long time to live it down. Jason had actually called on another matter, and he was surprised at himself for doing it. Damian had mentioned that the Marchioness of Queensdown was holding a ball in Damian and Jane's honour, and Jason and Patrick were naturally both invited.

Patrick had let slip that he was going to ask Felicity to accompany him, and on hearing this Jason knew that he could not let him do that.

Miss Anderson had got under his skin! He didn't know what it was, but he knew he wanted to see her again. He wanted to try and erase that dreadful incident when they had first met. His behaviour on that occasion had haunted him ever since. Daughter of such a person.

How could he ever have suspected Mr Anderson's?

He had therefore called to ask Lady Douglas if he could escort Felicity to the ball, and accordingly when he found Mr Anderson at Grosvenor Square, he felt it easier to ask him if he would allow him to escort his stepsister to the ball. Mr

Anderson knew nothing of the event, but knowing Jason, he was only too pleased to know that Felicity would be in good hands. Lady Douglas, too was delighted. Felicity had nothing to say in the matter, and it was later that evening that Lady Douglas told her of Jason's call. She hadn't met Jason since that first time, and so it was with some trepidation and yet some excitement that she looked forward to the ball.

Felicity's dress had been delivered and she and Jane had spent most of the morning trying on the various gowns which had arrived. The excitement mounted.

Meanwhile, having achieved his object, Jason returned home to find a message from Castlereagh. All arrangements had been made and they had to leave London on the morning of the 5th October. Jason was relieved to find that this was the day after the marchioness of Queensdown's ball. No explanations would have to be given for missing it. He had been wondering whether he had been foolhardy in making such a firm intention of attending it. He had wondered, *whether it would have been better to have just chanced a meeting with her and taken the risk of her having a dance free for him*. He was sure Felicity would be very popular, and unless he got there early, there wouldn't have been much chance for him. Therefore he had taken the risk and asked to escort her. There could be many raised eyebrows amongst the mamas and their daughters when they saw him with a beautiful stranger. Still, he could have his excuses ready for any questions; after all, she was his stepsister. He would be away the following day too, and might not return? Not return he hadn't really bothered before about it, but suddenly he wanted to return, with surprise he found himself thinking what it would be like never to see those beautiful green eyes of hers again. *Heavens above, man, get a grip on yourself,* he said to himself, "A pair of pretty eyes and you're in trouble if you don't take care?"

The last thing that he wanted was to find himself unable to concentrate on the job in hand at this time, and so he forced himself to plan for the trip.

He must get in touch with Damian and Patrick, and they must meet to finalise everything.

Castlereagh had said that he would be at the Queensdown's ball, and would let them know anything else that had arisen since the note.

Also, the Prince Regent would be there, and he wanted to have a word with the three of them before they left. Castlereagh thought the Ball would present a fine public occasion which should not give rise to any suspicions. Jason knew that any slip would mean their deaths, and so he too was careful not to leave any signs of his forthcoming journey for servants to see. Everything was packed or destroyed. However, he failed to notice that part of Castlereagh's note had slipped to the floor and fallen under his chair. He decided that he must see Damian and Patrick immediately, so he rang for his servant to have his carriage brought round for him. He hastily gathered his cloak, hat and gloves from the footman and dashed off to find the others.

Meanwhile, Claude had met another man from the 'French Embassy' and it was made quite clear to him that in return for either Jason's death or a substantial sum, he must obtain for them details of Jason's next visit to France. This came as a complete surprise to Claude, who had never dreamed that Jason spied for the English Government. He then realised what he had let himself in for. Wretchedly he agreed, and it was made quite clear to him that his life was of no consequence to them, and that if he failed, well, that was it.

Claude was no coward, but he realised only too late that what was asked of him to was impossible. It was treason. He knew that Jason would never give him the information. How was he going to get it? He went into a tavern to think seriously about it, and whilst he was there, he came to the conclusion that perhaps it would be better to make a clean breast of everything to Jason. He would truly repent and promise to mend his ways. Even take a job if necessary! Therefore, he decided the best thing was to go immediately whilst he had the courage to face him, so on presenting himself at the door of Jason's home, he was upset to find Jason was not in.

The footman, of course, knew Claude and suggested that perhaps he might like to wait for his brother. He decided that he would. It would be as well, and so he was shown into the library. The footman had advised Masters, the butler, who entered quickly with sherry on a silver solver.

"A sherry, my Lord," he said. "I'm sure his Lordship will not be long. He has ordered dinner for half past five, and he cannot, therefore, be very long."

"Thank you, Masters, a sherry will go down nicely. I will wait for a while."

Whilst he was talking to Masters, he had seen a piece of paper on the floor by the foot of his chair, and when Masters left, he curiously picked it up and read what it said:

"…meet M. Hainault at *Rue des Concierges*. He will let you know how to make contact. He will pick you up on the 12th same place he left you."

Claude couldn't believe his eyes. Here's his chance! Put in his lap for him! He sat for a few minutes, wondering why the Devil was tempting him! He had come here with the very best of intentions. To ask Jason's forgiveness and help, and here he was with the bit of evidence that could swing matters round the opposite way! Holding his breath, he slipped the piece of paper into his pocket and grabbed his hat and gloves from the startled footman.

With no explanation, he ran down the steps and beckoned a cab; with luck, he would be able to get hold of Fouquet at the club, and he was safe. Within minutes of Claude's departure, Jason returned home. He was worried. He knew that the message from Castlereagh had been on two sheets of paper, but he could only find one when he got to Patrick's.

Fortunately, he knew the message, but where he had lost it, he did not know. He had searched his cloak and the few pockets he had. He had searched his carriage and given a quick look round the steps as he entered his house.

Now he searched the library and was disturbed to see Masters standing in the doorway. He had not heard the door open.

"Masters, have you picked up a note from the floor whilst I've been out?"

"No, my lord, indeed, the only time I came in was to give Mr Claude a glass of sherry!"

"Mr Claude!" exclaimed Jason. "Good heavens, man, why did you let him go?" Masters looked flabbergasted at this, but then Jason realised he was being unfair as he hadn't told him that he was looking for Claude.

He hurriedly apologised and changed his tone, and assured the hustler that everything was all right. However, when Masters went on to explain Claude's hurried departure, Jason put two and two together and wondered what use Claude could have for part of his note. There were only a few words on it, and he didn't think Claude had any contacts with the French agents or knew he was connected in any way. Still, it might be wise to let Castlereagh know that part of the contents of his note might have got into the wrong hands.

Jason knew that whatever the French agents found out, they had to go ahead now with the journey. It was too late to change it, and many lives would be at stake. For the moment, they would have to play it by ear and hope that the message did not make sense to whoever had it now.

Chapter 11
The Ball

The morning of the 4th October dawned, and both Felicity and Jane woke early, full of excitement. The Ball was an event of some consequence as the Prince Regent had agreed to attend, and practically everybody who was somebody in Society had declared their intention of being present if invited.

The Marquis and Marchioness of Queensdown were now very elderly and the bulk of the arrangements had fallen on the shoulders of Jane's parents. Therefore since their return to Grosvenor Square, there had been constant comings and goings in preparation for the great day.

The time passed so slowly for the girls, and eventually, when they were finally dressed by their maids and ready to set off, they presented a beautiful picture. Jane, with her golden hair, blue eyes and delicate complexion, was in an exquisite aquamarine silk gown with the finest golden embroidery, and she wore a matching set of aquamarines – necklace and earrings and a circlet in her hair, which were a gift from her fiancé. Her long hair had been teased into long curls that framed her oval face, and the jewels shone like stars amongst them.

Felicity, in complete contrast with her dark hair was simply dressed in that beautiful gown she had chosen from Miss Starkey's. The pureness of the white silk, the delicate gold and silver gauze and the pastel pink roses emphasised Felicity's wonderful colouring, which was to win over so many of the eligible young men that evening. However, that is jumping too far ahead Damian arrived first and looked so handsome, especially to Jane. He was tall and dark, not quite as broad or as tall as Jason, though, Jason soon arrived, and together the two young men waited for their young ladies to descend. Felicity did not want to meet Jason alone, so together, the two young girls came down that grand staircase; Damian going up to Jane and Jason looked up to Felicity. He's quite taken aback; she was beautiful, his heart beat quite wildly for seconds, but then he stepped forward and feeling rather self-conscious she greeted him with a low curtsey and hoping she wouldn't faint in front of him, Felicity's heart sang with delight. For a young lady to be attending her first Ball in society, escorted by such a handsome young man, was almost too much for her. She had got over her first shyness, and whilst there was some quick chatter amongst the party of people preparing to leave, she stole another good look at him. Yes, he was good looking, and she was a very fortunate young lady to have a stepbrother like him. Jason had unconsciously chosen an evening cloak of the green of Felicity's eyes – or was it just that he had been unable to get her eyes out of his mind when he instructed his valet to lay out his clothes for the evening's festivities! However, whatever the reason, together, the young couple were ready to depart, and the coach was waiting for them. The footmen handed the ladies is into the coach, followed by their escorts, the doors were closed and the two horses set off at a steady pace. Lord and Lady Douglas had already departed as they were anxious that everything was ready for the evening. There wasn't a great distance to go, and soon the crowd grew and gathered around the coaches as they drew up at the front of the imposing Queensdown residence, which was lit from end to end. Many flunkeys were rushing hither and thither, whilst the ever-mounting hubbub from the crowd prevented much conversation. Indeed Felicity was so excited that she couldn't think of anything to say. Jane, Damian and Jason had, of course, been to many such events and to them it lost some but not all of its excitement. There was an undercurrent of excitement in the carriage because tonight all was for them, that is for Jane and Damian, and there was so much ahead of them. Tomorrow they would wonder how they managed it all. As their coach drew up and the footmen opened the door, the crowd cheered because the word was soon passed around who they were.

As they mounted the steps escorted by flunkeys holding flaming torches, Felicity and Jason followed behind and suspecting that she was finding it a little overpowering Jason put a steadying hand under her elbow and soon they were all in the magnificent reception hall. To Felicity, everything was too wonderful for words, and whilst Jane and Damian went over to Jane's parents and grandparents and Damian's grandfather having been divested of cloaks, gloves, etc., Jason found himself alone at last with his stepsister.

They paid their respects to their hosts, but being part of the family party found themselves having arrived slightly earlier than many of the other guests. The musicians were already playing in the gallery and rather than dance in solitary state and also draw attention to themselves, Jason who knew the Queensdown residence quite well, suggested to Felicity that she might care to see some of the magnificent rooms, especially the famous paintings of Gainsborough and Reynolds in the Long Gallery. Jason enjoyed showing these art treasures to Felicity, and he realised that she had definite ideas of her own as to beauty and design. When they had gone the length of the Long Gallery, Jason remembered the handsome face collection, which a previous Marquis of Queensdown, who had travelled all over the world including China, had gathered together and was now considered priceless. Knowing how things of beauty appealed to her, he resolved to get the permission of the Marquis to show it to her. However, he realised that their absence from the ballroom by now would probably have been noticed by their friends, so promising to show it to her another time, they made their way back to the Ballroom. By now, the room had filled, and the glittering chandeliers, the music, the excited chatter all added to the magnificent picture, which presented itself to the young couple on their entrance to the ballroom.

There were so many beautiful ladies and handsome lords, many of whom were in magnificent uniforms being officers waiting to cross the Channel and join Wellington's forces in Spain. The ladies' gowns were of every possible hue and fabric, and the diamonds, rubies, sapphires and emeralds, not to mention the many decorations worn in their hair and upon their persons, added to the fabulous picture which Felicity was seeing for the first time. As Jason and Felicity entered the Ballroom, Jason could feel the murmur and glances which came in their direction. To Felicity, nothing was apparent, as she was just too excited taking in all the wonders of the 'high society'. However, Jason knew that every mama and every eligible female was devouring Felicity, her bearing, her clothes, jewellery, manners – everything would be torn to shreds if he, Jason, were to show too much affection. No, he must play the part of just an escort to his stepsister, but he was beginning to realise that he felt far more than that. After all, there was no blood tie, there was no reason, but no, no he was not able to think of such things as yet. Let this evening be just a social occasion when he could introduce Felicity to those he considered suitable and see that she enjoyed her first Ball. "My lord, it is a long time since we saw you at such an event," exclaimed a rather aged dowager, sitting a foot or so away from where Jason and Felicity were standing.

"Your Grace," replied Jason, "I'm afraid I am kept rather busy at Charnwood. On such occasions as this, however, when friends are so happily acclaimed, it is a pleasure to put work aside for a few hours. Your Grace, may I present my stepsister, Miss Felicity Anderson, who is also a very close friend of Lady Jane's. Miss Anderson and Lady Jane were at school together and Miss Anderson is going to be a bridesmaid for Lady Jane."

That will stop the tongues of the old crones waging, thought Jason. It was well known how much trouble mischievous gossip could cause in London society these days. He knew of the old dowager duchess's garrulousness and that every word of his would soon be circulating the ballroom.

"My dear," said the dowager. "I am pleased to know that you are a friend of Lady Jane's for we all love her dearly. I hope you are enjoying yourself. I hope his Lordship," she indicated Jason with a slight movement of her head, "has not claimed every dance, for my grandson," here she turned sharply in her chair and motioned rather sternly to a rather podgy and pimply youth to come forward, "has expressed much pleasure in having the honour of a dance with you." Poor Felicity was quite startled as she had not thought of dancing with anyone else, and had quite forgotten that her card would be claimed by many of the young lords whenever and if Jason left her for a moment. Quickly she gathered her thoughts, because she didn't know whether Jason would want to have most or even any of the glances with her or would be content with just a few turns around the floor. She looked up hastily at him, and he too was rather unsettled, although he hoped he didn't show it. He had forgotten to mark her card whilst he had the chance and now she was the centre of attention and he hadn't claimed any! Still, if he had claimed many or all the dances, the tongues would wag once more. Perhaps it would be as well if this young grandson of the dowager duchess had this dance and so to Felicity's dismay, she heard him say, "I am sure, your Grace, that Miss Anderson would be delighted for Lord Spencer to mark her card for a dance. Shall we say, the next waltz?" Calmly, at least outwardly, he reached for Felicity's card as she was standing there looking and feeling rather helpless and entered Lord Spencer's name against the next dance. Jason was really rubbing salt in his wound, as the waltz would mean that Lord Spencer would be beholding what he, Jason, Earl of Lindsey, had been dreaming of all the previous night. Lord Spencer himself was rather amazed at his good fortune, because his grandmother, the Dowager Duchess of Exmouth, was intent on procuring an heiress for his wife as their family fortunes were in poor straits. To dance with a beautiful girl overawed him, and for some time, he couldn't think of a word to say, and Felicity on her part had nothing to say either. She was feeling very disappointed that her first dance hadn't been with Jason. Personally, she would rather have not danced at all and just talked to Jason rather than dance with this gawky, podgy young lordling.

Jason knew of the poor position of the Exmouth family fortunes and guessed that the crafty dowager was, in fact, testing him, Jason, to see whether it was true that Felicity was just his stepsister. She would know that Felicity had no fortune – she would have heard of Jason's mother's second marriage to Felicity's father – nothing was missed in society gossip – so the dowager duchess had no reason for pushing forward her grandson for the attentions of Miss Anderson. Pangs of jealously ran through Jason as he watched the couple dancing, and he was pleased to see that hardly a word passed between the couple. Gradually, however, Felicity found herself enjoying the dance, she knew the steps from her days at the Misses Frobisher's dancing lessons, and once or twice a natural smile came through, and Lord Spencer found the courage from somewhere to pass a comment. Jason saw these smiles and standing no more of it, he begged her Grace permission to leave, and he found himself across the room near the entrance. Just then, Castlereagh arrived and seeing Jason, he passed the usual pleasantries for all to hear, and then very quietly asked if he had heard anything of Claude or his friends. They gradually drew into one of the window recesses where they could see everything going on and be seen, but not overheard. Castlereagh and Jason were soon joined by Patrick, and casually the conversation covered all the topics that needed to be finalised.

Jason would tell Damian the final details at a suitable occasion, as it was rather difficult for Damian to slip away from his betrothed on this his betrothal ball.

"There is nothing new from our end, and if Claude's friends are going to do anything, it will be on the other side of the Channel. They wouldn't dare risk anything in London," said Jason.

"Keep on your guard every minute of the day and night, and don't be side-tracked. These men are dangerous, and it is important that you all, and I mean all, get back safely," ordered Castlereagh.

"You can be certain of that," agreed Jason. "No one more than I want to return to England."

As soon as Jason said that he knew it to be so very true; the more he saw of Felicity, the more he wanted her. Now he had some reason to get back home, Horne to England to Felicity – if she would have him.

Castlereagh looked at him in surprise at the intensity of his remarks – he had seen Jason with a pretty girl on his arm, but he wasn't aware of any romance in the offing. It was one of the ways of his life – pretty girls, many of them – a typical Regency buck with time, money and love to lavish on the pretty things of the day – an image Jason had created deliberately. Quickly, Castlereagh explained various things which had come to hand since their last meeting. It promised to be a stormy crossing, and, therefore, Castlereagh wanted to make sure that Jason knew the exact place to land.

Those safe landing places were rather rare in such troublesome times, and it was only with the help of a few trusted Frenchmen, who had learnt to hate what Napoleon Bonaparte stood for, that agents could be landed safely.

"Two flashes of a lantern, two seconds in darkness and then three flashes of the lantern. This means all clear. If two flashes only, then this means Boney's agents are in the area and you get away as quickly as you can. No heroics either, my lords. If you can't land, then the whole mission is cancelled. The whole scheme is something of a mystery, and until we get to know who and what is at the bottom of it, then I don't trust anyone. You've got the names of your contact. Try not to take an active part – let the local partisans do it, but if it is certain that Napoleon Bonaparte can be crushed, then you can assure them of our support. I've no idea of what they need. One of you may need to get back here quickly. The well will be within lantern distance on the evening tide from the 10th onwards, and there will also be a boat within reach just before sunrise each morning to pick anyone up if necessary. Of course, if French patrols are in the area, then there will be a delay, but we shall do our best – I know you will do yours Good luck, God guides you, my friends."

Castlereagh classed each of the friends' hands in turn and they could tell that his thoughts would be with then throughout their arduous and nerve-wracking task.

Whilst Jason had been talking to Castlereagh, the waltz had finished and Felicity had found herself surrounded by young lords of all shapes, sizes and ages, and was quite bewildered until Lord Douglas suddenly appeared on the scene, which he took in at a glance.

"I've come to claim my dance, Felicity, as promised," he said.

"With pleasure, my Lord," Felicity demurely replied, sighing inwardly with relief. She could not see Jason anywhere and she was really annoyed with him for leaving her to herself. Surely he could have waited until the end of the dance. He knew how she would feel surrounded by so many young gentlemen and suddenly, however, she sew him in the alcove talking to Patrick and a distinguished gentleman, who Lord Douglas told her was Lord Castlereagh, and she realised that business was coming before pleasure!

"Are you enjoying your first ball?" enquired Lord Douglas.

"Oh, yes, my Lord, it is so exciting and so wonderful!" she exclaimed.

After a few more pleasantries, the dancing stopped once more, and Lord Douglas found just the person he needed to help Felicity, because he too had seen Jason over the side of the room and he knew that he couldn't very well interrupt Lord Castlereagh. What on earth Castlereagh wanted with Jason and Patrick at that particular moment he didn't know, but that he had to find someone suitable to look after Felicity.

Lord Douglas led Felicity over to Lady Jersey, who was well known for her slight to Lord Wellington, and also, she was one of the most sought after hostesses of the London Society. Without her approval, it was very difficult, nay impossible, to gain entrance to Almacks, that worthy venue of Society.

Lord Douglas was relieved to see Sally, as he knew the Countess of Jersey, and so he said, "Lady Jersey, may I present Miss Felicity Anderson to you. She is the stepsister of the Earl of Lindsey, who is otherwise occupied at the moment, and she is a school friend of Jane's. She is also going to be her bridesmaid too."

"My dear Felicity, are you enjoying yourself? How I wish I were as young and fresh as you are – you have the whole world in front of you. I always remember my first ball. Oh, it was quite grand and magnificent, and I know just how you feel."

Indicating the seat beside her, she asked Felicity a few questions, but without Felicity knowing it, she had got all the information she wanted from her. Felicity only saw an elderly lady with extremely well-kept silver-grey hair, paper-fine skin stretched over well-defined bones, twinkling eyes full of kindness. Although of mature years, Lady Jersey was dressed in the latest fashion in a lilac spider gauze over an under-dress of rose satin, and a lace veil over her diamond tiara.

Suddenly there was a fanfare of trumpets, which announced the arrival of the Prince Regent, resplendent in a mulberry satin coat and white breaches, diamonds sparkling on his shoes and elsewhere on his person. After parading around the room, being bowed low to by everyone present, he reached his special place and sat down heavily. Damian and Jane had, of course, been presented to him and very soon after the music started again and the dancing continued. By now, Jason and his party had dispersed, and with some concern, Jason remembered Felicity. How could he have left her? What had happened to her? Where was she? Frantically, he scanned the room, and with inward sigh of relief, he saw her sitting next to Lady Jersey.

As quickly as good manners allowed, he made his way across to Felicity, and bowing low before Lady Jersey, he managed to snatch a look at Felicity to see how she was taking his abandonment of her. Felicity gave away no sign of how she felt. Really, she was furious, but as soon as she saw him, the anger melted.

"Lady Jersey," Jason exclaimed, "I see you have met my charming stepsister."

"Indeed I have, and where have you been young man, when you should have been looking after her?" she asked him rather sternly, raising her quizzing glass to her eyes. She knew how embarrassing it could have been for Felicity to have been left to herself.

"A thousand apologies, my Lady, I was detained by Lord Castlereagh, and unfortunately was unable to absent myself from him until now. I am indeed extremely grateful to you for rescuing my sister."

He felt the need to stress the relationship because Lady Jersey was looking at him with a very sharp twinkle in her eye, and Jason imagined she had guessed where his heart lay. She, too, had known such moments.

Just then, the next dance was announced, and Jason claimed it immediately. Overjoyed but not showing it. Determined to make him pay for his lack of attention, Felicity allowed herself to be led on to the floor and soon as he took her in his arms, all was forgiven. She really began to enjoy the evening.

No expense had been spared for the buffet supper, with champagne flowing freely, lobsters, game pie, chicken, venison, aspic jellies, hams, chantilly, creams and frothing delicacies, fresh fruit and such concoctions only to be seen on such tables where chefs of distinction could show their talents.

After supper, Jason could tell that Felicity had forgiven him, and he found himself enjoying the occasion far more than he thought possible. He saw one or two glances from acquaintances, and indeed some of his friends had asked to be introduced to Felicity, enquiring who the beautiful young lady was whom he had brought that evening. Felicity was certainly surprised to find herself the centre of such attention, and in particular, one young gentleman, Lord Richard Trenchard, was very attentive until Jason insisted on having the remaining dances.

Just then, the Prince Regent, who had decided it was time to leave the proceedings, was passing and he stopped on seeing Jason. He knew of the nature of Jason's work for Castlereagh, but couldn't very well say anything in front of the assembly. However, Jason took the opportunity of presenting Felicity to the Prince Regent, who immediately took a liking to her and told Jason to take great care of her. By this, Jason knew that the Prince was also meaning him to take great care of his mission and get back safely to her. It was the only way the Regent could get a message to him, but it was reassuring to know that the highest personage in the land was taking an interest in the mission.

Meanwhile, Felicity was so excited at being presented to the Prince that Jason thought it wiser to dance and not just stand or sit around. To Felicity, it was dreamland – to be held in Jason's arms. To Jason – unknown to Felicity, he was thinking exactly the same thing. They floated on the air, or thought they did and wanted it to last forever. However, reason prevailed and Jason couldn't help but wonder whether he would ever hold her in his arms again – tomorrow he was away – would he come back? Unconsciously in the waltz they were then dancing, he tightened his hold on her, and when she looked up at him enquiringly, he felt himself dissolve into those liquid pools of green sea gazing up at him. Her lips were so tempting, and her hair framed the beautiful picture; that he started to bend his head, but suddenly realised where he was and instead whispered, "Have you seen the gardens yet?"

"Of course not, my Lord, how could I?" Felicity replied in amazement.

"Forgive me, I was forgetting," he replied, quickly realising what an idiotic thing to ask in October. Instead, he remembered the jade collection, and as Lord Douglas was just nearby, he moved over to him and asked his permission to show it to Felicity. "Of course, Jason," replied Lord Douglas. "You know here. It is, the key is in that. Desk in the study – the top left-hand drawer."

Jason knew he just had to get Felicity away from the rest of the milling throng. He didn't want this moment to escape him. He knew he had little time. He had to set out in a few hours for Dover, and yet he wanted a few precious moments alone with Felicity. In mid-summer, the gardens would have been perfect, Queensdown being famous for their rose arbours and fountains, but in October at practically midnight, no lover could expect any results from those surroundings. However, knowing Felicity loved beautiful things as he had found out earlier in the evening, he knew she would want to see this precious collection gathered from all corners of China and other parts of the world.

Slipping away from the dancing proved to be fairly easy – some may have seen, but he didn't care any longer. Lord Douglas had meant his father's desk, but Jason knew this, and so quietly, they slipped away to the Chinese Gallery. Some of the pieces were rather ugly, but the different shades of jade and some of the delicate figurines were exquisite.

"This piece is the colour of your eyes," Jason murmured to Felicity. The candles in the room which they had brought with them rather than get a servant to light up the room, flickered slightly and Felicity wasn't quite sure that she had heard Jason correctly. However, she was left in no doubt when the candle flames flickered in his eyes, and she saw his tenderness for her. He saw her upturned face, her innocence ends her trust, and he could bear the bonds of silence no longer – he put the candle bra down, put his arms on her shoulders and drew her to him.

"Oh, Felicity," he whispered quietly, "I love you, I love you so much."

She felt as though time stood still, and she couldn't breathe. She just continued to look up at him, Her lips slight apart as though she wanted to speak, and he bent his head and kissed those tempting lips, gently and then more passionately as he felt her respond.

It was the first time she had ever been kissed, and it was as wonderful as she had ever dreamt it would be.

He lifted his head, and she leant her head on his shoulder and murmured, "Jason, I love you too, I can't believe it's true."

"Hush, my darling, it's so, so true. I've waited a long time to find someone like you."

Minutes passed by, more endearments said, but then Jason came to his senses and reason reared its ugly head. He realised that tomorrow would soon be upon him, and he would be miles away. He might never come back. He might never see her again. He could promise her nothing, and he could tell her nothing.

Taking his arms away from her, he hold her at arms' stretch and slowly he looked at her, it every inch of her, so that he could always picture her, whether he was in a French prison or at the end of a rope ready to fall away into the dark pit beyond. He would always remember her, standing there in the candlelight, surrounded by those priceless jade figurines, her dark curls slightly awry from learning of his love and his passion, and those eyes – oh, he would remember her eyes until his dying day.

In bewilderment, Felicity kept so still. She didn't have an inkling of what was going through Jason's head, but she realised that he was looking at her so intently as if to remember every detail as though he may never see her again. How right she was.

"Felicity, I love you, and you love me, and there is nothing in the 'world' which would stop me from marrying you except one thing and that unfortunately is something which exists and which I cannot reveal to you. Please, please trust me. I love you from the bottom of my heart, and if it is possible, then I intend to marry you. I can say nothing at the moment to your father or to anyone, but please do not let me lose your love. I have a job to do, and I may die, and there may be no future together for us – that is as much as I dare say, so please keep my love, don't give it away, don't forget it, but I cannot possibly ask you to not enjoy yourself whilst I'm away. But please do not accept any of the many, many proposals you are bound to get until you hear again from me. It may be a month, two months, but I hope, I only hope it will be one day in the very near future.

"Trust me, please, Felicity, my darling."

To say that Felicity was bewildered would be an understatement. One moment she was being told she was the only one for him, that he wanted to marry her, and then he couldn't – at least not yet! She felt as though her world had fallen apart. He said he may die – what on earth was he going to do. "Oh, please, please, Jason, don't go, don't leave me."

"My darling, I have to. I have to leave tomorrow morning –, and there is so much more that you do not know about nor could understand, please don't ask me to explain. I love you so very, very much, but I cannot marry you yet. If ever," he added under his breath.

Felicity didn't hear the last couple of words, which was just as well.

"My darling, Felicity. I had no right to tell you I love you. It was wrong of me to speak so soon, but I couldn't help myself knowing how you will be overwhelmed with proposals from the dukes to the plain misters whilst I am away. I have loved you ever since you accused me of being the thief in Lady Douglas's drawing room."

This brought a weak smile to Felicity's face, and he gently wiped away the tears.

"Please, please, believe me, darling, that I will do everything in my power to come back to you as quickly as possible."

Sensing, rather than knowing about it, Felicity knew the struggles within him, and putting her hands up to either side of his face, she whispered, "Jason, I love you. Whatever it is that you are going to do, I will wait for you. No matter what happens, I will love you always."

Putting his arms around her, he held her tightly. So much so that a ring he was wearing of an unusual design caused her to cry out sharply. It was an unusual ring in that it was, in fact, two rings joined by a secret fastening.

Taking it from his finger, he took it apart and gave one to her.

"Take this, my love as my token of my very deep affection and love, and when my mission is over, if I cannot come straight to you, I will send this other part of the ring and you shall know I am safe and will soon be with you."

In a daze, all she could say was, "Jason, please, please remember I shall wait for you no matter how long. Don't forget me please, wherever you are."

"Forget you, my darling! Never, never in all my days shall I ever have you out of my mind."

Drawing her once more to him, he kissed her lovely lips for the last time, and touched her dark curls as though to make sure they were real, and they slowly moved back down the Gallery. Giving the candlebra to a flunkey and putting the key back in the desk gave them time to hide their emotions.

Taking glass of champagne from a footman hovering around the ballroom for each of them, they silently toasted each other and were gradually drawn once more into the brilliance of the ballroom the merry throng.

The assembly was gradually drawing to a close, and after a few more dances and general conversation, everyone started back home, and later that morning then she and Jane finally got to bed, Felicity wondered if it had, in fact, all been a dream. No, it couldn't be – had his ring – not that she had shown it to anyone, in fact, it was hidden amongst her own jewellery in her jewellery casket, but that was fact and that was enough to send her to sleep with such sweet dreams.

Chapter 12
France

Jason had got back to his home hardly realising where he was, being so full of joy and happiness because Felicity was his, his for evermore, they got back safely. He could only think of her upturned face waiting to be kissed, but the next minute Robert, his servant, was there waiting for him to undress and urging him to get a few hours' sleep before the long journey began. Over and over again in his sleep, he murmured, "Felicity, my love, my darling one," and eventually, he slept fitfully, if not soundly, until Robert woke him by shaking him awake and saying that it was dawn and shouldn't they be on their way?

Robert had stayed up late whilst Jason was at the ball and had been surprised to see a parcel on the table in the hall when he returned from the alehouse nearby, his usual evening haunt. The parcel was addressed to Jason, so Robert took it into the study, put it into one of the drawers in the desk. It was wrapped in a piece of brown paper and loosely tied, and so seemed of no consequence. Certainly, nothing to waste time about before Jason set out in the morning. Little did he know that his master would have given him a year's wages to have seen that particular parcel.

In the early morning air, Jason shivered as he met Damian and Patrick as arranged, and soon in the pale morning light, they were on their way to Dover. A message had already gone to Captain Thelwall to prepare to sail for France as soon as the three men were aboard, and as soon as they were sighted, the ship's boat collected them. A quick nod from Jason and the anchor was weighed. Soon in the freshening wind, with her yards and decks alive with seamen, the 'Firefly' skimmed over the waves towards the French coast. In the clear morning light now, the 'Firefly' looked lively and beautiful, and soon the white cliffs of the southern coast of England were out of sight.

Down in the cabin, the passengers were partaking of a hearty breakfast, none of them having felt like eating much before riding to Dover. Celebrations could still be well remembered. Captain Thelwall had now joined them, and soon there was complete agreement on the plans for landing them in France and for keeping within distance in case of need from the 10th onwards.

"Well, Captain, do you think the landing at the *Daie dos Anges* will be difficult?" Jason asked.

He had never been in this area of the French coast before under such circumstances, Brest and the Brittany coast being his previous haunts. He knew, however, that the captain was to be relied upon. Navigation was a strong point with him, and so it was no surprise to Jason when Captain Thelwall replied, "Unless the Froggies know we are coming, there'll be no difficulty at all, m'lord!"

"Good," said Patrick, "I don't want wet feet for the journey to Paris."

"You'll be lucky if that's all you get this time," said Jason warningly.

"Yes," agreed Damian. "We'll have our work cut out."

"We know that there is a chance that our arrangements may be known to Bonaparte's spies, as you know. Up to now, though, I understand that there has been little movement to apprehend any of our contacts named in the note. We have sent word to them to be extra careful and to report if they suspect anything," Jason said.

"I think they are waiting for the bigger fry and will wait until we get there," said Damian. "It will probably be best to tread warily and make a trial run first."

"Agreed. That is what I had thought of," replied Jason. "I think it will probably be best if one of us contacts M. Hainault and let him think that only he has come over. Then, if there are no repercussions, then we can follow up together. However, if I'm caught, then it is up to you both to do what you can."

"You!" exclaimed Patrick and Damian in unison. "It would be far better for one of us to make contact first," continued Patrick, but Jason would not hear of it, and despite their repeated and insistent demands, it was finally agreed that Jason would make the first approach, and then see if there were any suspicious results. Jason knew that he was taking a great risk because they knew that one of Bonaparte's agents in London had travelled to Dover in haste two days earlier. Castlereagh had warned Jason of this, and they both assumed that this was as a result of the information gleaned by Claude.

They had no intention of trying to land at *Le Baie des Anges* in the daylight, as despite its angelic name, there were nasty rocks a short distance outside the bay, and the ebb tide would surely bring disaster to the 'Firefly', and also it would announce their arrival to any watchers on the cliffs; Le Treport not being too far distant for casual workers to be in the area, in the daytime at least. The inside of the small cabin gave no indication of the trials that lay ahead of its passengers, and it was with reluctance that Jason disturbed Patrick's slumber to announce that very shortly they would be disembarking.

Up on deck, Captain Thelwall was waiting, his dark features inscrutable as he touched his hat and said formally, "Boat ready, m'lord."

"Thank you, Captain," acknowledged Jason, and put his hand forward to take that of the elderly man in whose capable hands he and his future lay.

"Good luck, sir!" His handclasp giving more indication of his feelings than did his face. "We'll lay in wait just off more each evening and just before dawn until you all return".

Jason looked towards the dark cliffs and then at the little boat, which tossed in the lively waves. He could just see the white foam, which showed just how near they were to the rocks. He knew that the captain had judged the tide and current nicely and that they should have no difficulty in getting ashore quickly, as the expected storm which had given them a bit of a rough time during the crossing, had now died away.

They were all on deck now, and the three of them checked that they had all they required. It had been arranged with their contact ashore for horses to be waiting for them, so quickly over the side, they went, down the rope ladder to the little boat, which was rocking in the slight swell, and very soon, the 'Firefly' had faded into the night, and they only knew she was there because they had just left her. No light, no sign, no sound. The captain was used to these kind of manoeuvres, and Jason was very thankful.

Then suddenly, a small lantern light flashed from the top of the cliffs – twice, then a pause, then three flashes – all was safe. Quickly the two sailors from the 'Firefly' who had rowed the boat had them at the edge of the beach, and no sooner were the three Englishmen out, then the sailors were rowing away, and they too soon faded out of sight.

Quickly, they took their bearings and headed for the cliff path, which their briefing in London had indicated. It was Patrick who found it and soon they were up on top of the cliffs, and it was easy to follow the path to the small cottage which their contact used as a base. In fact, it looked quite deserted, and Damian echoed all their thoughts when he whispered,

"Are you sure this is the right place, Jason?"

"Yes, and all previous information has been correct from this source, so we had better scout around and check the back of the place and find who flashed the lantern."

Patrick went round the back, Jason approached the Front door of the cottage, and Damian kept a lookout as best he could along the dark pathway. However, when Jason gave the arranged knock on the door, it opened quickly, and a wizened little man darted out, exclaiming, "Messieurs, Messieurs, don't make so much noise please."

To Jason, they hadn't made a sound, but he knew that any movement, stone kicked or twig snapping would echo in the silent darkness to someone whose nerves would be taut, such as their contact's would be.

"Have you the horses as arranged, Monsieur," whispered Jason.

"Naturally, Monsieur. It was arranged and Demerges never lets you down," the old man retorted, again in a whisper.

"Come round to the back of the place, and you'll see what fine specimens I got for you. It was difficult, Monsieur," he said in an ingratiating whine, but Jason was firm and rather brusque because he knew that Castlereagh would have paid handsomely on their behalf. No further money should be necessary.

The old man had indeed got them three fine horses, and with relief Jason gave him an extra gold piece, just in case they needed his help on the return journey. Castlereagh did not believe in using the same man for the inward and the return journey, as the less each agent knew the better. They couldn't reveal more than they knew, could they! However, Jason knew that if necessary Castlereagh was agreed to them making for an agent for a second time if an emergency arose, and Jason rather thought that it might just be this time.

They were soon on their way, and much to their relief, the road which they had been told existed did materialise suddenly and they were on their way to Paris. The French roads were not in the best of the condition at that time of the year, and they kept to the sides when possible, mainly to deaden the sound of the hooves. It was not unknown for travellers to pass that way during the night, and not many peasants were brave enough to challenge the right of anyone to travel through the night. However, to avoid contact with any of Napoleon's guards where possible, they avoided going through the centres of the small villages which were strung out along their route.

As dawn broke, they found themselves just outside the city, and as planned, they headed for a small inn where they knew 'friend' could be found.

In fact, the innkeeper had known Patrick when he was a young lad, and it was with relief that they unsaddled their horses and sat down to a hearty meal which the innkeeper's wife, Madame Paulette, placed before them.

"Your beds are ready for you as soon as you have eaten, Messieurs," she assured them, and the innkeeper confirmed that their horses would be looked after for them and kept well out of sight. Anybody found acting suspiciously or asking questions would be 'dealt with'. It was also wiser that the young men kept to their rooms during the daylight hours and moved at night if possible.

To this Jason, who was now yawning from the effect of the good food and warmth from the big fire roaring up the chimney, replied that they would rest for hours and perhaps later in the day, they could be wakened as they wanted to get inside the city not too long after nightfall.

As soon as their heads touched their pillows, they were all fast asleep and snoring gently, not in rhythm, but perhaps one could say in harmony.

As arranged Jason rode alone to make contact with someone, he only knew as Monsieur Hainault, or rather Citizen Hainault. He knew that according to the neighbours Citizen Hainault was a very well-respected and honest merchant of Paris, so between them Castlereagh and Jason had decided that Jason would be a buyer of fine materials from Brest, being in Paris to obtain special materials for the trousseau of one of the daughters of his very best customer, *Le Due de Moncenis*. As it was nearly closing time when

Jason walked into the premises of Citizen Hainault, he was relieved to find it empty, and on asking the clerk for Citizen Hainault, the clerk went into the rear of the premises to bring forth a portly gentleman with high colour in his cheeks and no hair on his head.

"Ah, Citizen Macon, it is a pleasure to make your acquaintance. I have long awaited your visit. It is indeed an honour to help you choose materials for the daughter of so distinguished a patron," he said, holding his hand out to Jason. "You have had a long journey, please come and share a glass of cognac with me to get rid of the winter chills, which are setting in early this year."

At this, Jason moved towards the doorway through which Hainault had come, but the merchant guided him towards another door, which Jason had not seen.

"This, Citizen, is to my private apartments. Where best to enjoy a good cognac, eh," he chuckled.

Jason agreed, and together they left the clerk sorting out some papers at his desk. As soon as they were the other side of the door, the merchant stopped and holding up his hand to Jason, motioned for him to keep still and surprisingly for one of his girth, he bent down to the keyhole of the door through which they had entered and checked that his clerk was still at his desk. He turned the key to his apartment very quietly, and Jason knew that it must be well oiled for there was no sound of it turning at all. Silently, the merchant beckoned to Jason to follow him down the corridor and finally up some stairs to a very comfortable room, in which Jason could see Hainault used it as his living quarters.

"Now, my friend, I think we can talk safely," Hainault said quickly and quietly. "Up to now, there have been no indications that I am under suspicion, but following the information from London, I have been extra careful. I have not made contact with my friend and I judged it better to wait for that when you arrived just in case anything went wrong along the way. I thought that now you are here, we can go ahead. I have just had some very fine materials delivered from my agent in the East, and I have every reason to call and see my agent at the warehouse, which is in the vicinity of my friend's abode, wait on me tomorrow at the same time, and I shall have arranged a meeting for you as soon as possible, and there will be some magnificent materials for you to look through to satisfy that curious clerk of mine down below."

With that, Jason had to be satisfied. He could understand the Frenchman's reluctance to do anything before he knew Jason was ready, and so on those terms, it was agreed that Jason should return tomorrow, purporting to have come socially; to see the new materials from the Orient. In this clerk's presence, they made their adieux, and Jason left Paris as inconspicuously as possible and returned to the inn, where Madame Paulette had yet another sustaining meal for them. Jason explained to the other two what had happened, that he knew nothing more about what was happening, but that tomorrow he might be able to say if there was anything for them. Although he couldn't confirm it, he thought he hadn't been followed nor watched throughout his journey.

The next day dragged along slowly, and to make matters worse, it was a warm day for October, so they had to do the best they could shut up in their room out of sight. They managed to get down to check their horses, and all were well. Finally, Jason set out once more and as arranged met Citizen Hainault and discussed the beautiful fabrics which the merchant had deliberately set up in the warehouse in full view of the clerk. Jason knew enough about such materials to make an intelligent conversation and was able to bargain for certain quantities of the material for his customers.

As in the best of traditions, they agreed to seal their transactions with another glass of cognac, and together they mounted the stairs as before.

This time the merchant deliberately went straight up the stairs and into his room and closed the door. However, after about five seconds, he opened it very quietly and silently crept along the corridor to check on his clerk. Well, all was well, and with relief, Jason learned that Hainault had got an appointment for him that evening. Jason hadn't mentioned that he had friends with him, so thinking it over quickly he never mentioned them, and he arranged to go with Citizen Hainault to meet the contact of the group who were the current antagonists of the Bonaparte regime. Jason hadn't a clue what to expect, who they were, or what their plans were, and only Hainault knew who he was and where they were going. For all Jason knew, Hainault could be working for Boney and be leading him into a trap. However, he had no way out and so, making an excuse to his clerk, that he wanted to show Citizen Macon some more materials in another warehouse, the merchant took Jason across Paris.

Chapter 13
Intrigue

Through back alleys and down cobbled lanes, Hainault led Jason until finally stopping before a shabby refuge in the Passage Saint-Pierre, at an obviously pre-arranged signal the door was opened and Jason was led down into a dimly lit room. The light was sufficient for him to see that there was only one person in the room, and he was wearing the dark clerical garb of a Spanish priest! So the Spaniards were in it too, immediately flashed through Jason's mind, but he held his tongue and just listened.

The person was introduced as the Abbe Lafon, but he looked more a man of action than a man of the cloth. His steely blue eyes looked straight at Jason and without further ado, he motioned for the two men to take a seat at the rough table in the room. There were just a couple of stools so Jason knew it was not a well-used rendezvous or habitation.

"What does England want out of this?" immediately asked Lafon.

"To see the end of Napoleon and his blockage of the Channel," replied Jason.

"What kind of help and when?" was shot back at him.

"Nothing obvious, but I'm sure gold would help your scheme – what is it?"

The Abbe looked a little startled as though he had expected England to send troops in to help, thought Jason, but this thought was farthest from the Abbe's mind. In fact, the coup was so secret that only a couple of parsons knew and he didn't want England really mixed up in it. The real reason behind his involvement was because Pope Pius VII had been brought a few months earlier from exile in Savona to Fontainebleau, by Napoleon for fear that the British Navy would attempt to liberate him. However, Abbe Lafon was part of a vast organisation based on a large section of the French clergy, which planned to liberate the Pope. The Bull of excommunication which the Pope had issued against Napoleon three years before when the French invaded the Papal States and which had caused him to be exiled from Rome, had never been published in France, but it had become known in secret ways through prelates, priests and the faithful adherents of the Catholic faith. The French clergy were divided, the majority remaining faithful to the Holy Father, but a minority supported the Imperial decree. Many of those faithful, bishops and archbishops had been arrested, whilst various Cardinals in the Pope's suite were put under arrest in the fortresses of Vincennes. Lafon, was considered inconsequential and so had been shut up in La Force in Paris. Some friends had managed to get him transferred to the hospital clinic of Dr Dubuisson, and here he had become acquainted with a certain General Malet, a life-long anti-Bonapartist. By very different ways, one and the same hatred had brought them both to that clinic, and that common hatred quickly established a friendship which seemed to have been lifelong. They confided everything to each other, united their projects, plans and hopes. It made no difference what lay behind them, what was the ultimate goal that inspired them. The immediate aim was the same, Napoleon's overthrow and the end of the Imperial regime.

"Yes, indeed, gold would help. We shall need all we can get to bring the troops over to our side. They are so poorly paid by now that we shall find good use. How much and how soon can you get it?"

"It will take a little time, how long have we got?" replied Jason.

"Haven't any with me, and I shall need to get word back to England."

"Hm, we planned to overthrow the tyrant on the 10th of this month, so you cannot help us at the beginning, but more and more gold will become necessary as we take over control. These greedy officials will soon change sides when they see what it is worth to them," replied the Abbe.

"But that's tomorrow," exclaimed Jason.

"Yes," replied the Abbe, "we have everything planned, and we see no reason to hold it back. Your gold can help us later."

"Can you tell me some of your plans? My leader will wish to know something about them if we are to help you?" asked Jason.

"At the moment, there are only four of us in this, and that is enough. When you see the result, when we are there in the Hotel de Ville, you can bring forth your gold, and your shipping will be free to go anywhere in the Channel once more," replied Abbe Lafon.

Through all this interchange Hainault had been outside the room soon after Jason had confirmed that England would help. He suddenly entered the room and whispered something to the Abbe, at which the latter immediately got up, held out his hand to Jason and said, "Keep in touch with Hainault, you shall not fail to hear of our success. Come to me when I can help you, and don't forget the gold. Shall we say, 50,000 gold Louis to start with?"

"I shall keep in touch," promised Jason, not knowing whether or not Castlereagh would think it worthwhile sending over such a sum, but as nothing was needed until there had been a coup and Napoleon was overthrown Jason saw no need to make any promises, just to wish the venture 'Bon Quickly, the Abbe disappeared through another door in the room and Hainault quickly pushed Jason out of the one they had originally come successfully through. Why the rush Jason knew not, but then one didn't ask such questions at such times. He knew enough of this kind of intrigue to move with haste silently.

Back at the merchant's premises, Jason joined Hainault in a glass of cognac, and together they toasted the success of their particular *coup d'état*.

By then, it was rather late, and though there was no curfew, it was difficult to get out of the city. However, Jason decided to risk it, and so he heeded the warning of the merchant and kept to the darker streets and alleys, on a watch though for any gangs lurking around.

That was one thing that Napoleon had done – his National Guard was a credit to him when they wanted to be, and the mob rule of the revolution era had long been a thing of the past.

Back at the Inn, Patrick and Damian wanted to know all the news, not expecting Jason to have already been in touch with members of the underground movement to overthrow Napoleon. They were staggered when they learned of the plans already in hand and the imminent data of the coup.

"One of us shall have to get back to Castlereagh and let him know and also bring back some gold to show good faith if it is a success," said Patrick.

"Yes," replied Jason. "If it is a success."

"Aren't you sure of them, then," Damian said.

"I don't know enough about this Abbe or General Malet. I've heard of Malet before, and he's supposed to be in a clinic out of the way of doing harm to the Imperial regime. The Abbe inferred that it was easy to get out of the clinic, indeed he too is supposed to be there, and as he was out of the clinic when I met him, presume it is easy enough, but I'm not easy in my mind about the whole affair. Still, we are not expected to take part in it, and Castlereagh cannot complain about that as long as a result is what we are all working for."

"Does M Hainault know anything more of the Abbe?" asked Patrick.

"No, nothing much, but he seems to trust him. Apparently, the Philadelphes are mixed up in it somewhere along the line, and this is where Hainault comes in."

"Who shall go back to Castlereagh," asked Patrick, not wanting to go, but obviously someone must, and it had to be either him or Damian.

"Damian, I think – Jane will be grateful," Jason adding with a smile, thinking too that she could also ease Felicity's mind that they were all well. Jason hadn't mentioned anything to Patrick or Damian about his fondness for Felicity, so no other meaning was thought of, and Damian was suitably grateful for the chance to return so soon to his beloved. Captain Thelwall will be at the rendezvous as planned and when you see Castlereagh tell him not to put too much faith in this idea of Lafon and Malet. Dreams in a clinic tend to become too real whilst they are inside, but reality presents many problems. "There is no doubt that Malet is a clever and dangerous man, but as to the Abbe, I just do not know."

"If he belongs to the Pope's entourage, he will have other resources at hand, I am sure and will probably let Malet do most of the obvious work and then take over when success is assured," said Jason.

Damian had soon packed his few belongings, and the innkeeper had his horse brought round to the back door because Damian could make many miles in the dark hours still left before daybreak. He might get to the *Baie des Anges* in time for the dawn rendezvous, but if not, he could hide in a barn until the evening because he knew that the Captain would look for someone both at dusk and dawn.

"Right, Damian, a quick, safe journey and give our love to Jane and Felicity," said Patrick with a smile, and Jason too agreed with his sentiments, hoping Damian would take it from him in the same spirit he took it from Patrick, who was known to like the ladies, and gathering the reins Damian was off into the night and Jason and Patrick made their way back into the inn.

All the following day, the 10th October, Jason and Patrick stayed in their room, knowing that if the coup had been a success, the news would soon be around. However, everything was quiet, and they risked sitting in the tap room drinking ale during the evening, keeping out of the way in a dim recess, hoping that no nosey villager would give them more than a passing glance.

Being on what was a fairly well-travelled route, strangers were not rare, and so they thought they could risk leaving their room, which by now they were heartily sick of, despite the efforts of Madame Paulette.

Nothing happened; everyone was just as before. The innkeeper who knew they were expecting news came over to them when finally the door was closed on the last drinkers and said, "Is no news good or bad news, messieurs?"

"Bad news, I think, my friend," replied Jason.

"I must get into Paris first thing in the morning and see what went wrong."

"Do you want me with you," replied Patrick, who by now was getting rather fed up with staying at the inn, although there was a very attractive young girl who helped Madame Paulette. Patrick had taken advantage of Jason's absences to flirt light-heartedly with her, but he had come for adventure, not flirting – he could do that in London society easily enough.

"No, Hainault doesn't know of your existence, and if the coup didn't succeed, then you'll have to ride to the coast to warm Damian and get back to London."

"What about you, Jason?"

"He stays a little while longer if it hasn't come off and try to see if anything else is being planned. If the conspirators have been caught, then I'll join you at the coast as quickly as possible. Leave a message at that small inn, 'The Anchor' just outside Le Treport, if you are to come on to Paris, back here to the Paulettes or back to England as fast as you can."

"The message will be from a Monsieur Dupont, that's a common enough name and shouldn't give much trouble. The message will be something like – Paul has the fever, Paul being your nephew say, that being not to come, and Paul hopes you will call on him if I need you back in Paris."

"Well, I hope Paul extends his invitation, I shall be very disappointed not to see my nephew after such a long time away," replied Patrick laughingly, knowing full well that Jason had every intention of playing the major part in this venture, and that he could only do what Jason told him. Still, he was getting away from the inn for a short time, at least.

The next morning Jason was soon off and away into Paris, and as soon as Hainault saw him, he motioned him over to look at some silks, saying under his breath:

"One of the main guards on whom we had to rely got himself so drunk, he was put in the guardhouse, and everything had to be forgotten."

"What now?" asked Jason, equally guardedly because the clerk was not too far away.

"The next convenient night is the 22nd to 23rd of October and don't worry, this time nothing will go wrong. The Abbe is so sure that he will see you tonight and give you a little more information to reassure you. General Malet too may well be able to come too, but if not Madame Malet, who knows of the complete venture will come in his place."

"Very well," said Jason, not really wanting to come back into Paris again that night, but it might be as well to see how much he could get to know and see if this was yet another of those supposedly fool proof plans which men dream of when locked in prison cells for months on end.

Jason returned to the inn and gave Patrick the news.

"I'll leave then now or when you come back tonight?" asked Patrick.

"Perhaps it will be as well to wait until I've seen the Abbe and the General. If it is a lunatics dream, then we shall both go back to England and waste no more time."

When Jason returned to the warehouse that evening, the clerk was not there and so after locking up securely, the two men slipped off into the night, not this time to the Passage Saint-Pierre, but to the *Rua de l'Universite*. A middle-aged lady opened the door, and Jason was introduced to Madame Malet.

It was only through her endeavours that the General was at the Clinic.

He had been in La Force for quite a time, but now he would soon be returned there as the money he got from his army pay was due to be cut off and without that, there would be nothing to meet the bills of Dr Dubuisson. This was a make-or-break venture for him.

The Abbe and the General and another young man introduced as Monsieur Balance were sitting in the room, and whilst Hainault went into the kitchen, the five persons connected with the forthcoming coup sat and weighed up each other. Jason had, of course, only met the Abbe before, so he waited and let the General make the first move.

He seemed to be the obvious leader or wanted to be. The young man known as Balance was a trim, slight young man, and took little part in the conversation which followed. It appeared, however, that he was to take over the position of Prefect of Police when Pasquier was arrested. That's moving a little ahead though of the General's plans, and he proceeded to tell Jason some of their intentions.

It appeared that on the night of the 22nd to 23rd of October, he, the Abbe, Balance and a certain Corporal Rateau who had been the drunkard on the earlier occasion were going to go to the main barracks at Popincourt, wake the guard, give the password which Rateau would supply, and announce to the bewildered Commandant that Napoleon had been killed on the 7th October beneath the walls of Moscow. Malet was to assume the name of a fellow General as his own was too well known as an anti-Bonapartiste, and they intended to arrest certain officials and proclaim a new provisional government.

"You will see, *mon ami Anglais*, from the list that we shall once more bring France back to her glorious days. There will be 15 members, being Moreau, who will be the Prime Minister of the Provisional Government, Carnot, will be his deputy; then General Augereau, General Oestutt-Tracy, General Lambrecht, General Volney, General Garat. We shall keep Frochot as Prefect of the Seine – he'll change sides when he sees what is happening. Then Mathieu de Montmorency, Alexis de Noailles, both Aristocratic enemies of the Imperial regime, then there is Bigonnet, florent-Guyot, Jacquemont, former members of the Legislative Assembly. We shall also ask Admiral Truguet and finally, myself.

"The Abbe has no wish for such a position. As you know, he works to free the Pope, and we are agreed, are we not my friends, that our causes are allied and complete."

Whilst the General had been mentioning all these names, Jason had been struck by his positiveness and complete mastery of the plot. There was no doubt he had everything planned down to the last detail. Provided he was not let down by others, there was a chance of success. He knew of Generals Laharie and Guida, but nothing of the person called

Bocchaciampe, the three persons Malet was relying upon to be released from La Force Prison to take up the important positions prior to it being announced to the populace that Napoleon had been killed.

"We shall be glad of your English gold, my friend," said Malet. "We must not forget the old soldiers. They have had enough of the Corsicans travels through Europe. They will welcome the general peace, which we shall announce immediately with all our former enemies. They will all return home. Give them extra pay, promotion, and they will do what we ask. We'll abolish conscription but retain the Legion of Honour. Simple things like this will end the Imperialist regime. Whilst he's under the walls of the Kremlin, his walls in Paris will totter. Down with Napoleon, Long live the Provisional Government, gentlemen. I give you a toast – success to our return to sanity." Madame Malet had provided glasses and a bottle of cognac, which soon disappeared. Many other things were discussed, but when Jason asked about documents they would need and such other administrative details, the Abbe set his mind at rest.

"Do not worry; those are already – just the date to be put on when we start. That corporal of yours had better not let us down this time, *Generali.*"

By the time all the important things had been discussed, Jason made excuses to leave – he must get a message to Patrick to get going and give him his impressions now that he knew a bit more of what was behind this particular plot.

Hainault got him back to the outskirts of Paris where Jason had left his horse, and soon back at the inn, Patrick was all ready for travel and had been idling his time in the small taproom, dangling the barmaid on his knee.

However, as soon as he saw Jason appear in the doorway, he tipped her off, and with a rue smile, she pouted and threw him a kiss which quickly was returned in a more practical way which she had hoped – a coin which would join her little hoard up in the attic. She had already found that travellers were appreciative of her particular charms, and she had no intention of staying in that inn any longer than necessary.

"Off on your way, Patrick," said Jason. "Tell Castlereagh, the plan is simple and good. It could work and all we shall need to do is to provide the ready money to oil the works a little. The Abbe wants the Pope freed, Malet wants to get rid of Napoleon and sees himself as running the whole thing eventually, but I doubt if the others will let him do that, but it should, if successful, be the end of Napoleon."

"How long do we have?" asked Patrick.

"Well, the next convenient date is the night of the 22nd to 23rd of October, so that gives you plenty of time to get back here. I don't think there is any need for Damian to come back. We have nothing to do but sit and wait. You can come back and stay if you want when you bring the money. I expect that young doxy I saw you with will welcome you back with open arms, eh?" He laughed.

"If there is any trouble before then, I'll send the warning to the inn outside Le Treport, or M Paulette will have the news if I've no time to get a message out." Laughing, Patrick vaulted into his saddle and was soon off into the night.

Jason wished he too could go back home to Felicity, but it would be as well to stay here and keep out of sight but in touch with the conspirators. Ten days to sit and wait – what to do? Perhaps he too should have gone back with Patrick and seen Felicity, but he knew he wouldn't want to come back to France once he had left it.

"Well, Monsieur Paulette, can you put up with me for ten days or so?" he said to the innkeeper on returning to the tap-room.

"I'm sure Madame Paulette will be only too pleased to be able to cook for someone who so obviously enjoys her cooking. I'm afraid I have to watch my weight a bit these days," he said, laughing as he poked at his rather large paunch.

"It makes a change to have someone sitting down and eating all put before him," agreed Madame Paulette, knowing full well that it was a rather delicate subject between her and her husband that when he ate her cooking he put on weight, and she preferred him rather less weighty, as he had been when she married him. But then, how many innkeepers stay slim?

Chapter 14
Action

The ten days soon passed, and Jason had found himself able to help Paulette with many odd jobs. If anyone from the Court of the Prince Regent could have seen their elegant Earl of Lindsey hauling up beer barrels from the cellar and helping with travellers' horses, they just would not have believed it. Jason had thought it wiser to help the Paulettes in this way rather than just hang around the inn. There was no way of knowing who was spying for who. Simone, the pretty wench who had flirted with Patrick, had to be given a story because she knew that Patrick hadn't been without some money. His clothes and attitude had been above her standards, and she had seen Jason and Damian too, but it was decided to tell her that Jason had lost his money and was wanted by the government for some minor offence. His friends had gone to sort it out and in the meantime, he was helping the Paulettes in the only way he could. Simone found she liked Jason, but her little tarty ways didn't appeal to Jason, but he had to try not to show it. She tried to find out more about him, but he was wise to such things, and she finally gave up when a much handsome and wealthier traveller arrived at the inn. Working the cellars and in the stables had provided Jason with a good unclean appearance and although he hated it, he didn't try to tidy himself up too much. A cellar man cum stable-boy usually only had the rags they stood up in, so when Patrick arrived, he didn't recognise him at first.

"*Garcon, mon cheval – donnez-lui un bon repas du fainet de l'eau tout de suite.*"

"*Oui, Monsieur, immédiatement,*" replied Jason.

Patrick started and gave another look at the stable boy. "Jason, what on earth."

"Hush, Patrick, there's nothing wrong, just go on in as though you had arrived normally. I'll join you later."

After doing all he had to do with the horses and bringing up some more barrels of ale for Monsieur Paulette, Jason finally staggered up to the room where Patrick was now installed.

"I'll explain everything when I've had something to eat and drink," said Jason before Patrick could even get a word in.

Madame Paulette brought up a tray and both men tucked into a chicken with vegetables and some savoury sauce. There was apple pie and cream to follow, and all this washed down with a jug of the best ale.

"Ten days is a long time to stay at a place like this, so whilst you were gone, I've been helping to look after the horses and bring up barrels from the cellar and so on. That wench Simone had to be given some kind of story, so as far as she is aware, I am the one in hiding, and you and Damian had gone away to sort out all my problems. Now you are back, we can tell her that it is sorted out and we can get away. What did Castlereagh say, and did you bring anything back with you?"

"Well, Castlereagh agrees that we sit and wait for the result of the coup. He's rather glad we are not to be involved in any other way. He doesn't want to be involved in liberating the Pope, as that would cause too many complications, but there's enough gold there, producing a couple of soft leather bags to give proof of our help."

"Good," replied Jason. "I've not been in touch with Hainault at all, and I think it best to keep away until the 21st. I'll then slip in and say that we've got what they want, and we wait to hear from them."

"Well, we've got one day left before then, what do we do with it," asked Patrick.

"I'm going to sleep, and sleep and sleep," replied Jason. "It gets rather hard going day after day lugging up those barrels."

Patrick laughed.

"Well, you did insist on staying. Now if it had been me, I think I would have been in bed instead of down in the callars! I wonder if Simone missed me, by the way, Jane and Felicity send their love!"

Jason started, "Had anything been said or was it just a phrase used so commonly nowadays." After all, Jason had known Jane for a long time and as far as everyone else was aware that Felicity was his stepsister.

"Oh well, time would tell."

Patrick looked at Jason keenly when he said that last phrase. When he had seen Jane, who had been thankful that Damian hadn't had to return, it was she who had sent her love, and felicitations to Jason, and on doing so had turned to include Felicity in the farewell phrase. Quite unexpectedly, Felicity had blushed and whilst Jane thought nothing of it,

Patrick had wondered after all they had been missing for quite a bit of the last part of the Grand Ball, and Jason had been rather determined to return. Well, perhaps the 'old man' had at last succumbed to a maiden's charms. Yes, he rather thought he had. He had added it deliberately at a time when he knew Jason had relaxed, and he saw the startled but quickly hidden look. *The lucky devil*, thought Patrick, who had been hoping to win Felicity's heart.

The next day, Jason did indeed stay in and slept…late, and when he finally staggered down to the dining room, he was greeted by Patrick, who was being fussed over by Simone.

"Ah, here's the sleepy head. Now all is well for him; all he does is sleep."

Simone giggled and Patrick pulled her down on to his knee and began to kiss and fondle her.

"Now, now, Monsieur – this is not the time; perhaps tonight, eh?"

With a laugh off, she danced, and Patrick gave her a rather expressive look and made it rather obvious that he was only too willing to share his night with her. Little did she know that it would be the last night because Jason and he had decided that should the coup be successful, they would deposit the gold and get back to the coast to give the news to England. It was up to the French people to carry on if the General and the Abby's plans were successful. By the end of the day of 23rd October, they would know one way or the other.

The rest of the day and night passed uneventfully for Jason, although he kept waking up, wondering how things were going on. Had the corporal given the correct password, would General Malet pass himself off as another lesser-known General? Would Commandant Soulier in charge of

Popincourt Barracks accept the news as true? Would Bault, the Head Warder of la Force allow Lahorie, Guidal and Bocchachiampe out of prison on the papers provided by the General? Would the military discipline instilled into the National Guard make them do exactly what their leaders told them to do? Did they really hate the Imperial regime? Would there be any resistance to it, or would gold really change them over, plus all the other extras Malet had planned on. What about the L'Aiglon, or the Eaglet, the King of Rome, Napoleon's son by the Empress Marie Louise? Were there any supporters who would declare themselves for him and say he was the next in line of succession? Looking at his watch, and that daylight was gradually coming over the fields, Jason could imagine the company of the 10th Cohort of the National Guard, which consisted of men exempt from active service because they were unfit for service or specially favoured instead of being in Russia or Spain; he could imagine them marching along the rue Saint-Sebastien, rue Saint-Claude, rue Saint-Louis, rue Saint-Antoine which had the sordid prison, La Grande Force. The French people still passed by it in fear, remembering those days when the September massacres had taken place, and the *Princess de Lamballe* had been struck down there.

Jason could not lie down any longer. Had Frochot, the Prefect of the Seine come over to their side, what about Savary, that man so hated by everyone He had been the man responsible for the murder of the *Due d'Enghien* and had become a duke himself, *Due de Rovigo*, who grew rich sending soldiers to be killed, hunting recalcitrant conscripts, shooting deserters enlisted by force even though half-blind and crippled. Jason doubted if he would last long once the protection of Napoleon was ended. There was then General Hulin, the Commandant of Paris. Malet himself had decided to attend to General Hulin's arrest. He alone could thwart their plans.

The minutes, the hours passed by, and Jason was now joined by Patrick, who had spent a better night in the arms of Simona, who had been very generous with her favours.

The inn where they were staying was not so far from Paris that news of the death of so great a person as the Emperor would not have reached it by mid-afternoon. Indeed, if the coup had been successful and the death of Napoleon believed, there would have been messengers on every road out of Paris within hours. "No, something had gone wrong, but what, I'm going into Paris to find out," said Jason.

"You're not going alone," insisted Patrick.

Both spoke French without any English accent, and there was little danger for them to be seen in Paris even in daylight. Jason doubted that anyone knew of their connection with the plot. There was only Hainault, who had been the contact. It would probably be as well to go to the warehouse and see what he had to say.

Arriving quite openly, Jason want into the warehouse leaving Patrick with their horses, and the clerk who knew Jason as Monsieur Macon, could only tell Jason that Monsieur Hainault was not there, had not been there all day and that if he could help Monsieur, he would be only too willing to do so. However, Jason thought it wiser to say nothing and just said he had called to say farewell and thank Monsieur Hainault for the many fine fabrics which he had been able to supply him with for his customers.

With that Jason left the premises and joined Patrick outside, mounted his horse and looking at each other, they moved away from the warehouse and out of sight of it paused, and looking at each other, both said, "What next?"

Little did they know, however, that the coup had indeed failed. Guidal had got drunk on the headiness of freedom and had not carried out all the plans he had had to do, and General Hulin had had minutes warning, which was enough time to denounce General Malet, who was pretending to be a General Lamotte. Lahorie and Guidal were captured; eventually, Balance disappeared, Rateau was arrested, and everyone known to have been in touch with any of these conspirators were arrested.

The Abbe Lafon, however, was another matter.

He just disappeared, and nothing more was heard of him. Monsieur Hainault had, in fact, been arrested too because the clerk, that insignificant person sitting at that large desk, had been only too pleased to curry favour, and he had put two and two together. He had followed Hainault and Jason that time when they had gone to General Malet's apartment. He had really finished work and left, but returning to collect some minor article had seen Jason arrive and the two of them leave. Being naturally curious, he had followed, and when the news of General Malet's plot became known, he had denounced Hainault to the authorities. Now, they also knew about Jason or the merchant from Brest as the clerk knew him. He had had his suspicions from the start for some reason or other – he was that way inclined. He had been brought up in the times of the Revolution, and it was ingrained in him to suspect everyone. Now, though, here was his great chance. He signalled to one of the beggars standing lounging about the doorway of another warehouse down the street, and that dirty looking individual sped away down the maze of back streets which abound in that quarter and was shortly to be seen entering a hostelry by the back entry. His information prompted the departure of another shabby person by the front door of the place, and so was set in motion a chain of messages. Meanwhile, Jason and Patrick unknowing of their danger, set off for the centre of Paris not in undue haste to draw attention to themselves, and unfortunately, it was at a pace which enabled them to be followed.

"It's no good, Patrick, we'll have to make enquiries," said Jason.

"There is an air of excitement about the place. Perhaps a drink at that sordid bordello might give us some news."

Dismounting and giving a coin to one of the many urchins to look after their horses, they entered the tavern, and after getting a jug of wine, they gradually joined in a conversation which was taking place at the next table. At this table were two elderly men, who had obviously once been part of the Grande Armee, which Napoleon Bonaparte had used to bring Europe down to her knees. Now, however, they no longer took any part having been disabled through battle injuries and were some of the many similar beggarly persons to be seen around Paris. It was obvious that there had been some event that morning because the old men were jabbering away, and when Jason and Patrick began to draw into their circle, they were only too willing to pass on their news, ably lubricated by the jugs of ale which were brought to the table at frequent signals by Patrick.

"But what exactly happened, Monsieur Viellard?" asked Jason. "How on earth could anyone just go up to the barracks and tell them Napoleon was dead."

"Well, Monsieur, it appears that all the documents were correct, and of course the youngsters who were on duty were not fully awake, you know, Monsieur, hmm not like the old days, my friend."

"Indeed, Monsieur, if it hadn't been for that great old soldier, General Hulin, we would now have a new government and Napoleon would be no more.

"It appears that one of the conspirators got drunk with his freedom and did not appear at the correct time to arrest certain members of the government and so on, Monsieur. One cannot trust the demon drink, eh." He cackled away to himself, for he too was well on the way to the hazy world of the drunkard.

"What happened to the conspirators, my good friend?" Jason asked the other old soldier, who seemed to be holding his drink a little better.

"All arrested, and many more – everyone who they think had anything to do with it. Of course, the old General, Malet I think his name was, was in a clinic, you know, not quite there touching his forehead with a grimy finger. They've even arrested his wife and some of their friends, but they say that some of them got away in time. One of them, a General Guidal was, of course, a spy for the English, so they could have been at the back of all this. Indeed, they say that an Englishman is being sought after as he was seen leaving the apartment of General Malet only the other night."

This was a shock to Jason, for he thought that his part had not been known to anyone other than Malet, the Abbe, that young man Balance and Hainault. It explained Hainault's absence too. If Jason had been seen, Hainault had.

Of course, they would have kept a watch on Hainault since they got the message via Claude from England, but everything had been careful, and Hainault, in particular, had gone to great lengths to make sure all was safe. Still in this business, one just never knew what was going to happen the next minute. And Jason and Patrick didn't know either that only a minute away was a company of the National Guard. The spies had been at work, and their location was known.

Realising that they had got to know all they possibly could, and also that their companions were now almost at the table, Jason and Patrick rose from the table, paid for the drinks and made for the door. The doorway was framed by an officer of the National Guard, who suddenly said, "Messieurs, I have reason to believe you are English, yes?" and with his hand on his sword and a company of soldiers just behind him, Jason knew that they had little chance of escape that way, realising that Patrick too was rather up against a table to his right, he knew that if they could both work together, they could block that entrance for a second just to give them time to get away. There was always a back door to this place, but on whose side was the patron?

All these thoughts and the following action happened in seconds of time, and as it had happened in the past, Patrick knew just what to do. Grabbing hold of one of the flimsy tables, he flung it at the Officer, and another one came from Jason took with accompanying chair and glasses and wine bottles, all adding to the confusion.

"Monsieur, this way," hissed the patron, indicating a door behind the bar. Jason and Patrick found themselves in an alley, which the soldiers would soon find themselves in, and they would either be surrounded or shot to death escaping. Facing them was another doorway, and so hurling themselves at it, they found it gave way into an old tenement and quickly closing the door, they took a quick look at their surroundings. They knew they hadn't much chance. Their horses were outside the inn, so they couldn't get them.

There must be another way out of this derelict place, so opening rotting doors and pushing planks for wood, which served for furniture out of the way; they stumbled into what seemed to be the kitchen of the house. The occupants, who were elderly, were as amazed as Jason and Patrick, who thought the place uninhabitable, but before the old folk could say or do anything, they were out of the place and in another alley.

"Quick this way, away from the inn," said Patrick. "We shall have to get ourselves horses elsewhere."

"We could do with finding ourselves a change of clothing too; they'll know who to look for now, although it was rather dark in that place. The officer may not have had a chance to see much of us having come in from the glare of the outside light."

By this time, they were well down the maze of alleys, which led down into the centre of Paris. They took care not to walk too quickly, and any side alley served their purpose. Soon they were on the way to the outskirts of the City, but they knew that at the entrance into the city itself, the guards would have been warned and they were still without horses. "Have you any money on you Patrick?" asked Jason.

Laughingly, Patrick said, "Half the gold in the world," and he told him how he had put one bag of the gold louis under his jerkin and the other in his saddle bag, both being a little heavy to carry on his person.

"Well, we can then buy horses. There is no trouble there, but where from?"

"There's an inn just there at the end of the road, perhaps it may be as well to book a room there and wait until the search has died down a little. We may be able to exchange clothes with someone!" said Patrick. "There'll also be horses in the stable."

Not liking to stay in the city longer than necessary Jason was against this at first, but soon realised that there was not much else they could do. They were both tired and more obvious on foot than on horses in their present clothes.

They could also possibly leave during the night and hope the guard at the Gate was not as wide awake. It had worked for Malet apparently at the Popincourt Barracks, perhaps it would work for them at *the Barri re du* Nord.

The inn was not a very welcoming place, but there was no suspicion in the innkeeper's eyes when the two men entered. Patrick had noted down one of the alleys that a blacksmith was busy shoeing some horses, so they said they had left their horses with him to be attended to and that they would be brought round to the inn's ostler for stabling later that evening or possibly in the morning.

They climbed rickety old stairs up to a room which held one bed and little else, and between them, they could just manage to get around. However, it was better than being out in the open, waiting to be surrounded by the militia. They had been told that there was a cold meal ready for them as soon as they were wanting it, and after a quick wash in some substance which passed for water, they went down to the dining room. The meal was nothing of consequence but was just what they had expected, and it served the purpose. It put new heart into them, and a few glasses of cognac soon eased their nerves. "It will be as well if we retire fairly early, and we can get some sleep but get away before everyone is up in the morning. There's an old fellow over there who is about your size, and I expect there'll be something around in one of the other rooms that will do me," said Jason.

"Shall we wait until they retire or go up now whilst they are all here in the dining room?" asked Patrick.

"You go up and have a quick look whilst there is a chance. See where things are, and then in the dark, we shan't have too much trouble. I'll stay down here, and if anyone makes a move, I'll try to warn you," said Jason.

Patrick found some reason to go back to their room, and although it seemed ages to Jason, it wasn't long before he was back.

"The old chap over there has a spare cloak in his room hanging on a peg just inside the door, and there's no lock on the door, so I'll be able to grab that whilst he is in bed. The only other thing is that the ostler is your build, and perhaps he may have something more suitable for you.

"We can go over and see if our horses have arrived, see what stock there is in the stable, and perhaps find out if there is anything of the ostlers that will do you. If not, then you'll have to make do."

"Yes, at least it will be dark, and there is a chance the soldier may be colour blind," replied Jason, a little of his humour coming back with the fire of the cognac in his belly. In due course, they made their way to the stables, and fortunately, the ostler was not there. A quick search produced a rather filthy looking cloak which Jason quickly appropriated and hid under his present one. However, the horses were the problem. No horses to look after. The ostler was presumably missing because he had gone, The old gentleman in the dining room was either not a rider, but a passenger on some coach or again perhaps his horse had gone to the blacksmith.

"The smithy," they said in unison. Quickly they left the inn, and as it was now going dusk, they were able to get quite unobtrusively down to the smithy. Yes, thank the lord, he had a few horses in the rough stables at the side of his forge.

Just in case those horses were to go out early in the morning to their owners, they returned to the inn, pretended to their host that they were tired and retired to their room. Unfortunately, the inn was quite a popular place during the later hours of the evening, and it was some time before the place was quiet enough for them to leave their room.

Patrick had managed to get some candle grease on the hinges of the door so that it wouldn't creak, and although he couldn't remember the old fellow's bedroom door squeaking earlier in the evening when he was looking for a cloak, he hoped that that hadn't developed one since. They moved on to the landing, in complete darkness. Patrick made for the door of the old traveller, opened it, no squeak, no cloak.

God, no, now what could he have done with it. He would have undressed to go to bed, not dressed ah, that was it, probably being an old man the coverings on the bed were not enough – perhaps he had put it on over the moth-eaten bedspread. Hoping not to have had needed to open the door widely, Patrick had now to do so, and to his relief, it did not squeak. His heart stopped beating for a second though, and he froze, the old fellow was there, but, yes, his eyes were closed and, was sitting up in bed, with his nightcap on and a dressing gown, and yes, the cloak was over the top of the bedding. Oh, a silent sigh of relief went through Patrick, but he now had to get across the room without waking up the old man, for it appeared the chap had fallen asleep whilst sitting propped up by his pillows. Going carefully, Patrick could see by the moonlight which filtered through the thin rags called curtains that there was no obstacle before him, but he couldn't know about creaky boards. Well, he had to do it, Jason would be wondering what *was* happening. Holding his breath, he started off across the room and got within inches of taking the cloak when the old chap moved. Patrick dropped out of sight beneath the edge of the bottom of the bed, which was quite a high one.

"Ah, foolish, foolish me," muttered the old man. "Fancying falling asleep sitting up," and he proceeded to put his pillows straight and snuggle down under the clothes. Soon he was breathing heavily, and Patrick just had to take the chance that he had soon got off to sleep again. Pulling ever so gently at the cloak, he found to his relief that the old man in his changing of position had not caught hold of the cloak, and gradually it slipped to the floor. Patrick silently gathered it up and once more crept to the door. This time he wasted no more effort, and it was open and shut in a flash, and he was down those stairs as fast as possible in the dim light available. "God in heaven, where've you been," uttered Jason, who by this time had been wondering whether to risk going back up the stairs. There had been no disturbance within the household, so Patrick was not discovered, so he knew something had held him up. Jason had the ostler's grimy cloak and with that on and Patrick with the old chap's old-fashioned cape, they both climbed over the wall at the back of the stables into the alley. They found the smithy's stables and yes, the horses were still there.

"Check that they are all shoed, because we don't want one letting us down too soon on our journey," whispered Jason.

The horses were a bit restless, but soon calmed down and quickly Patrick saddled one horse.

"This is newly shoed and seems very fit – take this, and I'll get that black he seems to have plenty of life in him," he said to Jason.

Jason opened the smithy door as quietly as possible. A horse stamped its feet a bit, but they were lucky, the black horse Patrick liked was also newly shod and so as quietly as they could with the horses, they closed the stable door and were off away to the *Barriere du Nord*.

They knew their way fairly well but tried to go as quietly as possible.

Travellers at that time of night were not rare, but unwise and so it was as well not to make oneself obvious. They were soon within a distance of the gate, and although the barriers were across the road, the guard was nowhere to be seen.

"The only thing is to attract his attention, and I'll creep up behind and knock him out. There should only be one on around now. He's due to be relieved soon, so he'll be rather fed up and tired."

Patrick waited moments for Jason to creep up in place, and then he made for the barriers.

"Hey, there, you in there, open this confounded thing."

A rather bleary-eyed sentry appeared, and he never knew what hit him. The gate was soon open, and they were on their way back to the coast.

They made good time but unfortunately were not able to get to the coast in time for the dawn rendezvous with the 'Firefly'.

"We'll head the way of The Anchor just outside *Le Treport*. The contact there will know how things are in the area. If there's any activity or anything suspicious, he'll know, and we'll have to find a barn," said Jason.

"Why go there? What about that place on the top of the cliffs where we first landed. It's not far away, and we'll be out of sight. I bet that old crone doesn't live there during the day, only on 'special' nights. If there's anything suspicious or we have to make a run for it, the 'Firefly' shouldn't be too far off, even if we have to swim about for a few hours!"

"Heaven forbid that we'll need to do that. That's one thing I can't do, at least not for long – I mean swim," replied Jason, when Patrick looked at him rather blankly.

"Oh, I'll hold you up, I won't let you drown down, old chape," he said with a twinkle in his eye. It was agreed that they would head for the hovel on the top of the cliffs. Dawn was breaking, but no one was in sight, and it was perhaps the best thing to do.

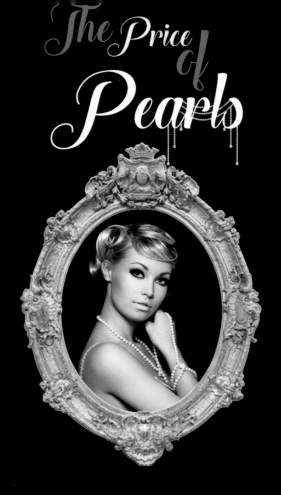

The Price of Pearls

Doreen Rawsthorne

AUSTIN MACAULEY PUBLISHERS™ LTD
CGC-33-01, 25 CANADA SQUARE,
CANARY WHARF, LONDON, E14 5LQ
UNITED KINGDOM

Chapter 15
A Discovery

Whilst the three young men had been journeying to France; the two girls had woken the following morning in their beautiful bedrooms, full of excitement and happiness. The ball had been a wonderful success, and Felicity was so happy for Jane. Felicity wondered at first, it had all been a dream, but she saw the ring Jason had given her amongst her jewels in her box – not a dream, reality.

Chattering excitedly, they finally went down for some breakfast, very late breakfast in fact, and so it was with surprise that Felicity found a note for her by her place at the table.

Quickly opening it, she said, "Jane, my father is ill. I must go to him at once."

"Your father ill he looked so well a few days ago when he was here. What has happened, Felicity?" asked Jane and her mother, anxiously.

"Apparently, he caught a cold on his journey back to Ravenwood, and he is very ill. The doctors fear greatly for his life. He hates riding in a coach, and he must have got very wet travelling by horse. My stepmother has written me this note and urges me to return with all haste."

"Oh, dear Felicity, we must tell Pa immediately, should we not, Mother? He can then arrange for you to travel home in our coach, and we shall know you will arrive there safely."

"I fully agree with you, my dear," said her mother, who immediately rang for the servants. All the arrangements were made through Jane's papa, who wanted a servant to travel with Felicity, but she would not have it, and she insisted that she would be quite all right for after all she would not have to stay away a night in an inn or such – the journey could be made in the day.

Meanwhile, collecting her thoughts and pushing away her fears for her father's life, she thought of getting a message to Jason. Har maid was packing her things for her; there was nothing she had to do. She knew Jason wouldn't be at home because she knew that he was going to leave well before breakfast on the morning after the ball, but if she could leave a message, he could set out for Ravenwood immediately on his return as not only did she want him with her, but she knew her stepmother, Jason's mother, would value his assistance. Claude would not be of the slightest use, and of course, no one knew where he was, nor did they want to!

Her stepmother, she might also soon be her mother-in-law – what complications.

She knew, though, that she would like her stepmother far better now since she had left home and known her through her son. *How love changed people*, she thought. She quite looked forward to seeing her, but for the moment would not mention Jason's love for her to his mother, as it was right that Jason should speak first to her father, whenever Jason returned, choking with emotion she hurriedly decided to send Jason a note, but if she gave it to a footman to deliver, Jane might see her do it and ask questions, so she decided she must go herself and deliver it she quickly told Betsy what she was doing, and putting her pelisse and a bonnet over her morning dress, she slipped out of the big house and walked quickly round to Jason's place, which was not far away. It had been pointed out to her last night from the coach on the way to the Ball.

The butler opened the door, as the footman had been allowed time off as the master was away, and he was very surprised to see a young lady of such a genteel disposition to be out by herself, never mind calling on a young man s establishment before noon! However, on hearing her name and putting two and two together, having heard from Jason's manservant that he had been muttering "Felicity" over and over again all through his sleep after the ball, he ushered her into the study, and she explained to him that she wished to leave a message for his master. She hadn't given the matter much thought in her haste to get around to Jason's before the Marquis's coach came for her, and so the butler suggested that she write a note on a piece of paper which he was sure she would find in the writing desk in the study. He would be certain to give it to his Lordship immediately upon his return. She found some paper but nothing to write with, so she opened one of the small drawers, and to her surprises, she saw a rather loosely packed parcel on top of a writing quill. Moving the parcel aside to pick up the quill, the contents spilt out, and to her amazement, a cascade of pearls fell out of it. She looked at the butler in amazement and he too was stunned. Hurriedly, they rewrapped them, but suddenly Felicity saw something that stopped her in her task of wrapping them. The clasp was broken, taking up the pearls, she had a good look at them, and she knew at once that they were hers.

"Masters, how long have these been here?" she asked the Butler. "Surely, a safer place is needed for them. They look very valuable," she added, feeling the need to soften the first part of her sentence.

"My lady, I have no idea. They could have been there a long time for all I know as I do not look in my lordship's desk," he replied haughtily.

Felicity realised that she too should not have been looking in the desk, and that Masters was, in fact, rebuking her, but she couldn't care less about it. She knew those were her pearls. The ones that had been stolen. Surely Jason couldn't have taken them, he hadn't seemed to be that kind of person, and he didn't need them for the money. But perhaps he did, perhaps these journeys of his were something to do with money. Perhaps he was a highwayman in secret. She knew this was not true, but her mind was racing over many thoughts, and she knew not what to believe. Her imagination was running riot.

Should she take the pearls or leave them there? Should she mention them in her note?

Should she leave her note now? Did she still want to marry him? She never gave it a thought that perhaps Jason had found the pearls for her because she thought that if he had, then it must have been before the ball last evening and he could have told her then that he had found them. There could have been no better opportunity. Surely he had left too early this morning to have found them since the ball. Getting more and more upset, she knew that she had to see Jason again and hear his explanation before agreeing to marry him. She couldn't accept this mystery. Returning to the present, however, she told Masters to put the pearls in a safe place, and she would write her note for His Lordship. Masters then retired to the hall, and she just wrote on her note that her father…was ill, and she had to return to Ravenwood to look after him. She hoped he would get in touch with her on his return as she was not sure she could marry him. She wondered how to sign the note – she could not put with love affection or regard since she didn't know now what her real feelings were. So just 'Felicity' would perhaps be the best, and at that, she left it.

She then gave it to Masters, who promised to deliver it to His Lordship immediately upon his return, but he stressed that he didn't know when that would be. It might be a few days or a few weeks, but as soon as he did, he would be given the note. Privately to himself, he thought he had better remind His Lordship about the pearls, just in case they had been overlooked. He didn't know his master's business, but he had seen the dismay on Felicity's face when she saw the pearls, and he knew that much happiness was at stake.

Felicity returned to the house, and as soon as she entered the door, Jane was at the top of those lovely marble stairs with ornate bannisters, decorated with gilded flowers. All the previous occupants of that great house and family looked down on the living family from the walls of that grand staircase, and Felicity had felt wonderful coming down it last night dressed for the ball. She quickly ran to Jane and explained that she had left the message for Jason. Drawing Jane aside into her room, she also mentioned the pearls. "Jason has the pearls!" she exclaimed.

"How on earth did he get them? If he had them, why didn't he say so last night at the ball or when he came to collect us?"

"That is what I asked myself when I saw them there in the drawer," said Felicity. "But perhaps there was a reason for saying nothing," she added, her love and generosity supporting the cloud now over Jason's head – a thunderous cloud according to Jane, who was greatly perplexed about the whole mystery.

"Oh, men, how stupid can they be?" stormed Jane. "If he had them, he should have told you."

"There must be some reason for it. I can't believe that Jason ever stole them, I just can't believe it," cried Felicity now practically in tears.

"Oh, Jane, what shall I do? Do you think he is short of money? He doesn't seem to be, but perhaps he has some gambling debts?"

"Gambling debts, Jason, Never! It is more likely that Claude has the debts, and stole the pearls. Jason found out, got them back at a price from the pawnbroker and for some reason, forgot to tell you last night," replied Jane staunchly defending Jason.

"Do you think so? I hope that is true. It would break his mother's and my father's hearts to know he was a thief and in trouble like Claude."

"It would break my heart too," she continued under her breath, nearly fainting from all the confusion and emotion she was suffering from. "Now cheer up, Felicity, I am sure there is a very good reason. Perhaps, he didn't even know they were there – but he should have done – it was his desk. Still, Father's carriage is at the door now, and you must get off to Ravenwood as quickly as possible. Your father will be happy to see you, and you will speed his recovery when he sees you home once more, but do come back as soon as you can. There are so many fittings for dresses, and the rest of my trousseau, I shall be quite distraught without your help."

"Yes, I must forget the pearls and Jason for the time being and make sure that my father gets restored to health." She was also thinking she must get to know her stepmother a little better too, although if she and Jason were to marry, she would become the mistress of another home even larger than Ravenwood she must find out about the pearls first before such thoughts took hold. With that, Felicity gathered up her things and went downstairs to bid goodbye to Jane's parents, who insisted that she return as soon as her father was well again. Jane had in fact persuaded Felicity to allow Betsy to travel with her as Felicity's own maid Meg was no longer at Ravenwood to look after her, and it was not thought likely that Mrs Anderson had had time to think of such things. Together in the luxurious coach with the crest on the door and the magnificent horses being handled with such skill, Felicity looked back at her journey such a short time ago under such different circumstances. Little did she know then that she would be travelling back to Ravenwood in such a grand manner, and loved by one of the most eligible bachelors of London society. What would the future bring? She couldn't really bear to think of it, but that was almost impossible she had really only those few precious moments to remember when he had taken her in his arms and told her he loved her.

The outskirts of London soon passed by and quickly it seemed that they were out in the country once more. The roads for part of the way were fast and free of damaging potholes, but for the last few miles just before Stan Bourne, the pace had to slow down, not only for their sakes but for the horses and the coach. Felicity didn't mind, though, because she knew that Ravenwood was only a short distance away over the next hill. As they topped the rise, there was that lovely home nestling in the trees in the gentle valley, now becoming shrouded in the evening mist, but looking oh so wonderful to the returning daughter of the house.

Chapter 16
Flight

About a week later, Jane was overjoyed to see Damian waiting for her in the drawing room. He had only just arrived, and she had walked in from the garden, not expecting to see anyone there. With her arms full of late flowers from the glasshouses, she looked a picture and it was some time before Damian could find a suitable opportunity to tell her that Jason and Patrick had stayed behind in France. She was disappointed for Felicity's sake. She knew how the mystery had upset her. She mentioned the mystery to Damian, who was at a complete loss too to explain it, but thought that if Jason had known they were in the desk, then he would have found some way of letting them or Felicity or her father know, of their safety.

Ha thought it best to wait until Jason returned, which shouldn't be in the too far distant future and all could be explained. With that matter safely decided upon, they turned to other more urgent matters and in his arms, Jane forgot to ask why they had gone to France this time. She knew of the various mysterious journeys the friends made, but she hadn't known they went abroad. Her only relief was that Damian was back and was not going away again.

The days passed by, and the lovers made their plans and the marriage arrangements went ahead. So it was with some surprise that Damian was visited by Patrick. When he heard what had happened to the coup planned for the 10th, but that Jason thought there was a chance for the scheme for the 23rd October, then he wished he could be of more help. However, the two friends went to see Castlereagh who agreed with Jason's assessment of the situation, and giving Patrick the required gold, all arrangements were made for him to get back to France as quickly as possible. It was only natural, though, that he should go with Damian to see Jane, and by good fortune, Felicity had that moment returned from Ravenwood. Her father had really only had a severe chill, and her stepmother had panicked, but it gave both the ladies of the house an opportunity to get to know each other that much better, so the visit home was not in vain. Mr Anderson soon recovered, and he was well enough to ride with Jane's carriage, which had been sent for Felicity, and see his daughter well on the road to London once more, but this time certain of her destination.

She was, of course, surprised too to hear that the friends had been in France, and they were both sworn to secrecy. However, Felicity's heart went faint when she heard that Jason had stayed there by himself, and as she was thinking only of him, when Jane wished Patrick a safe journey and sent the love of Felicity and herself, a general sounding sentiment, it was with quite a surprise that Felicity heard it, but she hoped she had stopped herself giving away their secret. She echoed Jane's sentiments, and tried to act as innocently as possible

Patrick was fortunate in his travel and, as is known, was able to get safely back to Paris and Jason. Perhaps it was as well that the young ladies of Grosvenor Square did not know what was really happening across the sea. It had come as a great shock to both Jane and Felicity to learn of what the gentlemen did for their country. Jane was fortunate that Damian was now out of it, but she was so proud of him. She wasn't even allowed to tell her parents, and so the only person she could talk to was Felicity, who was only too pleased to talk about it and Jason. After all, Jason was taking the greatest risk. All this for his country. No, he was no thief; she knew that in her own mind, so she put the subject out of her mind and together, the girls planned Jane's trousseau, and want to visit and were visited. Indeed Felicity had her fair share of callers too and it was becoming more and more difficult for her to refuse the many gallants who now called to visit with her.

Perhaps it was as well that Felicity hadn't any real idea of what was happening in France. Jason and Patrick had managed to find their way to close by the hovel where the agent had put the horses at the beginning of the venture, and cautiously they approached the top of the cliffs. Dawn had now broken, and they could see out to sea for miles and miles, but no sign of the 'Firefly'.

It had been a vain hope that they would have got there in time for the dawn landing of a boat from the 'Firefly', but it had apparently become too dangerous with visibility being so good, that Captain Thelwall had had to lie away from the sight of land until the evening.

Jason swore. "To be held up now of all things, so near and yet so far away. I think I can almost see the cliffs of Dover – perhaps I am imagining it, though."

Patrick held the horses, whilst Jason clambered down the cliff path in case there was any small boat hidden amongst the rocks, but there was nothing there.

"We shall have to get off this cliff top soon, Jason. Any patrol would soon see us, and by now, they will have discovered the *sentry at the Barriere*."

"We must find that old man at the hovel. If he's not there, then we'll have to chance our luck that there is no one else using it and stay there out of sight until evening. If I remember, the stables were quite reasonable, and the horses will be well hidden. Quick, let's go," Jason replied and was on his horse and away down the track as quickly as possible.

Springing into his saddle too, Patrick hastily followed, and they made their way along the cliff edge until they found the tumbled down place, which looked much worse in daylight than at night time. There was no sign of any occupant, and forcing entry through the back door, they found that there was absolutely nothing in the place. The old man must just have used it for that night. Now, what to do. They had no food. The water in the well was brackish. At least there was a little hay for the horses. They would have to just sit, wait, watch and listen carefully. "But we'll have to watch not only the sea, the cliff top and inland too. Keep quiet unless someone tries to come in. There's no reason for anyone to suspect us here. Let's hope Thelwall hasn't been nabbed by the French fleet. I don't fancy staying here for long," said Jason, looking rather grimly at his surroundings.

Patrick had put the horses in the stables, and he asked Jason if he thought they should let the horses go. They shouldn't need them again, and any sound away from them might give their hideaway to anyone searching.

"It's a good idea, but what if the 'Firefly' doesn't turn, she may not. What do we do then? It's a long walk to Calais or anywhere else for that matter."

"Hmm, it's a problem. Perhaps if I took them down the path to the beach and put them in one of the caves which aren't covered at high tide, they might be safer. They won't drown, any sound they make won't be heard up above and yet they will be there if we need them."

"Yes, do that, but leave the saddles here. Don't take them with you. We might find a use for them, there's not even a mattress to lie on in this dump."

Patrick disappeared once more and Jason set to work. There were some mouldy crusts in the larder, but hungry as he was, he couldn't stomach those. There was nothing at all to drink. They had managed to see a little of their dinner from the previous evening, but it had been deucedly difficult to put any aside under the host's watchful eye, so stomachs rumbling and no water to drink was their lot for that day. They had a wash in the brackish water from the well and rinsed out their mouths, but ugh – it was horrid. The time passed slowly. The brilliant sunshine gave them the advantage that they could see for miles, but it would also help any pursuers.

Up to now, through the murky window in the hovel, they had not seen a sign of pursuit, not a single soul, not even a seagull for company. The day went on and on and Jason watched whilst Patrick slept, and Patrick watched whilst Jason slept. Soon, although it had seemed days since they left Paris, the night fell, and it was pitch dark. A slight mist had come in on the evening tide. The enveloping darkness seemed to swallow up the little hovel and its occupants. The absolute quiet pulled them into a false sense of security. They must both have nodded off to sleep when suddenly the crunch of footsteps on the gravel woke them with a start.

"There's no one in here in this mud hut," grumbled a French voice.

"What the hell can we do about it if English aristos are down here?"

"Shut up, you fool. If they are here, they will have heard you for miles around. Shut your bleeding mouth, and get inside that hovel and check," barked another French voice out of the night.

Shaken and startled out of their stupor, Jason and Patrick feverishly gathered their things together, trying not to bump into each other in the dark and trying to get everything and not leave anything for them to find. "Quick," hissed Patrick, "he's gone to the front door, out through the back into the stables."

Trying to see if they'd missed anything, Jason hurriedly followed Patrick. The back door, fortunately, was partly open as the lock didn't work, and so it was a matter of seconds to slip out.

They were only just in time, because the grumbler soon found out the front wouldn't open, and he came stumbling around to the back door, which he crashed open with the butt of his rifle. He held a lantern in one hand and swinging it on high; he could see that there was nobody there.

"No, I told you so. They'd not be here in this rat hole. They'll be miles away from here by now. I know those aristos. I followed them during the Revolution, and caught many a skulking one on this cliff top."

Who he was talking to, no one knew because there was no one else in sight. Suddenly though, he stopped muttering and bent down, bringing his lantern low. Bending down to the ground, he picked up a glove.

"Damn, damn, damn," hissed Jason, "I must have dropped it on my way over here. Quickly is there another way out?"

"No, there's only this way, the way we came in," replied Patrick, now frantically looking around the stables.

The old man outside was still looking at the glove, and it must have suddenly sunk into his thick skull that it couldn't have belonged to anyone other than the English aristos. His cry of alarm rang out through the night, and immediately the place was surrounded by similar men. The leader pushed his way forward to where the old soldier was standing.

"Well, man, what've you found?" he cried harshly, snatching the glove from him.

"The Aristos, men, there around here. This is one of their gloves. Quick spread out and search every inch. A week's pay to whoever finds them," he roared.

It would be seconds before they were discovered. Frantically, Jason and Patrick prodded at every board in the walls of that stable. Suddenly Patrick hissed almost silently, but loud enough for Patrick to hear, "Here's a loose one."

They both got through somehow. It was so narrow that Jason, who was the larger of the two, found it difficult, but it's amazing what one can do when faced with death, which it would surely be if they were caught – English aristo spies in France. They had to leave the saddles behind, but then there was nothing incriminating in those. Patrick had divided the money between them, but that was all they had kept on them. Fortunately, the place was so dark that they were able to escape into the night. Once they were heard and a voice asked if that was George. Patrick quickly replied in a coarse French dialect which he hoped sounded right, "*Mais out, mon amil.*" It served its purpose, however, for soon they were running away from the noise, and they found themselves running away from the cliffs. Flopping down in some bushes which gave a little protection, they looked back at the sound of the searchers. Soon a glow lit the inside of the hovel, and it was soon ablaze, shining like a beacon on Beachy Head. The thatch must have been very dry, for it was soon just a bright glow, and the searchers were moving away into the distance.

"What shall we do now, Jason?" asked Patrick. "Stay here or go down to the beach?"

"Go down to the beach, I think," he replied. "If the 'Firefly' is anywhere around, they will have seen that blaze. The mist is only just skimming the top of the sea, and there should be a lookout in the crow's nest who'll see that blaze. Thelwall will probably send a boat into the bay to see what's the trouble."

Quickly they retraced their steps, feeling their way cautiously, and fell rather than climbed down the cliff path. They found the sea air rather chilly, but certainly, it was safer down there. They made their way to where the boat had dropped them off on their incoming journey, checking to see if the horses were still safe. They were making their way nicely across the pebbles, when suddenly a gruff French voice accosted them, "Not so fast, my English spies, we're not all as dim-witted as those stupid bastards up on the cliffs there."

With sinking hearts, the two men came to a standstill, realising that they were caught fast in the net of the French who were seeking them. Just then Jason heard the slight splash as though someone had slipped an oar quietly out of a boat, and he whispered out of the side of his mouth to Patrick,

"I think 'Firefly' is somewhere out there in this mist, and if we put up a fight and draw their attention to our exact spot, they may be able to help us." Quickly catching hold of Jason's idea, because the place was so dark, it would be impossible for anyone out there in the sea mist which had come in on the evening tide to see what was going on, Patrick lunged at the man who had challenged them, and Jason did the same to his companion who had just joined the group. However, Jason was not as lucky as Patrick, and the newcomer managed to get a shot off before Jason could stop him. Patrick had knocked down his guard, and turning he was horrified to see Jason sprawled on the pebbles. He couldn't see him very well, but he could feel blood running down Jason's face, and there was no movement at all from the body.

"Oh, God no Jason, quickly, come on, let's get going, Jason I'll try to carry you." But Patrick found this impossible and the pursuers from the top of the cliff were now well down the path, the shot having drawn them down to the beach and pinpointed the group.

Patrick was torn between staying with Jason, but what could he do if Jason was already dead – he himself would be hanged too. Torn with shock and sobbing with grief, he stumbled along the beach until suddenly, he saw figures at the edge of the water in a rowing boat, and he managed to get to them. "Firefly," he gasped, "Aye, my lord, quickly into the boat, the rascals are catching up." At that moment, a shot splashed into the water near the boat.

Quickly the men dragged Patrick into the rowing boat, and they quickly got out of range of the men on the beach, who were now more interested in their victim who lay there dead or unconscious as only time would tell.

"What happened to my Lord Lindsey, my lord?" asked the Bosun rather anxiously. "We couldn't see you anywhere, and it was only the fact that the lad in the crow's nest saw that blaze that brought us into the beach. We knew something was up, but the mist prevented us from corning too near.

"The mist isn't very high and up there the lad could see the glow of a beacon. He thought the Frenchies were celebrating Boney's death, but it looks as though it's the opposite from what you appear to have gone through."

Patrick could make no comment. How could he explain to everyone why he had left Jason lying there. He couldn't have carried him to the boat, the pursuers were so near and he looked and felt so dead, Jason, oh no! Poor Felicity – how could he possibly tell her?

The boat crew pulled Patrick aboard the ship, and Captain Thelwall, too was dismayed to hear the news, but as he said, "Better to have one of you than none at all."

As soon as the anchor was hauled up and they were off into the night and the safety of the English Channel, Captain Thelwall joined Patrick in the cabin, making sure that the young man had had something to eat, after having a change of clothing, wash and plenty of brandy to keep his spirits from sinking too low. Soon Patrick was asleep, and the 'Firefly' was heading through the Channel back to England. The sea was choppy and a rather brisk wind he'd soon cleared any mist, Patrick slept on numb from shock and the effect of the brandy.

Later, when the ship neared port, and Patrick awoke, he could only look back at the previous night as a nightmare. He just couldn't believe Jason was dead. No, he must have just been knocked unconscious and perhaps their next mission would be to rescue him from a French prison. He must get back to Castlereagh and get things organised.

Their luck had certainly been against them on this journey – an unsuccessful coup and a lost friend. At least he could tell Castlereagh that the French didn't really want Napoleon Bonaparte, but that there was no one strong enough to oust him. It would have to be a battle between troops on land in Europe that would see the 'Little Corsican' falter and fall as history would soon tell.

Chapter 17
Survival

Back on the beach, the Frenchmen had found the body of Jason and excitedly they all began talking about how much they would claim as a reward for an English spy. They failed to notice that Jason had in fact recovered consciousness, the bullet had grazed a deep furrow along his head, as he had knocked down the guard. He had managed to knock out the man, but in doing so, he jerked the guard's gun and it had gone off sending the bullet a hairs breadth from his brain. It may not have killed him, but he was gravely wounded and he was so confused and weak from loss of blood, that it was his moaning that suddenly drew one of the guard's attention to him. "Eh, lads, he's not dead, don't count that bounty yet! He's probably worth more alive than dead!"

Excitedly, the French gathered around Jason, who was more confused than ever. Where was he? Who were they? He could understand them, but they seemed to be so far away, but in fact, he was slipping back into unconsciousness.

The French realised that he was indeed worth more alive than dead – they could get information from a live spy. Quickly they improvised a stretcher, and the leader sent one of his men up the cliff to the nearest village to warn the doctor he was needed urgently.

It was a rather rough journey up the cliff side and along the path to the village, but somehow Jason survived it. The doctor looked rather uneasily at the unconscious person presented to him, but when he had washed away the blood and had a good look at the wound, he assured the French leader that his captive would live, but would not be able to give any information for a few days, if not weeks. The days passed by and gradually the fog disappeared from Jason's sight, and he saw that he was in a small room, lying on a small bed, so small that his feet were hanging over the end of it, but the sheets were clean, and there was a small cupboard at the side with a jug of water and a glass on it.

Through the window, which was only big enough to let in enough light to see where he was, he could see a little bit of blue sky, and he could hear the birds singing. How long he had been there he did not know, but he could tell that it must have been a long time – he had a beard, he lifted his arm and saw how thin and scrawny it was. He tried to lift his head, but that was too much – the pain that shot through his head was unbearable, and the 'fog' came d own again.

Hours later, perhaps the same day – he did not know – but he knew that it was now evening – there was a candle lit on the small cupboard at the side of his bed – he again came too and this time he did not try anything foolish. He just lay there and tried to remember where he was and who he was. Nothing at all would come back to him – as far as he knew he had no past, he was no one. He was frightened – everyone was someone who was he? Why was he here? Who had hurt him, or had he hurt himself?

Tormenting himself like this did not help either, because he just did not know the answers.

It seemed like hours before he heard any noise in the other rooms in whatever place he was in. Suddenly the door opened, and a young girl popped her head around the door, obviously not expecting him to be conscious, because she went out quickly, not really taking any notice, but she stopped and looked again.

"Maman, maman, the prisoner is awake! He is awake!"

Prisoner – oh no! Thought Jason, *I'm a prisoner am I? But who is keeping me prisoner and why? Wretched, wretched memory – why let me down like this?*

At the girl's cry, an elderly couple came quickly into the room, and the man bent over Jason and looking deeply into his eyes, he said, "Don't worry, my man, I am a doctor, and I am looking after you."

As he spoke in French, Jason automatically replied in French – to him, it was an automatic reaction, and yet it probably saved his life.

He realised that for some reason the French had him a prisoner and yet he knew the language – was he too a Frenchman? He didn't think so, but he wasn't sure?

The doctor continued to examine him, whilst the old lady went back downstairs and came back with a bowl of broth, which she gave to Jason on a spoon, feeding him like a child – he was too weak to even lift his head. He knew what had happened last time he had lifted his head, and he didn't want to run the risk of being unconscious again. He wanted to get to the bottom of this problem as quickly as possible.

"Monsieur, *le d octeur*, who am I and where am I?"

"You ask me, Monsieur, I do not know. You were caught on the beach near Le Treport and you were left with me for dead. In fact, at one time, we gave you up completely, but you were in good health when injured and your body has certainly done its work well. You have amazed me. I am told by the guards that you are an English spy, but you have papers on you that say you are a buyer of materials from Brest. Whether that will help you to discover your past, I do not know, but perhaps it would be as well to be the buyer from Brest, eh?"

Jason realised that the doctor was giving him his chance to escape the guillotine. Obviously, he didn't want him killed, having just brought him back from the dead, so thanking him, Jason gradually realised what lay ahead of him.

Over the next few days, Jason gradually regained his strength, but he was unable to remember anything more than he was told by the doctor. Somehow he knew he was not French and not a buyer of materials, but who was he? The weeks went by, and it was gradually apparent that soon Jason would be well enough to be moved to Paris. The sergeant of the local militia who had caught Jason on the beach had left strict instructions to be advised of the invalid's progress. It seemed to Jason that the doctor was very reluctant to let his patient go, and he heard him arguing more and more with the sergeant, but finally, the word came that Jason had to be moved to Paris.

"I'm sorry, M. Macon, but the sergeant he insists that you are now fit enough to be moved, and I am unable to disagree – I can find no more excuses. I have made every excuse I possibly could to give you time to regain your strength and your memory, but I'm afraid that you must now go with the guards," the doctor said sadly.

He would be sorry to see his patient go. He knew that once in prison, the cruel ministrations of the jailers would soon undo all his work of the past weeks. He had not told Jason that whilst he had been very ill, he had, in fact, spoken some words in English. Fortunately, the doctor had been alone in the room, and if he had said them again whilst his wife or daughter had been watching him, they would have mentioned it. He had, therefore, thought it wiser not to mention anything before, but now he was unable to watch over him, he believed he must tell Jason exactly what he had said. It may help him to regain his memory, but knowing of similar cases, he knew it was time and time alone, which could heal the damaged brain, if ever.

"Monsieur, there is one thing which I must tell you before you leave my care. I did not tell you before in case it preyed on your mind and you repeated it whilst you were unconscious or asleep, but now before you go, I must warn you that whilst you were unconscious in those early days soon after your capture, you mentioned a few words in English, and they were; Felicita, where are you? Wait for me, my darling."

There was no doubt, Monsieur, that it was in English for I knew a few words of it myself, but I took care that you were never left alone with someone I could not trust after that. Since then, Monsieur, you know you have spoken French all the time, so I can only assume that you are an Englishman with knowledge of France, perhaps living here for a time?

Jason knew immediately then that the doctor was right. He knew he was not a Frenchman, but not having heard any English spoken, he had not realised how easily it came to him to speak in English. "Doctor, thank you, thank you so very much."

"Hush, Monsieur, the guard outside may overhear speak in French."

"I'm sorry, Monsieur le Docteur, of course, I understand, and I would not wish to cause you any trouble. You and your family have been so kind to me. I understand what you have told me, but I am afraid I am no wiser. The name means nothing to me, but it is a start I shall have to try to remember."

"There is also another thing, Monsieur. When you were brought in, and I attended to your wound, the guards overlooked a ring you were wearing.

"I took the precaution of removing it because it would have soon disappeared in the pockets of those rascals. I kept it until today, and I suggest that you hide it somewhere on your person so that it cannot be found, but it may one day prove to be of some assistance to your ring – do you remember it?"

It is a strange Jason took the ring, but it meant nothing to him at all. He found it fitted his finger perfectly – he had gained weight during the last few weeks and looked more like the Jason that Patrick and his friends would have known. Whether they would have recognised him, though, is another matter because he had grown a beard, and it had altered the shape of his face. Perhaps it would deceive anyone who knew him in Paris – there he would be at a disadvantage. They may know him, but he wouldn't know them and he would have to be continually on his guard. What a position to be in, there was evidently some girl in his life; someone called Felicity; he must love her, and she loves him; where was she now? Did she think of him dead? As for the ring, it had a peculiar look about it, and suddenly, Jason realised that it was half of a crest his family crest? It must be one of those rings which split into two – who had the other? Felicity? Jason came to from his dreaming with a start – there were sounds of heavy boots outside the cottage, and the doctor's wife came rushing into the room.

"Husband, the guards are here – quickly, is Monsieur ready for them?"

"I do not want them in my house for any longer than necessary. Good luck, Monsieur – I hope you find out who you are soon and perhaps one day you will come back and let us know – eh?"

With an unexpected smile, because ever since he had awakened from that foggy past, he had never seen her smile, he stood up carefully – he had still to take care otherwise he found himself becoming dizzy – he sketched an elegant bow to her – it came so naturally that he realised that he must have done it often before, and the old lady blushed like a young maiden –

It was obvious that she was not used to such things either, and the doctor took his arm, and said, "Monsieur, it is things like that which you must watch. That is a salute which an aristocrat from Court pays to a lady at Court – not a merchant or a peasant from Brest. You must do it like so," and he showed Jason just how different his manners should be – not so exaggerated or demonstrative. "When you arrived here, Monsieur, you had a little money on you, and I kept it for you in case the day should come when you would need it to bribe a jailor or pay for your burial. Here it is now – you will certainly need it in La Force! Be careful with it; do not let those jailors see exactly how much you have. See, my wife has made you a secret pocket in your breeches – be careful no one is your friend in prison. Be on your guard all the time."

With those few hasty words of guidance, the doctor took up Jason's hat and cloak and opened the door.

"Messieurs, the invalid is ready to move now."

"About time too. He's been abed long enough. The sooner we're in Paris the better. The wine's not as good in this dead-hole of a village. Bah!"

"Wine, do you call it – I can think of better things to call it…" he said turning to his companions, who beat the table and called it all the names they could think of. No wonder the doctor's wife wanted them out of the way as soon as possible. At this rate, they would soon have no table or chairs left! Jason had not ridden a horse during his convalescence, and so it was with some trepidation that he put his foot in the stirrup and mounted it. He knew that this would be a terrible journey, but his guards' wouldn't bother about that. Somehow he had to keep in the saddle and not fall off unconscious.

The guards didn't bother to tie him up too realised that he was in no fit state to try to getaway. It took him all his time to stay on the horse at the steady pace, which the guards took. They had their orders to get him safely to Paris, and they knew that they had to get him there alive now that he was able to move at long last. Napoleon had returned and was demanding that the English spy be questioned. Why they had not tried anything whilst he was ill at the doctor's he did not know – surely that would have been the best place of all whilst he was so weak, but for some reason, they had left him in peace. Little did he know that there had been other things occupying Napoleon Bonaparte's mind – such as the trouble in Spain, and the fact that the people had dared to support the plot to overthrow him.

It was early January when Jason was finally delivered up to the main entrance of the prison known as La Force. The gaunt building, which gradually came into view – old thick walls which had seen a long passage of time and heard many murderous screams and seen many atrocities – gave no reassurance to Jason. The sergeant in charge of the guard rapped on the thick door of the Head Warder's office, and as soon as they saw who had arrived, the door creaked open and Jason was pushed inside where he faced an individual who stared intently at him.

"Is this supposed to be the English Spy who helped those fools in the October rising?" he asked.

"Certainement," replied the sergeant. "He's been recovering from a head wound at Le Treport, and we have brought him here as ordered. He's yours now," he cackled with glee, knowing how inmates of this place were treated. He had no sympathy with the English spy, although he hadn't heard him say a word in English throughout the journey. Right man!

He hoped he had brought the yes, he must have. That old doctor wouldn't have been such a fool as to pass off someone else. It was well known that the spy found on the beach had had a bad gash on the head, and this man they had brought all the way to Paris certainly had had such a wound. He had seen it when he had taken off his hat to wipe his brow. The exertion of the riding, although at a very reasonable pace, had not helped Jason at all. In fact, it took him all his time to keep on his feet whilst facing this rough-looking individual who was now in charge of this fortress. He knew that the future was grim, but at least he couldn't tell them anything, he didn't know anything…except the name Felicity. Somewhere there was a girl, but where?

Chapter 18
From France

Back in London, Felicity and Jane were still enjoying the Season and with Damian home, and so many offers to accompany Felicity, the girls were having a wonderful time.

Back at Ravenwood, Mr Anderson was fully recovered, and when he saw that his wife and Felicity were doing their best to get on good terms, he was very pleased. He had not really mentioned much about Claude and the missing pearls, but after Felicity left for London the second time, he thought it only wise to tell his wife the full story. She had seen how weak Claude was and how she had helped to foster this weakness by paying his debts whenever he had appealed to her for help. Mr Anderson told her that Claude would never be allowed to visit Ravenwood again and that under no circumstances was she to help him.

She accepted this as the right thing. She knew that if Claude had accepted the blame at the right time and confessed his debts etc.

Mr Anderson might have helped, but to put the blame on a young helpless maiden who was not there to defend herself was the final straw.

Nothing Claude could do now if he ever appeared, would restore her son to her. She felt no love for this son of him who had been so deceitful. She didn't want anything to spoil her happiness at Ravenwood. Like Felicity, she had come to enjoy the country atmosphere and the warmth of the local country society. They visited friends and were often visited by the local county gentry and she knew that she was happy.

Since Claude had left the pearls on Jason's doorstep, he had led a miserable life. He hadn't enough money to pay his debts. The Frenchmen had got back the pearls for him. That was his fee for the information. In the meantime, he had had to live on what he could steal or filch from others as unfortunate as he. He dared not go to his mother or to any of his friends. Such was his misfortune. He lived in dread of hearing of Jason's death, and it was with trepidation and fear that he sneaked a look at any papers he could find to see there was any mention of the death of such a well-known person and friend of the Prince Regent.

In fact, there was no news given out by Castlereagh, for Patrick had not been firm enough about the accident to say that Jason was indeed dead, and rather than cause a scandal and also cause Claude to inherit the earldom, it was decided to say if anyone asked that Jason was away in the country, and his continued absence was due to pressure of estate work.

His friends covered up for him, but in the meantime, Castlereagh had tried to make contact with others who were in a position to know if Jason had been killed, and they just had to wait. Jane and Felicity were stunned by the news, and Felicity knew that she had been unable to keep back from her friend just how much Jason had meant to her. Her friends had done their best, but after Jane and Damian's wedding, which was such a grand occasion, Felicity decided that she should return to Ravenwood and Patrick promised to come and keep her in touch with whatever news they could get.

Everyone searching for him had fully expected such an important capture to be taken to Paris immediately, and a death if that had been the case would certainly have been reported. Therefore, nothing was discovered about Jason's location or health, and gradually not even Castlereagh's gold could find out any more.

It was, therefore, around Christmas when Patrick arrived at Ravenwood, and found himself aching to hold Felicity and comfort her, but he knew that she never even knew he existed. He must wait – if Jason did not turn up, then perhaps he had a chance, but he knew that until there was the final proof that Jason had died, then she was waiting for him.

He had known that when he had told her that in spite of intensive inquiries, no death had been reported of any Englishman resembling Jason nor of a Monsieur Macon, which had been Jason's cover name. Jason must be somewhere, but no one knew where.

Christmas was not a very festive occasion at Ravenwood. No one felt like celebrating, but a brave face was put on when the local villagers came to the front door singing carols. Mr Anderson invited them in afterwards and they were given warm drinks and mince pies – something a little stronger for the grown-ups.

Soon another year came in, and the old year slipped by – a year full of adventure, hope, love and finally sadness for all those at Ravenwood. Felicity was grateful to Patrick for his kindness to her. At least she could talk to him of Jason – it was difficult talking to his mother and her father, but Patrick was able to give her some of the details of Jason's past adventures. Not all the details but enough to satisfy her curiosity and also to keep Jason's memory alive more vividly. She had the ring on a golden chain around her neck, usually hidden, but once when it had slipped into view, Jason's mother had seen it and recognised it. Felicity had then had to explain why she had it, and so her parents too realised just how much Felicity had lost.

1813 was to be an eventful year in Europe, and soon Patrick had to return to London. Castlereagh had sent a message to him that he wanted to see him. So bidding Mr and Mrs Anderson and Felicity farewell, he returned to London promising to return as soon as he could, with, he hoped, news which they all wanted. Little did he know that indeed Castlereagh had had some news, which by putting two and two together, he knew meant that Jason was alive.

One of his many contacts in France had sent a message to him that he had heard a member of the National Guard giving very explicit details to a friend of how the wine in Paris was better than that at Le Treport, where he'd been detailed to go with a guard to collect an English spy who had been recovering from a wound received whilst avoiding arrest a few months ago. Apparently, the spy had lost his memory and been severely injured and was now only able to be moved to Paris.

"Loss of memory – no documents to prove he was English – all conspirators in Paris arrested and the leaders executed – there was, therefore, no need, no urgent need to have Jason in Paris," explained Castlereagh to a stunned Patrick.

"Napoleon is now safe, he has returned from Russia and all is under control. He knows that it was an internal coup –

with no English help and he has no proof that the man they have caught is English. Unfortunately, my informant was not able to find out exactly where Jason is interned, probably La Force, but it could be anywhere – if his memory has gone, he can tell them nothing, so he could be in any French gaol or who knows. Perhaps I could go to Paris and try to find him," Patrick requested with an air of urgency and determination. He was determined that Jason, if alive, was not going to rot in a French dungeon.

"For the moment, no, my lord," replied Castlereagh firmly.

"It would be more dangerous for you at the moment than for Jason. If you were caught, you have no excuse – no loss of memory – and the security in Paris has been strengthened since the coup, so, no, definitely not."

Patrick realised the futility of any further argument, but he did get an assurance from Castlereagh that should any further news come from France, he would be the one to go.

"Certainly, I agree to that, but don't forget that if Jason has lost his memory, it is not certain it will ever come back. If it does, then he will be sufficiently intelligent enough to keep quiet about it. He will then try to get out himself. However, if his memory does not return, he could be anywhere in France with no way of finding him – a very difficult and I would say impossible task – you cannot look at every person in France, my lord. Also knowing the state of French prisons.

"Jason may have changed beyond recognition – weeks, never mind months or years, can do that."

To Patrick, though, it was at least reassuring news that Jason, for they both knew that it must be Jason to whom the guard had been referring, was alive. He could take back some hope to Felicity, but he knew that he had now lost her for himself. Until he could prove Jason was dead, Jason would always be alive and loved by Felicity. He knew though that he wouldn't want it any other way. He too loved Jason – their friendship had stretched back over many years and through many adventures. He would not take away his friend's love whilst there was a chance he could come back to claim it.

Chapter 19
Reprieve

Back in Paris, Jason realised how grateful he should be to the doctor who had insisted on keeping him away from Paris for so long. He was still very weak, but his head no longer worried him. The wound had healed nicely, and the headaches no longer gripped his head. However, his jailors thought this meant that his memory too had recovered, and so they went to work with the many implements devised during the Revolution to torture the poor inhabitants of La Force at that time. Their ideas of torture were devised to break not only the body but the spirit of any mortal, and with the warning by the doctor that he could at times speak in his sleep in English, and also therefore at the extremity of torture, Jason persevered in believing himself French, and insisted on speaking to anyone and everyone in French. He forgot his English, he couldn't remember England, so that was no problem, but he dreaded that unfortunate slip. He knew that their only evidence was the fact that he was on the beach at the time and had resisted arrest.

He had no papers on him other than his false ones, making him out to be a materials buyer from Brest, M. Macon, and so over and over again, he repeated this to his persecutors.

Finally, one day towards the end of January, the door of his miserable, dark, stinking cell opened, and blinking in the light from the lantern held by an officer, he saw a squad of soldiers in the corridor. His heart sank – this was the end – a firing squad. However, be that as it may, he would not crawl out of this place, so dragging himself up as straight as possible, for those fiendish contraptions had made a physical wreck of him, he was pushed and shoved down the corridor, half-carried by a couple of the guards. Suddenly he was out in the open, oh, that wonderful fresh air! The daylight hurt his eyes, so he could hardly see his surroundings, but he was pushed quickly into a carriage, and his hands and feet tied together. *How could they expect him to get away from so many of them in his state,* he thought in despair.

Gradually, he realised that he could see his surroundings, the many alleys running off the main street through which the carriage was being driven.

It was the first time he had really seen other people and houses and streets since he and Patrick – with a jolt; he realised that he had got a flash of the past – something he and someone called Patrick had done in the past. He and this Patrick must have been here in Paris – yes, he could see a room with tables – a bar or bistro – and suddenly soldiers arriving in the doorway, yes, with his head spinning, he realised that some things were coming back to him. It was the sight of those streets and the ordinary people of Paris – if only he could get out and see things for himself, perhaps other things would come back. For example, who was Felicity? Every night on his slab covered with a straw mattress, he had tried over and over again to bring to mind a portrait of a girl – someone who could be Felicity. After all, he had only seen the doctor's family his fellow companions on the journey to Paris and the guards in La Force, ever since the knock on the head on the beach, so this was, in fact, the first time he had seen crowds, people. There was no glass in the window and door openings of the carriage, so gradually, Jason realised just how cold it was. He had still got his own clothes on, those in which he had been found on the beach, which had included the miserable cloak they had pinched from the stable at that inn, but during all the past weeks, they hadn't stood up very well and were now in a pitiable condition. These rags, therefore, gave him no protection against the January wind, which was blowing through the carriage. The guards were well wrapped up, but they cared nothing for their prisoner. *Still,* thought Jason, *if I'm going to die, I'll soon be colder than this!* It was not to be though, as Jason soon found out, because the carriage stopped, Jason's feet were untied, and he was led into a courtyard and up into a building which was the military justice headquarters in the *Ruedu Cherche* – Mid is. Little did he know that many hours of painstaking work by the Public Prosecutor and his assistants had put together the full story and facts of the October conspiracy, but they could not find concrete evidence that this Monsieur Macon had had anything to do with it. The head warder at La Force had been given strict instructions to try and prise something, anything in English, from the prisoner.

The Chairman of the Military Commission, General Count Dejean, with the other members of the Bench, being five judges, two generals, two colonels and a major, entered the room, and the proceedings began.

First of all, a young man whose name was given as Andre. Boutreux, appeared before the commission. It was quite obvious to Jason that it was just a formality. He didn't know, but the main conspirators, who had been caught in the act, had already been sentenced and were long since buried in the ground or alive in some terrible hole known as a French prison. A similar fate as Malets awaited Boutreux, and he was led away to face a firing squad of twelve fusiliers in the *Plaine de Grenelle*, and his body joined the others in the common grave in the Vaugirard cemetery.

Then came a brief summary of a person named Abbe Lafon' who was not present before the Commission. It was decided by the Court that though he had received the conspirators in his house, on the recommendation of the Minister of Police, Abbe Lafon was depicted as harmless and not really responsible.

The search for him was, therefore, to be abandoned.

A person named Cajamano was the next, and he was sentenced to remain in prison and continue to be kept there as a detainee for the remainder of his natural life.

To Jason, these names meant nothing, neither did the next one or the person who appeared. It was the Citizen Hainault, a very miserable and ill-looking person, who even if Jason had kept his memory, it would have been difficult for him to recognise that portly gentleman who had offered him cognac in his rooms many months ago. Now he had lost a considerable amount of weight, and his colour was far from healthy. Ever since his arrest, he had wondered what had happened to the Englishman. No one had mentioned Englishman/to him in gaol, and he too hardly recognised Jason. Not only was he physically changed through the hardship of the 'pressure' put on him, but his now luxuriant beard also completely changed his features. It was only the name Monsieur Macon which gave Hainault a clue as to who this person in front of him really was, and he knew that it would do neither of them any good if he did admit it was the Englishman. He, Hainault, had already been sentenced for his part, and he knew that he would only send the Englishman to his death if he confirmed the story, so he denied that he had ever seen the prisoner before and hoped that somehow or other the young man would one day be free – it would be a long time before he himself would see freedom – if ever. Jason had showed no reaction on seeing Hainault, as of course he just did not remember him, so when the head warder was brought forth to give his statement, and a medical opinion was sought from the doctor who attended the prisoners at La Force, there was no way they could prove that Jason was an Englishman thought to have taken part in the uprising in October.

The doctor confirmed that such a head wound would bring about loss of memory if not death in most instances, and he could not foresee that the prisoner's memory would return at any specific time. It might – it might not!

Jason throughout the whole period of the trial, had been silent unless asked a question he could answer. To occupy the blankness, he had tried to fit in the name Patrick. Who was he? It was an English name, not French.

After a lengthy discussion amongst themselves, finally, the Chairman of the Military Commission indicated that they had decided their course of action, and the prisoner was requested to stand for the sentence.

Well, this was the beginning of the end. The end if he was found guilty, but perhaps the beginning of who knew what if found not guilty.

"The Court finds Monsieur Macon not guilty of being an English spy as there was no evidence to confirm this statement, but he is found guilty of resisting arrest on the beach at Le Treport, and for giving no reason for being on the said beach with someone who escaped on an English ship," intoned the Clerk who read the verdict of the Commission.

With an inward sigh, Jason began to breathe again, but how long would he have to wait in a French prison before he could search for his identity, and was it Patrick who had escaped on the English ship yes, it must have been. The sentence was 12 months from the date of the trial in L'Abbaye prison, which under the circumstances was a fairly lenient sentence in those days. The trial was now over, and everyone was hurrying out of the Military Justice headquarters, eager to get away from it all. Ever since General Malet had appeared that morning at the Popincourt Barracks with the false news of the death of their beloved Emperor, Napoleon Bonaparte, on the battlefield outside the walls of Moscow, there had been a witch-hunt for conspirators, and all concerned sighed with relief – perhaps now life could get back to normal.

To Jason, though, now of no political importance, but a common criminal, he found the difference was that he was treated even more inhumanly – if possible – and he soon found himself handed over to the gendarmes, and on a rough cart which rattled over the cobbles to the Quartier Saint-Germain and the prison which awaited him.

He was put in a cell with others, who hid in the dimness to avoid attracting the jailer's attention, and it was only when the locks were turned and the bolts put back in their sockets that the occupants eased their tired limbs back into their usual sordid places.

The place stank of human odours, rodent occupation and the dark, dank and dismal life which was to be his for a year – a year in a hell like this – O*h God, where are you now,* Jason cried to himself. He cried soundlessly to himself, as he too eased his wretched body to the ground. At least there would now be an end to the torturous implements used to pressure him, but how on earth would he regain any physical or mental strength in this, the lowest of low abodes! Mental and physical lethargy set in, and the strain of the past few months now began to tell, now that he could relax. He was beginning to drop off into a stupor induced by the rank and airless conditions of the cell, when he felt fingers probing around his waist pretending to fall sleep, his head rolling on to his shoulder, he let the fingers explore his waist belt – it was not as if there was anything of use in it – and then suddenly he rolled over quickly, summoning a strength from heaven knows where, and grabbed his pickpocket. His sudden movement shocked all the occupants of the cell, and in the dim light, he could make out the weasel features of a body which writhed in his grip.

"Not so fast, my friend," he hissed, keeping a firm grip on the pickpocket.

He knew that he had to make it quite clear from the beginning that he was stronger than them, and knowing that he couldn't have a fight with his opponent he just didn't have the energy or strength, but he had to pretend he did – he gathered every ounce he could find, and hurled the scrap of humanity across the room, it bounced off the wall and solid into a heap at the bottom of it.

How he managed to do it, Jason just didn't know, but he got up and staggered over to see how the wretch had suffered.

He was relieved to find the man breathing, but obviously stunned from the crash into the wall. Turning wearily, he looked at each of the other occupants, and making it quite obvious what would happen to them if they tried anything, he pointed to the unconscious form at the bottom of the wall and warned them all that it would happen to them too. He also showed them his empty waist belt to make it even more obvious they would be wasting their time. They all cringed away from him. Who was this stranger in their midst. Oh, well, why bother – let's leave him in peace – we only want a quiet life until we can go free – it wasn't worth risking any trouble for a sous or two.

Jason resumed his position on the wooden bench now instead of the floor; it was perhaps safer from the human and animal life in the cell there.

He recollected the smell of rodents as he entered the cell an hour or so earlier. They were not in evidence at the moment, but it was obvious they would show up later, probably at night whilst they tried to sleep.

Somehow or other, he must try to get out of here into better conditions. He needed money or something to bribe the jailor – money; the doctor mentioned something about putting some in a secret pocket. He hadn't needed any in La Force, but now well, the position was changed, and perhaps it would be as well to use it for that. *How much have I?* He wondered. He couldn't count it now whilst they were all awake watching him. Somehow he'd have to get it out whilst they were asleep. Yes, that would be best. He'd manage one night in this place, but it was only going to be one night if he had his way.

Chapter 20
Patrick Joins
Wellington in Spain

Back in England, Jane and Damian were happily married, and there was no news of a happy event towards the end of the year. Felicity had joined them for the Season and had enjoyed it, but all the time, she had not really entered fully into the spirit of everything. She knew all her friends were doing the best to take her mind off the worry and anxiety over Jason. The rumours had started to flow around the town that something was wrong with Jason, and it was found wise to say that he had been ill, and was now convalescing abroad; no one said exactly where and one heard South America one minute, Ireland by another and elsewhere. Mr and Mrs Anderson did not join Felicity in London, feeling that there would be too many questions to avoid, so Lord and Lady Douglas were hosts once more to Felicity;

Jane and Damian now living in their own home nearby for the season, it was very easy for the girls to see each other every day, but it was thought better for Felicity to stay with Jane's parents and they felt that they were doing something to help as well, apart from enjoying her youthful company. They felt lost now that Jane was married.

Patrick had felt left out of everything, so he had volunteered to join Wellington in Spain, and was by June amongst the 100,000 men of the army fighting on the Peninsular.

During May–June, the crossing of the Elsa had taken place, and now the second stage of the incredible campaign had started.

"Farewell Portugal," cried Lord Wellington, turning his horse around and waving goodbye as he crossed the frontier for what he hoped was to be the last time.

From Toro instead of moving along the expected road to France with conventional ease and deliberation, he suddenly turned his army north again into the bleak hills, crowning his original flanking movement with another lightning sweep to the north-east, thus turning the French on the line of the Ebro. Such an astonishing move with the French border at the west end of the Pyrenees as its target only made sense if Wellington could get his supplies through to Santander on the Bay of Biscay. This he did and was, of course, a shorter route for vessels from England.

Patrick, being in the cavalry, had no problems, but it had been a wearisome journey for the infantry, but the valley of the Ebro was paradise to them – a land of lotus and vineyards. However, the weather was too good to stay and sit and eat, so Wellington hustled them along – his men were 'spoiling for a battle'.

Dawn broke on 21st June 1813 in the cold, drizzling mist, but as had happened before during Wellington's campaign on the peninsula, it heralded a glorious victory – this time at Vitoria.

The previous evening Patrick had climbed a hill to take a look at Vitoria. In front of it lay an enormous army whose campfires and torches twinkled in the dusk, and he wondered what the morrow would bring. He wondered what he was doing there – miles away from home – he had wanted adventure, alone life in London had seemed dull and singularly boring. He missed Jason. Damian had other interests now, and their life of earlier years seemed a dream. He wondered where Jason was, whether they would ever meet again if he would come through tomorrow's battle, would Wellington finally oust Bonaparte not only from Spain, but France too? Turning back to the camp, he felt that perhaps victory at last and peace for all was near at hand.

The battle of Vitoria was no easy battle, and at times, Patrick thought it was over for him. The 18th Hussars had been ordered to charge three solid squares of infantry protected by cannon and however anyone survived was a miracle. Colonel Colquhoun Grant called them off realising too late how imprudent his order had been. This was the enemy's expiring effort, though, and they were soon driven off the hill and village. Inch by inch, they gave way, and suddenly there they all were, guns, baggage, money, carriages, women and all. There were so many women in King Joseph's army that it has been described as a mobile brothel, and now it was all abandoned. King Joseph's coach had already been stopped by Captain Henry Wyndham of the 14th Light Dragoons and Lieutenant Lord Worcester of the 10th Hussars. The King had escaped, but Patrick and his fellow officers of the Dragoons acquired many treasures, especially Joseph's lordly *silver pot de chambre*, which they christened The Emperor.

Meanwhile, the treasure hunt was on, or pillage, as it was known throughout the Peninsular War. Treasure chests, ladies' boxes and noblemen's rewards for service to the Emperor lay in the road and all over the countryside.

The looted carriages were used to convey as much as possible; others were overturned as useless. State papers and love letters, as well as priceless canvases, the property of the Spanish king were found, and Marshal Jourdan's baton in an ornamental case of blue velvet embroidered with thirty-two gold sages finally found its way into Wellington's possession. He, in turn, presented it to the Prince Regent, who returned the honour by making Wellington a field marshal.

Patrick had come through the battle unscathed and the richer by many trophies of war. He was now eager to get into France and settle 'Boney' once and for all.

It was to be a few months later, and many more miles to be travelled before Boney was defeated. Meanwhile, in England, the news of the battle of Vitoria had caused public rejoicing at such a pitch, surpassed only/by the tumultuous revelling on the battlefield, when a tremendous night-long feasting, enlivened by wine, women and song soon made the battlefield look more like a fairground at home than a battlefield in Spain.

The Prince Regent had ordered a most splendid and magnificent fete to be held in Vauxhall Gardens, where there had been 8,500 people joining in the festivities. There were even 1,500 at the grand dinner. Felicity, Jane and Damian had joined in the festivities, and as was only to be expected, Felicity would have enjoyed it far more if only her beloved

Jason had been with her. However, the merry mood persisted, and the victory was celebrated with all the fervour of true patriotism by all concerned.

San Sebastian fell on the 31st August, but after a horrific siege and storming, the castle finally fell to the troops, who incurred the wrath of all by their sacking of the town.

The next push over the Pyrenees had to wait, and Wellington's army finally crossed the River Bidasoa into France on 7th October 1813. Everything went just as the omens wanted it to – a thunderstorm the night before, local folk advised that the Bidasoa estuary was just fordable at very low tide and it was, and Marshal Sault's impregnable right flank was turned by an army 'marching from the sea'.

On the 9th November, the battle of the Neville continued the progress, and they preferred Wellington's army was welcomed by the French peasants – the disciplined army of Wellington to their own plundering countrymen.

The winter months passed by, and suddenly spring was upon them. Soult was driven remorselessly back and back, and finally on 12th April 1814, Wellington rode into Toulouse at the head of his army. Napoleon Bonaparte had already abdicated on the 6th of April. The good news was brought by a Colonel from Paris, and it was announced during the grand dinner welcoming Wellington and his troops to Toulouse, that King Louis XVIII was back on the throne of France, there was a constitution, and that the Emperor was destined for Elba – for a short time!

Chapter 21
Life Begins Again for Jason

Jason found that money did indeed provide better quarters, and although time passed slowly, at least it was not in that horrible cell in which he spent his first night. How he had managed to get through that night, he did not know. He still had nightmares of the rats running about and climbing over the sleeping forms of his companions.

Then the next morning, the concoction put through the door for them all to eat was just too much for Jason's healthy constitution. Even in a Force, the conditions and food had been disgusting, but not quite the filth of his present place.

He managed to make it known to the jailers that he was prepared to pay for something better and it was finally agreed that he had his own cell, tiny, but vermin free, and he was allowed to have writing materials plus edible food – not quite the standard he had been used to, but he could push it down.

Time went by, and although his money was running short, he was not put back with the others, and he found it well worthwhile cultivating the friendship of some of the guards, especially his usual nightly guard, a chap called Marcel Fardot. The guards found him a person to trust, and although the temptation to escape was never put his way, he realised that soon the twelve months would be over and he would be free to make his own life – but where should he go, he now had hardly enough money to bribe the jailers and was there someone somewhere who was waiting for him. It was this last thought which tormented his nights. He still could not 'see' Felicity, no Patrick – although at times he remembered the smell of violets and lilac and newly mown hay, but it was all imagination, of course, because he was far, far away from such heavenly delights. He couldn't remember even what they looked like.

He had been kept advised of all the battles, especially when the Emperor was winning, but he could tell that gradually the French guards were realising that they were soon going to be on the losing side. Wellington's victories and progress in the Peninsular War soon were the topic of all conversations and especially when the battle of Vitoria took place. Still pretending to be French, Jason sympathised with the guards, and soon he was able to get to know more and more of what was happening in the outside world, especially when Fardot was on duty. It was a miserable job guarding the rabble that was housed in L'Abbaye prison, and as time went by Jason mentioned that he would soon be out of the place and free once more, but that not remembering anything he had nowhere to go to, nor could he get in touch with anyone. In fact, he would be completely at a loss and with not a sous to his name. Marcel Fardot was not a very intelligent person, but he was sympathetic to the plight of one of his fellow men and having joined the guard many months after Jason's trial, he was not aware of any implications of Jason's nationality. One evening in December about a month before Jason was due to be let out, Fardot mentioned to his wife about the prisoner who knew nothing about himself. "I think it would be only human and Christian, wife, to give him a helping hand when he comes out of that place," he said thoughtfully:

"If you think so, Marcel, then we have that little room at the top of the house. It's only used for rubbish at the moment. Jeanne and I can soon clear it out and put a bed in it. His head."

It will be somewhere for him to rest.

"Yes, that will do, and speak to Jacques about a job. I expect he will be glad of some work. I'll mention it to Jacques tomorrow, yes – that's what I'll do."

Satisfied in his own mind that he was doing something for that poor unfortunate prisoner in his section, he continued to carve the doll which their little Susette was getting for Christmas.

During the night whilst the other guards were playing cards or having a quiet drink, he managed to get a few words with Jason, who by now quite looked forward to his nightly chats with him.

"Have you thought about what you will do when you get out, Monsieur?" Fardot said quietly, not wanting the others to hear him.

"Alas, my friend, I know not. I cannot remember much about the outside world, and as you know, I've had no visitors, so no one must know me in Paris," replied Jason thoughtfully. "I cannot expect to start up in business again, and I do not know whether I should return to Brest or not," he continued, wanting to keep up the pretence of his identity as long as possible. Once he was outside these walls, perhaps he could find something to jog that memory of his.

"Lately, he had dreams of countryside and horses, and then he would hear music and see people dancing, but nothing fitted in with anything he knew. Perhaps this was part of his past – who knew how one's memory worked. It could play tricks too – he had dreamt once that he was free and running through the streets of Paris, but that he was caught. He woke to find the captor's hand was the jailor's, shaking him awake."

"Well, if by the time you are set free, no one has come to get you, you can share a room in my house until you get your feet on the ground again," murmured Fardot.

"I've had a word with the wife, and it has all been arranged, so don't worry about that. Once you're out, you'll soon remember things."

"I might even be able to get you a job – with horses – would that suit you?" he asked anxiously.

This was more than Jason had even expected or dreamt for. If he had a base and friends, he could make discreet enquiries in the meantime.

"Thank you, my friend, thank you," he assured Fardot warmly. "My faith in mankind is restored."

Fardot was rather overwhelmed by the fervour of Jason's thanks, but he brushed them aside saying urgently, "No word to anyone else, though." Then gripping Jason's arm tightly, he said, "My job would be at stake if they knew I'd helped anyone in here."

"Of course, I'm just so grateful. You can't imagine what it's been like all these months, not knowing who I was, or who were my friends, or indeed if I had any friends. It is a soulless position to be in, a terrifying life, not knowing what is around the corner," replied Jason.

"I'll speak to Jacques about the job as soon as I can, but it may be that he'll want to see you first; in that case, we'll have to wait until you're out of here."

With that, Fardot returned to the table where the other guards were sitting, some drinking, some arguing, some sleeping – there was nothing here to disturb their peace. They had no one of importance in this section. Jason could not sleep that night. He tossed and turned, but sleep would not come. There was something to look forward to. He must not lose this chance to have a base in Paris. Perhaps someone would recognise him.

He had indeed put on a bit of weight but was still rather gaunt about the face, but his beard which he trimmed whenever he could with a knife, did help to disguise the hollow cheeks and dark rings under his eyes – those dark blue eyes which Felicity could remember so well.

When Jason had a few days left of his sentence, Fardot came to him one night and said quietly:

"Your room is ready, and I'll meet you outside the gate of the prison when you are freed. It would not do for me to be seen, but there is a bar down the road, and I'll be in there waiting for you."

"Thank you, my friend. Thank you," whispered Jason.

On that day for which Jason had waited so patiently at the end, but despairingly during the early months, the Head Warder of the prison came himself to Jason's cell. It was a new man, and he had not been involved in the original placing of Jason in this prison. He knew that Bonaparte was coming to the end, and he wanted no enemies, so he thought it prudent to see every departing prisoner and see if he could help them in their new start. However, Jason assured him that there was

nothing he could do. He said he intended to return to Brest –
perhaps it was as well to retain the identity which had been
forced on him. His papers taken from him when arrested were
returned to him to his surprise, so he was now a free man and
able to go wherever he wished and do whatever he wanted to
do.

Now he was free, though, he didn't know just what to do.
It was as though a caged bird had been set free in a wood, and
it didn't know what it was supposed to do – stay on the branch
or fly into the wood. He was not frightened, but wary of the
next step.

The gate of the gaol was opened. He stepped out and
breathed in the fresh air. It was heady, just like champagne,
free, free at last. He wasn't going to stay on the branch – no,
he would see what lay ahead for him in the wood. Having
made his decision, he stepped out along the cobbled street and
there he saw the bar – he knew Fardot would be there –
perhaps here he could find his future and remember his past.

Madame Fardot's cooking and the lively company of their
young family, especially Jeanne, soon brought about a change
in Jason, and he found himself treated like a member of the
family. Marcel had been true to his word and had got Jason a
job with his friend Jacques who was in charge of all the horses
used by Government officials. Jason found he liked horses, he
knew a great deal about them and once Jacques himself
commented on the fact. He liked the job, it was a healthy one,
and often, he was allowed to drive the carriages when a
member of the government required it, and there was not an
official coachman available. He had made no headway in his
search for his identity, and nothing rang a bell. He didn't
remember any of the places he visited in the evening with

Marcel. He enjoyed his life, and when Jacques suggested that he take over a vacant driving job, he was delighted to do so. Perhaps he would now visit other parts of the city which he might know better than this place – the Quartier Saint-Germain. This was not to be, though, because time was running out for Bonaparte. The forces of the Russians, Prussians and Austrians had begun to head for Paris. Soon Jason found himself being sent either and thither, and he had to be careful he was not sent up to the battle line. That brave fighting force of Bonaparte's was now a shambles, and it was soon apparent to the citizens of Paris, that their enemies would soon be in their city, and their Emperor would be defeated. The outlying fortresses of Paris fell, and on that fateful day of March 31st, 1814, early one morning, the Allied Officers set out from Meaux on the right bank of the Marne, some twenty miles northeast of Paris for their triumphal entry into Paris, capital of France.

Jason, together with the other members of the Fardot family, made his way towards the centre of the activities – the welcoming procession of the Allies. Marcel carried young Susette on his shoulders, and Jeanne clung to the arm of Jason, whilst Madame Fardot did her best to keep with them. The rejoicing was everywhere – Boney was done for now – soon, he would abdicate and the Bourbons would be restored. White Bourbon lilies were everywhere. Everyone had a white cockade in his hat.

Czar Alexander headed the triumphal procession of the Allies on a magnificent black stallion. A great defender of human rights, he was being called 'The Liberator of Europe', and being treated almost as a God by the French people. His tall, grey astrakhan headpiece, ending in two sturdy horns fashioned from lambs' feet, gave him a diabolical appearance. Aside from the headpiece, an ancient symbol of that mighty nation, the czar's uniform was in the French fashion with a tall stiff collar richly embroidered in silver, topping his green redingote. His foamy white silk cravat was held together by another symbolic piece of jewellery – an angry bison bull with lowered head caught in the moment of attack. The buttons of his uniform were all gold.

"*Vive Alexandre,*" was the cry from thousands of throats, including Jason's.

Everyone, not only from the city but from miles around Paris – from the surrounding countryside – had flocked to see this great man and the triumphant, not only the armies. There were not only actors and actresses from the Comedie Francaise in their gay clothes, but princes and princesses, dukes and duchesses, comtes and comtesses of the Ancient Regime who had returned to seek power under the new Bourbons. Many had fled to England and most knew whether or not friends and relatives had survived the terror of the Revolution, but in some instances, there were tearful reunions with friends and relatives feared dead for many years. All the city's inhabitants seemed to be there, from chimney sweeps to bakers, from seamstresses to pastry cooks – all wanting to see their great liberator. Talleyrand was there, Barras too – but many who had served their Emperor devotedly were obviously missing – dead by misdeed or with valour on the battlefield – no one knew or cared at this moment – it was the beginning of a new regime, and it was as well to be on the right side once more.

It was difficult to keep together in the crowds, and more than once, Jason and Jeanne were separated from Marcel and his wife with Susette, but Jason was enjoying every moment of it. It was the first time he could remember such an occasion, and he felt too it was a celebration of his freedom and his new life. Everyone now called Jason by his adopted French name of Jean Macon, and so when the procession had finally passed.

Marcel turned to Jean and asked whether or not; they extended their day by visiting the Luxembourg Gardens.

"Oh, yes, Jean, please – let us go there. It's wonderful, and we'll see all the pretty ladies and gentlemen," urged Jeanne.

"Certainment," replied Jason. "I have only passed it whilst driving the carriage, so it will be just as exciting for me too."

"We must stay together, though, because there will be so many people there, now don't get lost," emphasised Marcel.

Everyone seemed to have the same idea and soon sitting on the grass, they watched the ladies of Paris flirting with their companions, and they talked with other families who had had the same idea. Madame Fardot had brought a picnic lunch along with them, and it was a wonderful time for them all.

Time flew by, and soon they all had to return to their homes. They had been out since eight o'clock that morning, and everyone was now tired out by the excitement of the day.

"I noticed no English in the procession, Marcel," enquired Jason.

"No, they were beaten to it, but I expect that there will be another time. They say that Wellington will be bound to come to Paris to celebrate his victories now. That will be a splendid sight," Marcel said with a sigh.

"Well, I must get a few hours' sleep as I have to be up early – Jacques is shorthanded, and I expect there will be many extra horses to be looked after. Did you see that magnificent stallion that the Czar was riding – I'd like a ride on that," Jason said enviously.

"Ask him to sell it to you," replied Marcel jokingly. "You must have a few spare sous now."

"Sous," exclaimed Jason. "It would need a hell of a lot of those to buy that animal, my friend." He was now almost half asleep, and yet he felt he was somewhere else. "I've seen a horse like that somewhere else, and yet I cannot remember where. It can't be here in Paris – there's not a decent horse left – where have I seen good horses before," he mused.

"Perhaps, Jean, in your life before you were in prison, your memory is returning, *mon ami*?" enquired Marcel.

Jason had told Marcel that he occasionally had fleeting glimpses of the past, but Marcel knew as much as Jason did about it all. Jason never mentioned the names of Felicity and Patrick, though. That was his own secret, and he didn't feel like sharing that.

"I doubt it, Marcel," replied Jason. "I just at certain times get glimpses of things, but I cannot put them together because I do not know where they are or what I was doing."

"Never mind, Jean. One day, something will happen, and that will be it. You will remember everything. It has happened before. You need something to jolt your memory. Something or someone from your past to meet you, and voila, you will remember."

"But when, Marcel, when should I go to Brest, or should I stay in Paris? I feel safer here, *man ami*, and I do not know what I shall find in Brest?"

Jason had not the slightest intention of going to Brest, but he thought it wiser to pretend that Brest was his home place.

"A merchant from Brest might one day see you, and come up to you and say, Jean, my friend, where have you been. We've all missed you, and there you are, you will know who you are," exclaimed Marcel.

"Perhaps, Marcel, perhaps that will happen, but in the meantime, I have to work, and I'd better get that sleep. It will soon be too late to go to bed," replied Jason. "Goodnight, Marcel, I don't know what I would have done without you and your family."

"Oh, that's all right, Jean," responded Marcel. "We like having you, and one day, you'll see, you will remember."

Making his way up the winding stairs to his little room, Jason pondered over this subject for a while, but he knew it was futile. He hadn't enough money to travel any distance, and he really didn't know where to go to.

Also, as all his documents said he was French, so how could he turn up at an English port, saying he was really English, but he didn't know where he came from. He might come from London, he might not. He might have been a wanted man in London, and again no one might know him, so he would be no better off there. No, it would be wiser to stay here a little longer.

He had started to have these flashes of the past more frequently these days, so perhaps it was just a matter of time, and his memory would return.

Chapter 22
Recognition

Jason was kept busy by the vast amount of foreign troops now in Paris, and there were horses and their equipment to be looked after. He was also kept busy driving one visitor after another to various government departments.

He told Marcel one evening that all he seemed to do was eat, breathe and sleep horses.

"I get up and arrive at the stables. There are so many horses to be looked after, and some of those lazy louts cannot even clean a saddle properly, never mind groom a horse. They think now they are the city's liberators that we should do everything for them. Do this, Jean, do that Jean oh, I'll be glad to see the back of them. I hear that there is to be another triumphal procession, this time with everyone present, including the English. Even the Duke of Wellington is supposed to be coming too from Toulouse."

Jason was becoming rather weary of all the extra work foisted on him.

He knew his job and did it well, and some of the men who had been taken on to look after the influx of foreign troops hadn't the same interest in the job, so it was only natural that the keen officers of the Russian, Prussian and Austrian forces wanted a man who looked properly after their horses. It was, therefore, no surprise to Jacques, the man in charge of the stables, when a special request was received that the man, Jean, was to be sent round to the quarters of the Czar. He didn't mind it too much, the horses there which he was to look after would certainly be better than some of the horseflesh left in the French stables. He was looking forward to seeing the magnificent black stallion at close quarters.

He settled into his new job well and took great pride in his work.

The horses and their equipment shone, and he was allowed to exercise them during the early hours of the morning before the Czar, and his entourage were astir. There was great excitement in the city as the day of the Grand Parade before Louis XVIII took place. The 3rd May 1814 was another day in the history of France, and this time Jason had been hard at work before the majority of the inhabitants went to bed the previous evening. He had been detailed to get the Czar's horse ready for the parade and there was such an amount of equipment to be checked and burnished, and then he had to exercise them so that they would not be too frisky amongst the crowds. He didn't want the Czar to give him any trouble that day.

He wanted to get out amongst the crowds and see some English men at long last. Wellington, and his troops were riding in – they had marched up from Toulouse, and it was said that everywhere Wellington went, he was received like a saviour. He had brought the people out to see him wherever he went.

There was a great stir amongst the crowd as the whisper spread that the Duke of Wellington was coming. Emperors and Kings wanted to see this conquering hero too. Wellington was astride a white horse as he came into the view of the crowds, riding between the half-brothers.

General Stewart and Lord Castlereagh. Dressed in a plain blue frock-coat, up white neck-cloth and round top hat, he presented such a contrast to the bejewelled and glittering figures of the Emperor of Austria, the King of Prussia and the Czar of Russia. Suddenly Jason felt that he was with friends, his countrymen. Seeing the English troops ride by and hearing English voices, he knew deep down that he was, in fact, English and that no matter how much he had been immersed in the French atmosphere and life all these months, the overriding feeling deep down in him was that he was English, he belonged to that country called England and here before him was his fellow countryman.

So, Jason returned to the Czar's quarters when the parade had passed by, knowing that soon he would have as much work as ever to do. He had been proud of the horses ridden by the Russian troops, and especially that black stallion of the Czar's. It had become normal for the Russians to steal the scenes with their bravado, their Cossack style of riding, and their highly decorated uniforms, especially the officers who grabbed all the pretty French girls they could get their hands around. The gay Austrian hussars in their vermilion trousers, so tight they could hardly walk never mind ride or mount a horse, with their richly trimmed bright blue dolmans, high shako tied to the left shoulder by a thick golden cord and silver spurs, which offset the creak of the pale-yellow leather boots, by jingling at the wearer's every move. Birds of paradise were everywhere that day, but Jason was now back to reality – he had work to do. He knew that the cavalry under Wellington

194

were camped down not far away from his present quarters, so he managed to get away as early as he could, and he wandered over to the English camp. Several of the officers were still there, glad now to be in Paris, and that Wellington, now made the Duke of Wellington, had had his moment of glory, which all thought due to him. Jason heard these English voices, and the language sounded so familiar. He didn't want to join the group, but just to listen to English voices, but he was spotted by one of the guards and unceremoniously pushed into full view of the officers he had been watching.

"What have we here, eh, Ransome?" exclaimed one of the young officers.

"Looks like one of the Ruskies' stable hands, if I'm not mistaken, my lord," replied the young guard. "He was just standing there by the corner of the building – I've been watching him for a time. He didn't do anything; he was just watching and listening. He probably doesn't understand anything in any case, my lord, so shall I let him go," asked the guard.

"Hm, I'm not so sure – he may be waiting to see what we've got – perhaps seizing his chance to pinch a thing or two."

"Oh, no, no, my lord, I'm no thief," interrupted Jason quickly and in English. It was an automatic reaction, and to his dismay, it immediately drew everyone's attention to him, because he was obviously not one of their army.

"Oh, so he does speak English – spying eh, that's it," said the captain, grabbing Jason by the arm.

"No, my lord, I'm not spying, and I'm not a thief. I just wanted to hear English being spoken once again. I lost my memory many months ago, and I had French papers on me, but I know English, and I feel English. I just wanted to hear English being spoken once again. I've spoken French and been French for so long now that I had begun to doubt that I really was English."

"A fine story, my fellow. Do you really expect us to believe that? Who are you, then? What's your name? Where were you caught, and if you had French papers, why should you think you were English?" insisted the *Lieutemit* Lord Worcester.

"I was told I was captured on the beach at Le Treport trying to get on board an English ship. I was told an English spy escaped on the same ship, but they couldn't prove anything because I had only French papers on me, and I only spoke French. I had also had a bad head wound caused during the struggle on the beach, and I lost my memory. I couldn't say one way or another who I was. I have served a prison sentence for resisting arrest, and I have been living with a French family ever since. It was hearing your English voices, which drew me over here. I wanted to see if I could really understand you. Surely, you can tell if I am English. I have probably got a French accent by now – it is almost 18 months since I was captured, and I have never spoken any English during the whole time," pleaded Jason.

"What do you think, Henry?" asked Lord Worcester, turning to one of the other captains in the group.

"It could be true – I know that Castlereagh did have spies coming and going from France, but I knew none of them. We can't get hold of Castlereagh now he's the only one who would know if he was one of his men. Isn't he dining at Versailles with Louis tonight? You could keep him here under guard until tomorrow and then see what you can do," suggested Captain Henry Wyndham.

"A good idea. I don't want to spend any more time running around Paris tonight.

"I've had enough of all the celebrating. I must get some sleep – it's been three nights of celebrations, and there's the Royal review of my troops tomorrow, so perhaps one of your men can see to him, Henry."

"Patrick," shouted Captain Wyndham, to one of the other officers in the background. "Here a moment." The officer came over to the group and was given his orders to take the visitor to somewhere safe for the night. Jason quickly realised that he would be missed early in the morning, and the Czar would have his head off if his horses were not looked after, but this was his only chance of perhaps finding out his identity. To hell with the Czar, he was an Englishman, not a Russian – so why bother about them.

The new officer came up to the 'prisoner' and was about to take him away when he exclaimed, "Jason, my God, no – it can't be. Jason, don't you know me, it's Patrick!"

"Patrick," stemmed Jason hesitantly. "You are Patrick, and you know me?"

Of course, Patrick was not aware of the story Jason had given Lord Worcester, so when the others heard Patrick's exclamation and found out that Patrick knew him, or thought he did – then it was a different story.

A rather dazed Jason listened whilst Patrick explained that this rather shabby but healthily looking person before them was in fact, the Earl of Lindsey and had indeed been working for Castlereagh with him Patrick, when they had been attacked. Jason had been left for dead whilst he, Patrick, had escaped on the ship. He said enquiries had been made, but there had been no information at all about Jason for months, but eventually, they had heard that a Monsieur Macon had been imprisoned. Monsieur Macon being Jason's code name, then they knew he was alive, but it had been impossible to find him.

"Who is Felicity?" asked Jason.

"I was told by the doctor that in my sleep, I had mentioned her name, but can't remember her. Who is she, Patrick?" he said urgently, knowing that this Felicity could be his wife, fiancée, girlfriend, sister, or mistress.

"Don't you really remember her, Jason?" asked Patrick being very amused at this. "You'll know her as soon as you see her. Fancy forgetting Felicity," he continued in a teasing tone.

"But what relation is she to me?" persisted Jason.

"Well, I don't really know that Jason," said Patrick, knowing full well what the position was at Felicity's end, but he didn't like to torture him for too long. He could tell that this was the main thing as far as Jason was concerned. "She is your stepsister."

"Oh." Jason sighed. "I wondered if she was." Words failed him – somehow, he had thought she was closer to him. He had had that feeling whenever he said the name.

"You didn't let me finish," interrupted Patrick. "I have also been told that you told her you loved her, just before we all left on the 'Firefly' to come to France."

"Then she is my fiancé," said Jason eagerly. This was more like it. Now he knew that the name was something special to him. He knew now why it was one of the few memories left to him.

"Well, this rather changes things. You're certain, Patrick, of his identity?" asked Captain Wyndham. He had had no idea that Patrick had been involved with Castlereagh, but he knew the Honourable Patrick Lovelace to be a man who liked adventure, and highly recommended by Castlereagh when he joined the Dragoons earlier in the War in Spain.

"I'm quite certain, Captain, we've spent many hours together and seen many adventures. Perhaps he could share my quarters for tonight and then with a change of clothes and good barbering by my valet; we can see Lord Castlereagh early in the morning before he goes to his Royal function."

"Yes, that will be the best thing to do. What about your job and the family you've been staying with, Lindsey?"

"Perhaps a note could be delivered to the Czar's stables, saying that I'm unwell – rather than admit I've been an English lord looking after his horses. After I've seen Lord Castlereagh, perhaps I could go back to see my French friends. I would rather do that than just disappear and leave them a note.

"They have been very kind and were my only friends," requested Jason, now with a bit more authority realising that he was, in fact, their senior in rank.

Turning to Patrick, he held out his hands and said, "Well, my friend, you'll have to excuse any foreign mannerisms or any stupid questions. It's all rather bewildering, to say the least. It is now a dream rather than the nightmare it's been over the past months.

"I've tried and tried to remember things. I only found out at the trial that someone else had escaped on the ship, but I didn't know who. Then the name Patrick came into my head one day, so Felicity and Patrick have been my only links with that other world. Perhaps, if you'll tell me more of who I really am and what I was doing, things might come back to me."

Between them, questions never stopped throughout the night, and gradually Jason began to fit the pieces of the jigsaw puzzle back in place. He knew now about his mother marrying Felicity's father, about Damian and Jane, about his brother Claude, the mystery of the pearls, and finally all about that fatal trip to Paris. Patrick also confirmed that the ring Jason had kept throughout his imprisonment was indeed one showing his family crest.

Next morning, when Patrick's valet arrived to attend to Patrick's needs, he found that all the attention was required for Jason. On this occasion, Patrick looked after himself, and finally, after about an hour spent on shaving off Jason's beard, cutting his hair into the right style, cutting his nails and powdering himself, Patrick produced an array of garments which he had borrowed from fellow officers, who were only too pleased to be able to help one of their fellow men. What a change. Now, Jason was once more the aristocratic Lord Lindsey, not quite as immaculate or groomed as he would have been back in London setting out for Burlington House or Almacks, but certainly more than presentable to go and meet Lord Castlereagh.

News of Jason's presence had spread throughout the camp, and as he went on his way to the meeting, many former acquaintances came forward to shake his hand and greet him with delight. He had to admit that he didn't know any of them, but they took it all in good part. Lord Castlereagh too, had already been advised by Captain Wyndham of Jason's appearance, and so it was with true sincerity and warmth that he was greeted by that statesman. "This has crowned my visit to Paris, Jason. When Patrick returned to say he thought you had died, my spirit sank so low, I felt like resigning, but we all felt that you must be alive somewhere. A spirit like yours, so fit and physically strong, must survive, and it was with relief that I got news that someone using your false name was in prison. We tried and tried to find out where you were, but alas, it was impossible.

"Now you must have a good rest and return as quickly as possible to England. I shall return later this week – would you prefer to leave immediately or with Patrick and your friends here. Captain Thelwall of the 'Firefly' will be delighted to see you. His is one of the ships carrying our party back to England," enquired Castlereagh.

"The Firefly," mused Jason. "That sounds familiar." And so he decided that it might be as well if he didn't lose his newfound friends so soon. It was decided he would share Patrick's quarters and return with them all on the 'Firefly'.

Later that day, Patrick accompanied Jason back to his room and the family who had looked after him. Marcel had been worried about Jason's absence, but merely thought it was probably due to the extra work needed because of the previous day's parade. Now though, he didn't recognise the tall, dark, handsome Englishman who appeared on his doorstep. Jeanne did though. She had grown up during Jason's stay with them, and was beginning to fancy herself in love with her mysterious Jean. Now though she realised that it was impossible, but she would always remember her wonderful Englishman as she now called him. He had borrowed money from Patrick, who assured him that he would certainly be able to repay him, repay him a hundredfold if necessary as he was a wealthy landowner – to Jason's utter astonishment. Therefore, he had bought many presents for the family before he went to say his farewells, and after many assurances of always remembering him and on his side, the grateful thanks for their friendship in his time of trouble, Jason left that tiny house and his French nationality to return once more – this time he hoped permanently – to England.

A few days later, the English party accompanying Lord Castlereagh returned to England, and Jason was warmly welcomed by his old friend, Captain Thelwall, who was overcome with emotion on seeing him.

Chapter 23
The Price Is Paid

No news had travelled to London of Jason's survival, as he had never been posted 'missing' or 'presumed dead'. It was, therefore, no surprise to English society when he arrived back in England with Castlereagh's entourage. The story was spread that Jason had joined in the celebrations in Paris and for convenience had returned to London with his friends.

Continued grooming and attention to such details as perfectly fitting clothes in the latest fashion had certainly done their job. In the many months since Jason's disappearance and Claude's decline, the house in London had remained open although Jason's man servant Robert had little to do. He made occasional journeys to Charnwood for the purpose of maintaining the pretence of Jason's presence there. Claude could not come into the open as he knew he was a wanted man. Secretly, Claude hoped Jason was safe, but he found it rather strange that Jason had not been seen since that day he left for France. He wondered whether, in fact, the French had got him, and his conscience would never rest in peace if he thought he was responsible for Jason's death. He knew that he would never be allowed to inherit the earldom – it would die out because there was no one else to inherit – the Prince

Regent would never allow anyone of such disgrace as Claude's to inherit it. Claude often thought of his mother, and did manage to get a note to her, but on Mr Anderson's instructions, she did not reply to it.

Claude had taken to lingering outside Jason's London home for hours on end just to see if there was any sign of Jason. No one would have recognised him for Jason's brother anymore. He looked like the misbegotten beggars who haunted the streets of London in their thousands, pushing and shoving their way through the filth of the streets, the brothels, the gin mills, and taverns.

The misery and sickness which most of the gutter rabble finally ended up with had now got him in its grip, and was doing its best to make sure he would never get better. He had not shaved nor washed himself for months.

His clothes were wretched and stank to high heaven. He fell into the gutter often and usually had to be helped out of it by one of his kind. He now never noticed the filth on him. Gradually his features were beginning to change shape and get that deathly pallor, and decent passers-by avoided him whenever possible.

However, he was so determined to wait and see Jason alive that he just sat in an alley at the side of the place near Jason's home, becoming one on the pavement when a carriage pulled up at the front of Jason's door.

The first to do so for many, many months. Claude could have cried out with delight if his insides would have let him. He was almost choking when he saw Jason alight and saw him and his manservant Robert, who had joined Jason at Dover having received an urgent request by courier to be there when the ship's passengers landed with as much of Jason's belongings as Robert could convey. Fortunately, Jason had hardly changed physically; there was just a hardness there now which would never be removed, which had been brought about by the privation and hardship of a French prison. Otherwise, it was just as though he had only been away a few weeks – perhaps on holiday.

Claude knew that once that door was shut, the footman would never allow him to enter, no matter who he said he was. Stumbling across the road, faster than he had moved for many months, he managed to get there before Jason, who had been talking to his coachman, was able to reach the door.

Claude clutched at Jason's arm, and not taking a good look at him, Jason flung off the hand, shuddering at its filth. He had seen such bodies in gaol and recognised the degradation.

"Take him away," he snapped at the servants. "Fling him where he belongs – in the gutter."

"Jason, please don't do that. It is I, Claude," the creature croaked. "Jason, please, please don't go away, Jason, I've waited so long for your return Jason…" The voice trailed off and the vermin covered wretch fell limply to the ground.

"Claude!" exclaimed Jason, horrified. "It can't be," he bent over to look at the person closely, holding a handkerchief to his nose for the stench was positively shocking, and he recognised, but only just, the once-proud features of his brother.

"Good God."

Turning at once to the servants, he said, "Quick Robert, get a doctor and Mrs Johnson immediately."

His housekeeper, a white-haired motherly sort of person, rushed down the steps. She had been looking forward to seeing Mr Jason, but now she knew that it was Claude who needed her attention most of all.

"Mr Claude, oh, Mr Claude, whatever has happened? Where have you been?" she exclaimed.

"Mrs Johnson, I think a good hot bath, or should I say baths, will be the first necessary thing the doctor will recommend, and burn those rags immediately."

"Yes, Mr Jason, I'll see to it immediately. It's wonderful to have you back again, my lord," she said so genuinely that Jason felt rather overcome with emotion. First of all, Claude like this and now even Mrs Johnson was pleased to see him.

As she hastened off to get the maid to fill up the tub with steaming water, Robert and some of the other manservants managed to carry Claude up to his room. Mrs Johnson had been with the family for many years, and she had in fact, been the nurse to both boys from birth. She was dismayed to see the state that Claude was in, and he was hardly conscious when they finally managed to get him cleaned up and into bed. The doctor had arrived by then, and after prescribing a sleeping draught and plenty of nourishing soup, he drew Jason aside.

"I'm afraid, my Lord, there isn't much we can do for him now. Wherever he's been living these past months, it hasn't been a very healthy place, and the pox thrives on men in his condition. No, my lord, I'm afraid he's only got a few days left in this world. I'm deeply sorry, my Lord, but I thought it best, you should know the true position."

Jason was staggered. His only brother at death's door! Nothing he could do would save him. Suddenly he realised that he had recognised Claude – and Mrs Johnson too – his memory was back, and immediately his mind was filled with a charming picture of a young lady with dark curly hair and beautiful deep green eyes – it must be. It was Felicity. With a sigh, he slipped away from everyone – he needed to be alone to sort out all his emotions and thoughts. He must send a note round to Patrick to tell him the news – it must have been the shock of seeing Claude in such a state which gave him the necessary trauma to clear the fog which had been so persistent. Now he must also write to Felicity – what could he say – there was so much he wanted to, but it was going to be a very difficult letter to write. He really wanted to be with her, to hold her in his arms, but he could not now that Claude was here, and in all probability had the 'pox, and not likely to live very long.

It had to be a letter, therefore and hadn't they arranged that he would send his half of the family ring to her, when he got back home if he couldn't get to see her straight away. Yes, that was the solution. He descended the stairs slowly, remembering quite easily where his study lay, and he looked around him, feeling a warmth and love for this old family home, which he had not known about during those dreadful months which were now in the past.

In the study, he searched for writing materials and suddenly came across a note addressed to him, signed 'Felicity', saying that she wasn't sure if she could marry him. What was this – Patrick had said she was his fiancé, and in their long talks during the journey back to England, he had made Patrick talk and talk about Felicity, and how she felt for him was quite obvious from all Patrick had said. Therefore, why this note? He rang for his butler, Masters, and realising that it had probably been there for a long, long time, wondered if he knew anything about the note which he had found.

"Oh, yes, my lord, it was on the morning of your departure on your last mission, the young lady arrived in a hurry and was insistent on leaving you a note. She searched for writing materials, and whilst doing so came across a rather loosely wrapped package containing a pearl necklace – this seemed to upset her most dreadfully, my lord, and she left in some agitation. She suggested before she departed that I lock the necklace in your safe for safety. I did this immediately, my lord, and in fact, your safe has never been opened since. No one has ever mentioned the pearls to this day, my lord."

"Pearls, Masters?" queried Jason puzzled for a moment, then suddenly he remembered the missing pearls and Patrick mentioning something about them whilst in France.

"In my safe, are they, Masters?" he said, getting to his feet and taking a key from his key ring, he proceeded to open the safe, and there before him was a package. He opened it carefully, exclaiming in genuine amazement when he saw their beauty.

"Have you any idea, Masters, how these pearls arrived in my desk?" he asked an equally amazed Masters.

"I did make some enquiries during that day when they were found, my lord, and it appears that one of the footmen found them on the doorstep, he put them on the hall table, not knowing of course what was in the package, and when Robert saw them the next day, he decided to put them away, knowing that you would not be back for a few days, or so we thought at the time, my lord," replied Masters.

"I must see Claude, and perhaps he will know how they got there on the doorstep," said Jason quietly and more to himself than to Masters. In a louder voice, he then asked Masters to pass a message to Robert that he wished him to make a journey and to come to see him in his study in half an hour's time for his instructions.

Jason quickly went upstairs, and although Claude was very ill, he was conscious and now that he had been cleaned up and was feeling more comfortable than he had for weeks, he was able to tell Jason most of the story of his downfall – about Lucy, the theft of the pearls, the Frenchman who wanted information, the finding of the note and finally these last desperate months. Jason knew that it was really through Claude that there had been so much trouble – he had had to pay a terrible price for the information which Claude had given to the French to try to get the pearls back, but now Claude was going to pay an even greater price.

It took Jason rather longer than half an hour to write his letter to Felicity, but finally, after many attempts, he managed to convey not only the news and reason for Claude's illness, the reason Felicity found the pearls where she did, but also his undying love for the girl he had left behind him on that fateful day. Dare he hope that she still loved him? He told her how his only connection with his past had been her name, which the doctor had told him he had spoken in his unconsciousness, and also how he had kept his part of the ring hidden over the many months, and now he was sending it to her to let her know that he had returned home safely and with only one thought in his mind how soon they could be together.

It was a week later that Jason was finally able to do the many things he had been wanting desperately to do. Many things had happened in that week since he had arrived home.

First of all, after many dreadful hours of pain and sickness, Claude had finally died, having pleaded Jason's forgiveness, which Jason did/give, but he knew that he would never forget the eighteen months or so which he had gone through because of Claude's treachery.

Jason also sent a note round to Castlereagh, informing him of the information Claude had given him. He doubted whether it was of any use now, especially as Bonaparte was finally on his way to Elba, but he also told Castlereagh that he officially resigned from his 'service'.

No doubt through the stories of Jason's reappearance, especially when some of the troops returned from France and told of some of the stories they had heard their captains telling of how Lord Lindsey had been held a prisoner and had been a spy for England, Jason was becoming something of a hero, and he was being greeted on every side by former acquaintances whenever he went out. Now though, especially after the funeral, the house in London was closed, and the servants sent down to Charnwood, where Jason hoped to spend most of his time. Robert had returned from Ravenwood, but he said that the young lady was not at home, so he was not able to bring back any message to His Lordship.

Felicity had, in fact, been visiting some friends and only returned on the day that Jason was setting out to ride to Ravenwood. When she arrived home, she was pleasantly happy. It had been a very interesting visit. She had known her hosts for many years, so when her stepmother came running down the front door steps to greet her excitedly, hugging her and kissing her, she was truly astonished.

"Mother, now then, what is the matter? I've not been away for so long, why are you crying, and yet you're laughing too? What has happened?" she asked her stepmother anxiously, not expecting to be told such news which Mrs Anderson had had for the past couple of days.

"It is Jason, he's back, and all is well. He was in Paris and had lost his memory. He had been in prison, and he did not know who he was, and then he saw some English soldiers, and Patrick was there, and he was able to identify him. Robert, Jason's manservant, came to tell us, and there is a message for you too. Do come, my love, and tell your father and I that all is well for you both."

Felicity just could not believe it Jason back home – a letter for her – she was so overcome that it was in a dream that she opened the letter from Jason. She found first of all the other half of the ring, and she knew immediately it was true. She took that first of all and joined her half with it, then reading the letter, she knew immediately that she had been right that Jason had knew nothing about the pearls, and to see written clearly before her, that he still loved her and would soon be with her, as soon as he possibly could, she took the now complete ring and wore it proudly on her finger.

Not her engagement finger – no, that would be for Jason to do – to place it officially and at last when he came to her.

Most of the horses from the London stables at Jason's home had been sent down to Charnwood, but Robert had kept the best one for Jason to ride on for his journey to Charnwood, and immediately he saw it, he remembered that black stallion of the Czar's, for there before him was his own black stallion. He knew he had seen such an animal before, and there and then renamed his own stallion 'Czar'.

He had naturally not heard anything from Felicity during the past week, although a message had come back by return from Mr and Mrs Anderson to express their gratitude for his deliverance and assuring him of a very warm welcome as soon as he could possibly come to Ravenwood. Claude's death was not a surprise to Mr and Mrs Anderson, for they had feared him dead too many months ago. They had known he had fallen low, but it was with a very sad heart that Mrs Anderson heard of Claude's sickness and anticipated death. She had loved him as a little boy, but she could never forgive him for his treachery towards not only Jason but also to Mr Anderson and Felicity.

It was a beautiful day when Jason travelled down to Ravenwood – the leaves were a very fresh shade of green – they had not long since opened after a very severe winter – the birds were joyful and singing all day, and there were spring flowers blooming freely along the countryside roads which Jason travelled along with such a happy heart.

He had set out early deliberately – he wanted to get down to Ravenwood as quickly as possible, and he knew that his dreams would soon be fulfilled. He knew that Felicity had been faithful to him. Indeed Patrick had said rather ruefully that he had only been welcomed when he had news of Jason, and Felicity could talk of no one else but Jason and their adventures together, poor Patrick! Perhaps one day he would find his true love.

The miles soon passed by, and 'Czar' seemed to be flying across the muddy potholes down the country lanes, which led to Ravenwood. He passed through Stan Bourne, which he remembered was where he had heard of Felicity boarding the London coach. Soon, he would be in sight of Ravenwood. He hoped Felicity had returned from her visit – it would be an anti-climax if he had to wait for her – but Robert had said that her visit was only a short one.

In fact, he made such good time that Felicity had only had time to read the letter and go upstairs to change from her travelling clothes, when she heard a horse's hooves on the drive in front of the house. Looking out of the window, she could see a black horse, and a tall, dark-haired gentleman dismounting and turning to kiss her stepmother.

"It's Jason, Polly," she said excitedly to her maid, who had replaced the maid Jane had lent her.

"Oh, quickly, the rose-pink muslin gown, Polly, and my hair, oh, it's such a mess, oh, quickly, Polly. I must get down there immediately." The poor little girl who had taken over the lady's maid job was so bewildered by all these instructions that Felicity herself had to do most of the work, but in minutes she had dressed and brushed her hair. She knew that she wanted to look her best for Jason, but she wanted to see him now, immediately, after all those months of waiting and not knowing if he was still alive, she ran down the stairs, and Jason had just handed his cloak to the footman, his arm around his mother, who had tears in her eyes. Mr Anderson was trying to guide the party to the nearest suitable room when they all heard the patter of flying footsteps along the upper corridor, and then down the stairs they saw a vision of loveliness – at least that was how Jason described it to Felicity some hours later as they sat in the garden, with his arms holding her tightly. Immediate warm welcome from everyone, Mrs Anderson and Felicity reluctantly to leave to finalise what they were doing when Jason had arrived, so he and Mr Anderson were able to have a few quiet words. Jason explained Claude's part in the mystery of the pearls, which he now handed over to Mr Anderson, and how they had come to be in the desk where Felicity had seen them. He had mentioned most of this in letters to them, but he felt that he needed to tell them in his own way. He also wanted confirmation from Mr Anderson that he would allow him to marry Felicity. All the time he had been kept in London, he had to wait for this moment, and now words failed him, but Mr Anderson pet him by saying:

"What of the future, Jason? What part does Felicity play in it?" He could sense Jason was nervous – after all, he had felt the same himself once.

"I'm hoping that with your permission, sir, she will play the major part," replied Jason, glancing at Mr Anderson in suspense.

"Well, I think you had better ask her yourself. I can hear her footsteps coming along the corridor. Your mother and I have looked forward to this ever since Felicity told us."

With a gasp of relief and happiness, Jason grasped Mr Anderson's outstretched hand and rushed quickly into the hall, where Felicity was pretending to arrange some flowers. She had guessed what the men were talking about, so had hesitated to enter the study, but she knew from Jason's warm smile that all was well.

After a luncheon which was now a celebration, at which toasts were proposed not only to Jason's safe return to England, but into this happy family, and especially to the future of the young couple Jason and Felicity.

It seemed like hours later to Jason and Felicity that they were finally able to be alone, and together they strolled along the lane towards that small copse where this story had begun some twenty months earlier. Now the bluebells were out, and the blackbird hopping madly along the fence warning all of the newcomers to the wood were quite invisible to the eyes of the young couple. They were only aware of their happiness and the fact that at long last, they were reunited. Felicity had

Jason's ring on her correct engagement finger now, and together they looked forward to years of happiness at Charnwood.

Suddenly in the quiet lull which pervaded the copse, Jason spotted a red fox slinking through the undergrowth. Felicity immediately remembered seeing one on that fateful day when she decided to run away to London. Now she knew that it would have been better for the victim of the sparrow-hawk to have been left to the wiles of the fox. There was always a chance of escape when a chase was on, but a quick snatch by the sparrow-hawk, and it was all over. Jason had had such a lucky escape – for he had managed to deceive his pursuers, but if he had spoken English that time and not French, he would have been finished with immediately.

She felt a chill run through the air in remembrance of all the events which had taken place, so turning to Jason, she said, "Hold me tightly, my love, don't ever let me go again!"

"With all my heart, my darling, and I'll never let you go again. Never. I've paid the price over and over again for leaving you that night. We'll be together always," Jason reassured her, bending his head to kiss those warm and tender lips.